P9-DDL-828

Download Forms on Nolo.com

You can download the forms in this book at:

 **www.nolo.com/back-of-book/RUNSF.html**

We'll also post updates whenever there's an important change to the law affecting this book—as well as articles and other related materials.

More Resources
from Nolo.com

 ### Legal Forms, Books, & Software

Hundreds of do-it-yourself products—all written in plain English, approved, and updated by our in-house legal editors.

 ### Legal Articles

Get informed with thousands of free articles on everyday legal topics. Our articles are accurate, up to date, and reader friendly.

 ### Find a Lawyer

Want to talk to a lawyer? Use Nolo to find a lawyer who can help you with your case.

NOLO
LAW for ALL

11th Edition

Legal Forms for Starting & Running a Small Business

Attorney Fred S. Steingold

ELEVENTH EDITION	MARCH 2020
Editor	JESSICA GILLESPIE
Cover & Book Design	SUSAN PUTNEY
Production	SUSAN PUTNEY
Proofreading	IRENE BARNARD
Index	VICTORIA BAKER
Printing	BANG PRINTING

ISSN: 2164-3946 (print)
ISSN: 2332-7030 (online)
ISBN: 978-1-4133-2731-1 (pbk)
ISBN: 978-1-4133-2732-8 (ebook)

This book covers only United States law, unless it specifically states otherwise.

Please note

We believe accurate, plain-English legal information should help you solve many of your own legal problems. But this text is not a substitute for personalized advice from a knowledgeable lawyer. If you want the help of a trained professional—and we'll always point out situations in which we think that's a good idea—consult an attorney licensed to practice in your state.

About the Author

Fred Steingold passed away in 2017. He practiced law for over 40 years in Ann Arbor, Michigan where he was well-known and highly regarded by the local legal community. Fred wrote and updated several best-selling titles for Nolo, including *Legal Guide for Starting & Running a Small Business* and *The Employer's Legal Handbook*, which continue to be updated and published by Nolo. Over the 25 years that Fred wrote for Nolo, he worked with many editors and other Nolo employees, and he always graciously thanked them for their enthusiasm and assistance. We appreciated Fred's commitment to his work, his professional competence, and his kindness. We will miss working with him.

Table of Contents

Your Small Business Legal Companion

The most important rule when making any business agreement is: Get it in writing. In some situations—such as a contract to buy or sell real estate—only a written agreement is legally enforceable. Similarly, a contract that can't be carried out in one year, or a contract to sell goods exceeding a certain value set by state law (typically, $500), must be written.

But even in the situations where an oral contract is legally sufficient, there are many practical reasons to prefer writing down your agreement. Two years from now, you and the other people involved in any business transaction may have significantly different recollections about what you collectively agreed to. So putting agreements in black and white is an important memory aid. A well-drafted contract also confers several other important benefits on its signers. For one, it serves as a framework within which to resolve disputes. And even if this proves impossible and a court contest ensues, it will be far easier to prove the terms of a written contract than an oral one.

Still another important benefit of drafting a written agreement is that the act of putting your contract together can help you and the other party(ies) focus on the key legal and practical issues, some of which might otherwise be overlooked. And by starting this process with a well-designed form—like those in this book—your chances of creating a thorough document are further enhanced.

To help you create sound legal agreements, this book provides convenient, ready-to-use forms for most of the common transactions your small business is likely to encounter. Whether you're borrowing money, buying a business, leasing an office or store, hiring employees, or contracting for goods or services, you'll find well-drafted contracts that are simple to customize to fit your needs.

Happily, the fill-in-the-blanks contracts in this book are a lot easier to use than most similar legal documents. Not only have we avoided legalese, we have also adopted a clean and clear layout. But don't let the lack of gobbledygook fool you: These forms cover all the important legal bases.

Because a legal form without good background information and instructions is almost valueless, each chapter provides comprehensive legal and practical information that you need to create sound agreements. Unfortunately, even a book as chunky as this one doesn't have enough space to provide in-depth coverage of every practical and legal issue covered by every contract.

That's where other Nolo products come in. Throughout this book we'll refer you to other Nolo titles where you can learn even more about a specific topic, from hiring employees to choosing a domain name. When you need it, these books will provide you with detailed information and practical tips to get your business up and running—and keep it running. Some of the other small business titles Nolo offers are:

- *Legal Guide for Starting & Running a Small Business*, by Fred S. Steingold and David M. Steingold. Everything you need to know about starting your business, from which business structure is best for you to hiring employees to tips on obtaining business insurance.
- *Tax Savvy for Small Business*, by Frederick W. Daily. An indispensable guide to tax deductions your small business shouldn't miss, as well as in-depth information on the taxation of different kinds of business entities.
- *The Employer's Legal Handbook*, by Fred S. Steingold. Covers hiring, personnel practices, employee benefits, wage and hour rules, taxes, health and safety, discrimination and harassment, disciplinary action, and termination.
- *Negotiate the Best Lease for Your Business,* by Janet Portman. A downloadable book that explains how to analyze space needs, find the ideal location, and negotiate a lease that protects your legal and financial interests.
- *The Complete Guide to Selling a Business,* by Fred S. Steingold. When the time comes, selling your business will be a significant transaction, involving tens—or often

hundreds—of thousands of dollars. This book explains how to get your business ready for sale, set a price, prepare a sales agreement, and have a smooth closing.

- *Business Buyout Agreements: Plan Now for All Types of Business Transitions,* by Bethany K. Laurence and Anthony Mancuso. If you're starting a business with a co-owner, this book contains invaluable information on creating a buy-sell agreement and provides forms for you to create and customize your own agreement.

- *Incorporate Your Business: A Step-By-Step Guide to Forming a Corporation in Any State,* by Anthony Mancuso, shows you how to form a corporation in all 50 states.

- *Working With Independent Contractors,* by Stephen Fishman. If you're thinking of hiring independent contractors, this book is an invaluable resource. You'll learn the pros and cons of hiring independent contractors instead of employees, including the rules government agencies use to classify workers and the special tax issues associated with hiring independent contractors.

- *The Corporate Records Handbook: Meetings, Minutes & Resolutions,* by Anthony Mancuso. This book contains all the minutes and resolutions you'll need to keep your corporate record keeping on track.

- *Form Your Own Limited Liability Company,* by Anthony Mancuso. This book is a guide to forming your limited liability company in all 50 states and includes information and forms to help you reserve a name, file your articles of organization, and create an operating agreement.

- *Form a Partnership: The Complete Legal Guide,* by Denis Clifford and Ralph Warner. If you want to form a partnership, this book is an indispensable guide to partnerships and contains forms to help you create your own partnership agreement.

Four Practical Ways to Use the Forms in This Book

This book is a flexible resource that you can adapt to fit your needs and work style. There are at least four ways you can use the forms provided in this book.

- Because all forms are available to you electronically, the most efficient approach is to open, fill in, and print out a form, customizing it as needed. If you do use the electronic forms, be sure to read "Tips for Using the Downloadable Forms," below.

- Or, you can get the job done the old-fashioned way, by photocopying a form right out of the book and then filling it in with a typewriter or by hand.

- In some instances, especially where a form will be used repeatedly, you might want to print out or photocopy a pile of blank forms, filling them in later (by hand or typewriter) as needed.

- If someone else has already prepared a proposed contract and presented it to you for signature, you can use the appropriate form in this book as a sort of checklist to make sure that the proposed contract has all the recommended ingredients. If it doesn't, you can have the preparer use the book's form as a model when making modifications or additions.

CAUTION

Think twice before using the only copy of a form. Although it's possible to use the forms directly from this book, this is a poor idea because you'll be left without a clean copy if you need a similar document in the future. So if you decide to use a form, photocopy the form before you fill it out.

Tips for Using the Downloadable Forms

If you're using the downloadable forms—rather than the forms from the back of the book—you might notice that sometimes the instructions don't quite match up to the form. This is because, in some cases, you might need to fill out the downloadable form slightly differently than you would fill out the form in the back of the book. Here's what you need to know about filling out the forms electronically.

Checkboxes. On the downloadable forms, you don't need to use the checkboxes to mark which clauses you want to use. Instead, just delete any clause you don't want to use and include the ones you do. Also, delete the brackets (checkboxes) and any instructional text. The final product should read completely and smoothly. Here's an example from Form 2B, Partnership Agreement.

Book form:

> **3. Partnership Duration.** The partnership
> [X] began [ ] will begin on <u>January 1, 20xx</u> .
> It will continue
> [X] indefinitely until it is ended by the terms of this agreement.
> [ ] until _____ , unless ended sooner by the terms of this agreement.

Electronic form:

> **3. Partnership Duration.** The partnership began January 1, 20xx. It will continue indefinitely until it is ended by the terms of this agreement.

Word choice. Occasionally, a form will give you a choice of two or more words. On the downloadable forms, this choice is indicated by "[*choose one*:]."

For example, here is the first sentence in the example above before it was filled in:

> **3. Partnership Duration.** The partnership [*choose one*: began/will begin] on _____ .

Just include the correct word, deleting the instructional text, so that the sentence reads smoothly, like this:

> **3. Partnership Duration.** The partnership began on January 1, 20xx.

Fill-in text. When you fill in text on your downloadable forms, you can replace the entire blank line with your text: For example:

Book form:

> **2. Partnership Name.** The partnership will do business as a partnership under the name of <u>Four Brothers Construction</u> .

Electronic form:

> **2. Partnership Name.** The partnership will do business as a partnership under the name of Four Brothers Construction.

Final check. Before you print out the final draft of your document, check to make sure you've deleted any brackets, instructional text, and unnecessary clauses. Also, if you've deleted or added any clauses, double-check to make sure you've properly renumbered the clauses.

TIP

Read over the explanatory materials in each chapter before filling out the forms. This book is designed to be used as needed, rather than read through in its entirety. If you want to perform a particular task (like borrow money for your business), you can go right to the appropriate form (for example, Form 4A: Promissory Note). Just be sure to first read the introductory information at the beginning of the relevant chapter and at the beginning of the relevant section rather than jumping directly to the form and its instructions.

Do You Need a Lawyer?

Most small business transactions are relatively straightforward. Just as you routinely negotiate business deals involving significant dollar amounts without formal legal help, you can usually just as safely complete the basic legal paperwork needed to record your understanding.

But, like most generalizations, this one isn't always true. Creating a solid written agreement will occasionally mean seeking the advice of a lawyer to cope with a problematic issue. Fortunately, even when you decide to get a lawyer's help, the forms and information set out here should help you keep a tight rein on legal fees. You'll have gotten a running start by learning about the legal issues and perhaps drawing up a rough draft of the needed document, allowing you and your lawyer to focus on the few points that may not be routine.

Ideally, you should find a lawyer who's willing to serve as your small business legal coach—one who respects your ability to prepare drafts of routine paperwork and who stands ready to review and fine-tune your work when requested. A word

of caution here: Some lawyers still subscribe to the old-fashioned notion that they and only they are the repository of all legal information and expertise. In their view, you should turn every legal question and problem over to them, and your participation should be limited to promptly paying their bills. It should go almost without saying that even if this were an efficient way to run your business (it isn't—you clearly need to be involved in making all key decisions), you couldn't afford it.

To find a lawyer who's genuinely open to helping you help yourself and is sensitive to your need to keep costs down, talk to people who own or operate truly excellent small businesses. Ask them whom they've chosen as their legal mentors. Speak as well to your banker, accountant, insurance agent, and real estate broker—all of whom undoubtedly come into frequent contact with lawyers who creatively represent business clients.

TIP

Of the million or so American lawyers in private practice, probably only one in ten possesses sufficient training and experience in small business law to be of real help to you. And even when you locate a lawyer skilled in small business law in general, you need to make sure that he or she is knowledgeable about the specific job at hand. A lawyer who has a vast amount of experience in handling the sale and purchase of small businesses, for example, might have limited knowledge about the fast-changing world of commercial leases (not ideal if there's an unusual rent increase clause you want to discuss) and know next to nothing about dealing with state or federal regulatory agencies (not good if you need to appeal the suspension of your liquor license). In short, always ask about the lawyer's background in the particular area of law that affects you.

RESOURCE

Finding a good lawyer. When you need a lawyer, asking someone you trust for a referral is a good place to start. You can also try one of these excellent and free resources:

- **Nolo's Lawyer Directory.** Nolo has an easy-to-use online directory of lawyers, organized by location and area of expertise. You can find the directory and its comprehensive profiles at www.nolo.com/lawyers.

- **Lawyers.com.** At Lawyers.com you'll find a user-friendly search tool that allows you to tailor results by area of law and geography. You can also search for attorneys by name. Attorney profiles prominently display contact information, list topics of expertise, and show ratings—by both clients and other legal professionals.

- **Martindale.com.** Martindale.com offers an advanced search option that allows you to sort not only by practice area and location, but also by criteria like law school. Whether you look for lawyers by name or expertise, you'll find listings with detailed background information, peer and client ratings, and even profile visibility.

RESOURCE

Learn more about finding and working with a lawyer. You can get free information about finding and working with a lawyer at www.nolo.com/legal-encyclopedia/lawyer.

Get Updates and More Online

You can download any of the forms in this book at:

www.nolo.com/back-of-book/RUNSF.html

And if there are important changes to the information in this book, we'll post updates there, too. You'll also find other useful information, including author blogs.

Contract Basics

 FORMS

    To download the forms discussed in this chapter, go to this book's companion page on Nolo.com. See Appendix A for the link.

Most of the forms in this book are contracts—or promissory notes, which are just a particular type of contract. With any contract, you must understand what it says and make sure that it suits your needs. Also, you face two other important issues:

- How do you properly identify the businesses and individuals who are parties to the contract?
- How do the parties sign the contract to make it legally binding?

Rather than repeat the instructions for dealing with these issues many times throughout the book, we discuss the legal context and give you our recommendations in this first chapter.

Similarly, in this chapter, we also explain two other basic contract concepts that appear throughout the book. The first involves a disputes clause, which establishes a structure to allow the parties to resolve any disputes that could later occur. The second deals with modifying or adding to a contract, which could arise at any time.

But don't worry about having to memorize this basic information now in order to later complete a particular contract form. Along with the instructions for each form, we'll provide cross-references to the instructions in this chapter as needed.

Names Clause: Identifying the Parties to a Contract

At the beginning of most forms in this book, you'll need to fill in one or more names to identify the parties (individuals or businesses) who are agreeing to the contract. While this seems easy enough, it can sometimes be a little tricky, because how you identify the parties will vary somewhat depending on the types of business entities that are parties to the agreement.

For example, suppose you need to borrow money from your Uncle Al and want to put the loan in writing. First, you'll need a promissory note form (such as those in Chapter 4). Because both you and Uncle Al are individuals, you'll need to include both your names—you as borrower, Al as lender—with no additional identification needed.

In a business context, however, a promissory note—or for that matter, any other contract—can be used by people owning or managing any of a half-dozen types of legal entities. (See "Types of Business Entities," below.) So it can be a little more complicated to determine the correct name format to use for a business.

First, you need to make sure that you correctly name the business. Second, you must designate its legal structure (partnership or corporation, for instance), and if the business is other than a sole proprietorship, you must also note the state in which the company is organized.

Assume, for example, that Maria Jones is in the coin-operated laundry business as a sole proprietor and decides to buy the assets of a laundry owned by Clean Times, Inc., a corporation. The corporation's shareholders are Alice Appleby and Richard Reardon, who are respectively the president and secretary-treasurer. How do you state the buyer's and seller's names in the first clause of the contract to purchase the business?

Maria Jones (Buyer) and Clean Times, Inc., a California corporation (Seller), agree to the following sale.

Because a sole proprietorship is not legally a separate entity from its owner, you need not identify the state in which the business is organized. However, for a corporation, partnership, or an LLC, the state in which the buyer's business is organized should be included. For instance, if the buyer's corporation has filed its articles of incorporation in California, it's a California corporation.

If a sole proprietor does business under a name that's different from the sole proprietor's legal name, this is called a fictitious business name, an assumed business name, or a dba (doing business as).

You should include that different name in your contract. For instance, if Maria Jones of the above example operates her laundry business under the name CleanMat Laundry, she should include the fictitious name in the contract. The best way to do this is to add the fictitious name after the sole proprietor's name and the phrase "doing business as," as in "Maria Jones, doing business as CleanMat Laundry (Buyer)." A sole proprietor who doesn't use a fictitious business name can fill in his or her name as the buyer.

Likewise, a corporation, an LLC, or a partnership might also use a fictitious business name if for some reason the official business name is different than the trade name the business holds out to the public. For example, the partnership whose official name is "Adams & James" or the LLC formally organized as "XYZ Games, LLC" could do business as "Games & More." In that case, it should also include the dba, as in "XYZ Games, LLC, a District of Columbia limited liability company doing business as Games & More (Buyer)."

We've included a names chart, below, to consult whenever you need to fill in the names clause in any form. The chart gives the recommended format for completing the names clause.

Formats for Names in Legal Forms	
Type of Legal Entity	**Identification**
Individual/sole proprietor	John Smith
Two or more individuals/ sole proprietors	John Smith, Jane Jones, and Terry Thomson
Sole proprietor with a fictitious name	John Smith, doing business as John's Diner
General partnership	Smith & Jones, a California partnership
General partnership with a fictitious name	Smith & Jones, a California partnership doing business as John's Diner
LLC	Good News LLC, a California limited liability company
LLC with a fictitious name	Good News LLC, a California limited liability company doing business as John's Diner
Corporation	Modern Time, Inc., a California corporation
Corporation with a fictitious name	Modern Time, Inc., a California corporation doing business as John's Diner

FORM

You can also find the recommended formats for names in the downloadable form Names.rtf.

Signature Clause: Signing a Contract

For a contract to be legally binding, you must obtain the signature of the person or people with authority to legally bind each business. A sole proprietor signs the contract personally. For partnerships, LLCs, and corporations, one representative of the business usually signs the contract on the business's behalf. Some businesses, especially general partnerships, might require more than one owner to sign contracts.

A partnership's partnership agreement and an LLC's operating agreement should specify which owner or owners have the authority to sign sales contracts and bind the partnership or LLC, and should specify how many owners' signatures are required.

If the buyer is a corporation, an officer—usually the president or chief executive officer (CEO)—signs major contracts. However, the corporate bylaws might specify that more than one officer must sign contracts in order to bind the corporation.

For minor contracts that are part of a company's routine, someone who's less senior than a president, CEO, or manager might be able to sign the contract. Always include the signer's title (such as

Types of Business Entities

- **Sole Proprietorship.** A one-owner business in which the owner is personally liable for all business debts.
- **General Partnership.** A business entity formed by two or more people, all of whom are personally liable for all partnership debts. When two or more people are in business together and haven't formed a limited partnership, corporation, or limited liability company (LLC), they're treated as a general partnership by law even if they haven't signed a formal partnership agreement. A partnership doesn't pay federal income taxes; a partner's share of the profits or losses is reported on his or her personal tax return.
- **Limited Partnership.** A business entity formed by one or more general partners and one or more limited partners. Ordinarily, only the general partners are personally liable for the partnership debts.
- **Corporation.** A business entity formed by one or more shareholders. Ordinarily, a shareholder is not personally liable for the corporation's debts. This is true whether the corporation is organized for tax purposes as a regular (C) corporation or an S corporation; the two types of corporations differ only in terms of tax treatment. The big difference is that the undistributed income of a regular corporation is taxed at the corporate level. That's not true with an S corporation; for tax purposes, income and losses pass through to the individual shareholders as if they were partners in a partnership.
- **Limited Liability Company (LLC).** A business entity formed by one or more members. Ordinarily, a member is not personally liable for the LLC's debts and is taxed in the same way as if he or she were a partner (unless the LLC chooses to be taxed as a corporation).

"CEO" or "Sales Manager" in the space provided). Make sure that this is your routine business practice, and that the person who signs the contract has a grant of authority—written or otherwise—to do so. If a lot is at stake in a transaction, and the corporation you're dealing with intends to have someone other than its president sign a legal document on behalf of the corporation, it makes sense to ask to see the bylaw or directors' resolution authorizing the other officer to sign.

The parties should sign at least two copies of the contract—doing so creates an original document for both parties. (One exception is a promissory note. The borrower should sign only one promissory note, which the lender will keep until the debt is paid off.) After the contract is complete, each party should keep its copy of the document with other business records or, if the party is an individual, in another safe place.

Signature Formats

Signing a document might seem like a simple and obvious task, but you must do it in the proper format. Let's consider what format should be used to sign the contract between Maria Jones and Clean Times, discussed above. As sole proprietor, Maria Jones must begin with (1) her name or her fictitious business name, if she has one, followed by (2) the type of business entity it is—here, a sole proprietorship—followed by (3) her signature, (4) her name printed out, (5) her title in the business—in this case the owner, and (6) her address, like so:

Buyer

CleanMat

A sole proprietorship

By: _____

    Maria Jones

    Owner

    1234 Lucky Street

    White Plains, New York

Signature Formats

Sole proprietorship without fictitious name:

Dated: _____

By: _____

[Name of owner]

[Address]

Sole proprietorship with fictitious name:

Dated: _____

By: _____

[Name of owner] , doing business as [Fictitious name]

[Address]

General partnership without fictitious name:

[Partnership name] _____ ,

a _____ [State] _____ partnership

[Name of owner]

[Address]

(repeat this block for multiple signers)

Dated: _____

By: _____

[Name of signer]

[Title of signer]

General partnership with fictitious name:

[Partnership name] _____ ,

a [State] _____ partnership doing business as

[Fictitious name]

[Address]

(repeat this block for multiple signers)

Dated: _____

By: _____

[Name of signer]

[Title of signer]

Corporation without fictitious name:

[Corporation name] , a _____ [State] _____ corporation

[Address]

(repeat this block for multiple signers)

Dated: _____

By: _____

[Name of signer]

[Title of signer]

Corporation with fictitious name:

[Corporation name] _____ ,

a [State] _____ corporation doing business as

[Fictitious name]

[Address]

(repeat this block for multiple signers)

Dated: _____

By: _____

[Name of signer]

[Title of signer]

Limited liability company without fictitious name:

[LLC Name] _____ ,

a [State] _____ limited liability company

[Address]

(repeat this block for multiple signers)

Dated: _____

By: _____

[Name of signer]

[Title of signer]

Limited liability company with fictitious name:

[LLC Name] _____ ,

a [State] limited liability company doing business as

[Fictitious name]

[Address]

(repeat this block for multiple signers)

Dated: _____

By: _____

[Name of signer]

[Title of signer]

The selling corporation includes the same information.

Clean Times, Inc.
A New York Corporation
By: _____
    Alice Appleby
    President
    123 Chesterfield Boulevard
    White Plains, New York

We've included a signature chart, above, to show you how to deal with signatures in all common business contexts.

FORM

The signature formats are also in the downloadable form Signing.rtf.

A Business Owner's Personal Liability

How a business is legally organized is critical to determining whether or not a business owner who signs a contract or other document is personally liable if things go wrong. This is an important issue: When you're the person signing, you want to know if you're putting your personal (nonbusiness) assets at risk. And when someone on the other side of a transaction is signing, you need to know if you can go after his or her personal assets if the business fails to meet its obligations.

If a business is organized as a sole proprietorship or general partnership, an owner is automatically personally liable for meeting the terms of all business contracts. (In a limited partnership, only the general partner(s) would be liable.) If the contract terms aren't met, the person or business on the other side of the deal can sue and get a judgment (a court determination that a sum of money is owed) against not only the business but its owner as well, and the owner's assets can be taken by the creditor to satisfy (pay) the judgment amount.

However, if a corporation or an LLC fails to meet the terms of a contract, only the business is liable. This means that the person or business on the other side of the deal is only able to get a judgment against the business (not the owner) and can only collect from the business's assets (not the owner's)—unless an owner of a corporation or an LLC voluntarily waives this barrier to personal liability by personally guaranteeing the contract, as explained below.

EXAMPLE 1: Harold signs a five-year lease for a car repair shop he plans to run under the name of Hal's Garage. Because he doesn't incorporate or form an LLC and no one else owns the business with him, the law describes his business as a sole proprietorship. Harold's business never takes off and, after six frustrating months, he closes. The landlord sues for unpaid rent and gets a judgment against Harold personally. The landlord can collect not only from the few paltry dollars left in the business's bank account, but can go after Harold's personal bank account, his car, and his house (although Harold might be eligible to invoke debtor's exemption laws to limit what the landlord can take).

EXAMPLE 2: Spencer forms a corporation called Spencer Enterprises, Inc. The corporation leases space for five years to run a car repair shop; Spencer signs the lease as president of Spencer Enterprises, Inc. After six months, the business closes. The landlord can only get a judgment from the corporation and collect from its meager assets. Although Spencer loses all the money he put into the business, his car, bank account, and other personal assets are safe.

A Business Owner's Personal Guarantee

When an owner of shares in a corporation or a member of an LLC signs a contract, promissory note, or lease in his or her capacity as an owner of the corporation or LLC (with his or her title listed below his or her name), he or she does not become personally liable. The contract, note, or lease makes it clear that the owner is signing on behalf of the business, not as an individual. If the corporation or LLC defaults on payments, the seller, lender, landlord, or other party must get a court judgment against the LLC or corporation and will be able to collect from the business's assets only.

For that reason, the seller, lender, landlord, or other party might want to get a personal guarantee from one or more of the owners of the corporation or LLC, making the owner(s) personally liable for repayment. In this case, an owner would sign as president of the corporation or manager of the LLC and also as an individual, to personally guarantee payment.

! **CAUTION**

Corporate and LLC owners beware. You should think very carefully about personally guaranteeing a loan. A personal guarantee means that your personal assets are at risk if the loan is not repaid. Because the primary purpose of forming an LLC or corporation is to limit the owners' personal liability for business debts, owners should understand that they are giving up this limited liability when they sign a personal guarantee. On the other hand, most commercial lenders will not lend money to new corporations or LLCs without a personal guarantee. Giving up limited liability might be the only way to obtain the loan.

If the parties agree that a personal guarantee is appropriate, the language shown below can be added to the end of a contract, promissory note, or lease to provide that guarantee.

▤ **FORM**

These optional guarantee clauses are in the downloadable form Guarantee.rtf. If you decide to use one of the guarantees, copy the appropriate form and paste it into your document.

Customized Guarantees

Sometimes a guarantor will agree to be liable for only a certain amount of money or for only a limited period. You can tailor the guarantee accordingly, for example:

Guarantee for a limited amount:

> In consideration of _[name of lender]_ lending funds to _[name of corporation or LLC]_ , I personally guarantee the timely payment of the above promissory note. The maximum amount of my liability, however, is $5,000.

Guarantee for a limited time

> In consideration of _[name of landlord]_ signing the above lease with _[name of corporation or LLC]_ , I personally guarantee the performance of all obligations of _[name of corporation or LLC]_ for the first twelve months of the above lease.

! **CAUTION**

Preprinted guarantees could be more complicated. The forms in this book are more straightforward than some forms you might encounter in the commercial world. A bank's form for a loan guarantee could, for example, contain a sentence like the following, which asks the guarantor to "waive notice of acceptance, notice of nonpayment, protest, and notice of protest with respect to the obligation covered hereunder." Lying behind this linguistic fog are statutory rights that might allow a guarantor to stall—or even prevent— a lender from collecting on a guarantee. For obvious reasons, a commercial lender will want you to waive, or give up, these rights. It's often okay to waive these statutory rights, and it might be difficult to obtain a loan from a commercial lender if you don't. But as with any legal document you're asked to sign, if you don't fully understand the terms, it's best to consult a lawyer.

Personal Guarantee of a Contract—Single Guarantor

In consideration of __[name of other party]_____

signing the above contract, I personally guarantee the performance of all obligations of __[name of_____

__corporation or LLC]_____ in the above contract.

Dated: _____

Signature: _____

Printed name:_____

Address: _____

Personal Guarantee of a Contract—Two or More Guarantors

In consideration of __[name of other party]_____

signing the above contract, with __[name of corporation or LLC]_____

we jointly and individually guarantee the performance of all obligations of __[name of corporation or LLC]

in the above contract.

Dated: _____

Signature: _____

Printed name:_____

Address: _____

Dated: _____

Signature: _____

Printed name:_____

Address: _____

Personal Guarantee of a Promissory Note—Single Guarantor

In consideration of __[name of lender]_____ lending funds to

__[name of corporation or LLC]__ , I personally guarantee the timely payment of the above promissory note.

Dated: _____

Signature: _____

Printed name:_____

Address: _____

Personal Guarantee of a Promissory Note—Two or More Guarantors

In consideration of __[name of lender]_____

lending funds to __[name of corporation or LLC]_____ ,

we jointly and individually guarantee the timely payment of the above promissory note.

Dated: _____

Signature: _____

Printed name:_____

Address: _____

Dated: _____

Signature: _____

Printed name:_____

Address: _____

Requiring a Spouse's Signature

If one party is signing a document in a capacity that makes him or her personally liable for a business debt or other business obligation, the other party might ask that his or her spouse sign as well. This is most likely to happen, for example, if you're personally borrowing money that you'll use in your business or if you're personally guaranteeing a debt or other obligation of a corporation in which you own shares or of an LLC in which you're a member.

Similarly, you might find yourself in a situation in which you'd like to have the spouse of the other party sign a document. In addition to the situation just mentioned, this could happen if you're lending money to or entering into an agreement with an individual whose spouse is financially well-off and could repay the debt if the borrower defaulted.

Not surprisingly, having your spouse sign a document can substantially increase the other party's legal rights. For example, in most states if you alone sign for a loan or agree to be liable for any other obligation, the creditor can get a judgment for nonpayment against you but not against your spouse. This means that, ordinarily—except in community property states, where all marital, or community, property can be taken to pay for the debts of both spouses—a creditor will be able to reach the property that you own in your own name, but not the property that you and your spouse own in both your names.

However, if you and your spouse both sign a contract and then don't abide by its terms, the other party will be able to sue and get a judgment against both of you. In addition, the creditor can then enforce the judgment by seizing your joint bank account or jointly owned real estate as well as property you own in your name alone. The creditor will also be able to go after property that's in your spouse's name alone, as well as garnish your spouse's paycheck.

If the parties agree that a spouse's personal guarantee is appropriate, you can use one of the personal guarantee clauses discussed above.

Community Property States

The following are community property states:

Arizona	Louisiana	Texas
California	Nevada	Washington
Idaho	New Mexico	Wisconsin

(Also, in Alaska, South Dakota, and Tennessee, a couple can sign a written document agreeing that all property will be treated as community property.)

In community property states, a married couple's property tends to be primarily community (joint) property regardless of the names in which it's held. Each spouse might also own separate property, but—especially in longer marriages—most property tends to be owned by both. A creditor can go after the community property of you and your spouse to pay off a debt, even if you alone signed for the loan.

If your spouse does have separate property— property a spouse owned before getting married, property acquired after marriage by gift or inheritance, or property agreed in writing to be kept separate—his or her separate property is normally beyond a creditor's reach. But if your spouse signs a personal guarantee, his or her separate property will be at risk if you default on your payments.

Witnesses and Notaries

Very few legal documents need to be notarized or signed by witnesses. In fact, only one form in this book needs to be notarized (Form 5F: Seller's Affidavit: No Creditors in Chapter 5), and in some states notarization isn't even required for that form. For business forms, notarization and witnessing are usually limited to documents that are going to be recorded at a public office charged with keeping such records (usually called the county recorder or register of deeds). State laws require witnesses or notaries to sign some other types of documents, such as living trusts or powers of attorney.

> (!) **CAUTION**
>
> **Having a document notarized doesn't guarantee that the person signing the document has the authority to do so.** When a notary public witnesses a signature and enters that information into the notary's record book, the notary is only certifying that the person signing the document is who he or she claims to be. Whether that person has the authority to sign a document on behalf of a business is another matter entirely. Consider asking for resolutions from the business's shareholders, members, or partners approving the transaction and granting the person the authority to bind the business to the contract. For more information on these kinds of resolutions, see *The Corporate Records Handbook: Meetings, Minutes & Resolutions* and *Your Limited Liability Company: An Operating Manual*, by Anthony Mancuso (Nolo).

Standard Clauses

If you were to look at a handful of business contracts—loan agreements, sales contracts, or leases—you'd find that many of them include identical clauses, often found at the end of the contracts. These clauses address issues that often come up in any contract, such as:

- whether the parties intend the contract to be modified in writing only
- how each party will communicate with the other regarding the contract, and
- what will happen to the rest of the contract if a judge decides that one part of it is not legal.

Instead of writing clauses to address these issues from scratch, lawyers find it quicker to consult form books, where they find them already written and ready to drop into almost any contract. These clauses are known as boilerplate clauses (boiler-plates are sheets of steel that can be cut to form the shell of any boiler). The essence of a boilerplate clause is that no one is likely to argue much about the precise language of the clause—but whether you and the other side want to include the clause is, of course, a matter of negotiation.

That said, the clauses that follow should elicit little, if any, resistance from the other party to your contract. That's because most of the time, the ones we've chosen will benefit both of you. For example, one boilerplate clause we recommend allows you and the other party to specify which state's law will apply in the event of a disagreement over the meaning or implementation of your contract. Without that clause, if you and the other side get into a dispute over the contract, you might spend time and money arguing over that preliminary issue—*before* you even get to the heart of your dispute!

Let's look at each clause and see why it's useful to have it in your contract. Each of these clauses is included in most contracts in the book, generally at the end.

Entire Agreement

Before you sign your agreement, you and the other party will negotiate certain points. Hopefully, the points you and the other party agree on will end up in your contract. But sometimes you and the other party will talk about a point or an issue and leave it out of the final agreement. The language in this section, sometimes called an integration clause, means that only what is written in the agreement (not what you discussed) is part of the contract between you and the other party. Although it's not foolproof, including an integration clause in your agreement can help prevent the other party from claiming that you agreed to something that's not in (or conflicts with something in) the contract, and use those prior conversations to prove that you did agree to it.

Similarly, sometimes you and the other party will have negotiated your contract by writing letters back and forth, or will have written up a temporary agreement to govern your relationship until you have time to create a more formal contract. This clause also prevents those previous writings (any letters, memos, or other agreements or contracts) from being considered part of your contract if,

somewhere along the line, the terms of your contract conflict with what's written in those other documents.

Successors and Assignees

After you sign the contract, you might decide to sell or merge your company. Will the new company or your heirs gain your rights under the contract? Or, suppose you'd simply like to get someone else to take over your rights and obligations under the contract—can you do so without having to get the other party's permission? The successors and assignees clause attempts to address these issues.

In case one party sells or gives away (assigns) its rights under the contract to another company or person (or leaves the rights to an heir after death), the agreements in this book provide that the terms of the contract are binding on anyone who receives a right or obligation.

This agreement does not require the buyer or seller to get permission before assigning its rights under the contract. Sometimes a party might understandably object to this; for instance, if you contract with a specialty manufacturer to create custom goods for your company, you wouldn't want the manufacturer to be able to assign this duty to someone else. If that's the case, you can modify this clause to provide that the contract can be assigned only with the other party's written permission.

Notices

Because you and the other party might not be seeing each other frequently, it makes sense to exchange mailing addresses and agree on how you'll send written communications about the contract to each other. Also, if you need to deliver an important legal notice to the other party, such as a warning that the other party is in breach of the contract, or notice to a landlord that you're terminating your tenancy, you should make sure you deliver notice in one of the ways set out in this paragraph (in person, by certified mail, or by overnight courier), since this is how you and the other party have agreed to get in touch with each other. Generally, you'll fill in your address by your signature at the end of the contract.

Governing Law

Although you and the other party to your contract probably won't end up in court over your contract, it makes sense to designate which state's law will apply to the contract before you get into a dispute. If you don't choose a state now, you might waste time fighting over this issue later. Usually, you and the other party to the contract will be in the same state, so fill in that state.

If you and the other party are located in different states, designating the governing law is even more important. If you don't designate a state to govern your agreement, you could spend precious time arguing over the law that will apply to your contract, instead of trying to resolve the actual dispute.

If you can negotiate it, it's usually advantageous for you to have the laws of your home state govern an agreement. This is because every state has different laws regarding general contract interpretation, and you and your attorney will probably be most familiar with the laws of your home state.

Counterparts

Counterparts is legal jargon for identical copies of a document. This clause allows you to send copies of the contract to the other party or parties, asking them to sign and return the signature page to you. When you put the other signature page(s) together with your signature page, you have a complete set of signatures that makes your copy an original and fully signed document.

Modification

After you've signed your agreement, from time to time you and the other party to the contract might discuss various aspects of your agreement and even talk about changing some of its provisions. To prevent a casual conversation with the other party from turning into a full-scale amendment of the agreement, the modification clause requires any amendment to the contract to be in writing and signed by both of you. That way, you and the other party can make sure you've thought about the changes and agreed to them.

Waiver

Failing to enforce a right you have under a contract can sometimes cause you to lose (waive) that right. Your agreement attempts to prevent that from happening by requiring all parties to agree in advance that if one of them doesn't enforce a right, it doesn't mean that party has permanently given up that right.

For example, if the buyer is late on an installment payment and the seller doesn't immediately try to terminate the contract for breach, this clause says that the seller isn't prevented from exercising its rights under the contract at a later time.

> **CAUTION**
>
> **Clauses like this don't always work.** This clause isn't foolproof. A judge could ignore it and infer from a party's behavior that it has permanently waived a right. For example, if the buyer is consistently three days late with every installment payment for three years, a judge might not allow the seller to suddenly terminate the contract for breach. To avoid this, if the other party misses an obligation or violates a term of the contract, send a letter saying you are willing to overlook the missed obligation or violation this time, but that you're going to enforce your rights in the future.

Severability

There's always a possibility that you'll get into a dispute with the other party and a judge will need to interpret your agreement. Some courts, upon discovering an unenforceable or invalid clause in a contract, will make the entire contract unenforceable—which is probably not what either of you intended. This clause tries to preserve the rest of the contract if part of it doesn't pass muster with a judge by severing the unenforceable provision or provisions from the contract, leaving the enforceable provisions intact.

Resolving Disputes

Sooner or later, even the most conscientious business is likely to run into a legal dispute involving a contract. One way to resolve it is through a court fight. This approach is usually a poor one, since trials are typically expensive, prolonged, emotionally draining, and, in some instances, even threatening to the survival of the business. It usually makes far more sense to attempt to resolve disputes through other means, such as:

- **Negotiation.** The parties to the dispute try to voluntarily work out their differences through open discussions that often result in each compromising a little to put the matter to rest.
- **Mediation.** The parties try to achieve a voluntary settlement with the help of a neutral third party (the mediator) who helps disputants craft their own solution. Mediation is inexpensive, quick, confidential, and effective about 80% of the time.
- **Arbitration.** The parties allow a neutral third party (the arbitrator) to arrive at a binding decision in order to resolve the dispute. Normally, the decision is solely up to the arbitrator. In some situations, however, the parties establish certain limits in advance of the arbitration—for example, X employee can be awarded anywhere between $25,000 and

$100,000 if the supervising personnel of Y employer have sexually harassed her. Where limits are set by the parties, the arbitrator is bound by them. Arbitration is almost always speedier and usually much less expensive than litigation.

Ideally, you'd like to be able to settle disputes through negotiations conducted by you and the other parties involved. This is usually a speedy, inexpensive way to put disagreements behind you and move on with your business. Unfortunately, however, even when everyone tries in good faith to negotiate a settlement, they don't always succeed.

Recognizing this, the dispute resolution paragraph set out below lets the parties agree in advance on a framework mandating noncourt alternatives, such as mediation and arbitration for resolving disputes.

FORM

This clause is also in the downloadable form Disputes.rtf. You can add it to any contract in this book that doesn't already include this dispute clause.

As you see, this dispute resolution system allows the parties to make one of three choices:

- **Litigation.** You go to court and let a judge or jury resolve the dispute. Although this is the traditional method, as mentioned, it's also usually the most expensive, time-consuming, and emotionally draining.
- **Mediation and Possible Litigation.** The parties agree to let a mediator help them reach a voluntary settlement of the dispute. If mediation doesn't accomplish this goal, any party can take the dispute to court. You can name the mediator when you prepare the form or agree on one when the need arises.
- **Mediation and Possible Arbitration.** This is similar to the previous choice: The parties start by submitting the dispute to mediation. Here, however, if mediation doesn't lead

Disputes

(*Choose one*)

☐ **Litigation.** If a dispute arises, either party may take the matter to court.

☐ **Mediation and Possible Litigation.** If a dispute arises, the parties will try in good faith to settle it through mediation conducted by:

☐ _____ .

☐ a mediator to be mutually selected.

　The parties will share the costs of the mediator equally. Each party will cooperate fully and fairly with the mediator and will attempt to reach a mutually satisfactory compromise to the dispute. If the dispute is not resolved within 30 days after it is referred to the mediator, either party may take the matter to court.

☐ **Mediation and Possible Arbitration.** If a dispute arises, the parties will try in good faith to settle it through mediation conducted by:

☐ _____ .

☐ a mediator to be mutually selected.

　The parties will share the costs of the mediator equally. Each party will cooperate fully and fairly with the mediator and will attempt to reach a mutually satisfactory compromise to the dispute. If the dispute is not resolved within 30 days after it is referred to the mediator, it will be arbitrated by:

☐ _____ .

☐ an arbitrator to be mutually selected.

　Judgment on the arbitration award may be entered in any court that has jurisdiction over the matter. Costs of arbitration, including lawyers' fees, will be allocated by the arbitrator.

☐ **Attorneys' Fees.** If either party brings a legal action arising out of a dispute over this agreement, the losing party will reimburse the prevailing party for all reasonable costs and attorneys' fees incurred by the prevailing party in the lawsuit.

to a settlement, the dispute is submitted to arbitration. The arbitrator makes a final decision that will be enforced by a court, if necessary. You can name the arbitrator when you prepare the form or agree on one when the need arises.

- **Attorneys' Fees.** This provision can make both parties pause and think before rushing to start a lawsuit. The outcome of a lawsuit is rarely 100% predictable. For this reason, the possibility of having to pay the other side's costs can encourage the contracting parties to resolve their differences through a negotiated settlement, perhaps with the help of a mediator. On the other hand, if you prefer the normal practice in the United States of having litigants bear their own costs, you should not choose this provision. *Use this provision only if you checked the "Litigation" or "Mediation and Possible Litigation" boxes discussed above. This clause is not compatible with the "Mediation and Possible Arbitration" clause.*

RESOURCE

For a comprehensive and practical discussion of mediation and other methods of resolving disputes, see *Mediate, Don't Litigate: Strategies for Successful Mediation,* by Peter Lovenheim (Nolo), (available as an e-book only at www.nolo.com).

Attachments

No legal form is likely to be a perfect fit for every transaction it could be used for. You'll sometimes need to tinker with one of our forms to make it work for you. Large chunks of material can best be added to a contract *before it's signed* by using an attachment to the form.

An attachment is the routine place to put lengthy material that doesn't easily fit in the form we provide. As long as the attachment clearly refers to the contract to which it is being attached, this

approach is as legal as it is sensible. For example, a lengthy legal description of real estate you're buying, the specifications for the remodeling of your business space, or a list of parts for a machine you are ordering would all appropriately go in an attachment.

This book includes a specific attachment to a lease (Form 6J) and a specific attachment to a real estate purchase contract (Form 7E). For attachments to other types of contracts, you can use the general form shown below.

Instructions for Form 1A: Attachment

FORM

All the forms in this book are provided in Appendix B and on the Nolo website. To access the downloadable forms online, use the link provided in Appendix A.

When preparing two or more attachments, number them consecutively—that is, Attachment Number 1, Attachment Number 2, and so on.

As you read the instructions for form 1A, you might want to refer to the form in Appendix B or open the form on your computer so you can follow along. (Before you use the form in Appendix B, be sure to photocopy it so you'll have a clean copy to use later.)

1. Names

List the parties in the same order that they appear in the contract to which the attachment belongs.

2. Terms of Attachment

In the first blank, enter the title of the main contract. Most contracts have a title located at the top of the document that describes the type of contract, such as "Sales Contract." If your contract includes a title like this, enter it here. If your contract does not have a formal title, make up a title that indicates the subject of the agreement. For instance, if you are amending a contract to buy or sell business equipment, you might call it "Purchase Contract."

Attachment Number _____

1. **Names.** This attachment is made by _____

_____ and _____

_____ .

2. **Terms of Attachment.** We agree to the following attachment to the _____

_____[*insert title of document*]_____ dated _____ concerning:

_____[*state in general terms the subject of the contract*]_____

_____

_____[*state in specific terms the subject of the attachment*]_____

_____

_____

_____

_____

_____

_____

_____

_____

_____

_____

Dated: _____

Name of business: _____

a _____

By: _____

Printed name: _____

Title: _____

Address: _____

_____

Name of business: _____

a _____

By: _____

Printed name: _____

Title: _____

Address: _____

_____

In the second blank, enter the date of the main contract. This is usually the date the contract was signed. You can usually find this information in the first paragraph of the main contract or at the end of the contract with the signatures.

In the third blank, briefly state what the main contract is about. For instance, if it is a contract to rent business equipment, your description might read "the rental of business equipment and furniture from Sun Ray, Inc."

Finally, in the last blank, describe in detail the information you want to include in your attachment. This is usually something like a long list of items one party is purchasing from the other that doesn't easily fit into the original agreement. For example, let's say Racafrax, Inc., is selling its business and is assigning all of its equipment leases to the buyer. Rather than list these equipment leases in the purchase contract, Racafrax creates an attachment to the contract and lists the numerous leases there. Here are samples of what the terms might look like:

Sample 1:

> The following leases are assigned to the buyer:
> - Equipment Lease dated September 18, 20xx between Racafrax, Inc., and Equipment Co.
> - Equipment Lease dated May 27, 20xx between Racafrax, Inc., and Packaging Machine Co.
> - Equipment Lease dated July 22, 20xx between Racafrax, Inc., and Fred's Audio Visual, Inc.

Sample 2:

> Portable exhibit unit Model 600 shown in Seller's current catalogue shall be modified to include a third exhibit wall, 10' x 8', in a curved-wall configuration with spaces for three electronic graphic panels, 2.5' x 2.5' each. The entire exhibit shall be professionally finished in gray fabric #205, and the laminate finish for the shelving shall be wheat.

Sample 3:

> Seller agrees to deliver ten bookcases on the first day of each month for four months, beginning July 1, 20xx. Buyer will pay the balance of the purchase price in four installments of $900 each. The first payment will be due on July 1, 20xx; the second will be due on August 1, 20xx; the third on September 1, 20xx; and the fourth on October 1, 20xx.

Signatures

All parties to the main document should sign the attachment, and the attachment should be dated.

Amendments

Once a contract has been signed, it can be changed only if all the parties agree and sign an amendment. This book includes a specific amendment of a lease (Form 6I) and a specific amendment of a real estate purchase contract (Form 7F). For amendments to other types of contracts, you can use the general form shown below.

How to Make Small Modifications

There are a couple of ways you can modify a contract:

With your computer. If the parties have not signed the contract, and you are creating a form using a downloadable form, you can use your word processing program to change or add to it to suit your needs.

Make small changes by hand. After a form is printed (or even handwritten), it's often necessary to make changes. It's both practical and perfectly legal to make small changes by crossing out language that doesn't apply and using a pen to add new material. After you do so, have all parties initial and date the changes to show that they agree. This can be done next to the changed wording, if there's room, or in the margin.

Amendment Number _____

1. **Names.** This amendment is made by _____
   _____ and _____
   _____ .

2. **Terms of Amendment.** We agree to the following amendment to the ___ [*insert title of document*]
   _____ dated _____ concerning:
   [*state in general terms the subject of the contract*] _____

   _____

   _____

   _____

   _____

   [*state in specific terms the subject of the amendment*]

   _____

   _____

   _____

   _____

   _____

   _____

   In all other respects, the terms of the original contract and any earlier amendments will remain in effect. If there is conflict between this amendment and the original contract or any earlier amendment, the terms of this amendment will prevail.

   Dated: _____

   Name of business: _____

   a _____
   By: _____
   Printed name: _____
   Title: _____
   Address: _____
   _____

   Name of business: _____

   a _____
   By: _____
   Printed name: _____
   Title: _____
   Address: _____
   _____

Amendment Number 1

1. **Names.** This amendment is made by Village Rentals, LLC, a New York Limited Liability Company and Claudia Redgrave, doing business as Sunnyside Café .

2. **Terms of Amendment.** We agree to the following amendment to the Equipment Rental Contract dated October 17, 20xx concerning: the rental of two Sun Ray Model space heaters.

    Paragraph 4 is amended to reduce the rent from $120 per week to $100 per week beginning December 1, 20xx.

In all other respects, the terms of the original contract and any earlier amendments will remain in effect. If there is conflict between this amendment and the original contract or any earlier amendment, the terms of this amendment will prevail.

Dated: November 25, 20xx

Name of business: Village Rentals, LLC

a New York Limited Liability Company

By: *Louis Dickens*

Printed name: Louis Dickens

Title: President

Address: 125 State Street, Ithaca, New York

Name of business: Sunnyside Café

a Sole Proprietorship

By: *Claudia Redgrave*

Printed name: Claudia Redgrave

Title: Owner

Address: 1020 University Avenue, Ithaca, New York

! CAUTION

Don't use amendments for multiple changes.
Amendments to existing contracts work fine when a couple of items are being changed (for example, a completion date is being extended or a dollar amount raised or lowered), but can cause confusion when lots of items in the original contract will be changed. Where changes will be extensive, it often makes sense to redo the entire document to avoid the possibility of confusion.

Instructions for Form 1B: Amendment

All the forms in this book are provided in Appendix B and on the Nolo website. To access the downloadable forms online, use the link provided in Appendix A.

Number amendments consecutively—that is, Amendment 1, Amendment 2, and so on.

As you read the instructions for form 1B, you might want to refer to the form in Appendix B or open the form on your computer so you can follow along. (Before you use the form in Appendix B, be sure to photocopy it so you'll have a clean copy to use later.)

1. Names

List the parties in the same order that they appear in the contract being amended.

2. Terms of Amendment

In the first blank, enter the title of the contract being amended. Most contracts have a title located at the top of the document that describes the type of contract, such as "Sales Contract." If your contract includes a title like this, enter it here. If your contract does not have a formal title, make up a title that indicates the subject of the agreement. For instance, if you are amending a contract to buy or sell business equipment, you might call it "Purchase Contract."

In the second blank, enter the date of the contract being amended. This is usually the date the contract was signed. You can usually find this information in the first paragraph of the contract or at the end of the contract with the signatures.

In the third blank, briefly state what the contract being amended is about. For instance, if it is a contract to rent business equipment, your description might read "the rental of business equipment and furniture from Sun Ray, Inc."

Finally, in the last blank, describe in detail the information you want to include in your amendment. Include the changes you are making to the contract and a paragraph or provision number, if possible. For example, if you are deleting a paragraph or clause in your agreement, your amendment might read "Paragraph 16 of the original contract is deleted in its entirety." If you are changing a portion of an agreement—for instance, you are raising or lowering an equipment rental fee—your amendment might read "Paragraph 4 is amended to reduce the rent from $120 per week to $100 per week beginning December 30, 20xx."

Signatures

All parties to the main document should sign the amendment, and the amendment should be dated.

Forming Your Business

 FORMS

    To download the forms discussed in this chapter, go to this book's companion page on Nolo.com. See Appendix A for the link.

When you start a new business, you must choose a legal format. For most small businesses, the choices come down to these:

- sole proprietorship
- general partnership
- regular corporation (sometimes called a C corporation)
- S corporation, or
- limited liability company (LLC).

Other legal formats—limited partnership, professional corporation, and nonprofit corporation —are unlikely to meet the needs of the typical small business.

If you start a one-person business or work as a freelancer or independent contractor, your business will automatically be treated as a sole proprietorship unless you establish a corporation or an LLC. Similarly, if you start a business with two or more people, your business will automatically be treated as a general partnership unless you form a corporation, an LLC, or a limited partnership.

The most important factors in deciding which way to go are:

- **Personal Liability.** Will you be personally liable for business debts? (Personal liability means that a business creditor—a person or company to whom your business owes money—can get a judgment against you for the debt. The creditor can then collect the judgment out of your personal assets such as a personal bank account or your home.) The fast answer is that as a sole proprietor or a partner, you'll face personal liability for business debts. But as the owner of shares in a corporation or as a member of an LLC, you'll generally face no personal liability—unless, of course, you voluntarily agree to assume it by signing a personal guarantee (such as for a business loan).

TIP

Limited liability isn't a big deal for many microbusinesses. A great many small service and retail businesses simply don't subject their owners to significant debt or lawsuit risk. And often even in the few cases where they do, a good insurance policy will provide needed protection. This means that there's often no compelling need to form a corporation or an LLC when you're just starting out.

- **Taxes.** Will you and the other business owners simply report your portion of profits and losses on your own income tax returns, or will the business itself be taxed on its profits? Sole proprietors, partners, owners of S corporation stock, and members of LLCs need only contend with one level of taxation: All taxes are paid by the owners on their individual returns. By contrast, a regular or C corporation pays taxes on its corporate earnings in addition to the taxes paid by the shareholders who receive dividends. (Also, LLCs can choose corporate-style taxation without converting their legal structure to a corporation.)
- **Time and Expense.** Will it be time-consuming and costly to form and maintain the business? Sole proprietorships and partnerships are relatively easy and inexpensive to start and keep up. Corporations and LLCs typically require more time and effort and cost a bit more—but the cost needn't be a tremendous burden. You can handle all or most of the paperwork yourself by using one of the Nolo books listed below.
- **Fringe Benefits.** Will the business be able to provide fringe benefits (health insurance, retirement plans, and the like) to the owners and deduct the cost of those benefits as a business expense? This question is only

relevant to businesses with enough income to pay fairly generous fringe benefits in the first place. But if your business is lucky enough to be in this category, the regular C corporation offers the best tax-saving opportunities.

Form Your Entity Online

With Nolo's online formation service, forming your LLC or corporation can be quick and easy. You'll complete a comprehensive interview about you and your business. Then Nolo will file the necessary forms.

To start your formation now, go to www.nolo. com/products/business-suite/business-formation/online-business-formation-services.

RESOURCE

For in-depth information on choosing a legal format for your business, see Chapter 1 of *Legal Guide for Starting & Running a Small Business*, by Fred S. Steingold and David M. Steingold (Nolo). For specifics and useful forms to create various types of business entities, see the following publications from Nolo:

- *Form Your Own Limited Liability Company*, by Anthony Mancuso, shows you how to establish an LLC in all 50 states.
- *Incorporate Your Business: A Step-by-Step Guide to Forming a Corporation in Any State*, by Anthony Mancuso, shows you how to form a corporation in all 50 states.
- *Form a Partnership: The Complete Legal Guide*, by Denis Clifford and Ralph Warner, shows you how to form a partnership and create a lasting partnership agreement.
- You can also find lots of useful and free information about starting a business on Nolo's Business Formation page at www.nolo.com/legal-encyclopedia/llc-corporations-partnerships.

TIP

It's often smart to start with the simplest legal format and convert later if necessary. It can be eminently sensible to start out as a simple, inexpensive sole proprietorship or partnership. Later you can convert to a corporation or an LLC if your risk of personal liability increases or there are compelling tax reasons to do so.

To guide you through the steps you must take to form any type of business, read Form 2A: Checklist for Starting a Small Business.

The other forms in this chapter help you start a partnership, a corporation, or a one-owner LLC. No formal document is required to start a sole proprietorship. However, there are several practical and legal steps you must take to put your business on the right track. (This is covered in Form 2A: Checklist for Starting a Small Business, mentioned above.)

Partnerships. If you are starting a partnership, preparing a written partnership agreement allows you to provide a sound footing for your legal relationship with your partners and helps prevent or resolve disputes that may later arise. Use Form 2B: Partnership Agreement for this purpose.

Limited Liability Companies (LLCs). Many business owners who want to limit their personal liability prefer the simplicity and flexibility of the LLC over the corporation. To form an LLC, owners must file articles of organization with the state and sign an operating agreement. If you are starting an LLC and you will be its sole owner, you can use Form 2F: LLC Operating Agreement for Single-Member LLC to help preserve your limited liability status. (This book does not provide an operating agreement for multimember LLCs; however, the instructions for Form 2A: Checklist for Starting a Small Business give other resources for multimember LLCs.) If you wish to give each member of your LLC a document showing his or her ownership interest in the company, you can use Form 2G: LLC Membership Certificate.

Corporations. If you decide to form a corporation, this book offers three useful documents for this purpose. Before forming the corporation, it's sensible to have all shareholders agree in advance on the basic elements of the business, including the name and purpose of the corporation, how many shares each owner will acquire, and who will serve on the board of directors. Use Form 2C: Preincorporation Agreement to record this information.

To form the corporation, owners must file articles of incorporation with the state and create corporate bylaws. Form 2D: Corporate Bylaws lays out the legal rules for running the corporation and covers such matters as how many people will serve on the board of directors, when and where regular meetings will be held, who may call a special meeting, and what officers the corporation will have.

Unless all shareholders create an agreement to restrict the sale or transfer of their shares, any shareholder can freely transfer them. Free transfer is okay for publicly traded stock but can create havoc in a small corporation where the shareholders (owners) usually run the business. If you're in business with two other owners, for example, you probably wouldn't want Owner #3 to sell his or her stock to a complete stranger, because the new person may have a completely different vision about how to run the company. Accordingly, Form 2E: Stock Agreement allows you to provide in advance what will happen if a shareholder wants to transfer shares or dies.

Finally, with Form 2H: Stock Certificate, you can give each shareholder a document showing his or her ownership interest in the corporation.

Form 2A: Checklist for Starting a Small Business

This checklist makes a great to-do list for starting your business.

Instructions for Form 2A: Checklist for Starting a Small Business

The checklist and all of the forms in this book are provided in Appendix B and on the Nolo website. To download the checklist and forms online, use the link provided in Appendix A. This next section describes each task listed in the Checklist for Starting a Small Business.

Evaluate and Develop Your Business Idea

First, before you invest a lot of time and money in your business idea, you should determine if you've chosen the right business and if the business can make money. If you pass these tests, it's time to do some initial planning and brainstorming. Next you should create a business plan, consider sources of financing, and think about a basic marketing plan.

Analyze Your Business Idea. To determine if your business idea makes sense for you, you might want to read "Start Your Own Business: 50 Things You'll Need to Do," a free article on Nolo's website (www.nolo.com).

Can Your Business Make Money? To determine if your business can be profitable, you should do a break-even analysis with expense and sales estimates. To learn how, read "Will My Business Make Money?" —a free article on Nolo's website (www.nolo.com).

Creating a Business Plan. Creating a business plan is important even if you won't be seeking outside money from banks or investors. For more information on developing your business plan, including how to create a profit/loss forecast and a cash flow analysis, see Nolo's book *How to Write a Business Plan*, by Mike McKeever.

Getting Loans or Equity Investments. To explore ways to raise money for your small business, read *Legal Guide for Starting & Running a Small Business*, by Fred S. Steingold and David M. Steingold (Nolo), Chapter 9. If you decide to borrow money from friends or family members (rather than a bank or other financial institution), see Chapter 4 of this book for promissory notes you can use to specify the details of the payment arrangements.

Market Your Idea. For lots of free information about marketing, go to the Marketing & Advertising section of Nolo.com at www.nolo.com/legal-encyclopedia/marketing-advertising.

Decide on a Legal Structure for Your Business

Next, you need to decide what type of ownership structure you'll choose; that is, whether you'll operate your business as a sole proprietorship, a partnership, a corporation, or an LLC.

Most business owners start out as sole proprietors, or if there are two owners involved, as a partnership. If their businesses are successful, they may consider becoming a corporation or an LLC.

Whether you're better off starting as a sole proprietor or partnership or choosing one of the more sophisticated organizational structures depends on several factors, including the size and profitability of your business, how many people will own it, and whether it will entail liability risks not covered by insurance.

To learn more about the various legal structures, see *Legal Guide for Starting & Running a Small Business*, by Fred S. Steingold and David M. Steingold (Nolo), Chapter 1.

Choose a Name for Your Business

Before you settle on a name for your business, you'll need to determine if your proposed name is available for your use. Once you find an available name, you'll have to register it as a fictitious or assumed business name, a corporate or an LLC name, if applicable, and possibly as a federal and state trademark.

Finding an Available Business Name. Before using a business name, it's wise to conduct a name search to avoid a conflict with a business that's already using the same or a similar name. If you're starting a small, local business, you can usually feel reasonably secure searching for name conflicts at the state and local level. If you're starting a larger company or one that will do business in more than one state, you might need to do a more sophisticated federal trademark search. For more information on doing name searches, see *Legal Guide for Starting & Running a Small Business*, by Fred S. Steingold and David M. Steingold (Nolo), Chapter 6.

Registering Your Business Name. In most states, if you do business under a name other than your own legal name, you'll need to register it as a fictitious or assumed name. (An example of an assumed name/fictitious name filing is below.)

If you're forming a corporation or an LLC, you'll register your business name with the office of the secretary of state or other agency when you file your articles of incorporation or articles of organization.

In addition, if you plan to do business regionally or nationally and will use your business name to identify a product or service, you should also look into registering your trademark or service mark at the state or federal level.

For more information on registering your business name, see *Legal Guide for Starting & Running a Small Business,* by Fred S. Steingold and David M. Steingold (Nolo), Chapter 6. You might also want to see *Trademark: Legal Care for Your Business & Product Name*, by Stephen Fishman (Nolo). You can also get lots of useful information in the Business Formation section of Nolo.com.

Prepare Organizational Paperwork

SKIP AHEAD
If you've decided to start out as a sole proprietor, you can skip this checklist item and jump ahead to "Find a Business Location."

If you've decided to create a partnership, an LLC, or a corporation, you'll need to take an extra step or two. For example, partners need to form a partnership agreement, LLC members need to create articles of organization, and corporate shareholders need to fill out articles of incorporation.

BN-15-R0305 ♻ printed on recycled paper

M.C.L.A. 445.1 et seq.
M.C.L.A. 445.2B
FILING FEE $10.00

LAWRENCE KESTENBAUM
WASHTENAW COUNTY CLERK/REGISTER

REMIT PAYMENT / MAIL TO:
WASHTENAW COUNTY CLERK
200 N. MAIN ST., SUITE 100, P.O. BOX 8645
ANN ARBOR, MI 48107-8645

THIS IS A LEGAL DOCUMENT
TYPE OR PRINT CLEARLY
USE BLACK OR BLUE INK

TELEPHONE (734) 222-6720

WASHTENAW COUNTY — CERTIFICATE OF ASSUMED NAME
THIS CERTIFICATE EXPIRES FIVE (5) YEARS FROM THE DATE OF FILING

THE UNDERSIGNED, hereby certifies that the following persons now owns (or) intends to own, conduct or transact business in the County of Washtenaw, State of Michigan, under the designation, name or style stated below:

1. AN ORIGINAL__X___   RENEWAL_____   CHANGE OF LOCATION_____   DISSOLUTION_____

2. NAME OF BUSINESS__Aardvark Café_____

3. PRINCIPAL ADDRESS OF BUSINESS_____555 State St.,_____Dexter, MI____44444____
                                          number & street   city   state   zip code

4. (PRINT) FULL LEGAL NAME(S) OF PERSON(S)   RESIDENCE ADDRESS(ES)

Edward   F.   Jones   111 Adam St.
  first   middle   last   number and street

                                                     Dexter,   MI   44444
                                                       city   state   zip code

  first   middle   last   number and street

                                                       city   state   zip code

5. NON-RESIDENTS OF MICHIGAN, MUST FILE A "CONSENT TO SERVICE" (BN-05). FILING FEE $2.00.

6. SIGNATURE(S) OF ALL PERSON(S) LISTED ABOVE — **MUST BE WITNESSED BY A NOTARY PUBLIC**.

(Signature) *Edward F. Jones*

(Signature)_____

(Notary Signature) *Sidney Smith*

STATE OF MICHIGAN   )ss.
COUNTY OF WASHTENAW)

Printed Name__Sidney Smith_____

Notary Public,__Washtenaw_____ County, MI

Subscribed and sworn to before me this

Acting In__Washtenaw_____ County, MI

day,__May____15,____20xx____
     month   day   year

Commission expires_June 1, 20xx_____

FOR OFFICE USE ONLY — DO NOT WRITE BELOW THIS LINE

Counter ☐   Mail ☐   Franchise Yes ☐   No ☐   Approved _____ / _____

CERTIFICATION OF RECORD

STATE OF MICHIGAN   )
                          SS
COUNTY OF WASHTENAW)

I, LAWRENCE KESTENBAUM, CLERK/REGISTER OF SAID COUNTY OF WASHTENAW DO HEREBY CERTIFY that the foregoing is a true and exact copy of the original document on file in my office.

Dated: _____

Lawrence Kestenbaum

LAWRENCE KESTENBAUM,
WASHTENAW COUNTY CLERK/REGISTER

FILE #

PREVIOUS FILE #

Partnerships. Partners should sign a written partnership agreement before going into business together. For more information on forming a partnership, see *Legal Guide for Starting & Running a Small Business*, by Fred S. Steingold and David M. Steingold (Nolo), Chapter 2.

Limited Liability Companies. To form an LLC, owners must file articles of organization (or in some states, a certificate of organization or certificate of formation) and sign an operating agreement. An operating agreement helps ensure your personal liability protection by showing that you have been conscientious about organizing your LLC. For more information on forming an LLC, see *Legal Guide for Starting & Running a Small Business,* by Fred S. Steingold and David M. Steingold (Nolo), Chapter 4.

If you will be the sole owner of your LLC, you can use Form 2F: LLC Operating Agreement for Single-Member LLC.

Corporations. To form a corporation, incorporators must files articles of incorporation—which in some states are called certificates of incorporation, articles of association, or charters. In most states, the secretary of state can give you a printed form for this essential document—or you may find the form online; all you have to do is fill in some blank spaces. Although details vary from state to state, you'll typically need to include:

- the corporation's name
- its purpose
- the name of the registered agent (in some states, called an agent for service of process or a resident agent)
- the number of shares authorized, and
- the names and addresses of the incorporators.

You'll file the form with the secretary of state (or other designated official) and pay an incorporation fee. Your corporation will also need to adopt bylaws. When you're ready, use Form 2C: Preincorporation Agreement, Form 2D: Corporate Bylaws, and Form 2E: Stock Agreement. For more information on forming a corporation, see *Legal Guide for Starting & Running a Small Business*, by Fred S. Steingold and David M. Steingold (Nolo), Chapter 3.

S Corporations. If you decide to form an S corporation, in addition to the regular corporate paperwork mentioned above, you'll also need to file IRS Form 2553, *Election by a Small Business Corporation*. For more information on S corporations, see *Legal Guide for Starting & Running a Small Business*, by Fred S. Steingold and David M. Steingold (Nolo), Chapter 3.

Find a Business Location

Unless you'll start out running your business from home (which many sole proprietors do indefinitely), you'll want to find suitable commercial space.

Identifying Your Needs. When choosing business space, you need to consider the size of the premises, the availability of customer parking, and the status of electrical and communications wiring, among other things. For help on identifying your minimum requirements and the maximum rent you can pay for your business space, see *Legal Guide for Starting & Running a Small Business,* by Fred S. Steingold and David M. Steingold (Nolo), Chapter 1.

Finding a Location. One key to choosing a profitable location is determining the factors that will increase customer volume for your business. For more information on looking for a location and using a broker, see the downloadable book *Negotiate the Best Lease for Your Business*, by Janet Portman (Nolo), Chapter 2.

Negotiating Your Lease. With a little effort, you can usually negotiate significant improvements to the landlord's lease terms. For lots of helpful information on negotiating lease terms, see *Negotiate the Best Lease for Your Business*, beginning at Chapter 5. To create your own lease, see Chapter 6 of this book for a number of forms you can use.

Home Businesses. Following are a few issues that concern most home businesses—in most cases, a few precautions are all that's needed to avoid unexpected legal difficulties. For more information, see *Legal Guide for Starting & Running a Small Business*, by Fred S. Steingold and David M. Steingold (Nolo), Chapter 14.

- **Insurance.** Make sure you have adequate liability and property damage insurance; your homeowners' insurance policy might not cover business use of your home. For example, if a UPS delivery person trips on your porch step while delivering a business package to you or if your dog bites a visiting client, you might not be covered. Similarly, you might find that homeowners' coverage won't pay for a business computer that gets stolen. An insurance agent or broker can probably extend your policy to cover your business use for a modest additional premium.

- **Lease and Homeowner Restrictions.** Be aware that you might not have an unlimited right to do business from your home. If you're in a rented unit, your lease could prohibit business operations. In a private home, you might be bound by "covenants, conditions, and restrictions"—rules that apply to all owners in a subdivision, condo, or planned-unit development.

- **Review Zoning Ordinances.** Local zoning ordinances might not allow businesses to operate in the district where you live. Learn about the local zoning restrictions; you could be able to abide by them, or at least meet their spirit. Or, you might need to get a home occupation permit for your business. Check with your local zoning or planning office. A neighbor or municipal zoning ordinance will probably not stop your business use if you keep a low profile. Limit your signage, keep deliveries to a minimum, and don't see too many customers or clients at your home. Neighbors are unlikely to complain if you run a quiet, low-traffic business that doesn't affect them.

- **Taxes.** Taxes—especially the rules on the home-office deduction and depreciation— are another concern for home-based businesses. You should review IRS Publication 587, *Business Use of Your Home.* This publication is available from the IRS website at www.irs.gov. For more information on taxes for home businesses, see *Home Business Tax Deductions*, by Stephen Fishman (Nolo).

File for Licenses and Permits

You will need to complete general business registration requirements. You might need to obtain a business license from your municipality or state, an employer identification number from the IRS, a seller's permit from your state, a zoning permit from your local planning board, and other licenses or permits.

Federal Taxpayer Identification Number. If you are forming a partnership or corporation or your business will hire employees, you need to obtain a taxpayer ID from the IRS. You can do this online on the IRS website or by filing IRS Form SS-4, *Application for Employer Identification Number*, included in this book.

Licenses. In most locations, every business needs a basic business license, or tax registration certificate. And, in addition to a basic business license, you might need a specialized business license—especially if you sell food, liquor, or firearms or work with hazardous materials. States also require licensing of people practicing traditional professions, such as lawyers, physicians, pharmacists, and architects and can require licenses for other occupations, such as barbers, auto mechanics, pest control specialists, and insurance agents—the list varies from state to state.

Permits. In addition to a business license, you might need a zoning permit or variance to carry on your intended business. And if you plan to run a regulated business, such as a restaurant, bar, taxi service, or waste removal company, you'll probably need a special permit from state or local authorities. Again, the list varies from location to location so you'll need to inquire with the appropriate municipal and state offices.

Your state's Small Business Development Center or other agency may offer a one-stop shopping website that advises you on the licenses and permits you need for your particular type of business. To learn more about licenses and permits, see *Legal Guide for Starting & Running a Small Business*, by Fred S. Steingold and David M. Steingold (Nolo), Chapter 7. You may also want to see *The Small Business Start-Up Kit: A Step-by-Step Legal Guide* or *The Small Business Start-Up Kit for California*, both by Peri H. Pakroo (Nolo).

Obtain Insurance

Although business insurance is not generally required, it's a good idea to purchase enough insurance to cover your company's assets.

Property Insurance. It's sensible to carry insurance to replace or repair your property if it's stolen or damaged by fire, flood, windstorm, earthquake, vandalism, or any of dozens of other hazards. The insurance should also cover the theft of, or damage to, property that a customer leaves in your care—for example, a valuable piece of equipment.

Liability Insurance. You want the peace of mind of knowing that you have liability coverage in case someone is physically injured on your premises (slipping on a wet floor, for example) or as a result of your business operations (getting struck by a company van). Be sure you're also covered if an employee driving his or her own car injures someone while on company business. And if you'll be manufacturing a product or selling dangerous items, look into product liability insurance so you're protected if a product you've made or sold injures someone.

Other Insurance Coverage. Review your business operations with an experienced insurance agent or broker to learn what other coverage might be appropriate. There's no substitute for establishing a good working relationship with a knowledgeable insurance agent or broker. For more information on obtaining insurance, see *Legal Guide for Starting & Running a Small Business*, by Fred S. Steingold and David M. Steingold (Nolo), Chapter 12.

Set Up Tax Reporting and Accounting

Before the end of your first year, you'll need to learn how to report your income, which can vary depending on how your business is structured. To optimize your tax savings, you should become familiar with how to write off expenses and asset purchases as well as keep good records—before you begin to incur start-up costs.

How Your Business Is Taxed. To learn about taxes for sole proprietors, see *Tax Savvy for Small Business*, by Frederick W. Daily (Nolo), Chapter 7.

To learn about partnership taxation, see Chapter 10 of that book.

To learn about corporate taxation, see Chapters 8 and 9.

To learn about LLC taxation, see Chapter 11.

Deductions and Depreciation. Just about any necessary and reasonable expense that helps you earn business income is deductible. For information on deducting expenses, see *Tax Savvy for Small Business*, Chapter 2. You'll also find excellent guidance in another Nolo book, *Deduct It! Lower Your Small Business Taxes*, by Stephen Fishman. Special rules apply to deducting the cost of business equipment and assets, which usually must be depreciated over a number of years. See Chapter 3 of that book for more information.

IRS Publications. Form 2A alerts you to two IRS publications about federal taxes for small businesses, as well as a helpful tax calendar with important filing dates. You can get these publications from the IRS website (www.irs.gov).

Record Keeping and Accounting. You'll need to decide on a method of accounting, a tax year, and a method of bookkeeping.

- **Cash vs. Accrual Accounting.** Most small service businesses use the cash method of accounting, but if your business will stock inventory to sell to the public or use in manufacturing, the IRS requires you to use the accrual accounting method. For information about the difference between cash and accrual accounting, see *Tax Savvy for Small Business*, Chapter 4.

- **Calendar vs. Fiscal Year.** Most small businesses use a calendar year (January 1 to December 31). To choose another tax period, you must have a good reason and get permission from the IRS. For information about choosing a calendar or fiscal year, see *Tax Savvy for Small Business*, Chapter 4. To choose a tax period other than the calendar year, use IRS Form 8716, *Election to Have a Tax Year Other Than a Required Tax Year.*

- **Bookkeeper vs. Software.** Depending on the volume and complexity of your business finances, you might benefit from hiring a part-time bookkeeper or consulting an accountant who can show you how to set up a simple bookkeeping system. Or, you might find that business accounting software, such as *Quicken Home and Business* or *QuickBooks* (both by Quicken) will be sufficient. For information on bookkeeping, see *Tax Savvy for Small Business*, Chapter 4.

Hire Workers

Chances are you will need to hire employees or independent contractors before long, if not right off the bat.

General Information on Hiring Workers. *The Employer's Legal Handbook*, by Fred S. Steingold (Nolo), provides excellent information on wage and hour laws, antidiscrimination statutes, and leave policies. You'll find additional help in "Hiring Your First Employee: 13 Things You Must Do," a free article on Nolo's website. Below you'll also find a discussion of employment forms included in this book, as well as links to government agencies and important websites.

Independent Contractors. When you're just starting out, hiring independent contractors can save a lot of time and money. However, you need to be careful not to mistakenly or falsely characterize workers as independent contractors. To qualify as an independent contractor under IRS rules, a worker must control both the outcome of a project and the means of accomplishing it. In close cases, the IRS prefers to see workers treated as employees rather than as independent contractors. For more information on the difference between independent contractors and employees, see *The Employer's Legal Handbook*, Chapter 12. If you decide to hire an independent contractor, use Form 9F: Contract With Independent Contractor.

Employer Identification Numbers. If you don't have an Employer Identification Number (EIN) already, you'll need one when you pay employer and employee income taxes, Social Security taxes, and Medicare taxes. The easiest way to get an EIN, is to apply for one online using the question-and-answer feature available at www.irs.gov. Or, if you prefer, you can phone in the information or fill out a paper version you can mail or fax to the IRS. See www.irs.gov for details. We've included the form, IRS Form SS-4 *Application for Employer Identification Number,* in this book and on Nolo's website (see Appendix A).

Unemployment Tax. You'll have to make payments to your state's unemployment compensation fund, which provides short-term relief to workers who are laid off. First, you'll need to register with your state's employment department or similar agency. To find the proper agency, go to www.statelocalgov.net.

You'll also need to file IRS Form 940, *Employer's Annual Federal Unemployment (FUTA) Tax Return,* to report your federal unemployment tax each year. You must file this form for any year in which:

- you paid wages of $1,500 or more in any quarter, or
- had one or more employees for at least part of a day in any 20 or more different weeks. Count all full-time, part-time, and temporary employees, but don't count partners if your business is a partnership.

Form 940 is included in this book and on Nolo's website. It's also available from the IRS website (www.irs.gov).

Form SS-4
(Rev. December 2017)
Department of the Treasury
Internal Revenue Service

Application for Employer Identification Number

(For use by employers, corporations, partnerships, trusts, estates, churches, government agencies, Indian tribal entities, certain individuals, and others.)
▶ Go to *www.irs.gov/FormSS4* for instructions and the latest information.
▶ See separate instructions for each line. ▶ Keep a copy for your records.

OMB No. 1545-0003

EIN

Type or print clearly.

1 Legal name of entity (or individual) for whom the EIN is being requested
Progressive Court Reporting Service, LLC.

2 Trade name of business (if different from name on line 1)

3 Executor, administrator, trustee, "care of" name

4a Mailing address (room, apt., suite no. and street, or P.O. box)
123 Courthouse Square

5a Street address (if different) (Do not enter a P.O. box.)

4b City, state, and ZIP code (if foreign, see instructions)
Berkeley, CA 99999

5b City, state, and ZIP code (if foreign, see instructions)

6 County and state where principal business is located
Alameda County, California

7a Name of responsible party
Sally Adams

7b SSN, ITIN, or EIN
999-99-9999

8a Is this application for a limited liability company (LLC) (or a foreign equivalent)? ☑ Yes ☐ No

8b If 8a is "Yes," enter the number of LLC members ▶

8c If 8a is "Yes," was the LLC organized in the United States? ☑ Yes ☐ No

9a **Type of entity** (check only one box). **Caution.** If 8a is "Yes," see the instructions for the correct box to check.

☐ Sole proprietor (SSN) _____
☐ Partnership
☐ Corporation (enter form number to be filed) ▶ _____
☐ Personal service corporation
☐ Church or church-controlled organization
☐ Other nonprofit organization (specify) ▶ _____
☑ Other (specify) ▶ **Disregarded Entity**

☐ Estate (SSN of decedent) _____
☐ Plan administrator (TIN) _____
☐ Trust (TIN of grantor) _____
☐ Military/National Guard ☐ State/local government
☐ Farmers' cooperative ☐ Federal government
☐ REMIC ☐ Indian tribal governments/enterprises
Group Exemption Number (GEN) if any ▶

9b If a corporation, name the state or foreign country (if applicable) where incorporated

State

Foreign country

10 **Reason for applying** (check only one box)
☑ Started new business (specify type) ▶ _____
Limited Liability Company
☐ Hired employees (Check the box and see line 13.)
☐ Compliance with IRS withholding regulations
☐ Other (specify) ▶

☐ Banking purpose (specify purpose) ▶ _____
☐ Changed type of organization (specify new type) ▶ _____
☐ Purchased going business
☐ Created a trust (specify type) ▶ _____
☐ Created a pension plan (specify type) ▶ _____

11 Date business started or acquired (month, day, year). See instructions.
September 1, 20xx

12 Closing month of accounting year

14 If you expect your employment tax liability to be $1,000 or less in a full calendar year **and** want to file Form 944 annually instead of Forms 941 quarterly, check here. (Your employment tax liability generally will be $1,000 or less if you expect to pay $4,000 or less in total wages.) If you do not check this box, you must file Form 941 for every quarter. ☑

13 Highest number of employees expected in the next 12 months (enter -0- if none). If no employees expected, skip line 14.

Agricultural	Household	Other

15 First date wages or annuities were paid (month, day, year). **Note:** If applicant is a withholding agent, enter date income will first be paid to nonresident alien (month, day, year) ▶ **September 30, 20xx**

16 Check **one** box that best describes the principal activity of your business.
☐ Construction ☐ Rental & leasing ☐ Transportation & warehousing
☐ Real estate ☐ Manufacturing ☐ Finance & insurance
☐ Health care & social assistance ☐ Wholesale-agent/broker
☐ Accommodation & food service ☐ Wholesale-other ☐ Retail
☑ Other (specify) ▶ **Court Reporting Services**

17 Indicate principal line of merchandise sold, specific construction work done, products produced, or services provided.

18 Has the applicant entity shown on line 1 ever applied for and received an EIN? ☐ Yes ☑ No
If "Yes," write previous EIN here ▶

Third Party Designee

Complete this section **only** if you want to authorize the named individual to receive the entity's EIN and answer questions about the completion of this form.

Designee's name

Designee's telephone number (include area code)

Address and ZIP code

Designee's fax number (include area code)

Under penalties of perjury, I declare that I have examined this application, and to the best of my knowledge and belief, it is true, correct, and complete.

Name and title (type or print clearly) ▶ **Sally Adams, President**

Applicant's telephone number (include area code)
555-555-5555

Signature ▶ *Sally Adams*   Date ▶ *2/1/20xx*

Applicant's fax number (include area code)
555-555-5555

For Privacy Act and Paperwork Reduction Act Notice, see separate instructions.   Cat. No. 16055N   Form **SS-4** (Rev. 12-2017)

Withholding and Payroll Taxes. Every business with employees must withhold a portion of each employee's income and deposit it with the IRS, and also make Social Security and Medicare tax payments to the IRS. Have each new employee fill out IRS Form W-4, *Employee's Withholding Allowance Certificate*, included in this book. This form does not need to be filed with the IRS, but it tells you how many allowances an employee is claiming for tax purposes, so that you can withhold the correct amount of tax from his or her paycheck. For more information, be sure to get IRS Publication 15, Circular E, *Employer's Tax Guide.* You can get this publication from the IRS website (www.irs.gov).

Workers' Compensation. Look into the workers' compensation insurance requirements in your state. You'll need this coverage in case a worker suffers an on-the-job injury, because such injuries aren't covered by normal liability insurance. To find your state agency's website, go to www.irmi.com/free-resources/insurance-industry-links/workers-comp-agencies.aspx. For more information on workers' compensation laws, see *The Employer's Legal Handbook*, Chapter 7.

Compliance With Other Government Regulations. Several federal and state agencies administer other laws in the workplace. Be sure to comply with the laws of each agency:

- **OSHA.** For information on compliance with Occupational Safety and Health Administration (OSHA) regulations, including creating an Injury and Illness Prevention Plan, go to the OSHA website (www.osha.gov). For more information on health and safety in the workplace, see *The Employer's Legal Handbook*, Chapter 7.
- **Department of Labor.** For information on posters you must display in your business, go to www.dol.gov/elaws/posters.htm. This online "Poster Advisor" feature will help you determine which posters you must display in your workplace. (The Advisor will ask you a series of questions, such as the number of employees and annual dollar volume, and then provide a list of posters you must

display and an opportunity to print them.) In addition, you must comply with your state department of labor's poster requirements. For a list of state departments of labor, go to www.dol.gov/whd/contacts/state_of.htm.

- **New Hire Reporting Agency.** For information on the new hire reporting program, which requires employers to report information on employees for the purpose of locating parents who owe child support, go to the Administration for Children & Families website at www.acf.hhs.gov/programs/css/employers/employer-responsibilities/new-hire-reporting. This website provides a link to state-by-state reporting information. Note that the new hire reporting agency in your state may or may not be your state's employment department.
- **U.S. Citizenship and Immigration Services (USCIS).** You must have each new employee complete USCIS Form I-9, *Employment Eligibility Verification*, to verify the employee's eligibility to work in the United States. The form need not be filed with the USCIS, but it must be kept in your files for three years and made available for inspection by officials of the USCIS. This form is included in this book. (As of press time, the USCIS was instructing employers to continue using the I-9 form with the August 31, 2019 expiration date until further notice. Be sure to check the USCIS website at www.uscis.gov for the latest version of the form before using the one in this book.)

Employment Applications. Form 9A: Employment Application requests information on the applicant's educational background, training, skills, and achievements.

Employee Handbook. If you have more than a few employees, you might want to create a handbook that explains your employment policies. This way, your employees will know what is expected of them and what they can expect from you. Your handbook should include policies on:

- at-will employment
- pay and benefits

- workdays, hours, and time off
- discrimination and harassment
- performance evaluations
- complaints and investigations
- substance abuse
- privacy in the workplace, and
- discipline.

For guidance on the legal and practical considerations as well as electronic versions of policies on each of the above topics, see *Create Your Own Employee Handbook: A Legal & Practical Guide for Employers*, by Lisa Guerin and Amy DelPo (Nolo).

Form 2B: Partnership Agreement

If you are creating a partnership, you should make a written partnership agreement. A partnership agreement spells out your rights and responsibilities and allows you to structure your relationship with your partners in a way that suits your business. Although the law recognizes partnerships without written agreements, there are huge benefits to putting yours in writing. For one, the process of creating a written agreement forces you and your partners to confront and talk through many important decisions, such as how much money each partner will invest in the business, how profits and losses will be allocated, how the partnership will be managed, and what happens if a partner withdraws from the business. What's more, a written partnership agreement can provide an invaluable framework to handle later misunderstandings and disagreements, which of course are likely to be part—hopefully a small part—of any business.

Another benefit of creating a formal agreement is that it allows the partners to adjust the operating rules of the partnership to suit their needs instead of being bound by the default rules that state law imposes in the absence of an agreement. For example, suppose you and another partner get into a dispute about the business and one of you sues the other. If you don't have a written partnership agreement, the judge will decide the case based on your state's partnership law—which might be different from what you and the other partner would like to happen. By contrast, if you have provided your own way of handling things in a written agreement, it will normally control and determine the judge's decision.

> **EXAMPLE:** Al, Barbara, and Carl start a partnership business. Since they're old friends and don't like paperwork, they never actually agree on the formula for allocating profits, let alone put it in writing. Because Al will be working full time in the business and Barbara and Carl will be working only part time, their joint assumption seems to be that Al will get 50% of the profits and Barbara and Carl will each get 25%. However, a year later, after a bitter falling out among the partners followed by a lawsuit, a judge is forced to consider this issue. Because there's no written agreement and the oral evidence is inconclusive, the judge must follow state law and rule that each partner is entitled to one-third of the profits.

What Is a Limited Partnership?

The fill-in-the-blanks form in this book is for a general partnership and not a limited partnership —a very different legal animal that combines some attributes of a partnership with some attributes of a corporation.

Most limited partnerships are formed for real estate or other investment ventures where one or more active partners will run a business financed by the investments of a number of silent partners. A limited partnership must have at least one general partner who has the same rights and responsibilities (including unlimited liability) as does a partner in a general partnership. It also must have at least one limited partner (and usually has more), who is typically a passive investor. A limited partner isn't personally liable for the debts of the partnership—as long as he or she doesn't participate in managing the business.

Because setting up a limited partnership is complicated, you should see a lawyer if you're going to start one.

Filing Paperwork With State or Local Governments

One advantage of a partnership over a corporation or limited liability company is that you don't have to file formation documents with a public agency along with a hefty fee. However, in some states, you will need to file a partnership certificate giving the names of the partners. And in a few states, you might also need to publish a notice in the newspaper informing the public that you've formed the partnership. Check with the county clerk or the secretary of state's office for details on your state's requirements.

RESOURCE

For more on partnerships, see Chapter 2 of the *Legal Guide for Starting & Running a Small Business,* by Fred S. Steingold and David M. Steingold (Nolo), and *Form a Partnership: The Complete Legal Guide,* by Denis Clifford and Ralph Warner (Nolo).

Instructions for Form 2B: Partnership Agreement

All the forms in this book are provided in Appendix B and on the Nolo website. To access the downloadable forms online, use the link provided in Appendix A. As you read the instructions for form 2B, you might want to refer to the form in Appendix B or open the form on your computer so you can follow along. (Before you use the form in Appendix B, be sure to photocopy it so you'll have a clean copy to use later.)

1. Partners

Insert the names of all partners.

2. Partnership Name

One of the first things you need to do is settle on a name for your partnership. There are two basic ways to choose your name:

- You can combine your own last names, such as "Johnson, Holmes, & Sanchez" as your official partnership name.
- You can make up the name under which you'll do business, such as "Three Guys Contractors," which is called a fictitious or assumed business name.

Before settling on a partnership name, it's wise to conduct a name search to avoid a possible conflict with a business that is already using the same name or a similar one. Typically, if your partnership is a small local business, you can feel reasonably secure if you've searched for name conflicts at the state and local level. Check the records of the state, county, or local offices where assumed or fictitious business names are filed and the state office where corporations and LLCs are registered. Also check the phone books and city directories covering your area.

If you plan to do business regionally or nationally and will use your business name to identify a product or service, you should consider doing a national trademark search and look into registering your trademark or service mark at both the federal and state levels. For more in-depth information on trademark searches and registration, see *Trademark: Legal Care for Your Business & Product Name,* by Stephen Fishman (Nolo).

If you decide to use a name that doesn't include the last names of all of the partners, you'll need to register your partnership's name as a fictitious or assumed business name—generally by filing a form at a designated county office. You might also need to publish your partnership name in a local newspaper. Many counties and municipalities have websites that provide more information about registering a fictitious business name and publishing required notices. See www.statelocalgov. net for a comprehensive list of state and local government sites on the Internet.

Insert the name of the partnership.

3. Partnership Duration

Insert the date the partnership began or when it is to begin. Your partnership will begin on whatever date you decide. This can be either a date in the future that you select now, or it can be the same day you sign your partnership agreement.

Next, check one of the boxes to indicate when the partnership will end. Most partnerships last indefinitely—as long as the partners want them to last. However, you can choose a date when your partnership will end. If you are setting up your partnership to complete a specific project, such as developing a particular piece of real estate, you might want the partnership to end on a date that you specify here. If you check the second box, insert a date for the end of the partnership.

4. Partnership Office

Insert the address where partnership records will be kept. Usually this will be the partnership's main business location. If the partnership's mailing address is the same as the partnership office, check the first box. If you have a separate mailing address—a post office box, for example—check the second box and fill in the mailing address.

5. Partnership Purpose

Insert the purpose of the partnership. Some examples are:

- to operate one or more retail stores for the sale of computer software.
- to manufacture and distribute equipment for the preparation of espresso, cappuccino, and other coffee-based beverages.
- to design websites for computer users and companies.
- to cater banquets, picnics, and other social and business functions requiring food service, and to rent equipment to be used in connection with such catering services.

6. Capital Contributions

Each partner must contribute some property to the partnership in exchange for an ownership interest. The partner can contribute cash, property, or both.

Depending on how readily available the partners' contributions are, this can be anywhere from a few days to a few weeks or even months after your partnership starts. The important thing to keep in mind is that your business needs to have enough money to operate until the partners make their contributions. In the first blank, enter the date by which the partners will hand over their contributions.

A. Cash Contributions
If partners will be contributing cash, fill in their names and the amount each will contribute.

B. Noncash Contributions
If partners will contribute property, insert the partners' names. Then describe the property and what value it will be given on the partnership's books.

Often, partners' initial contributions are equal, but not always. Unequal contributions are accounted for by granting the partners unequal rights to the partnership's profits and losses. For example, one partner contributes $6,000 and the other puts in $4,000. Future profits and losses of the partnership are allocated 60%/40%.

7. Capital Accounts

You don't need to insert anything here. A capital account is a bookkeeping technique for keeping track of how much of the partnership assets each partner owns. When a partner contributes cash or property to the partnership, the partner's capital account is credited with the cash amount or fair market value of the property contributed. The partnership will regularly add each partner's share of partnership profits to the capital accounts. Each partner's share of any losses and distributions will be deducted. In addition, if the partnership takes out a loan, the capital accounts should reflect each partner's share of the debt.

SEE AN EXPERT

Get help setting up your books. If you're unfamiliar with business bookkeeping, see an accountant to help you get started and to explain how capital accounts work. The accountant can also brief you on how to meet your federal and state business tax obligations. But first, you might want to consult *Form a Partnership: The Complete Legal Guide*, by Denis Clifford and Ralph Warner (Nolo), which explains the basics.

8. Profits and Losses

You'll probably want to check the first box. It says that the net profits and losses will be allocated to the partners in the same proportions as their capital contributions. Generally, a partner's reward for doing work for a partnership is a share of the partnership profits. Checking the first box—having the partners agree to split profits and losses according to their capital contributions—is the easiest and most common method for making such allocations. For example, suppose one partner puts in $20,000 and two other partners put in $10,000 each. The profits will be allocated 50%/25%/25%.

If you'd like to split up profits and losses in a way that isn't proportionate to the partners' capital contributions, check the second box and insert the percentages to be allocated to each partner. This method is called a special allocation. For example, suppose John and Anna set up a partnership to operate their consulting business. John and Anna put up equal amounts of cash, but they decide that John will be allocated 65% of the partnership's profits and losses for the first two years, and Anna will be allocated 35% of the partnership's profits and losses.

If you want to set up a special allocation, you must carefully follow IRS rules, so you'll need an accountant or tax lawyer to add special language to your partnership agreement to ensure that it will pass muster with the IRS. If the IRS refuses to accept your special allocation, it will deem the profits and losses to be distributed in the same percentage as the partner's capital contributions.

9. Salaries

You don't need to insert anything here. The assumption behind this section is that partners will be rewarded for their work based on the allocation formula set out in Section 8. Paying salaries to partners creates tax complications for the partnership and the individual partners. You could delete the language in this section, and insert language providing for salaries but, before doing that, seek the advice of a CPA or tax lawyer.

10. Interest

You don't need to insert anything here. If you would like a partner to receive interest, it's better to have the person lend money to the partnership. Be sure to document the loan with a promissory note. (See Chapter 4.)

11. Management

Here you'll need to decide how partnership decisions will be made—either through the unanimous agreement of all partners, through a majority, or through a combination of the two.

For a small partnership to succeed, the partners need to have both shared goals and confidence in one another's judgment. If those elements don't exist, pages of rules as to how decisions should be made won't help. When it comes to important decisions, it's smart to talk over the matter with all the partners and respect each other's opinions. If you agree to require unanimous agreement of all partners, choose the first option.

On the other hand, requiring unanimity on all decisions may be as unnecessary as it is hard to achieve—making it impractical to select the first option. Choosing the second option allows you more flexibility by requiring unanimous agreement on just the major business decisions that you specify, such as renting, buying, or selling real estate, or taking out a business loan.

Let's briefly look at the potential consequences of each type of decision to help you figure out whether you want to require unanimity for a particular decision.

Borrowing or Lending Money. When the partnership borrows money, each partner in a general partnership is personally responsible for repaying that money if the partnership doesn't. With such serious consequences, it's understandable that all partners would want to control the borrowing of money. Similarly, partners should always agree on lending money to outsiders before writing the check.

Signing a Lease. Especially if the partnership is leasing its first commercial space, all of the partners will probably want a say in the location, price, and lease terms. Even if it's not the first business space, it's likely that each partner will want to be involved in the decision because each partner is personally liable for the lease payments.

Signing a Contract to Buy or Sell Real Estate. Selling real estate, especially if it is one of the partnership's main assets, is another matter that the partners will want to agree on. Likewise, buying real estate will probably require a large commitment of the partnership's capital, so the partners will probably want to unanimously approve that decision as well.

Signing a Security Agreement or Mortgage. Your partnership might need a security agreement or mortgage when taking out a loan. A security agreement or mortgage will place a lien on partnership property; in other words, the partnership property will act as collateral for the loan. If the partnership defaults on the arrangement, usually by failing to make payments on a loan, the lender or creditor can take the property and sell it to pay the debt. Because this can have serious consequences for the business, it's advisable for partners to agree before pledging property as collateral.

Selling Partnership Assets. If the partnership wants to sell some or all of its assets, all of the partners should discuss the matter and agree. This will help to avoid confusion, arguments, and monetary losses to the business.

Other Decisions. There could be some other decisions for which you want to require unanimity that we haven't listed here. If that's the case, describe the action or decision in the space provided.

Sample

> Releasing any partnership claim, except upon payment in full.

12. Partnership Funds

Insert the name of the financial institution where you'll keep the partnership funds.

Then check a box to indicate who will be able to sign partnership checks. Many partnerships require the signature of only one partner on business checks, but others require two or more. If you check the last box, insert the number of partners who must sign. In a three-person partnership, for example, you might want to require that checks be signed by two partners.

The financial institution where you have the account will have a form of its own for you to fill out.

13. Agreement to End Partnership

You don't need to insert anything here. This paragraph makes it clear that the partnership can be ended if all the partners agree.

14. Partner's Withdrawal

Under the laws of most states, if one partner withdraws from the partnership, the partnership will automatically end: The partnership assets will be liquidated, bills will be paid, and the partners will be cashed out. Check the first box if this scenario is what you want.

You can, however, create a different outcome. Check the second box if you want to give the remaining partners the chance to keep the partnership alive by buying out the interest of the withdrawing partner. The partners will have 30 days to decide whether to continue or end the partnership. All remaining partners must agree to continue at that time. Technically, if the remaining partners choose to continue, they will form a new partnership with each other, but the business will continue as if there was no change.

15. Partner's Death

As with a partner's withdrawal, a partner's death will end the partnership—unless you agree to another outcome. Check the first box if you want the partnership assets to be liquidated and the deceased partner's share of the assets to be paid to that partner's estate.

Check the second box if you want to give the remaining partners the chance to keep the partnership alive by buying out the interest of the deceased partner. The partners will have 30 days to decide whether to continue or end the partnership. All remaining partners must agree to continue it at that time. Technically, if the remaining partners choose to continue, they will form a new partnership with each other, but the business will continue as if there was no change.

16. Buyout

Complete this optional paragraph only if you've provided for a buyout of a withdrawing partner's interest (Paragraph 14) or a deceased partner's interest (Paragraph 15). If you haven't provided for a buyout in Paragraph 14 or 15, either cross out this paragraph (in which case, all partners should initial the deletion) or insert the words "Not Applicable." (If you're using the downloadable form, just delete it and renumber the paragraphs that follow).

First, insert the number of days the partnership has to pay the withdrawing partner or the deceased partner's estate for that partner's interest. Keep in mind that the remaining partners already have 30 days to decide whether they want to purchase the interest and continue the business, so the number of days you select for payment of the buyout price should include this amount of time. For example, if you insert 60 days, the remaining partners will have 30 days to decide whether to buy out the interest and 30 more days to pay for it. The number of days should account for any time the partners will need to determine the value of the partner's interest, but it should not make the withdrawing partner or the deceased partner's estate wait too long after the buyout decision is made.

Next you must choose a way to value the interest of a partner being bought out. Here are the alternatives:

Capital Account. A partner's capital account is the amount of the partner's contributions, plus any unpaid allocations of profit, less any distributions already made to the partner. It should also reflect the partner's share of any partnership debts. This is the simplest way to value a partner's ownership interest: using the dollar value of the partner's capital account. However, this might not include the value of the business's assets, its yearly revenues, and profits and intangibles such as goodwill.

Appraisal Value. Another way to value a partner's ownership interest is to have your partnership's accountant determine the fair market value of the partner's interest. This might or might not be appropriate, depending on how knowledgeable the accountant is about your industry and how expensive it would be to have the accountant conduct an appraisal. (Most will charge an hourly or flat fee for this service.)

Other Valuation Methods. There are several other methods of valuing a partner's interest that use your company's financial statements from one or more years. These include the book value, multiple of book value, and capitalization of earnings methods. These methods are explained in more detail in *Legal Guide for Starting & Running a Small Business*, by Fred S. Steingold and David M. Steingold (Nolo). Depending on your business, one of these methods could be more appropriate than using a partner's capital account or an accountant's appraisal.

Check one of the first two boxes if it contains an acceptable formula for fixing the buyout price. If not, check the third box and fill in the method of setting the buyout amount. If you're not sure which method you want to use, you might want to consult your legal and accounting advisers and talk with other business owners in your field about how they would go about valuing their businesses.

Using Life Insurance to Fund a Buyout of a Deceased Partner's Interest

One way to provide the funds to buy out a deceased partner's interest is to buy life insurance. Although your agreement does not require you to do so, you and your partners can buy life insurance policies on each other in an amount sufficient to pay for the shares of a partner who dies.

If a partner dies, the remaining partners will receive the benefits from the life insurance policy, which they can then use to buy the deceased partner's interest from the partner's estate.

While many business owners do not like paying up front for a benefit that could be years away, insurance policies are cheaper than either saving or borrowing money. (You'd have to save much more money than the amount of your insurance premiums to achieve the same payout an insurance policy will give you, and this money wouldn't be available to help you expand your business.) An insurance policy also guarantees that cash will be available to purchase the shares of a partner who dies unexpectedly.

RESOURCE

For a more thorough discussion of the subject and a comprehensive agreement with different options, see *Business Buyout Agreements: Plan Now for All Types of Business Transitions*, by Bethany K. Laurence and Anthony Mancuso (Nolo). For instance, you might decide that you need a more customized agreement that covers more contingencies, such as what happens in the case of a partner's divorce or bankruptcy. Or you might want to include other payment options for purchasing a partner's interest, such as an installment plan or payments of interest only for a period of time. If you do decide to create a separate, more comprehensive buy-sell agreement, you would remove from this partnership agreement the provisions dealing with buyouts in the case of a partner's death or withdrawal.

Standard Clauses (Clauses 17–24)

The remainder of the agreement contains the standard clauses we discussed in Chapter 1. The only thing you'll need to fill in here is the name of the state whose law will apply to the contract in the paragraph called "Governing Law."

Date and Signatures

Fill in the date the agreement is signed. Each partner must sign his or her name, and their respective names and addresses should be typed in.

Form 2C: Preincorporation Agreement

A preincorporation agreement sets out the financial and organizational structure of a corporation being formed. Although not legally required, a preincorporation agreement can be a very useful aid to starting a new corporation. The process of drawing up an agreement allows you and other owners to focus on key business issues. Sometimes doing this can even cause you to abandon the idea of starting the business. If so, this should be seen as a positive development. It's much better to confront tough management issues early rather than after everyone has invested money, time, and energy in a business enterprise.

This form is designed for people who plan to incorporate a small business owned by a handful of shareholders, each of whom will actively take part in the day-to-day operations of the business. You might not need to create a preincorporation agreement if you fall into one of the following categories:

- You will be the sole owner of your corporation.
- You are incorporating an existing business with your co-owners.
- You've previously done business with those who will co-own your corporation.
- The owners of your corporation will be family members.

However, it can never hurt to create a quick preincorporation agreement, and it can help avoid financial and management spats later.

TIP

A preincorporation agreement is just the first step you take in starting a corporation. Among the other important things you must do are:

- Prepare and file the articles of incorporation (known in some states by other names— see instructions, below, for Paragraph 2).
- Select a board of directors.
- Adopt bylaws.
- Issue stock.
- Decide whether you want to elect S corporation tax status.

Instructions for Form 2C: Preincorporation Agreement

All the forms in this book are provided in Appendix B and on the Nolo website. To access the downloadable forms online, use the link provided in Appendix A. As you read the instructions for form 2C, you might want to refer to the form in Appendix B or open the form on your computer so you can follow along. (Before you use the form in Appendix B, be sure to photocopy it so you'll have a clean copy to use later.)

1. Shareholders' Names

Insert the names of all shareholders.

2. Incorporation

Insert the state in which you plan to incorporate. Corporations are created under state law rather than federal law, and each state has its own rules for how to start a corporation.

The best place to form your corporation is in the state where you and your co-owners live. Incorporating in another state, such as Delaware, does not make sense for most small corporations.

Though incorporation fees may be lower in another state, a corporation always has to register in the state where it actually does business even if it was formed in a different state. Registering in two states takes as much time and costs as much money as filing in just one state—so we recommend filing in the state where you live.

Usually, a state office—such as the Secretary of State—can provide a form for the articles of incorporation. Many Secretary of State offices provide incorporation forms and a list of filing fees on their websites. Check www.statelocalgov.net for a list of state government agencies on the Internet.

TIP

Legal jargon differs from state to state. Most states use the term articles of incorporation to refer to the basic document that creates a corporation, but some states (including Connecticut, Delaware, New York, and Oklahoma) use the term certificate of incorporation. Washington calls the document a certificate of formation, and Tennessee calls it a charter.

For single-owner corporations, the sole owner usually prepares, signs, and files the articles of incorporation. For co-owned corporations, all of the owners may sign the articles, or they can appoint just one person to sign them. Whoever signs the articles is called the incorporator. Select the option that fits your choice.

3. Corporate Name

You need to make sure the business name you want to use is available. Your state's corporate filing office will not let you use a name that is identical or very similar to the name of another corporation in your state. Check your state's corporate filing office to see if the name you want to use is available, and if it is, see whether you can reserve it. You can usually check business name availability online and reserve a name online or through a paper filing. Names can usually be reserved for a month or two (the exact period of time depends on your state's law) for a nominal fee.

Be sure the name you choose complies with the corporation laws of your state. For example, you may be required to include one of the following words or its abbreviation in the name of the corporation: Corporation, Incorporated, or Limited.

In addition to checking name availability with your state's corporate filing office, you will need to make sure your proposed name does not violate another business's existing trademark. If you will use your business name to identify a product or service, you should also look into registering your trademark or service mark at the state or federal level. For more information on naming your business and products, see *Trademark: Legal Care for Your Business & Product Name*, by Stephen Fishman (Nolo).

If your corporation will do business under a name other than the name that will appear on your articles of incorporation, you'll need to register that name as a fictitious or assumed business name. For example, Apollo Furniture, Inc., is considering doing business as either Apollo—a shortened form of its official name—or as Contemporary Studio—a name completely different from its official name. Whichever name it chooses, the company must register it as a fictitious or assumed business name with the county or counties where it does business. You can register a fictitious or assumed business name by filling out and filing a printed form at a designated county or state office, usually for a small fee. You might also need to publish the fictitious or assumed name in a local newspaper. Many counties and municipalities have websites that provide more information about registering fictitious business names and publishing required notices. See www.statelocalgov.net for a comprehensive list of state and local government sites on the Internet.

Fill in the name of the new corporation. Also, check the box if you're planning to use an assumed or fictitious name that's different from the official corporate name. Then fill in the name.

Samples

> Apollo Furniture, Inc. wants to do business as Apollo—a shortened form of its official name. It inserts the name Apollo in the space.

> Apollo Furniture wants to do business as Contemporary Studio—a name completely different from its official name. It inserts the name Contemporary Studio in the space.

TIP
You'll need to make your trade name a matter of public record. State law will probably require you to file an assumed name certificate with a state or county office. And in some states, you'll need to publish a notice in the newspaper informing the public of your fictitious name. This will let the public know that the business called Contemporary Studio, for example, is another name for Apollo Furniture, Inc.

4. Corporate Purpose

Insert the purpose of the corporation. Use simple language and describe the purpose broadly enough to cover all your intended and possible activities.

Samples

> … to operate one or more retail stores for the sale of computer software and to engage in any other lawful business for which corporations may be organized in this state.

> … to manufacture and distribute equipment for the preparation of espresso, cappuccino, and other coffee-based beverages and to engage in any other lawful business for which corporations may be organized in this state.

> ... to design websites for computer users and companies and to engage in any other lawful business for which corporations may be organized in this state.

> ... to cater banquets, picnics, and other functions requiring food service, and to rent equipment to be used in connection with these catering services, and to engage in any other lawful business for which corporations may be organized in this state.

5. Corporate Stock

Issuing shares of stock to the initial owners formally divides up ownership interests in the corporation and supplies the corporation with start-up capital. The initial owners provide money or other property to the corporation in exchange for shares of stock. Insert the total number of shares the corporation will be issuing to the shareholders signing the agreement.

> **CAUTION**
>
> **There's a difference between authorized stock and issued stock.** Your new corporation will be authorized under state law to issue a certain number of shares of stock. The number is usually established at the time you incorporate and in a few states will be tied to the fees you pay the state for incorporating. Just the same, it's a good idea to have plenty of stock authorized so that you'll have some in reserve after you issue shares to the initial shareholders—although if you run out, you can always get authority later for more stock.

This paragraph of the shareholders' agreement deals only with the shares you'll be issuing to the initial shareholders and not with the total number of shares authorized.

This paragraph assumes that all your shares will be common stock, meaning that there's no guarantee that dividends will be paid. Issuing preferred stock (under which owners receive a fixed dividend before dividends are paid to common stock owners) is too complex for most small businesses.

6. Stock Subscriptions

Here, each shareholder makes a commitment to buy a certain number of shares.

Fill in the price per share of the stock. Most new corporations charge $1 per share—a simple and commonsense approach that simplifies bookkeeping. Then, fill in the name of each person signing the agreement, the number of shares each is buying, and the total price each is paying.

The form that we've provided for the Preincorporation Agreement assumes that shareholders will pay cash for their shares. While this is normally the case, payment can also be made by contributing tangible assets to the corporation, such as a car or a computer. If this fits your situation, you'll need to add appropriate language describing the asset that the shareholder will contribute.

After you've incorporated and the shareholders have paid for their shares, the corporation will issue a stock certificate to each shareholder making it official that the person named has a designated number of shares in the corporation. It's usually signed by the corporation's president and secretary. You can buy blank stock certificate forms online or at an office supply store.

In some states you might also have to file a notice of stock transaction or similar form with your state corporations office.

7. Tax Status

This agreement states that all shares of stock will be issued under Section 1244 of the Internal Revenue Code. This language is included in your agreement for the benefit of shareholders who might eventually have to sell their stock at a loss. It permits such shareholders to deduct the loss as an ordinary loss from their ordinary individual income (such as salaries, dividends, and the like), up to $50,000 per year—or up to $100,000 per year if the shareholder is married and filing a joint return. Without this statement, any loss from the sale of stock would be treated as a capital loss, and could be used to offset only $3,000 of ordinary individual income in any year. For example, suppose a shareholder buys 10,000 shares of stock for $10,000, but sells it at a loss for $3,000 one year later. If the shares were issued under Section 1244, the shareholder can deduct that $7,000 loss from the rest of the shareholder's ordinary income. This should save the shareholder several thousand dollars in taxes.

If the shareholders want the corporation to elect S corporation status, check the optional box. (If not, and you're using the downloadable form, just delete it.) If so, shareholders will be taxed as if they are partners. Each shareholder's share of the corporation's profit or loss will be reported on his or her personal tax return. The corporation itself will pay no income tax.

There are two main reasons to choose S corporation tax status:

- An S corporation allows owners to deduct business losses on their personal income tax returns, using them to offset any income that they (and their spouses, if they're married) have from other sources. This can be helpful for corporations that anticipate start-up losses.
- When owners sell their S corporation, the taxable gain on the sale of the business can be less than if they operated the business as a regular corporation.

There are additional pros and cons to electing S corporation status. See *Legal Guide for Starting & Running a Small Business,* by Fred S. Steingold and David M. Steingold (Nolo), for further discussion. After reading up on this subject, you might still want to consult a tax adviser to help you decide whether to form an S corporation.

RESOURCE

Finding a good lawyer. When you need a lawyer, asking someone you trust for a referral is a good place to start. You can also try one of these excellent and free resources:

- **Nolo's Lawyer Directory.** Nolo has an easy-to-use online directory of lawyers, organized by location and area of expertise. You can find the directory and its comprehensive profiles at www.nolo.com/lawyers.

- **Lawyers.com.** At Lawyers.com you'll find a user-friendly search tool that allows you to tailor results by area of law and geography. You can also search for attorneys by name. Attorney profiles prominently display contact information, list topics of expertise, and show ratings—by both clients and other legal professionals.
- **Martindale.com.** Martindale.com offers an advanced search option that allows you to sort not only by practice area and location, but also by criteria like law school. Whether you look for lawyers by name or expertise, you'll find listings with detailed background information, peer and client ratings, and even profile visibility.

Complying With Securities Laws

Your corporation must comply with state and federal securities laws when it issues stock. Registering stock issuances with the federal Securities and Exchange Commission (SEC) and your state securities agency takes time and typically involves both legal and accounting fees.

Fortunately, most small corporations qualify for exemptions from both state and federal securities registration. For example, SEC rules do not require a corporation to register a private offering—that is, a nonadvertised sale to a limited number of people (generally 35 or fewer) or to investors who can reasonably be expected to take care of themselves because of their net worth, income-earning capacity, or relationship to the owners. Most states have also enacted their own versions of this SEC exemption.

In short, if your corporation will issue shares to a small number of people (generally ten or fewer) who will actively participate in running the business, it will almost certainly qualify for exemptions to federal and state securities registration.

If you're selling shares of stock to passive investors (people who won't be involved in running the company), complying with state and federal securities laws gets complicated. Get help from a good small business lawyer.

If you choose to elect S corporation status, all shareholders must sign IRS Form 2553 and you must file it with the IRS. You must file a similar form with the state tax agency. After filing Form 2553, your business will be taxed as a partnership if your corporation has more than one shareholder or as a sole proprietorship if yours is a one-shareholder corporation. Shareholders will be allocated a portion of profits (or losses) of the corporation according to their percentage of stock ownership in the corporation. If you change your mind, your corporation can revoke S corporation status and return to regular corporate tax status, but if it does this, it will not be able to reelect S corporation status for another five years.

RESOURCE

If you like the idea of having the profits and losses of your business pass through to the owners for tax purposes, you should know that this can be accomplished by forming a limited liability company (LLC). LLC owners automatically receive partnership tax treatment unless they elect to be taxed as a corporation. Again, consider talking to a tax adviser if you need help in choosing which way to go. For more information on small business taxation, see *Tax Savvy for Small Business*, by Frederick W. Daily (Nolo).

8. Board of Directors

You don't need to insert anything here. A corporation's directors make major policy and financial decisions for the corporation—for instance, they authorize the issuance of stock, approve loans to and from the corporation, and elect the officers. Your corporate bylaws will grant directors these powers. In a small business in which the owners actually run the business, it usually makes sense for all owners to serve on the board of directors.

In many states, the number of required directors is tied to the number of shareholders. For instance, a corporation with one shareholder would need only one director, while a corporation with two shareholders would need at least two directors

and a corporation with three or more shareholders would need at least three directors. However, no state requires a board to have more than three directors. Your preincorporation agreement will make all of the initial shareholders directors of the corporation. If you want to name different directors, you can do so at a later time.

9. Officers

Insert the names of the officers. You should name at least a president, a secretary, and a treasurer. In most states, however, one person can hold all of the required offices. Check with your state's corporate filing office if you want one person to hold all of the required positions or if you don't want to appoint a president, secretary, or treasurer.

Officers are responsible for the day-to-day operation and management of the corporation. Officers do not have to be shareholders, but in small corporations, they usually are. The president is usually the chief operating officer (COO) of the corporation. The secretary is responsible for the corporate records. The treasurer—sometimes called a chief financial officer (CFO)—is responsible for the corporate finances, although it's common to delegate everyday financial duties to a bookkeeper or accounting department.

10. Place of Business

Insert the address of your main location. This is the address where the records of the corporation will be kept and where official notices will be sent.

11. Bylaws

Form 2D, the next form in this chapter, can be the basis for your bylaws.

Standard Clauses (Clauses 12–19)

The remainder of the agreement contains the standard clauses we discussed in Chapter 1. The only thing you'll need to fill in here is the name of the state whose law will apply to the contract in the paragraph called "Governing Law."

Signatures

Each shareholder must sign his or her name, and each address should be typed in.

Form 2D: Corporate Bylaws

A corporation's bylaws are the internal rules that govern the company's day-to-day operations, such as how many directors will serve on the board and when and where the corporation will hold directors' and shareholders' meetings. You should prepare and follow bylaws for two reasons.

First, every corporation needs an orderly way to handle the legalities of corporate life. You need rules, for example, on how to elect the board of directors and corporate officers, how to hold meetings, and the number of votes required for shareholders and directors to take action. Bylaws deal with these and related issues.

Second, as you know, one big reason to do business as a corporation is to limit your personal liability. But to maintain limited liability status, you need to act like a real corporate entity—which means creating a paper trail that demonstrates your corporation is following the necessary business formalities. Doing this not only means adopting bylaws when your corporation is established but also keeping ongoing corporate records, such as minutes of regular and special shareholders' and directors' meetings. (See Chapter 3.) In short, good corporate record keeping will help protect you if the IRS or a creditor insists that your corporation is just a sham and tries to go after your house, car, bank accounts, and other property that you personally own.

The bylaws in this chapter are designed for a small corporation—one in which a handful of people own all the stock and are actively involved in the day-to-day operations of the business. At first, these bylaws might look complicated and even a little overwhelming. True, there are a lot of details, but these bylaws are sensible, written in clear language, and easy to put into practice.

 SEE AN EXPERT

You might need more customized bylaws. Our bylaws give you a reasonable measure of flexibility, but you could have other ideas about running your business that don't easily fit into this mold. Chances are your creative ideas will affect only one or two areas of corporate management. If so, you can use these bylaws for most provisions, but see a lawyer for help with appropriate wording to cover the troublesome areas.

Incorporators should formally adopt bylaws as soon as the incorporation papers have been signed and filed with the required state office. But the ideal time to prepare bylaws is when the incorporators are putting together a pre-incorporation agreement (Form 2C). This helps all shareholders learn whether they have really achieved a meeting of the minds on many of the key aspects of starting and running the corporation.

Instructions for Form 2D: Corporate Bylaws

All the forms in this book are provided in Appendix B and on the Nolo website. To access the downloadable forms online, use the link provided in Appendix A. As you read the instructions for form 2D, you might want to refer to the form in Appendix B or open the form on your computer so you can follow along. (Before you use the form in Appendix B, be sure to photocopy it so you'll have a clean copy to use later.)

Heading

In the first blank, insert the name of your corporation. In the second blank, fill in the state in which you filed your incorporation papers.

Article I: Meetings of Shareholders

Article I covers the procedures for annual and special meetings of shareholders.

1. First, insert the day of the month and the month when annual meetings will take place.

Sample

> The annual meeting of shareholders will be held on the first Wednesday in September.

Second, insert the time when annual meetings will start.

2. Insert the number of people who will serve on the board of directors. Typically, in a small corporation, all of the shareholders will want to serve on the board of directors. While most states permit a corporation to have just one director regardless of the number of owners, a few states require that a corporation must have at least three directors, except that a corporation with only two owners can have two directors and a corporation with only one owner can have just one director. If you would like your corporation to have only one or two directors, but you have more than one or two shareholders, check with your state's corporate filing office to see if this is allowed.

3. A special meeting of shareholders is one called and held between the scheduled annual meetings.

   Check a box to indicate whether the president or a number of shareholders or directors can call a special meeting of shareholders. If you check the second or third box, insert the number of shareholders or directors required to call a special meeting.

4. You don't need to fill in anything here. This section sets out the notice requirements for annual and special meetings.

RELATED TOPIC

For a notice form, see Form 3A: Notice of Shareholders' Meeting.

5. You don't need to fill in anything here. This section provides the minimum number of shareholders that must be present for a meeting to be valid. In order to take action at a meeting, a quorum of shareholders must be present— either in person or by proxy. Your bylaws provide that a quorum of shareholders at any shareholders' meeting consists of the owners of a majority of the shares outstanding.

6. You don't need to fill in anything here. Each share of stock constitutes one vote. In other words, each shareholder will have as many votes as he or she owns shares of stock.

7. You don't need to fill in anything here. Shareholders may authorize someone else to vote their shares at a meeting using a shareholder proxy. Your bylaws require all proxies to be in writing.

RELATED TOPIC

For a proxy form, see Form 3C: Shareholder Proxy.

8. For shareholders to take action, the action must usually be supported by a majority of the shares the corporation has issued. There are two exceptions. First, although it's rare, state law occasionally mandates a two-thirds or even three-fourths vote (called a supermajority) on some issues, such as a corporate merger or a dissolution of the corporation. Consult the corporation laws in your state to learn if any actions require more than a majority vote. Second, and far more commonly, shareholders themselves may use their bylaws to require a supermajority vote for certain significant actions such as purchasing or selling real estate, borrowing significant sums of money, or selling all or nearly all of the corporation's assets.

   If you wish to require a supermajority for some actions, check the box marked "Exception." Insert the type of action requiring a supermajority in the first blank and the percentages of votes required to pass the action in the second blank.

Sample

> Approval of the sale or purchase of real estate by the corporation requires the assent of two-thirds of the corporate shares that have been issued.

9. You don't need to fill in anything here. This section allows shareholders to take action by signing written consent—written approval of corporate actions—instead of holding formal meetings. A meeting, documented in formal minutes, is still the best way to deal with controversial issues, but for routine matters or actions that all shareholders agree on, written consents are a convenient way to proceed.

Article II: Stock

1.–4. Nothing needs to be filled in here. These sections discuss who must sign stock certificates and the requirements for keeping track of and transferring shares of stock. Read these requirements before you continue preparing your bylaws:

- Each stock certificate must be signed by the president and the secretary of the corporation.
- The corporation must keep records of which stock certificates have been issued to which shareholders and the number of shares each certificate represents.
- If a shareholder sells or transfers his or her stock, the corporation will cancel the original certificate and issue a new stock certificate to the new owner.
- If a shareholder sells or transfers his or her stock, the transfer isn't complete until the secretary makes the transfer in the corporation's books.

Article III: Board of Directors

1. This makes it clear that the board of directors will run the corporation. But because the shareholders and directors are often the same in a small corporation, the shareholders aren't typically delegating management to others. Insert the name of the state in which you filed your incorporation papers.

2. You don't need to fill in anything here. This section sets out a procedure for filling vacancies on the board of directors. Generally, a director vacancy is filled by calling a special meeting of shareholders to vote on a new director.

3. Check a box to indicate who can call a special meeting of the directors—the president, any director, or several directors. If you check the last box, insert the number of directors required to call a special meeting.

    Then, insert the number of days required for a notice of a meeting of the directors. The notice must be sent by first-class mail and must state the time, place, and purpose of the meeting.

4. Insert the number of directors required for a quorum at directors' meetings. A quorum is the minimum number of directors who must be present for the meeting to be valid. A one-director corporation should provide for a one-director quorum. Most other corporations provide that a quorum is a majority of the directors. For instance, if your corporation has three directors, two of the directors would have to be present at a meeting to make a quorum. Alternatively, you can choose the exact number of directors that will make a quorum. In many states, the minimum number of directors for a quorum is two directors or one-third of the directors, whichever is larger. For instance, a four-director corporation may provide for a quorum of two, but the minimum quorum for a nine-director corporation would be three.

5. Check one box to indicate the type of vote required for actions to be taken by the board of directors. If you check the last box, insert the minimum number of director votes required. The number of director votes needed to approve an action or make a decision is different from the quorum requirement. For example, suppose a four-director corporation requires a majority

quorum (that's three directors) and a meeting is held at which three directors are present. If the bylaws require a majority of director votes to take action at a meeting, action can be taken only by the affirmative vote of two or more directors at the meeting.

6. You don't need to fill in anything here. Typically, directors of a small corporation aren't paid for those duties but, of course, may get paid for the other work they do for the corporation. Suppose, for example, that you, Joe, and Alice each own one-third of the shares of a corporation and you each work in the business each day. The corporation will pay you each a salary for your work and may pay you each a bonus as well—but won't pay you something additional for the time you spend serving on the board of directors.

7. You don't need to fill in anything here. Your bylaws allow directors to take actions in writing (in legal jargon, by written consent) so they don't have to hold formal meetings to make a decision. Written consent requires the signatures of the same number of directors that would be necessary to take action at a face-to-face meeting.

8. You don't need to fill in anything here. Holding a meeting by conference call can be a great convenience.

Article IV: Officers

The officers of a corporation are responsible for running the business on a day-to-day basis. Many state laws require that a corporation have at least a president, a secretary, and a treasurer, although some states do not require corporations to have any officers. In most states, one person can hold all of the required offices. Check with your state's corporate filing office if you want one person to hold all of the positions or if you don't want to elect a president, secretary, or treasurer.

1. Check a box for each officer your corporation will have. You can check more than one box. (If you're using the downloadable form, delete the unused officer choices).

2. You don't need to fill in anything here. This section provides for the president to preside at directors' meetings.

3. Check a box to indicate whether the vice-president or the secretary takes over if the president can't act. The vice-president is the appropriate officer if there is one, but not every corporation has a vice-president.

4.–5. You don't need to fill in anything here. This section defines the roles of the secretary and treasurer.

6. You don't need to fill in anything here. This section gives the board of directors the authority to set salaries for the corporation's officers.

Article V: Fiscal

1. Indicate whether the corporate books will be kept on a cash basis or accrual basis. Most small corporations use the cash basis. Keeping your books on a cash basis means you take expenses into account when you actually pay for them (not when you incur them) and put income on your books when you actually receive it (not when you've just earned the right to receive it). Accrual accounting works a bit differently. With accrual accounting, you take expenses into account when you incur them and put income on your books when you earn the right to receive it. Some types of corporations are required to use the accrual accounting method. Consult an accountant or do some of your own research to decide which method is better for your business.

Sample 1

You purchase a new phone system on credit in January and pay $1,000 for it in March, two months later. Using cash method accounting, you would record a $1,000 payment for the month of March, the month when the money is actually paid. But under the accrual method, the $1,000 payment would be recorded in January, when you take the phone system and become obligated to pay for it.

Sample 2

> Your computer installation business finishes a job
> on November 30, 2020, and doesn't get paid until
> January 10, 2021. If you use the cash method, you'd
> record the payment in January 2021. Under the
> accrual method the income would be recorded in
> your books in November 2020.

RESOURCE

**For more information about the difference
between cash and accrual accounting,** see *Tax Savvy
for Small Business*, by Frederick W. Daily (Nolo).

2. You don't need to fill in anything here. This
section requires the treasurer to give financial
statements to the shareholders annually.

Article VI: Amendments

You don't need to fill in anything here. Only the
shareholders can change (amend) the bylaws.
Your bylaws specify that a vote of the owners of a
majority of the shares outstanding is required to
change the corporation's bylaws. Changes may be
made at an annual meeting or at a special meeting
called for the purpose of amending the bylaws.

RESOURCE

**For in-depth help in calling and holding
special meetings and adopting corporate resolutions,**
see *The Corporate Records Handbook: Meetings, Minutes
& Resolutions*, by Anthony Mancuso (Nolo). Also see
Chapter 3 of this book for several additional useful forms.

Date and Signatures

Fill in the date the bylaws are adopted. Each of the
shareholders must sign his or her name, and their
respective names and addresses should be typed in.

Form 2E: Stock Agreement

A stock agreement, also known as a buy-sell
agreement or shareholders' agreement, controls
who can own shares of stock in your corporation
and when a shareholder can be bought out by
the corporation or the other shareholders. Every
corporation with more than one owner should
have this type of agreement so that the owners can
maintain some control over who can become fellow
shareholders.

This stock agreement automatically restricts the
right of shareholders to sell their stock by giving the
corporation or other shareholders the first option
to buy a selling shareholder's shares (this is called
a right of first refusal). The basic idea is that before
an outsider can come aboard as a shareholder, the
corporation will first have a chance to buy the
shares. If the corporation itself doesn't purchase
the shares, the other shareholders then have the
opportunity to buy the shares. This agreement also
gives you the option of requiring the corporation to
buy the shares of any shareholder who dies.

Instructions for Form 2E: Stock Agreement

All the forms in this book are provided in
Appendix B and on the Nolo website. To access the
downloadable forms online, use the link provided
in Appendix A. As you read the instructions for
form 2E, you might want to refer to the form in
Appendix B or open the form on your computer so
you can follow along. (Before you use the form in
Appendix B, be sure to photocopy it so you'll have
a clean copy to use later.)

1. Names

In the first set of blanks, insert the names of the
shareholders. Then fill in the corporation's name.

2. Restrictions on Sale of Stock

Again, insert the name of the corporation.

3. Offer to Corporation

You don't need to insert anything here. This section says if a shareholder receives a good faith offer to purchase his or her shares, the corporation gets first crack at purchasing them at that price. A good faith offer is one that's freely negotiated and not rigged to artificially boost the price. If it's not a good faith offer, the corporation doesn't have to buy the stock, and the shareholder will not be permitted to sell it. After learning of the offer, the corporation has ten days to decide whether to buy the shares. If it decides to do so, it must purchase the shares from the selling shareholder at the same price and on the same terms as the original offer.

4. Offer to Shareholders

You don't need to insert anything here. This section lets the other shareholders buy the stock at the good faith offer price if the corporation declines to buy some or all of the shares. The shareholders can buy the shares pro rata (each shareholder purchases the same percentage of shares he or she already owns in the corporation) or the shareholders can agree to divide up the shares in a different way.

5. Remaining Shares

This paragraph says that if any of the selling shareholder's shares are not bought by the corporation or the other shareholders, the selling shareholder may, within 30 days, sell those shares to the person who made the original offer to purchase them, as long as the sale is on the same terms and conditions as in the original offer.

6. Continuing Effect

The terms and restrictions imposed by your stock agreement will last until the agreement is amended (changed) or until it is replaced by another stock agreement signed by all of the shareholders. The agreement's terms and restrictions apply to all shares in the corporation, whether or not they have been issued on the date this agreement is signed. Anyone who becomes a shareholder in the corporation at a later time is bound by the terms of this agreement in the same way as the initial shareholders.

7. Death of Shareholder

When a shareholder dies, there's a possibility that the shareholder's shares will be inherited by someone with whom the other shareholders don't want to share ownership of the company. To avoid this possibility, this stock agreement gives you the opportunity to require the corporation to purchase a deceased shareholder's shares from the shareholder's estate. To pay for the shares, the corporation is required to purchase a life insurance policy on the life of each shareholder in an amount sufficient to pay for the shares of a shareholder who dies.

Although many business owners do not like paying up front for a benefit that could be years away, insurance policies are cheaper than either saving or borrowing money. (You'd have to save much more money than the amount of your insurance premiums to achieve the same payout an insurance policy will give you, and this money wouldn't be available to help you expand your business.) An insurance policy also guarantees that cash will be available to purchase the shares of a shareholder who dies unexpectedly.

If you don't want to require the corporation to buy a deceased shareholder's shares, don't include this clause and renumber the remaining clauses.

If you do want to include this clause, you must either choose to have the corporation's accountant value the shareholder's shares by checking the first box, or enter a different valuation method by checking the second box. If you check the first box, your accountant will conduct an appraisal of the business, which will take into account the value of the business's assets, its yearly revenues and profits, and intangibles such as goodwill. However, it is often difficult for an accountant to subjectively but fairly value a private company's shares because the shares are not traded on a public exchange.

Moreover, unless an accountant has expertise in valuing businesses in a particular industry, he or she might not be able to provide an accurate assessment of the business's value.

You might want to enter your own valuation method, which can be less expensive than an appraisal. There are several methods of valuing your company's shares that use your company's financial statements from one or more years. These include the book value, the multiple of book value, and the capitalization of earnings methods. These methods are explained in more detail in *Business Buyout Agreements: Plan Now for All Types of Business Transitions*, by Bethany K. Laurence and Anthony Mancuso (Nolo). Depending on your business, one of these methods could be more appropriate than an appraisal.

If you choose to enter your own valuation method, check the second box and describe the method in detail. Here are some examples of how to describe various valuation methods:

Sample: Agreeing on a Fixed Price in Advance

> The agreed value of the company shall be $500,000, or such amount specified in a written statement signed by each Shareholder of the company after the signing of this agreement. The value of the deceased Shareholder's shares shall be the entire value for the company, multiplied by the Shareholder's percentage of ownership.

Sample: Book Value

> The value of the company shall be its book value (its assets minus its liabilities as shown on the balance sheet of the company as of the end of the most recent fiscal year prior to the Shareholder's death). The value of the deceased Shareholder's shares shall be the entire value for the company, multiplied by the Shareholder's percentage of ownership.

Sample: Multiple of Book Value

> The value of the company shall be two times its book value (its assets minus its liabilities as shown on the balance sheet of the company as of the end of the most recent fiscal year prior to the Shareholder's death). The value of the deceased Shareholder's shares shall be the entire value for the company, multiplied by the Shareholder's percentage of ownership.

Sample: Capitalization of Earnings

> The value of the company shall be determined on the basis of three times the average net earnings (annual gross revenues of the company minus annual expenses and any annual federal, state, and local income taxes payable by the company) for the three fiscal years prior to the Shareholder's death. The value of the deceased Shareholder's shares shall be the entire value for the company, multiplied by the Shareholder's percentage of ownership.

If you're not sure which method you want to use, you might want to consult your legal and accounting advisers and talk with other business owners in your field about how they would go about valuing their business.

While a mandatory buyout provision is common in small business stock agreements, it often results in the owner who remains alive the longest ending up with the whole business. This could be a reasonable outcome because the last owner to die will have managed or worked for the company for the longest amount of time. Nevertheless, because it forces a shareholder's estate to sell the shareholder's shares, it can work against the shareholder's survivors in some circumstances. You might want to explore more flexible buyout options for your stock agreement than we can provide here. For more information, see *Business Buyout Agreements: Plan Now for All Types of Business Transitions*, by Bethany K. Laurence and Anthony Mancuso (Nolo).

SEE AN EXPERT

Jointly owned shares need further attention. This book assumes the usual situation in which a stockholder owns shares in his or her own name only, meaning that the shares will become part of the shareholder's estate when the shareholder dies. Rarely in a small incorporated business will a shareholder own shares jointly with his or her spouse. If this does occur, the shares of the first spouse to die will belong to the surviving spouse rather than the estate of the spouse who has died. This paragraph won't work for jointly owned shares unless it's substantially modified—a task that will probably require a lawyer's assistance.

Standard Clauses

The remainder of the agreement contains the standard clauses we discussed in Chapter 1. The only thing you'll need to fill in here is the name of the state whose law will apply to the contract in the paragraph called "Governing Law."

Signatures

All shareholders must sign their names and fill in their respective names and addresses. In addition, even though all shareholders sign the document (as individuals), a representative of the corporation must also sign the agreement on the corporation's behalf to bind the corporation to the terms of the agreement.

A corporate officer, probably the president or chief executive officer, should sign the agreement on the corporation's behalf. However, your corporate bylaws may specify that more than one officer must sign contracts in order to bind the corporation. In that case, you'll need two officers to sign the agreement.

RESOURCE

Do you need a more detailed agreement? This stock agreement provides a limited number of ways to control the ownership of your company. It establishes fixed rules that govern the sale of corporate stock and it allows you to indicate whether the corporation will repurchase the shares of a shareholder who dies. However, you might want your agreement to cover other matters. For instance, you could want it to establish terms for buying out the interest of a retiring shareholder. You might also want to include more complex valuation formulas and payment plans in your agreement. For a stock agreement form that offers more alternatives, see *Business Buyout Agreements: Plan Now for All Types of Business Transitions*, by Bethany K. Laurence and Anthony Mancuso (Nolo).

Form 2F: LLC Operating Agreement for Single-Member LLC

The operating agreement for an LLC (limited liability company) is similar to the bylaws of a corporation. The agreement defines the internal rules that govern the company's day-to-day operations.

Even though you will be the sole owner (member) of your LLC, it is important to create an operating agreement to separate your LLC from you as an individual. Without the formality of an agreement, the LLC would look a lot like a sole proprietorship (which does not limit your personal liability for business debts). Creating a formal operating agreement helps reduce the chances that courts will refuse to recognize your LLC and hold you personally liable for the debts of your business. Just the existence of a formal written operating agreement, even a simple one, will lend credibility to your LLC's separate status.

Corporations and LLCs Use Different Terms

Although there are many similarities between corporations and LLCs, there are many differences as well—especially when it comes to terminology, as shown in the following chart.

Term	Corporation	LLC
What an owner is called	Shareholder	Member
What an owner owns	Stock Interest	Membership
What document creates the entity	Articles of Incorporation	Articles of Organization
What document spells out internal operating procedures	Bylaws	Operating Agreement

As you'll see from reading the operating agreement, maintaining an LLC can be simpler and requires less paperwork than running a corporation. And the LLC allows wide latitude in how you structure its management. For example, it can be run by one member, by a member who is selected as a manager, or by an outside manager. Also, a single-member LLC is taxed like a sole proprietorship. The business itself pays no federal income tax. Instead, the profits and losses pass through to the members (owners) who report their shares on their individual tax returns. Most small business owners prefer this arrangement. You can, however, elect to have your LLC taxed as a corporation. In that case, the business itself would be taxed. To do so, you file IRS Form 8832, *Entity Classification Election*. Your tax adviser can give you further guidance on this issue.

In every state, you can form an LLC with only one member. Typically, to set up an LLC you must prepare just two basic legal documents: the articles of organization, which is a public document you file with the state, and the operating agreement, which is the internal agreement that defines your rights and responsibilities. While most states use the term articles of organization to refer to the basic document that creates an LLC, some states (including Delaware, Mississippi, New Hampshire, New Jersey, and Washington) use the term certificate of formation and two other states (including Massachusetts and Pennsylvania) call the document a certificate of organization.

Form Your LLC Online

With Nolo's Online LLC, you can form your LLC quickly and easily online. First, you'll complete a comprehensive interview about you and your business. Then Nolo will file the necessary forms and will also create a comprehensive operating agreement for your LLC.

To start your LLC formation now, go to www.nolo.com/products/business-suite/business-formation.

In most states, preparing your articles of organization is surprisingly simple, especially if your LLC is a typical small business consisting of a handful of owners. Most states provide a printed form for the articles of organization—just fill in the blanks, sign the form, and file it with the LLC filing office. For step-by-step instructions on preparing articles of organization and other organizational documents for your single-member LLC, consult *Nolo's Guide to Single-Member LLCs*, by David M. Steingold. For help creating a multimember operating agreement or a more comprehensive operating agreement for single-member LLCs than the one offered here, see *Form Your Own Limited Liability Company*, by Anthony Mancuso (Nolo). If you will be applying for a loan on behalf of your LLC or investing a significant amount of money in it, you are better off creating a more comprehensive operating agreement than the one provided here.

Instructions for Form 2F: LLC Operating Agreement for Single-Member LLC

All the forms in this book are provided in Appendix B and on the Nolo website. To access the downloadable forms online, use the link provided in Appendix A. As you read the instructions for form 2F, you might want to refer to the form in Appendix B or open the form on your computer so you can follow along. (Before you use the form in Appendix B, be sure to photocopy it so you'll have a clean copy to use later.)

1. Names

One of the first things you need to do is settle on a name for your LLC. There are two basic ways to choose your name:

- You can combine your own last names, such as "Johnson, Holmes, & Sanchez" and add LLC at the end.
- You can make up the name under which you'll do business, such as "Three Guys Contractors, LLC."

Before settling on a business name, it's wise to conduct a name search to avoid a possible conflict with a business that is already using the same name or a similar one. Typically, if your LLC is a small local business, you can feel reasonably secure if you've searched for name conflicts at the state and local level. Check the records of the state, county, or local offices where assumed or fictitious business names are filed and the state office where corporations and LLCs are registered. Also check the phone books and city directories covering your area.

If you plan to do business regionally or nationally and will use your business name to identify a product or service, you should consider doing a national trademark search and look into registering your trademark or service mark at both the federal and state levels. For more in-depth information on trademark searches and registration, see *Trademark: Legal Care for Your Business & Product Name*, by Stephen Fishman (Nolo).

Your LLC name will have to include an LLC designator, such as "Limited Liability Company," "Limited Company," or "LLC," in the name. Depending on the state in which your business is located, one or more of the following names could be appropriate ways to indicate that your business is an LLC:

- Andover Services Limited Liability Company
- Andover Services L.L.C.
- Andover Services LLC
- Andover Services Limited Liability Co.
- Andover Services Ltd. Liability Co.
- Andover Services Limited Company
- Andover Services Ltd. Co.
- Andover Services L.C.
- Andover Services LC

Insert the name of the LLC in the first blank. Insert the state in the second blank. Insert your name in the third blank.

2. Formation

Each state has its own law covering the creation and operation of a limited liability company. Insert the name of the state in which your LLC is being formed, which will almost always be the state in which you live. Your articles of organization will describe the purpose of your LLC; you needn't repeat it here.

3. Offices

Your state law typically will require you to give an address for your registered office—the place where lawsuits and legal notices can be delivered. This usually will be your normal place of business or your home. Insert the address here.

Your state law will also require you to designate a registered agent—the person to whom legal notices can be delivered. Since you are the sole owner of the company, the form assumes that you'll be the registered agent of your LLC.

4. Management

You will be the sole manager of your LLC. But it's wise to name a trusted person to watch over your business if you die or become incapacitated and are unable to make business decisions yourself. If you wish to do so, check the box to include the optional paragraph and then insert the name of a trusted friend, relative, or business colleague.

CAUTION

Do you have a durable power of attorney for finances? Many people make durable powers of attorney for finances—the legal document that names someone to handle your finances if you become incapacitated and unable to handle your own affairs. A durable power of attorney sometimes covers business decisions along with other financial matters. If you have a durable power of attorney for finances, be certain that the power of attorney and your LLC operating agreement work together. If your power of attorney includes authority to make business decisions, you will probably want to name the same person to take care of your LLC that you named in the power of attorney.

5. Liability and Indemnification

You don't need to insert anything here. This section restates state law in that an LLC owner is not personally liable for the LLC's debts and liabilities (although there are a few exceptions to this general rule, such as when the owner specifically guarantees payment of a debt). The LLC agrees to pay attorneys' fees and other legal expenses for the member or any manager who is sued, if the member or manager did not act recklessly.

6. Capital Contributions

To establish a legitimate ownership interest in your LLC, you must contribute something to the business. It's best to start with just a token amount, such as $5,000. You can always lend additional funds to the business later, if the need arises. You should open an LLC bank account and put the start-up contribution into that account, along with any other funds you're lending to the LLC.

However, make sure you put enough money and/or property into your LLC to cover foreseeable short-term debts. If you don't put very much money in your LLC and you run up a lot of debts, a court might decide your LLC is a sham to prevent creditors from reaching your personal assets and take away your limited personal liability.

You can contribute cash, property, or both. If you're contributing cash, check the first box and enter the amount. If you're going to contribute property—such as a computer or real estate— check the second box and describe the property.

Sample

> MacBook computer, HP printer, and Fujitsu scanner.

TIP

You'll need additional paperwork to transfer property to your LLC. You should use a bill of sale to document the transfer of personal property, such as a computer, to your LLC. You can use Form 8C: Bill of Sale for Goods for this purpose. If you are transferring real estate to the LLC, you need to use a deed to document the transfer. To formalize the transfer you must file the deed in the county in which the property is located. Because preparing and filing deeds can be complicated, we recommend getting a lawyer's help.

7. Taxes

Normally, you'll want your single-member LLC to be taxed as a sole proprietorship. This means the profits and losses will pass through to you and you'll report them on Schedule C as part of your annual Form 1040. The LLC will not pay any federal income tax. If you and your tax adviser agree that this is best for you, then check the first box.

An alternative is to have your LLC taxed as a corporation, in which case the LLC will be taxed on its income and you will be taxed on any distributions you receive from the LLC. If your company is profitable, and if you're going to hold some profits in reserve for future use by the LLC, this option could reduce your taxes by allowing you to split the LLC's income between the LLC and yourself. If you and your tax adviser conclude that this is the better way to go, then check the second box.

TIP

If you choose corporate taxation, you need to file a special IRS form right after you start your LLC. File IRS Form 8832, *Entity Classification Election.*

8. Tax Year and Accounting Method

Tax Year. This section states that your LLC's tax year, or accounting period, ends on December 31, just like an individual taxpayer. To choose another tax period, you must have a good reason and get permission from the IRS. To choose a tax period other than the calendar year, you would have to file IRS Form 8716, *Election to Have a Tax Year Other Than a Required Tax Year,* (and change this operating agreement). For information about choosing a calendar or fiscal year, see *Tax Savvy for Small Business,* by Frederick W. Daily (Nolo), Chapter 4.

Accounting Method. Indicate whether your LLC will use the cash or accrual method of accounting. Most small businesses use the cash method, but if your business will stock inventory, the IRS requires you to use the accrual accounting method.

Keeping your books on a cash basis means you take expenses into account when you actually pay for them (not when you incur them) and you put income on your books when you actually receive it (not when you've just earned the right to receive it). With accrual accounting, you take expenses into account when you incur them and put income on your books when you earn the right to receive it.

EXAMPLE 1: You purchase a new computer on credit in November and pay $1,000 for it in February, two months later. Using cash method accounting, you would record a $1,000 payment for the month of February, the month when the money is actually paid. But under the accrual method, the $1,000 payment would be recorded in November, when you take the computer and become obligated to pay for it.

EXAMPLE 2: Your flooring business finishes a job on November 30, 2020, and doesn't get paid until February 1, 2021. If you use the cash method, you'd record the payment in February 2021. Under the accrual method the income would be recorded in your books in November 2020.

9. Funds

Nothing needs to be filled in here. This paragraph simply authorizes you to decide where you'll deposit LLC funds and provides who can sign checks. You do not have to list any authorized individuals in your operating agreement.

10. Additional Members

Nothing needs to be filled in here. This paragraph allows you to bring in additional members in the future. If you do admit members in the future, you'll need to amend your operating agreement, and possibly your articles of organization, to reflect the new situation.

11. Distributions

Nothing needs to filled in here. You'll be the sole judge of when to distribute cash and other LLC assets.

12. Dissolution and Termination of the LLC

You don't need to insert anything here. This section states that the LLC will continue indefinitely, even if the sole member dies, and lists two instances when the LLC will terminate (end): (1) when the member decides to dissolve the LLC, or (2) when a court or agency forces an involuntary dissolution.

Signature

Date the agreement. Then sign the agreement on behalf of the LLC. For more on signatures, see Chapter 1.

> **TIP**
>
> **Document major LLC events.** Although most state laws don't require a limited liability company to keep the same kinds of detailed records as a corporation, it's often a good idea to get the members' written consent to certain events anyway. It's wise to document major events, such as taking out a large loan, selling LLC property, or acknowledging the contribution of property from a member to the LLC. For a comprehensive guide to running a limited liability company and documenting these decisions, see *Your Limited Liability Company: An Operating Manual*, by Anthony Mancuso (Nolo).

Form 2G: LLC Membership Certificate

Historically, corporations have issued stock certificates to their shareholders to document that the shareholders have an ownership interest in the business. In some cases, this is required by the state's corporation statute. But limited liability companies (LLCs) do not have to follow the same paperwork rules or traditions that corporations do. In fact, one of the advantages that an LLC has over a corporation is that the paperwork is greatly reduced. Still, you and the other members of your LLC might wish to follow the corporate practice of issuing a document showing the owner's interest in the business. If so, you can use Form 2G for this purpose.

Instructions to Form 2G: LLC Membership Certificate

All the forms in this book are provided in Appendix B and on the Nolo website. To access the downloadable forms online, use the link provided in Appendix A.

As you read the instructions for form 2G, you might want to refer to the form in Appendix B or open the form on your computer so you can follow along. (Before you use the form in Appendix B, be sure to photocopy it so you'll have a clean copy to use later.)

Top of the Form

On the first line, insert the name of your company—for example, "Andover Services LLC." Then, in the next line, insert the name of the state where you filed the articles of organization for your company; this will probably be the state in which you reside.

In the following line, insert the certificate number and then the number of membership units (if your LLC uses membership units). For example, if your LLC has two equal members and you've provided in your operating agreement for a total of 1,000 membership units, you'd insert the number "500" in each of the membership certificates.

Middle of the Form

In the first sentence, insert the name of the LLC member in the first blank space. In the next space, insert the number of membership units the member owns and, in the final space, insert the name of your LLC.

In the last sentence, insert the date that your LLC's operating agreement was signed.

Bottom of the Form

Insert the date that the membership certificate is being signed. Then, beneath their respective signature lines, insert the names of your LLC's president and secretary—which, in a single-member LLC, might be the same person.

Form 2H: Stock Certificate

Corporations often use printed stock certificates to show the extent of a shareholder's ownership interest in the company. These printed documents look impressive and official, but you can prepare your own version that is just as effective from a legal standpoint. The stock certificate in this book will help you get the job done quickly and efficiently by filling in a few blank spaces.

Instructions to Form 2H: Stock Certificate

All the forms in this book are provided in Appendix B and on the Nolo website. To access the downloadable forms online, use the link provided in Appendix A.

As you read the instructions for form 2H, you might want to refer to the form in Appendix B or open the form on your computer so you can follow along. (Before you use the form in Appendix B, be sure to photocopy it so you'll have a clean copy to use later.)

Top of the Form

On the first line, insert the name of your corporation—for example, "Andover Services Incorporated." Then, in the next line, insert the name of the state where you filed the incorporation document (such as articles of incorporation) for your business; this will probably be the state in which you reside.

In the following line, insert the certificate number and then the number of shares the shareholder owns. For example, if your corporation has two equal owners and your corporation is issuing a total of 1,000 shares of stock, you'd insert the number "500" in each of the stock certificates.

Middle of the Form

In the first sentence, insert the name of the shareholder in the first blank space. In the next space, insert the number of shares the shareholder owns, and, in the final space, insert the name of your corporation.

In the last sentence, insert the date that your corporation's stock agreement was signed. If you don't have a stock agreement, you can delete this last sentence.

Bottom of the Form

Insert the date that the stock certificate is being signed. Then, beneath their respective signature lines, insert the names of your corporation's president and secretary—which, in a single-owner corporation, might be the same person.

Running Your Corporation

 FORMS

To download the forms discussed in this chapter, go to this book's companion page on Nolo.com. See Appendix A for the link.

To fulfill its legal and practical obligations, even a small corporation needs to hold key corporate meetings and keep a written record of important corporate decisions. Failure to do this can have serious consequences. For example, the lack of good corporate records makes you vulnerable if a creditor or the IRS challenges the legitimacy of your corporation. In a worst-case scenario, your failure to keep records like a corporation could allow a judge to decide that you and other shareholders are not entitled to the limitation against personal liability that a corporation normally provides. This could leave you to face personal liability for all of the corporation's debts.

To follow the required legal procedures, all formal actions taken by the shareholders and directors should be written in the form of minutes or written consents and kept in a corporate records book. Your records book needn't be fancy; an ordinary loose-leaf notebook will do the job. Day-to-day decisions made by officers and employees need not be documented in the corporate record book. What do need to be recorded are the minutes of corporate meetings.

At a shareholders' or directors' meeting, the participants discuss the issues and approve or reject motions put before them. The corporate secretary prepares minutes recording significant actions and decisions and keeps them in the corporate record book. These minutes serve not only to fulfill legal requirements, but also to show that decisions were made with the proper notice and votes and to remind you of the reasons decisions were made. Both shareholders' and directors' meetings fall into three general categories.

Annual Meetings. You should hold a shareholders' meeting and a directors' meeting at least once each year. Directors' meetings typically follow right after the shareholders' meeting. The main item of business at the shareholders' annual meeting is usually the election of directors, following rules set out in the corporation's bylaws. There may also be a discussion of the company's finances and plans for the coming year. At a directors' annual meeting, the corporate officers may be elected and finances and strategic planning are discussed.

Although it might not be technically required (because annual meeting dates are in the bylaws), it's a good idea to send advance notice of the annual meetings to everyone involved, listing all subjects you think will be covered. And it's especially smart to do this if unexpected, unusual, or controversial business will be addressed at the meeting.

Other Regular Meetings. Directors might find it makes sense to set up a schedule of periodic meetings—to be held quarterly, for example—that take place on certain fixed dates. Shareholders may do the same but, especially in corporations where most or all shareholders are also directors, shareholders have no real need to do so. (Shareholders don't directly manage the business, but, by law and under the terms of the corporation's bylaws, delegate that responsibility to the directors.)

Even though regular meetings might be scheduled ahead of time, the best practice is for the corporate secretary to notify the shareholders or directors well in advance of the time and place of the meeting.

Special Meetings. Usually the corporation's president, another officer, or a majority of directors or shareholders may call special meetings at any time between annual meetings or regular meetings. Shareholders might call a special meeting, for example, to fill a vacancy on the board of directors caused by resignation or perhaps to approve a sale of the corporation's major assets. Directors might hold a special meeting to pass a resolution needed to deal with important corporate business such as approving a bank loan, an executive employment contract, or the sale of real estate.

Notice of special meetings must be given in advance; usually the corporate bylaws set a number of days before a meeting by which the notice must be provided. The bylaws will normally provide that, at special meetings, the participants can vote only on the topics listed in the notice, unless all shareholders are present and agree otherwise.

Notice of Meetings. Most states require notice of meetings to be sent by first-class mail at least ten business days (for shareholders' meetings) or five business days (for directors' meetings) before the meeting date. The notice should state the time, place, and date of the meeting. Although not always legally required, the purpose for the meeting should also be in the notice. Some states have revised their corporate laws to allow for electronic notice for meetings, such as by email or fax. Check your bylaws and state law to see what's allowed or required. If you have dissident shareholders or directors or a controversial topic on the agenda, you will want to strictly adhere to notice rules.

To give written notice of various corporate meetings, you can use one of the following forms: Form 3A: Notice of Shareholders' Meeting or Form 3B: Notice of Directors' Meeting.

Minutes of Meeting. At a shareholders' or directors' meeting, the participants discuss the issues and approve or reject motions put before them. The corporate secretary prepares minutes recording significant actions and keeps them in the corporate records book. Form 3D: Minutes of Shareholders' Meeting and Form 3E: Minutes of Directors' Meeting can be used to do this.

Notice by Email, Fax, or Other Electronic Means

In certain situations, a corporation might decide to provide notice of a meeting by email, fax, or some other electronic means even if it's not specifically authorized by state law. This is more likely to be done with a small, closely held corporation where a few people own and run the corporation. If you do this, be sure to meet the substance of your state law or bylaw notice requirements. For example, if you email notice of a meeting, make sure it's done within the proper number of days prior to the meeting and contains all the required information. Then request an email response back confirming receipt of the notice and place a copy of the email notice and response in your corporate records book.

Corporate bylaws may permit meetings to be held through a telephone conference call. Form 3F: Minutes of Telephone Conference Directors' Meeting shows how minutes may be written for such a meeting.

Absence From a Meeting. If a shareholder can't attend a meeting, your bylaws may allow the shareholder to sign a proxy, which gives another person the authority to appear and vote the signer's shares at a shareholders' meeting. For this purpose, you can use Form 3C: Shareholder Proxy.

Written Consents. If you are worried that holding meetings will become cumbersome, there are some streamlined steps you can take. One way for shareholders or directors of a small company to take action is by signing written consents—that is, written approval of corporate actions—instead of holding actual meetings. Written consents are commonly used in place of a meeting in a situation where no controversial issues are outstanding and all shareholders or directors agree on whatever action will be taken. In this context, they offer a good way for directors and shareholders— especially those in corporations that have only a few owners—to take care of required paperwork without having to convene a formal meeting. Check your bylaws (which should mirror state law rules) regarding action by written consent. Most states allow action by written consent only if there is unanimous consent by the directors or shareholders. In some states and for certain issues, less than unanimous consent is allowed for shareholder action. Form 3G: Consent of Shareholders and Form 3H: Consent of Directors can be used for this purpose.

Missed Meetings. If you've missed holding and recording a required annual meeting, you can repair much of the damage by holding it later and recording the decisions made with minutes or by taking action through written consents, and then putting the documentation in your corporate records book.

RESOURCE

This chapter provides a quick survey of the requirements for holding and running corporate meetings, along with the basic forms to accomplish the job. For a much more comprehensive treatment of this subject, see *The Corporate Records Handbook: Meetings, Minutes & Resolutions,* by Anthony Mancuso (Nolo). This book gives detailed, step-by-step instructions on how to set up and run shareholders' and directors' meetings and provides over 80 legal and tax resolutions designed to document important corporate actions (buying or selling real estate or borrowing money, for example) for inclusion in corporate minutes or written consents.

When you've completed the forms in this chapter and obtained the needed signatures, place them in your corporate records book along with the corporation's articles of incorporation, bylaws, and other important corporate legal documents.

Form 3A: Notice of Shareholders' Meeting

A notice of shareholders' meeting is sent to each shareholder so that each shareholder knows when and where the meeting will be held, and the topics that will be covered. Corporate bylaws, following the dictates of state law, usually require that the corporation hold an annual meeting of shareholders and that notice be sent out beforehand specifying the date, time, and location. Check your bylaws to see how far in advance you must give the notice and how the notice should be sent. Your bylaws might require certified rather than regular mail, for example, or you might be allowed to send notice by email or fax (which is specifically authorized in some states).

Form 3A is designed to give shareholders notice of an annual, regular, or special meeting. Even if—as is common—your bylaws already establish the date, time, and place of the annual meeting or regular meetings and don't require that further notice of such meetings be given, it's still good practice to send a notice. A shareholder who forgets the meeting

date and misses the meeting may resent the fact that he or she was not reminded that an important action was to be taken. In short, the courtesy of sending a notice, even if it's not required, will help a small corporation run more smoothly.

Guidelines for Notices to Shareholders

To be in compliance with all states' legal notice requirements for shareholders' meetings, follow these rules:

Rule 1. Provide written notice of all shareholders' meetings.

Rule 2. Mail the notice at least ten business days prior to shareholders' meetings—unless your bylaws require a longer notice or a different type of delivery.

Rule 3. State the purpose of the meeting in the notice.

Source: *The Corporate Records Handbook: Meetings, Minutes & Resolutions,* by Anthony Mancuso (Nolo).

A notice is always required for a special meeting. And unlike a regular meeting, notice of a special meeting must specify the topics to be covered.

TIP

For annual meetings, one notice can do double duty. Where the shareholders and the directors are the same people—a common situation in small businesses—you can combine the notices of the annual meetings of both and send a single notice.

Instructions for Form 3A: Notice of Shareholders' Meeting

All the forms in this book are provided in Appendix B and on the Nolo website. To access the downloadable forms online, use the link provided in Appendix A. As you read the instructions for Form 3A, you might want to refer to the form in Appendix B or open the form on your computer so you can follow along.

(Before you use the form in Appendix B, be sure to photocopy it so you'll have a clean copy to use later.)

Introduction

In the first blank, fill in the name of the corporation.

Type of Meeting

Indicate whether this is to be an annual, a regular, or a special meeting.

Date

Insert the date the meeting will be held.

Time

Insert the time the meeting will start.

Place

If your bylaws specify that shareholders' meetings are to be held at the business's principal place of business, list that location. Otherwise, insert the place where the meeting will be held.

Purposes

You're usually not required to state in advance the matters that will be covered at an annual or regular meeting of shareholders. At such a meeting, shareholders are free to propose and vote on any matters that are brought up. As noted earlier, however, if an unusual or possibly controversial item will be considered, it's both courteous and a good business practice to list the agenda items so that shareholders can be prepared. In a notice of an annual meeting of shareholders, election of the board of directors is always an agenda item, so you may want to include it in the notice.

Sample

> To elect the board of directors of UpTown, Inc.

With a special meeting, you usually are legally required to list all items that will be voted on in the notice of the meeting. Topics not listed on the notice can't be legally approved, unless all of the shareholders are present at the meeting and they unanimously agree on the matter.

Issues that affect the basic character or structure of the corporation should be addressed at a shareholders' meeting. For example, shareholders would appropriately consider a proposal to merge with another business, to amend the articles of incorporation or bylaws, or to fill a vacancy on the board of directors. In preparing the notice of the meeting, you can describe these topics briefly in your own words:

Samples

> To consider the proposed merger of UpTown, Inc., with Tempo Associates, Inc.

> To consider amending the Articles of Incorporation to change the name of UpTown, Inc., to Chipco, Inc.

> To consider amending the bylaws of UpTown, Inc., to increase the number of directors from four to five.

> To fill the vacancy on the board of directors of UpTown, Inc., created by the resignation of Barbara Jones.

Whether you're holding a regular or special meeting, it's a good idea to include that other business may be transacted. That way you won't be limited to voting on the topics listed on the notice.

5. Special Meetings

If the notice is for a special meeting, include the special meeting paragraph and specify who called the meeting. (You can delete this paragraph if it does not apply.) Your bylaws should tell you who has the legal authority to call special meetings. If an officer, one or more directors, or one or more shareholders called the meeting, fill in their names. If another authorized officer called the meeting, be sure to include that officer's title. Also make sure they satisfy any requirement set out in the corporate bylaws or your state corporation laws. For instance, your bylaws (or your state laws) might require that only a certain number of shareholders, or shareholders who own a certain number or percentage of shares, may call a special meeting.

Signature

After your notice is finished, the corporate secretary should date and sign it and provide a copy to each shareholder who is entitled to receive notice of the meeting. The secretary should make sure that the shareholders receive the amount of notice to which they are entitled.

Form 3B: Notice of Directors' Meeting

Corporate bylaws often establish a date, time, and location for an annual meeting of directors. Your bylaws may also establish a schedule of regular meetings to be held more frequently than once a year, perhaps as often as quarterly. Bylaws also typically permit the president or a certain number of directors to call special meetings as needed.

Form 3B is designed to give directors notice of any of these types of meetings. As is true for shareholders' meetings, bylaws usually establish the time and place of the annual meeting so that official notice is not required. But it's still a good idea and courteous to always send a notice. If your bylaws do require you to notify directors of annual or regular meetings, there may also be requirements for how far in advance notice must be given and how the notice should be sent. Your bylaws might require certified rather than regular mail, for example, or you might be allowed to send notice by email or fax (which is specifically authorized in some states).

A notice is always required for a special meeting, and that notice must specify the topics to be covered. Again, check your bylaws for details on when and how notice is to be given. Your bylaws will also state who can call for a special meeting of directors. Often the president or another officer is given such authority or a specified number of directors can require that such a meeting be held.

In small, closely held companies in which the shareholders serve as directors, it might make sense to combine the shareholders' and directors' annual meetings into a single meeting. In that situation, it's fine to use one meeting notice for both meetings.

Guidelines for Notices to Directors

To comply with every state's legal notice requirements for directors' meetings, follow these rules:

Rule 1. Provide written notice of all directors' meetings.

Rule 2. Mail the notice at least ten business days prior to directors' meetings—unless your bylaws require a longer notice or a different type of delivery.

Rule 3. State the purpose of the meeting in the notice.

Source: *The Corporate Records Handbook: Meetings, Minutes & Resolutions,* by Anthony Mancuso (Nolo).

Instructions for Form 3B: Notice of Directors' Meeting

All the forms in this book are provided in Appendix B and on the Nolo website. To access the downloadable forms online, use the link provided in Appendix A. As you read the instructions for Form 3B, you might want to refer to the form in Appendix B or open the form on your computer so you can follow along. (Before you use the form in Appendix B, be sure to photocopy it so you'll have a clean copy to use later.)

Introduction

In the first blank, fill in the name of the corporation.

Type of Meeting

Indicate whether this is to be an annual, a regular, or a special meeting.

Date

Insert the date the meeting will be held.

Time

Insert the time the meeting will start.

Place

If your bylaws specify that directors' meetings be held at the business's principal place of business, list that location. Otherwise, insert the place the meeting will be held.

Purposes

Technically you aren't required to state in advance the purposes of an annual or regular meeting of directors. At such a meeting, directors are free to propose and vote on any issues anyone brings up. However, it's a good business practice to list the business to be transacted if you know about it in advance. This is particularly helpful if some surprising or possibly controversial topic is likely to be discussed and acted on.

A special meeting is another matter: You're usually required by your bylaws to list the topics to be discussed. If the directors vote on a nonlisted item, the vote won't be valid unless all the directors are present and the vote is unanimous.

One frequently asked question is, "How closely do directors have to manage a corporation?" There is no precise answer. The job of the directors is to determine the business policies of the corporation. How much the directors themselves do and how much they delegate to the corporation's officers will vary from business to business, but often the directors' approval is sought for such items as signing major contracts, leasing or buying space, borrowing money, and hiring top managers. You can state the agenda items briefly and in plain language:

Samples

> To consider exercising the corporation's option to extend its lease for an additional three years.

> To consider offering to Gene Baker the position of Research Director of RacaFrax, Inc., with a two-year contract.

> To consider borrowing $50,000.00 from First Thrift Bank to be used for renovation of the RacaFrax, Inc., corporate offices.

Whether you're holding a regular or special meeting, it's a good idea to include that other business may be transacted, to cover the possibility that new topics might come up that aren't presently anticipated. That way you won't be limited to voting on the topics listed on the notice.

Special Meetings

If the notice is for a special meeting, include the special meeting paragraph and specify who called the meeting. (You can delete this paragraph if it does not apply.) Your bylaws should tell you who has the legal authority to call special meetings. If an officer or one or more directors called the meeting, enter the officer's title or the directors' names in the blank. Make sure they satisfy any requirement set out in the corporate bylaws or your state corporation laws. For instance, your bylaws (or your state laws) might allow only one director to call a special meeting or they might require a minimum number of directors to call a special meeting.

Signature

After your notice is finished, the corporate secretary should date and sign it and send a copy to each director. The secretary should make sure that the directors receive the amount of notice to which they are entitled.

Form 3C: Shareholder Proxy

A shareholder proxy is a document that a shareholder uses to grant someone else, usually another shareholder, the right to vote the shareholder's stock at an upcoming meeting. It's unusual to use shareholder proxies in small corporations because the shareholders typically make it a point to be present at all important shareholders' meetings or ask the other shareholders to reschedule a meeting to make it possible for everyone to attend.

But if you're going to be out of town, for example, when the scheduled meeting will be held, and you can't get the meeting date changed, you might wish to give someone else the right to vote your shares—especially if you expect that action will be taken on a controversial matter and the vote will be close. By giving another shareholder your proxy, you'll be sure your vote will be counted.

Instructions for Form 3C: Shareholder Proxy

All the forms in this book are provided in Appendix B and on the Nolo website. To access the downloadable forms online, use the link provided in Appendix A. As you read the instructions for Form 3C, you might want to refer to the form in Appendix B or open the form on your computer so you can follow along. (Before you use the form in Appendix B, be sure to photocopy it so you'll have a clean copy to use later.)

First Blank

Fill in the name of the person who will hold your proxy—in other words, the person who will have the right to vote your stock at a meeting. Alternatively, if you are the corporate secretary and you are preparing this form for a shareholder, you may leave this blank and allow the shareholder to fill in the information later and send it back to you.

Second Blank

Insert the name of the corporation.

Annual/Regular/Special

Choose whether the proxy is for an annual, regular, or special meeting.

Third Blank

Generally, a proxy is valid for only one corporate meeting. Enter the date of the meeting for which the proxy will be granted.

Signature

Whether the corporate secretary sends this proxy form to a shareholder or the shareholder prepares this form on his or her own, the shareholder should date, sign, and return it to the corporate secretary before the meeting for which the proxy is granted. The corporate secretary should keep the proxy in the corporate records book, along with other records of the meeting.

Form 3D: Minutes of Shareholders' Meeting

When shareholders meet, you must prepare minutes to document any actions taken at the meeting. Use this form to record the decisions reached by shareholders at the meeting.

These minutes are streamlined to meet the minimum needs of an incorporated small business consisting of just a few shareholders—typically, the same people who serve on the board of directors and operate the company from day to day. These simplified minutes, for example, do not recite the traditional parliamentary procedures such as naming the shareholders who propose and second a resolution or motion, nor do they indicate the number of votes cast on each issue. This reflects the fact that shareholders in small corporations often do not strictly follow formal *Robert's Rules of Order* procedures in conducting meetings, preferring to make most decisions by consensus.

Corporations wishing a higher degree of documented formality should consult *The Corporate Records Handbook: Meetings, Minutes & Resolutions*, by Anthony Mancuso (Nolo). It contains excellent forms for minutes, as well as examples of wording for a large number of the most used corporate resolutions.

Instructions for Form 3D: Minutes of Shareholders' Meeting

All the forms in this book are provided in Appendix B and on the Nolo website. To access the downloadable forms online, use the link provided in Appendix A. As you read the instructions for Form 3D, you might want to refer to the form in Appendix B or open the form on your computer so you can follow along. (Before you use the form in Appendix B, be sure to photocopy it so you'll have a clean copy to use later.)

Introduction

In the first blank, insert the name of the corporation and then indicate the type of meeting—annual, special, or regular. (Annual meetings are scheduled in the bylaws, often for the election of corporate directors. Regular meetings are meetings held periodically throughout the year, such as monthly or quarterly, at which shareholders discuss and decide on routine corporate business. Special meetings are called to discuss urgent or nonroutine corporate matters, such as the sale of the business.)

Next, insert the date and place of the meeting and the time the meeting began and the time it ended. Remember to indicate "a.m." or "p.m."

Notice

Your minutes state that notice of the meeting was provided to the shareholders in accordance with the corporation's bylaws and state law.

If the meeting was a special meeting, include the extra provision and insert the name or names of whoever called the special meeting. (Your bylaws should tell you who has the legal authority to call special shareholders' meetings. For more information, see the introduction to this chapter.)

Quorum

A quorum is the minimum number of votes that must be present for shareholders to hold a meeting at which action is taken. You'll usually find your corporation's quorum requirements in the corporate bylaws. Most typically, each share of stock gets one vote and the holders of a majority of the shares must be present at a meeting to form a quorum.

Insert the names of shareholders who attended the meeting, either in person or by proxy. In the case of shareholders who attended by proxy, insert the name of the proxy.

Sample

Constance Baker by Joseph Chen, her proxy.

Actions Taken

Often—especially at regular or annual meetings—the shareholders will begin by reviewing and approving the minutes of the previous meeting. However, there is no legal requirement that they do so. If you did approve the minutes of the previous meeting, indicate if the last meeting was an annual, regular, or special meeting and fill in the date of that meeting.

Describe the actions taken and decisions made by the shareholders at the meeting in the space provided.

Samples

> The following people were elected to serve as directors until the next annual meeting or until their successors take office:
> - Barry Baker
> - Elaine Epifano
> - John Simpson
> - Kim Santiago

> The shareholders of Racafrax, Inc., voted unanimously to approve the sale of the building at 127 Main Street, Arkadelphia, Arkansas, to Venture Enterprises in accordance with the proposed contract presented by the corporate president, a copy of which is attached.

TIP

A majority vote of those shareholders present at a meeting might not be enough. The bylaws of some corporations might require a yes vote of a supermajority of shares—two-thirds, three-fourths, or even more—to approve certain important shareholder actions. Have the bylaws handy at every meeting so you know exactly how many votes a particular action requires for passage.

Signature

The corporate secretary should sign and date the minutes and insert his or her name and the name of the corporation. The minutes are then distributed to the shareholders for approval. Shareholder approval for the minutes is given either at the next shareholders' meeting or on a separate written approval form. The secretary should place the minutes in the corporate records book for future reference.

Form 3E: Minutes of Directors' Meeting

When directors meet, you must prepare minutes to document any actions taken at the meeting. Use this form to record the decisions reached by directors at a directors' meeting.

These minutes are streamlined to meet the minimum needs of an incorporated small business consisting of just a few directors and shareholders. They should work well to record what went on at most routine directors' meetings. However, you might need more specialized information if the directors plan to take unusual or highly specialized actions. The best source of sample minutes needed to accomplish this is *The Corporate Records Handbook: Meetings, Minutes & Resolutions*, by Anthony Mancuso (Nolo), which contains wording for 80 different kinds of directors' resolutions.

Instructions for Form 3E: Minutes of Directors' Meeting

All the forms in this book are provided in Appendix B and on the Nolo website. To access the downloadable forms online, use the link provided in Appendix A. As you read the instructions for Form 3E, you might want to refer to the form in Appendix B or open the form on your computer so you can follow along. (Before you use the form in Appendix B, be sure to photocopy it so you'll have a clean copy to use later.)

Introduction

In the first blank, insert the name of the corporation and then indicate the type of meeting—annual, special, or regular. (Annual meetings are scheduled in the bylaws, often for the election of corporate officers. Regular meetings are meetings held periodically throughout the year, such as monthly or quarterly, at which directors discuss and decide on routine corporate business. Special meetings are called to discuss urgent or nonroutine corporate matters, such as the sale of the business.)

Next, insert the date and place of the meeting and the time the meeting began and the time it ended. Remember to insert "a.m." or "p.m."

Notice

Your minutes state that notice of the meeting was provided to the directors in accordance with the corporation's bylaws and state law.

If the meeting was a special meeting, include the extra provision and insert the name or names of whoever called the special meeting. (Your bylaws should tell you who has the legal authority to call special directors' meetings. For more information, see the introduction to this chapter.)

Quorum

A quorum is the minimum number of directors who must be present for directors to hold a valid meeting and take action. Commonly, a corporation's bylaws require that at least a majority of the directors be present to constitute a quorum.

Insert the names of directors who attended the meeting. If any directors participated from another location, you can state that by adding "(by phone)" or "(by Skype)" after their names.

Actions Taken

Often—especially at regular or annual meetings— the directors will begin by reviewing and approving the minutes of the previous meeting. However, there is no legal requirement that they do so. If you did approve the minutes of the previous meeting, indicate if the last meeting was an annual, regular, or special meeting and fill in the date of that meeting.

Describe the actions taken and decisions made by the directors at the meeting in the space provided.

Samples

> The directors of Round Stone, Inc., unanimously approved the exercising of the corporation's option to extend its lease for the building at 27 Barksdale Street, Galveston, Texas, for an additional three years and authorize the president to send the appropriate notice to the landlord, Rypan Holding, Inc., of Fort Worth, Texas.

> The directors of Round Stone, Inc., voted unanimously to hire Gene Baker as the company's director of research under the proposed two-year employment contract presented by the president, a copy of which is attached.

The bylaws of many small corporations require an affirmative vote of as many as two-thirds or three-quarters of all directors to approve certain actions, such as authorizing the corporation to borrow money. If your corporation's bylaws require more than a simple majority of the directors to approve certain actions—for example, loans over $50,000—be careful to specify the number of directors who voted in favor of the action.

Sample

> The following four directors of Square Z, Inc., voted in favor of authorizing the president to arrange for a $75,000 loan from First Thrift Bank of Larchmont, New York, to be used for renovation of the corporate offices at 1002 Boston Post Road, Larchmont, New York: Joe Jacob, Karl Koch, Lawrence Lamont, and Mindy Maxwell. Director Ned Norris voted no.

TIP

You don't need director action for day-to-day business decisions. Directors are in charge of the overall management of the corporation—not the nitty-gritty details of everyday business decisions, which are best left to the corporation's officers and employees (some or all of whom might also be directors). Typically, a corporation will delegate considerable authority to the company president or other officers or employees, with the result that there will be many business decisions you're not required to document in directors' minutes. You might, for example, empower the president to hire and fire all employees except where an employee will be offered a contract of more than one year or a salary of more than $100,000, in which case, the issues must be bought to the board for prior approval.

Signature

The corporate secretary should sign and date the minutes and insert his or her name and the name of the corporation. The minutes are then distributed to the directors for approval. Director approval for the minutes is given either at the next directors' meeting or on a separate written approval form. The secretary should place the minutes in the corporate records book for future reference.

Form 3F: Minutes of Telephone Conference Directors' Meeting

If your corporation plans to hold a directors' meeting by conference call or other electronic means, you should prepare minutes to document any actions taken at the meeting. You can use this form to do so. This form is a streamlined, informal version of minutes, created for your convenience. If a controversial decision will be made, it's always better to hold the meeting in person.

Make sure your bylaws authorize you to hold directors' meetings in this way. (Most states' statutes governing corporate meetings are broad enough to allow meetings by telephone or other electronic means, such as Skype or videoconferencing.)

To be safe, you might want to document that such a meeting is agreeable to all. One convenient way to do this is to have each director email, fax, or mail in a consent form before the phone meeting. You can use Form 3H: Consent of Directors to do this. Keep any consent forms in the corporate records book along with the minutes of the meeting.

The same quorum requirements—generally found in the bylaws—apply to telephone conference meetings as to any other type of directors' meeting. Your president or secretary can begin the meeting by polling the group to be sure the required number of directors is on the line or present. Throughout the meeting, all the directors should remain in voice contact with each other.

Instructions for Form 3F: Minutes of Telephone Conference Directors' Meeting

All the forms in this book are provided in Appendix B and on the Nolo website. To access the downloadable forms online, use the link provided in Appendix A. As you read the instructions for Form 3F, you might want to refer to the form in Appendix B or open the form on your computer so you can follow along. (Before you use the form in Appendix B, be sure to photocopy it so you'll have a clean copy to use later.)

Introduction

In the first blank, insert the name of the corporation. Next, insert the date of the meeting and the time the meeting began and the time it ended. Remember to insert "a.m." or "p.m."

Quorum

A quorum is the minimum number of directors who must be present—or in this case participating in the telephone conference—for directors to hold a valid meeting and take action. Commonly, a corporation's bylaws require that at least a majority of the directors be present to constitute a quorum. Insert the names of the directors who participated in the conference call.

Actions Taken

Describe the actions taken or decisions made in the blank.

Samples

> The directors of Round Stone, Inc., voted unanimously to hire Gene Baker as the company's director of research under the proposed two-year employment contract presented by the president, a copy of which is attached.

> The directors of Round Stone, Inc., unanimously approved the exercising of the corporation's option to extend its lease for the building at 27 Barksdale Street, Galveston, Texas, for an additional three years and authorized the president to send the appropriate notice to the landlord, Rypan Holding, Inc., of Fort Worth, Texas.

The bylaws of many small corporations require an affirmative vote of as many as two-thirds or three-quarters of all directors to approve certain actions, such as authorizing the corporation to borrow money. If your corporation's bylaws require more than a simple majority of the directors to approve certain actions—for example, loans over $50,000—be careful to specify the number of directors who voted in favor of the action.

Sample

> The following four directors of Square Z, Inc., voted in favor of authorizing the president to arrange for a $75,000 loan from First Thrift Bank of Larchmont, New York, to be used for renovation of the corporate offices at 1002 Boston Post Road, Larchmont, New York: Joe Jacob, Karl Koch, Lawrence Lamont, and Mindy Maxwell. Director Ned Norris voted no.

Signature

The corporate secretary should sign and date the minutes and insert his or her name and the name of the corporation. The minutes are then distributed to the directors for approval. Director approval for the minutes is given either at the next directors' meeting or on a separate written approval form. The secretary should place the minutes in the corporate records book for future reference.

Form 3G: Consent of Shareholders

As mentioned above, there's more than one way for shareholders to take action. The most familiar way is for shareholders to meet and vote in person, but other ways of recording shareholders' votes are growing in popularity. In particular, the use of signed, written consents by shareholders in the absence of a meeting is quite common today, especially where one or more shareholders live or work a fair distance from the others.

Consents are most commonly used when the only purpose of a meeting is to document routine and noncontroversial actions, such as reelecting existing directors. Even if an action is unusual—for example, changing the name of a corporation—if all shareholders have already discussed and agreed to such a change, a written consent form will work fine.

Using a written consent in place of minutes makes especially good sense in the following situations:

- **A Meeting Was Missed.** If your corporation failed to hold an annual meeting of shareholders (or several of them) or missed another regularly scheduled meeting, you can fill the gap in your corporate records by having all shareholders sign a consent form that approves the routine actions that would have been taken at an in-person meeting. If, for example, the shareholders missed their December 15, 2020 annual meeting, they might all sign a written consent on February 15, 2021 approving the election of the board of directors, effective as of December 15, 2020. The consent resolution would be dated February 15, 2021—the date the shareholders actually signed it.

- **A One-Person Corporation.** If you're the only shareholder, there's no sensible way you can hold a meeting with yourself. At the same time, you still want to observe the traditional corporate formalities in case someone later claims your corporation is a legal sham. Using written consents for your actions as sole shareholder helps establish a paper trail should the validity of your corporation ever be challenged by the IRS or a business creditor.

- **A Small, Family-Owned Business.** If you own a corporation with your spouse, your kids, or a brother or sister, it's likely that you and these family business colleagues agree on all the important corporate issues. Holding a formal meeting to vote on business issues can feel awkward, or unnecessary, and can almost always be avoided by using written consents to meet the corporation's legal record-keeping needs.

Some states require unanimous consent for shareholders to take action by written consent. Others allow approval by the same number or percentage of shareholders as required for shareholder action at a meeting. Check your bylaws or state law for the rules in your state.

TIP

Make sure all shareholders are fully informed of all actions in the absence of a meeting. If you take action by written consent rather than by holding a meeting, your bylaws might require you to send prompt notice of the consent action to any shareholders who didn't sign the consent form. Even if the bylaws don't require such a notice, it's a good idea in order to avoid giving the impression that sneaky things are going on.

Instructions for Form 3G: Consent of Shareholders

All the forms in this book are provided in Appendix B and on the Nolo website. To access the downloadable forms online, use the link provided in Appendix A. As you read the instructions for Form 3G, you might want to refer to the form in Appendix B or open the form on your computer so you can follow along. (Before you use the form in Appendix B, be sure to photocopy it so you'll have a clean copy to use later.)

First Blank

Insert the name of the corporation.

Second Blank

Insert the actions agreed to.

Samples

Article I, Section 2, of the corporate bylaws is amended to read as follows:

"At the annual meeting, shareholders will elect a board of five directors."

The following people are elected to serve as directors of the corporation:
- Alice Andreas
- Bill Bonfield
- Connie Carter
- Donna Dowright
- Elena Ellis

Beginning April 1, 20xx the corporation will do business under the assumed name of Zanzibar Technologies. The secretary of the corporation is authorized and directed to file an appropriate certificate of assumed name with the Secretary of State's office.

Signatures

Each consenting shareholder should date and sign the form in the spaces provided, and the corporate secretary should place the signed consent form in the corporate records book.

RESOURCE

For more information about using consent forms for taking shareholder action and for examples of language to use, see *The Corporate Records Handbook: Meetings, Minutes & Resolutions*, **by Anthony Mancuso (Nolo).**

Form 3H: Consent of Directors

Most states allow directors to take action by written consent without a meeting. However, unlike with shareholders, usually unanimous consent is required for directors to take action by written consent without a meeting. Unless you think you will have unanimous consent by directors on an issue, you will need to hold a directors' meeting in person (or by other permitted meeting methods such as conference call or Skype) to take action on the item.

Many of the practical issues regarding when it makes sense to use written consents are discussed above in the introduction to the discussion regarding Form 3G: Consent of Shareholders. Review that section to learn when the use of consents for director action makes sense.

Instructions for Form 3H: Consent of Directors

All the forms in this book are provided in Appendix B and on the Nolo website. To access the downloadable forms online, use the link provided in Appendix A. As you read the instructions for Form 3H, you might want to refer to the form in Appendix B or open the form on your computer so you can follow along. (Before you use the form in Appendix B, be sure to photocopy it so you'll have a clean copy to use later.)

First Blank

Insert the name of the corporation.

Second Blank

Insert the actions agreed to.

Samples

> The following people were elected to serve in the offices listed following their names:
>
> | Barbara Alden | President |
> | Jeff Barton | Secretary |
> | Laura Crain | Treasurer |

> The president of RacaFrax, Inc., is authorized to negotiate and sign a two-year lease for the first floor of 12 Texas Street, Fort Worth, Texas, at a gross rent not to exceed $2,000 a month.

> The bank accounts of RacaFrax, Inc., will be transferred from State Bank to First Thrift Bank (Fort Worth Branch), and the president and treasurer are authorized to sign all documents necessary to make this transfer.

Signatures

Each consenting director should date and sign the form in the spaces provided, and the corporate secretary should place the signed consent form in the corporate records book.

Borrowing Money

 FORMS

    To download the forms discussed in this chapter, go to this book's companion page on Nolo.com. See Appendix A for the link.

Many small business owners need more funds than they currently have to expand a small business. And of course, extra cash might be necessary in an emergency to cover extensive unforeseen expenses or even just to cover low cash flow months. No matter what the reason, if you need to tap outside sources for a loan, you essentially have two choices: to borrow the money privately from friends or family members or to apply for a loan from a bank or another institution.

Whether you borrow money from a bank or someone you know, you'll sign a promissory note to document your assurance that you'll repay the money. A promissory note says, in effect, "I promise to pay you $_____ plus interest of ___%" and then describes how and when you're to make payments.

This chapter contains four promissory notes designed for use when your business borrows money from a friend or relative. Banks and other commercial lenders write up their own forms for you to sign, so if you're getting a loan from a commercial lender, you'll use their forms.

RESOURCE

Chapter 9 of the *Legal Guide for Starting & Running a Small Business,* **by Fred S. Steingold and David M. Steingold (Nolo), contains in-depth coverage on raising money for your business.**

Understanding Promissory Notes in General

A promissory note is a binding legal contract. As with all contracts, something of value is exchanged between two parties. In this case, you (the borrower) receive money. The lender receives your promise to repay the money with interest on specified dates. If you don't meet the repayment terms, the lender can sue and get a judgment against you for the amount you owe plus court costs and possibly lawyers' fees. With a judgment in hand, the lender can then collect the money owed from your bank accounts and other assets.

Before borrowing money and signing a promissory note, you need to fully understand the terms and details.

Interest

Unless otherwise specified in the note, interest is paid at the end of the borrowing interval—not in advance. For example, if you borrow money on January 1 and agree to pay interest each month on the first day of the month, your February payment will cover the interest for your use of the money in January.

State usury laws cap the rate of interest a lender can charge—often in the range of 10% to 20% for loans. A lender who charges more may face financial penalties and is not allowed to go to court to collect the excess amount. However, state laws generally allow a lender to charge a higher interest rate when a business borrows money than when an individual does—in fact, some states put no limit on the rate of interest a business may be charged. But friends and relatives aren't likely to charge excessive interest rates, so usury laws are rarely a problem. Check the usury law of your state only if the rate the lender wants to charge exceeds 10%.

TIP

Choose a fair interest rate. The sensible way to approach interest is to choose a rate that's fair and benefits everyone involved—slightly lower than one would pay a commercial lender and slightly more than the lender would earn in a safe investment (such as a money market fund).

CAUTION

A no-interest loan can have tax implications. If a generous family member is lending you more than $10,000, the promissory note should call for interest that at least matches the Applicable Federal Rate (AFR). You'll find the current AFR at www.irs.gov. Additional rules apply if a related party lends you more than $100,000. See a tax professional for details.

Personal Guarantee

If your business is organized as a sole proprietorship or general partnership, by definition you'll be personally liable for repaying the business loan. But if your business is organized as a corporation or limited liability company, and you were to sign a promissory note on behalf of the corporation or the LLC, you would not be personally liable for repayment. The lender would only be able to go after your business's assets for repayment.

For this reason, a bank or other commercial lender usually requires you to personally guarantee repayment of a loan to your corporation or LLC, in which case you make yourself personally liable for the debt. If your business doesn't repay the loan, the lender can sue you and go after your personal assets, as if you hadn't organized as a corporation or an LLC in the first place.

RELATED TOPIC
Personal guarantees are discussed further in Chapter 1.

Of course, commercial lenders aren't the only ones who want to be repaid. A financially savvy friend or relative might also ask you to personally guarantee the repayment of a loan to your corporation or LLC. Chapter 1 contains language you can add to a promissory note to personally guarantee a loan.

If your spouse is asked to guarantee repayment of a loan, be aware of the possible consequences. Your spouse's personal liability added to your own will place at risk any property you and your spouse own jointly, as well as your spouse's separate property and wages. Generally, a lender is more likely to require your spouse's guarantee if you're borrowing money for a sole proprietorship than if the loan is being made to a partnership, corporation, or limited liability company.

Equity Investment: Another Way to Raise Money

New or expanding businesses that need cash sometimes seek equity investors who will buy a piece of the business. Investors stand to make money if your business succeeds and to lose money if it fails. The advantage to this arrangement is that, unlike borrowing money, you normally make no commitment to investors that they'll get their money back if things go poorly. Of course, in exchange for this freedom from debt worries, there are significant disadvantages, because you relinquish (sell) a share of your business in exchange for the investment. If your business flourishes, your investors will own part of your success. And if your business prospers and you sell it someday, the investors will be entitled to a chunk of what you receive in proportion to their share in the business. In addition, your investor might have a say in how you run your business. (Depending on the arrangements you make, equity investors might or might not be entitled to participate in making business decisions.)

Special state and federal securities laws govern the sale of interests to these equity investors. If you're interested in pursuing this route, you'll need to learn more about securities laws requirements. Fortunately, there are generous exemptions that normally allow a small business to provide a limited number of investors an interest in the business without complicated paperwork. In the rare cases in which your business won't qualify for these exemptions, you have to comply with the complex disclosure requirements of the securities laws—such as distributing an approved prospectus to potential investors. In this case, it could be too much trouble to do the deal unless a great deal of money is involved. You should probably consult a small business expert to make sure you comply with these often complicated laws.

RELATED TOPIC

For a discussion of spousal liability and community property, see Chapter 1.

In some cases, a personal guarantee might not be enough. For example, if you're starting a new business, a lender could conclude that the business is not sufficiently creditworthy to qualify for a loan, even if you and your spouse personally guarantee repayment. The solution might be to ask a parent, aunt, uncle, or close friend—someone with greater financial resources than you—to guarantee repayment. If you do this, however, be sure to fully disclose all the risks to your friend or relative: A cosigner (also called a coguarantor) must be told that he or she is on the hook to repay the loan if you and your business can't. And a cosigner should understand that guaranteeing your loan could impair his or her ability to borrow money.

Security Interest

A lender might also want to obtain a security interest in the borrower's business assets or other property, such as the borrower's house or boat. Similar to a mortgage, a security interest gives the lender the right to seize and sell the property to pay off the loan if the borrower defaults (misses payments).

By contrast, if the borrower defaults on a loan for which the lender doesn't have a security interest, the lender will have to sue the borrower in court, get a judgment, locate available assets, and seize the assets to collect what the borrower owes.

A friend or relative who lends money isn't as likely as a commercial lender to ask for the loan to be secured with a security interest. Still, the borrower could decide that it's only fair to include one, or that it's a good enticement to offer the lender.

CAUTION

Don't pledge more property than necessary. When you pledge assets to secure the repayment of money you're borrowing, you should pledge only enough property to cover the loan. You want be free to sell your other assets or possibly to use them to secure additional loans.

The promissory notes in this chapter can be used for secured loans. In addition, use Form 4E: Security Agreement for Borrowing Money to secure the promissory note. For further protection, the security agreement acknowledges that the lender will prepare a second document called a Uniform Commercial Code (UCC) Financing Statement, which will be recorded (filed) at a public office to let third parties such as purchasers or other lenders know about the security interest. When the borrower pays off the loan, the lender must give the borrower an official termination of the financing statement, which can be filed at the same place where the financing statement was filed. This document is explained further in the instructions for the security agreement.

SEE AN EXPERT

Pledging real estate as security requires professional assistance. If you pledge your home or other real estate as security for a business loan, a security agreement won't be adequate to protect the lender. A well-informed lender will ask you to sign a mortgage or a deed of trust to be recorded (filed) with the county records office to establish a lien showing that the lender has an interest in your real estate. Procedures for preparing and recording mortgages and deeds of trust are somewhat technical and vary from state to state; it's wise to seek the assistance of a real estate lawyer.

Get Permission to Borrow

If your business is a corporation, the board of directors should adopt a corporate resolution approving not only the borrowing of money but also the pledging of corporate assets as security for the loan. And, even though it's probably not required by your bylaws or state law, it's a good idea to get written permission from any shareholders who are not also directors. This will forestall shareholder grumbling if the corporation can't repay the loan and corporate assets are liquidated by the lender. Also, a commercial lender will want to see the board of directors' resolution authorizing the loan. A friend or relative who lends you money is less likely to insist on seeing it.

RELATED TOPIC
You can use Form 3H: Consent of Directors and Form 3G: Consent of Shareholders for this purpose.

Similarly, if your business is an LLC, get written permission from all of the members before borrowing money or pledging LLC assets as collateral for a loan. See the instructions for forms 3G and 3H in Chapter 3 for sample language that you can use.

Acceleration Clause

Acceleration allows the lender to demand payment of the entire loan amount if the borrower doesn't make a required payment within a specified number of days after it becomes due. If the borrower still doesn't pay, the lender can sue the borrower for the entire amount owed.

The promissory notes in this book include acceleration clauses that allow the lender to collect the entire amount before it is due. Without an acceleration clause, the lender would have to sue the borrower each time a payment was missed or wait until all installment payments had been missed to sue for the whole amount.

Late Fee

A lender might want to include a clause in the promissory note tacking on a late charge for payments not made on time. Our agreements do not call for payment of a late fee, and you should argue against adding one if you're the borrower. Here's why: If a payment is late, interest continues to run on the principal balance owed, meaning the lender is already being compensated for your use of the money over more time. A late charge means the lender is double-dipping.

Prepayment

Paying some of the loan principal before it's due reduces the overall amount of interest on a loan. A borrower might do this by increasing each installment payment, making occasional additional payments, or paying the loan balance off early.

Some loans have prepayment penalties, meaning that if the borrower wants to pay off part or all of the loan before it is due, the lender can charge a penalty, usually 1% to 3% of the loan principal. The promissory notes in this chapter state that prepayment will be allowed without penalty. In other words, the borrower is allowed to pay off the loan early, without penalty.

CAUTION
Monthly installment payments must always be made. Even if the borrower prepays some of the loan, regular monthly installment payments must still be made. Suppose that on June 1 you make your normal monthly installment payment of $200. To reduce the principal amount, you pay $1,000 extra and ask that it be applied toward principal. Even though you might think you've paid five months in advance, you haven't. On July 1—and on the first day of each month after that—you still must make your normal monthly payment of $200 until the loan is paid off. In short, if you make extra payments toward principal, be sure you'll still have enough cash on hand to make regular payments as they become due.

Fees and Costs

The promissory notes in this chapter require you to pay the lender's costs and lawyers' fees if the lender must sue to collect on the note.

Signing and Storing Your Promissory Note

Sign only the original promissory note and give it to the lender to keep. Keep a photocopy of the signed note (marked "COPY") for your records.

The lender should return the original marked as "paid in full" to you when you've paid the note off.

Changing a Promissory Note

Occasionally, you and the lender might want to change (amend) the terms of an existing promissory note. The best way to do this is to prepare and sign a new promissory note containing the new terms. You should never rely on oral understandings about your rights or obligations under a promissory note, where your money and credit could be at stake.

In the new promissory note, you can add the following language:

This promissory note replaces the $_____ promissory note signed by Borrower on _____ , 20____ , and payable to Lender.

The lender should return the original promissory note to the borrower in exchange for the new note.

RESOURCE

For more information and forms for getting approval from corporate directors and shareholders for borrowing money and pledging assets, see *The Corporate Records Handbook: Meetings, Minutes & Resolutions*, by Anthony Mancuso (Nolo). For information and forms on getting approval from LLC members and managers for borrowing money and pledging assets, see *Your Limited Liability Company: An Operating Manual*, by Anthony Mancuso (Nolo).

The Promissory Notes in This Chapter

The main differences among the four promissory notes in this chapter concern how you'll pay back the loan:

- **Form 4A: Promissory Note (Amortized Monthly or Annual Payments).** This note requires you to pay the same monthly or annual payment for a specified number of months or years until the loan is paid off. Part of each payment goes toward interest and the rest goes toward principal. When you make the last payment, the loan and interest are fully paid. In accounting jargon, this type of loan is said to be fully amortized over the period that the payments are made.

- **Form 4B: Promissory Note (Balloon Payment).** This note requires you to make equal monthly payments of principal and interest until the balance is due in one payment, called a balloon payment. This type of promissory note offers definite benefits to the borrower—primarily, lower monthly payments during the course of the loan, thus keeping cash available for other needs.

EXAMPLE: Phil needs some start-up money for his new business. Cousin Edna is willing to lend him $20,000 at 7% interest, but she'd like to have all the money back in two years when she plans to modernize her kitchen and bathroom. Phil and Edna agree that Phil will pay back $200 a month for two years. At the end of two years, Phil will have reduced the loan balance from $20,000 to $17,589.94. (The rest of his payments will have gone toward interest.) Phil will owe this balance to Edna in one balloon payment. Phil is comfortable with this arrangement. If he doesn't have the cash to pay the balloon payment, he knows he can refinance his house with the bank to pay off Edna.

- **Form 4C: Promissory Note (Interest-Only Payments).** This type of note allows the borrower to repay the lender by making payments of interest at specified intervals, such as every month. During the repayment period, the borrower does not have to pay any principal. At the end of the loan term, you must make a balloon payment to cover the

Amortization Chart for Monthly Payment

Interest Rate	Number of Years								
	1	1.5	2	2.5	3	4	5	6	7
3.0%	0.0847	0.0569	0.0430	0.0346	0.0291	0.0221	0.0180	0.0152	0.0132
3.5%	0.0849	0.0571	0.0432	0.0349	0.0293	0.0224	0.0182	0.0154	0.0134
4.0%	0.0851	0.0573	0.0434	0.0351	0.0295	0.0226	0.0184	0.0156	0.0137
4.5%	0.0854	0.0576	0.0436	0.0353	0.0297	0.0228	0.0186	0.0159	0.0139
5.0%	0.0856	0.0578	0.0439	0.0355	0.0300	0.0230	0.0189	0.0161	0.0141
5.5%	0.0858	0.0580	0.0441	0.0358	0.0302	0.0233	0.0191	0.0163	0.0144
6.0%	0.0861	0.0582	0.0443	0.0360	0.0304	0.0235	0.0193	0.0166	0.0146
6.5%	0.0863	0.0585	0.0445	0.0362	0.0306	0.0237	0.0196	0.0168	0.0148
7.0%	0.0865	0.0587	0.0448	0.0364	0.0309	0.0239	0.0198	0.0170	0.0151
7.5%	0.0868	0.0589	0.0450	0.0367	0.0311	0.0242	0.0200	0.0173	0.0153
8.0%	0.0870	0.0591	0.0452	0.0369	0.0313	0.0244	0.0203	0.0175	0.0156
8.5%	0.0872	0.0594	0.0455	0.0371	0.0316	0.0246	0.0205	0.0178	0.0158
9.0%	0.0875	0.0596	0.0457	0.0373	0.0318	0.0249	0.0208	0.0180	0.0161
9.5%	0.0877	0.0598	0.0459	0.0376	0.0320	0.0251	0.0210	0.0183	0.0163
10.0%	0.0879	0.0601	0.0461	0.0378	0.0323	0.0254	0.0212	0.0185	0.0166
10.5%	0.0881	0.0603	0.0464	0.0380	0.0325	0.0256	0.0215	0.0188	0.0169
11.0%	0.0884	0.0605	0.0466	0.0383	0.0327	0.0258	0.0217	0.0190	0.0171
11.5%	0.0886	0.0608	0.0468	0.0385	0.0330	0.0261	0.0220	0.0193	0.0174
12.0%	0.0888	0.0610	0.0471	0.0387	0.0332	0.0263	0.0222	0.0196	0.0177

Interest Rate	Number of Years								
	8	9	10	11	12	13	14	15	20
3.0%	0.0117	0.0106	0.0097	0.0089	0.0083	0.0077	0.0073	0.0069	0.0055
3.5%	0.0120	0.0108	0.0099	0.0091	0.0085	0.0080	0.0075	0.0071	0.0058
4.0%	0.0122	0.0110	0.0101	0.0094	0.0088	0.0082	0.0078	0.0074	0.0061
4.5%	0.0124	0.0113	0.0104	0.0096	0.0090	0.0085	0.0080	0.0076	0.0063
5.0%	0.0127	0.0115	0.0106	0.0099	0.0092	0.0087	0.0083	0.0079	0.0066
5.5%	0.0129	0.0118	0.0109	0.0101	0.0095	0.0090	0.0085	0.0082	0.0069
6.0%	0.0131	0.0120	0.0111	0.0104	0.0098	0.0092	0.0088	0.0084	0.0072
6.5%	0.0134	0.0123	0.0114	0.0106	0.0100	0.0095	0.0091	0.0087	0.0075
7.0%	0.0136	0.0125	0.0116	0.0109	0.0103	0.0098	0.0094	0.0090	0.0078
7.5%	0.0139	0.0128	0.0119	0.0111	0.0106	0.0101	0.0096	0.0093	0.0081
8.0%	0.0141	0.0130	0.0121	0.0114	0.0108	0.0103	0.0099	0.0096	0.0084
8.5%	0.0144	0.0133	0.0124	0.0117	0.0111	0.0106	0.0102	0.0098	0.0087
9.0%	0.0147	0.0135	0.0127	0.0120	0.0114	0.0109	0.0105	0.0101	0.0090
9.5%	0.0149	0.0138	0.0129	0.0122	0.0117	0.0112	0.0108	0.0104	0.0093
10.0%	0.0152	0.0141	0.0132	0.0125	0.0120	0.0115	0.0111	0.0107	0.0097
10.5%	0.0154	0.0144	0.0135	0.0128	0.0122	0.0118	0.0114	0.0111	0.0100
11.0%	0.0157	0.0146	0.0138	0.0131	0.0125	0.0121	0.0117	0.0114	0.0103
11.5%	0.0160	0.0149	0.0141	0.0134	0.0128	0.0124	0.0120	0.0117	0.0107
12.0%	0.0163	0.0152	0.0143	0.0137	0.0131	0.0127	0.0123	0.0120	0.0110

entire principal and any remaining interest. This type of note offers definite benefits to the borrower—significantly lower monthly payments during the course of the loan, thus keeping cash available for other needs. But the disadvantage is that you end up paying more interest because you are borrowing the principal for a longer period of time.

- **Form 4D: Promissory Note (Lump-Sum Payment).** With this type of promissory note, you pay off the loan at a specified date in the future in one payment, which includes the entire principal amount and the accrued interest.

> **EXAMPLE:** Renee borrows $15,000 from her former college roommate for her graphic design business. The loan is at 8% and is to be repaid in one payment in seven years. Unless Renee pays back the loan early, she will owe $23,400 when the seven years are up.

TIP

Promissory notes can help preserve friendships and family harmony. It's smart to sign a promissory note, even if the friend or relative from whom you're borrowing assures you that such formality isn't necessary. Think of it this way: Documenting the loan can do no harm—and it can head off misunderstandings about whether the money is a loan or gift, when it is to be repaid, and how much interest is owed.

Form 4A: Promissory Note (Amortized Monthly or Annual Payments)

If you've ever taken out a mortgage or car loan, you're familiar with how this type of repayment works. You pay off the loan in equal monthly or annual payments over a set time, usually a number of years. Each of your payments is partly applied to interest and partly to principal. As the amount you owe declines, the amounts of each payment that go to principal and interest changes (the principal portion gradually goes up while the interest portion goes down). This is called amortizing the loan.

If you know the principal amount, the interest rate, and the number of years that payments will be made, you can consult an amortization calculator or schedule to arrive at the monthly payment. To use a free calculator, go to www.nolo.com/legal-calculators, or you can use software like *Quicken*.

If you don't have immediate access to the Internet or software to calculate the amortization, the chart above can help you determine what amount needs to be paid each month to pay off a loan over time. Here's how to use it:

Step 1. In the left-hand column of the chart, find your interest rate.

Step 2. At the top of the chart, find the period of time you'll have to repay the loan—the period between the making of the loan and the date all principal will be paid.

Step 3. Find the figure where the two columns intersect. For instance, if the interest rate is 10% and the loan will be paid over five years, the figure at the intersection point is 0.0212.

Step 4. Multiply that figure by the principal amount of the loan. The product is the monthly payment, which includes principal and interest.

> **EXAMPLE:** Vladimir makes a loan of $10,000 at 10% interest. The loan is payable in monthly installments over five years. Vladimir multiplies 0.0212 by $10,000 to get $212, the amount of each monthly payment.

Instructions for Form 4A: Promissory Note (Amortized Monthly or Annual Payments)

All the forms in this book are provided in Appendix B and on the Nolo website. To access the downloadable forms online, use the link provided in Appendix A. As you read the instructions for Form 4A, you might want to refer to the form in Appendix B or open the form on your computer so you can follow along. (Before you use the form in Appendix B, be sure to photocopy it so you'll have a clean copy to use later.)

1. Names

Insert the names and addresses of the borrower and lender. See Chapter 1 for a discussion of how to identify the parties in legal forms.

2. Promise to Pay

In the first blank, insert the principal amount of the loan. In the second blank, fill in the annual interest rate. For information on interest rates and usury laws, see the introduction to this chapter.

The phrase "For value received" is legal jargon meaning that you have received something—in this case, money—from the lender in exchange for your promise to pay money. It's there because the law requires that for your promise to pay to be binding, you must receive something of value from the other party.

3. Installments

Insert the number of monthly or annual payments you'll make to repay the loan and the amount of each installment. As noted above, the accompanying amortization chart and instructions allow you to quickly calculate the amount of each installment.

4. Date of Installment Payments

If you will be making monthly payments, insert the day of the month when payments will be made and the date the first payment is due. For example, if you borrow money on January 15, 2020, you might provide for payments to be made on the 15th of each month, with the first payment due on February 15, 2020.

If you will be making annual payments, insert the date when payments will be made and the date the first payment is due. For example, if you borrow money on March 15, 2019, you might provide for

payments to be made on March 15th of each year, with the first payment due on March 15, 2020.

5. Application of Payments

You don't need to insert anything here. Each payment automatically goes to pay accrued interest first. The rest goes toward the remaining principal. These allocations are easily handled by a free calculator (available at www.nolo.com/legal-calculators) or number-crunching software, such as *Quicken*. Basically, here's how it works: Assume that the annual interest rate is 8% on a $5,000 loan. To determine the annual interest, you'd multiply the loan balance by the interest rate. If you were making monthly payments, you'd divide the annual interest by 12 to determine the monthly interest portion of the payment. To illustrate:

Loan balance		$ 5,000.00
Interest rate	x	.08
Annual interest		$ 400.00
Payments per year	÷	12
Interest for first month		$ 33.33

If you're making payments of $200 each month, your payment for the current month would be applied as follows:

Interest	$ 33.33
Principal	166.67
Total	$ 200.00

That would leave a principal balance of $4,833.33 ($5,000.00 less $166.67) remaining on the loan. So next month, because the principal is less, the interest portion of your $200 payment will be a bit less and the principal portion will be a bit more.

6. Prepayment

You don't need to insert anything here. This paragraph allows the borrower to prepay the money borrowed—that is, pay all or part of the principal in advance. By prepaying, the total amount of interest paid is reduced.

7. Loan Acceleration

Promissory notes typically provide that if a payment is late by more than a specified number of days, the lender can declare the entire unpaid balance due. This is called an acceleration clause. Fill in the number of days after the payment due date that will trigger acceleration. Thirty days is often appropriate when the lender is a friend or relative.

8. Security

Check the first box if the note is unsecured, meaning that the lender does not have a lien on or security interest in any property.

Check the second box if the borrower is giving the lender a security interest in business property. Insert the name of the business. Be sure to also enter into a security agreement with the lender. (You can use Form 4E: Security Agreement for Borrowing Money.) The lender can then file a Uniform Commercial Code (UCC) Financing Statement with the appropriate state or county office. When the borrower pays off the loan, the lender must give the borrower an official termination of the financing statement, which can be filed at the same place where the financing statement was filed.

Check the third box if the borrower will give the lender a lien on real estate owned by the borrower or the borrower's business. Choose whether this will be done by a mortgage or deed of trust. (The practice varies from state to state.) Finally, insert the legal description of the real estate as found in your deed or title insurance policy.

If you're using the downloaded form, instead of marking the correct box, delete the security options you're not using, so that only the appropriate sentence(s) remain in the document.

> **SEE AN EXPERT**
>
> **Have a lawyer prepare the mortgage or deed of trust.** Because of the technical intricacies of real estate titles, it's best to have an expert draft the mortgage or

deed of trust that will secure the loan. After the loan is made, it's the lender's job to see that the mortgage or deed of trust gets recorded at the appropriate county records office. When the loan is paid, the lender should remove the lien (security interest) by giving you a release of the mortgage or deed of trust that you can record where the original document was recorded.

9. Collection Costs

Nothing needs to be filled in here. This paragraph requires the borrower to pay the lender's reasonable costs and lawyers' fees if the lender takes the borrower to court to collect on the note and wins the lawsuit.

Standard Clauses

The remainder of the note contains the standard clauses regarding Notices, Governing Law, and Severability discussed in Chapter 1. (Note that the other standard clauses discussed in Chapter 1 generally do not apply to promissory notes and are not included in this form.) The only thing you'll need to fill in here is the name of the state whose law will apply to the note in the paragraph "Governing Law."

Signature and Guarantee

As discussed above, the lender might want the borrower to have a personal guarantor sign the loan, to be personally liable for repayment. If this is the case, at the end of the promissory note, add the appropriate guarantee language from the downloadable form Guarantee.rtf.

 FORM

Guarantee language. Guarantee language that you can copy and paste into these promissory notes is included in the downloadable form Guarantee.rtf.

Only the borrower and guarantors, if any, sign the note. The lender does not sign it. (See Chapter 1 to read more about signing contracts.)

Form 4B: Promissory Note (Balloon Payment)

Suppose you borrow money and would like to pay it back over four years, but the burden of making installment payments sufficient to pay it off in that time would be too great. To allow you to conserve cash, the lender might agree to compute the monthly payments based on an eight-year amortization period—making the monthly payments substantially lower—but have you pay back the loan at the end of the four years. At the end of that period, you'd pay off whatever was still owing on the loan by making a lump-sum, or balloon, payment. Form 4B is designed for this type of loan.

> **EXAMPLE:** Phyllis will borrow $20,000 from her uncle Ted to start a transcription service for doctors who dictate their medical charts. They agree that Phyllis will repay the loan by making monthly payments over a four-year period and that the yearly interest rate will be 8%. Using an amortization calculator, Phyllis and Ted determine that it would take monthly payments of $488.26 to pay off the loan in full by the end of the fourth year. But this worries Phyllis, because in the first few months making payments of that size would pinch the tiny cash flow of her new business. To make things easier for Phyllis, she and Ted agree to the following: Phyllis will pay $282.73 a month—the amount it would take to amortize the loan over an eight-year period. At the end of four years, Phyllis will make a lump-sum payment of $11,864.27 to pay off the remaining principal balance.

TIP

Amortization computations may vary. The figures in the above example were derived using *Quicken*'s amortization feature. If you use the chart provided earlier in this chapter, you'll find that the computations are rounded off: The monthly installments for the four-year period are calculated at $488; the eight-year figure is $283, with a balloon payment of $11,900.

RESOURCE

Find free amortization calculators. Nolo offers free loan calculators at www.nolo.com/legal-calculators. Look under the header "Personal Financing" to figure out how much loan payments will be, how long it will take to pay off a loan, or to determine a loan rate.

Instructions for Form 4B: Promissory Note (Balloon Payment)

All the forms in this book are provided in Appendix B and on the Nolo website. To access the downloadable forms online, use the link provided in Appendix A. As you read the instructions for Form 4B, you might want to refer to the form in Appendix B or open the form on your computer so you can follow along. (Before you use the form in Appendix B, be sure to photocopy it so you'll have a clean copy to use later.)

1. Names

Insert the names and addresses of the borrower and lender. See Chapter 1 for a discussion of how to identify the parties in legal forms.

2. Promise to Pay

See instructions for Paragraph 2 of Form 4A.

3. Monthly Installments

Insert the number of monthly payments you'll make to repay the loan and the amount of each installment. As noted above, the accompanying amortization chart and instructions allow you to quickly calculate the amount of each installment. The amortization period used to calculate payments will be longer than the actual period over which the borrower will repay the loan. (Otherwise, there would be no balloon payment to be made at the end of the amortization period—the loan would be paid off.)

4. Date of Installment Payments

Insert the day of the month when the regular monthly payments will be made and the due date of the first payment. For example, if you borrow money on January 15, 2019, you might provide for payments to be made on the 15th day of each month, with the first payment due on February 15, 2019.

In the final space, insert the date by which you'll make the balloon payment covering the entire balance of principal and interest.

5. Application of Payments

You don't need to insert anything here. See the instructions for Paragraph 5 of Form 4A for how payments are allocated between principal and interest.

6. Prepayment

See the instructions for Paragraph 6 of Form 4A. You don't need to insert anything here.

7. Loan Acceleration

See the instructions for Paragraph 7 of Form 4A.

8. Security

See the instructions for Paragraph 8 of Form 4A.

9. Collection Costs

Nothing needs to be filled in here. See the instructions for Paragraph 9 of Form 4A.

Standard Clauses

The remainder of the note contains the standard clauses regarding Notices, Governing Law, and Severability discussed in Chapter 1. (Note that the other standard clauses discussed in Chapter 1 generally do not apply to promissory notes and are not included in this form.) The only thing you'll need to fill in here is the name of the state whose law will apply to the note in the paragraph "Governing Law."

Signature and Guarantee

See the instructions for Form 4A.

Form 4C: Promissory Note (Interest-Only Payments)

You and the lender may agree that you'll make monthly payments of interest only, and then pay off the entire principal in one lump sum at a date some months or years down the line. Form 4C is designed for this purpose. The advantage of this method is that the periodic payments you make will be lower than if you were to make payments that included both interest and principal. The disadvantage is that because you're borrowing the principal for a longer time, you'll be paying more interest.

> **EXAMPLE:** Peter borrows $20,000 at 8% interest from a family friend, Tracy, to expand his business. Tracy will need the entire amount back by the end of four years to make a down payment on a vacation cabin she plans to buy. Using an amortization calculator, Peter figures out that if he were to pay back the debt in equal installments each month for four years, each payment would need to be $488.26—a bit more than he can handle right now. But if he pays interest only, his payments will be only $133.33 a month. Peter and Tracy agree to this arrangement, giving Peter four years to raise the $20,000 that will be needed to pay back the entire principal. Peter isn't worried because he firmly believes his business will be strong enough by then that he'll have no problem refinancing through a bank loan, if necessary.
>
> Note the higher cost to Peter of doing it this way. He'll be making 48 payments of interest totaling $6,400 plus the repayment of the $20,000—which adds up to $26,400. If, instead, he were to amortize the loan over four years by making 48 monthly payments of $488.26 each, his total cost would be $23,436.48, which is nearly $3,000 less. Of course, the interest on business loans is a tax-deductible expense, which cushions the impact a bit.

> **TIP**
>
> **Interest-only payments afford the borrower maximum flexibility.** If a borrower gets a lender to agree to the interest-only method and then finds herself in the happy position of having a lot of cash on hand, she can prepay some of the principal, thus reducing the interest payments. But if cash flow isn't so great, she's under no pressure to pay any part of the principal until the end of the loan period, at which point she might have other alternatives, such as borrowing the necessary payback amount from a commercial lender.

Instructions for Form 4C: Promissory Note (Interest-Only Payments)

All the forms in this book are provided in Appendix B and on the Nolo website. To access the downloadable forms online, use the link provided in Appendix A. As you read the instructions for Form 4C, you might want to refer to the form in Appendix B or open the form on your computer so you can follow along. (Before you use the form in Appendix B, be sure to photocopy it so you'll have a clean copy to use later.)

1. Names

Insert the names and addresses of the borrower and lender. See Chapter 1 for a discussion of how to identify the parties in legal forms.

2. Promise to Pay

See the instructions for Paragraph 2 of Form 4A.

3. Interest Payments

Here you provide the repayment schedule. Check only one box: annual, monthly, or other (if you're using the downloadable form, delete the unused text).

Check the first box if you'll pay interest annually and insert the date of each annual payment—for example, "January 1." In the next blank, fill in the year you'll make the first interest payment. For the last blank, you'll need to calculate the amount of the interest payment. The following example assumes simple interest.

> **EXAMPLE:**
> The borrower borrows $10,000 at 8%.
> Interest is $10,000 x .08 = $800
> Each year, the borrower will make one interest payment of $800.

Check the second box if you'll make regular monthly interest payments. In the first blank, insert the day of the month—for example, the 15th day of each month. In the next blank, fill in the month that interest payments will begin—for example, January 2020. The lender might prefer monthly payments, because requiring monthly payments gets the borrower in the habit of paying regularly. For the last blank, you'll need to calculate the amount of the interest payment. The following example assumes simple interest.

> **EXAMPLE:**
> The borrower borrows $10,000 at 8%.
> $10,000 x .08 = $800
> $800 divided by 12 = $66.67 per month
> Each year, the borrower will make 12 interest payments of $66.67 each.

Check the third box if you plan to pay interest at intervals other than annually or monthly, such as the 15th day of January, April, July, and October, beginning April 15, 20xx. Use the blank to specify the details.

Samples

> ... quarterly on the 15th day of January, April, July, and October, beginning April 15, 20xx. The amount of each interest payment will be $200.

> ... semiannually on the 1st day of February and October, beginning February 1, 20xx. The amount of each interest payment will be $400.

Follow this example to calculate the amount of the interest payment. (The example assumes simple interest.)

EXAMPLE:

The borrower borrows $10,000 at 8%.

$10,000 x .08 = $800

$800 divided by 4 quarterly payments = $200 per quarter

$800 divided by 2 semiannual payments = $400 twice a year

Each year, the borrower will make four interest payments of $200 each or two interest payments of $400 each.

4. Principal Payment

Insert the date by which the borrower will repay the principal. Even if it's several years in the future, you need to set a date so that interest payments don't go on indefinitely.

5. Prepayment

See the instructions for Paragraph 6 of Form 4A. You don't need to insert anything here.

6. Loan Acceleration

See the instructions for Paragraph 7 of Form 4A.

7. Security

See the instructions for Paragraph 8 of Form 4A.

8. Collection Costs

Nothing needs to be filled in here. See the instructions for Paragraph 9 of Form 4A.

Standard Clauses

The remainder of the note contains the standard clauses regarding Notices, Governing Law, and Severability discussed in Chapter 1. (Note that the other standard clauses discussed in Chapter 1 generally do not apply to promissory notes and are not included in this form.) The only thing

you'll need to fill in here is the name of the state whose law will apply to the note in the paragraph "Governing Law."

Signature and Guarantee

See the instructions for Form 4A.

Form 4D: Promissory Note (Lump-Sum Payment)

If you and the lender prefer to keep things really simple, Form 4D might fit your needs. Here you agree to pay off the money you borrowed, plus interest, in one single payment. This works best for a short-term loan or possibly a loan from an affluent parent or grandparent to a child where the promise to repay is seen as an expression of the younger person's intent—not something that the lender would ever really enforce in court if the payment were delayed.

TIP

A will or trust can address fairness issues within a family. A large loan from a parent to a child can cause friction among siblings—especially if the parent dies before the child fully repays it. One solution is for the parent to provide in a will or living trust that any unpaid loan will be treated as a partial advance payment of that child's inheritance.

Instructions for Form 4D: Promissory Note (Lump-Sum Payment)

All the forms in this book are provided in Appendix B and on the Nolo website. To access the downloadable forms online, use the link provided in Appendix A. As you read the instructions for Form 4D, you might want to refer to the form in Appendix B or open the form on your computer so you can follow along. (Before you use the form in Appendix B, be sure to photocopy it so you'll have a clean copy to use later.)

1. Names

Insert the names and addresses of the borrower and lender. See Chapter 1 for a discussion of how to identify the parties in legal forms.

2. Promise to Pay

See the instructions for Paragraph 2 of Form 4A.

3. Payment Date

Check the first box if the loan will be due on a particular date, and insert the date by which the borrower will repay the entire amount of the loan plus interest.

Check the second box if the loan will be due after the occurrence of a particular event, and insert a description of the event (for example, borrower's receipt of a $10,000 Small Business Administration loan). Also insert a date by which the loan will be repaid in case the particular event does not occur. Make sure that the date is far enough in advance to allow enough time for the event to take place. The agreement provides that the loan will be due after the occurrence of the event, or on the alternate date you choose, whichever is sooner (in the agreement this is described as "the earlier of" the occurrence or the alternate date).

> **EXAMPLE:** On May 1, 2020, Tony agrees to lend Maggie $10,000 until she receives the proceeds of another loan that she hopes to get from the Small Business Administration. The parties agree that Maggie will repay the loan either when she gets the funds from the SBA or by October 1, 2020, whichever happens first.

The promissory note does not state the amount of the lump-sum payment; the exact amount should be determined on the payment date. However, you can estimate what the payment will be by multiplying the loan amount by the interest rate, and then multiplying that number by the number of years the loan is out. The following example assumes simple interest.

> **EXAMPLE:**
> The borrower borrows $10,000 at 8% for three years.
> $10,000 x .08 = $800
> $800 x 3 = $2,400 total interest
> $10,000 + $2,400 = $12,400 lump-sum payment
> The borrower will make one lump-sum payment of $12,400.

4. Prepayment

See the instructions for Paragraph 6 of Form 4A. You don't need to insert anything here.

5. Security

See the instructions for Paragraph 8 of Form 4A.

6. Collection Costs

Nothing needs to be filled in here. See the instructions for Paragraph 9 of Form 4A.

Standard Clauses

The remainder of the note contains the standard clauses regarding Notices, Governing Law, and Severability discussed in Chapter 1. (Note that the other standard clauses discussed in Chapter 1 generally do not apply to promissory notes and are not included in this form.) The only thing you'll need to fill in here is the name of the state whose law will apply to the note in the paragraph "Governing Law."

Signature and Guarantee

See the instructions for Form 4A.

Form 4E: Security Agreement for Borrowing Money

Those lending money to your business might feel more confident about the loan if they are given a security interest in the assets of the business. Then, if you don't repay the loan as promised, the lender can take the property you've pledged, sell it, and use the proceeds to at least partially repay the borrowed amount.

Before completing and signing a security agreement for a business loan, it helps to know how the law classifies property.

Real Estate or Real Property refers to land and the buildings attached to land. To grant a lender a security interest in (or lien on) real estate you own, you'd sign a mortgage or deed of trust. The lender would then record (file) the mortgage or deed of trust with a county land records office where it would become a matter of public record.

Personal Property includes all property that's not real estate. It can be property you use for personal purposes, such as your car, boat, clothes, or saxophone, as well as property used in or owned by your business, such as a business truck, machinery, a copy machine, a computer, or furniture. Personal property is of two types:

- **Tangible Personal Property**—property you can actually see and touch, such as a car or desk.
- **Intangible Personal Property**—property that's an abstract legal right, often represented by a document or certificate. It includes a bank account, certificate of deposit, stock in a corporation, the right to collect rent under a lease, accounts receivable, and intellectual property (a copyright, trademark, or patent).

Although it's possible for a business or an individual to pledge intangible personal property as security for a loan, it's far more common—and legally simpler—to pledge real estate or tangible personal property. Form 4E can be used where you're pledging some or all of your business's tangible personal property as security.

SEE AN EXPERT

See a lawyer if you'll use real estate or intellectual property as security for a loan. This form is intended only for tangible personal property. As explained in the introduction to this chapter, if you pledge your home or other real estate as security for a business loan, a security agreement won't be adequate to protect the lender. A well-informed lender will ask you to sign a mortgage or a deed of trust, which can then be recorded (filed) with a designated county

official to establish the lender's security interest in the real estate. Because title to real estate is a highly technical matter beyond the scope of this book, you should seek the assistance of a real estate lawyer before signing a mortgage or deed of trust. For similar reasons, you should consult an intellectual property lawyer for help in pledging intangible personal property, such as a copyright, trademark, or patent, as security for a loan.

 RESOURCE

Finding a good lawyer. When you need a lawyer, asking someone you trust for a referral is a good place to start. You can also try one of these excellent and free resources:

- **Nolo's Lawyer Directory.** Nolo has an easy-to-use online directory of lawyers, organized by location and area of expertise. You can find the directory and its comprehensive profiles at www.nolo.com/lawyers.
- **Lawyers.com.** At Lawyers.com you'll find a user-friendly search tool that allows you to tailor results by area of law and geography. You can also search for attorneys by name. Attorney profiles prominently display contact information, list topics of expertise, and show ratings—by both clients and other legal professionals.
- **Martindale.com.** Martindale.com offers an advanced search option that allows you to sort not only by practice area and location, but also by criteria like law school. Whether you look for lawyers by name or expertise, you'll find listings with detailed background information, peer and client ratings, and even profile visibility.

Instructions for Form 4E: Security Agreement for Borrowing Money

All the forms in this book are provided in Appendix B and on the Nolo website. To access the downloadable forms online, use the link provided in Appendix A. As you read the instructions for Form 4E, you might want to refer to the form in Appendix B or open the form on your computer so you can follow along. (Before you use the form in Appendix B, be sure to photocopy it so you'll have a clean copy to use later.)

! CAUTION

Get permission from directors, shareholders, and members before pledging assets. As explained in the introduction to this chapter, if your business is a corporation or an LLC, the board of directors or members should adopt a resolution approving not only the borrowing of money but also the pledging of company assets as security for the loan. And it's a good idea to get written permission from shareholders who are not directors or members who are not managers as well.

1. Names

In the first blank, fill in your name. In the second, fill in the lender's name.

2. Grant of Security Interest

You might need to check more than one box (if you're using the downloadable form, include just the appropriate clauses and delete the rest).

You'll probably want to select the first option, which refers to some or all of the tangible personal property that the borrower's business currently owns. The specific items of property will be listed in an attachment to your agreement. If you check the first box, also fill in the name by which your business is known.

The lender might also want a security interest in any other property you add to the business, including replacement inventory. In that case, check the second box as well.

Check the third box if you're going to pledge tangible personal property that you own personally or if you'll pledge a single item of business property— a car, for example—rather than all of the business's assets. (As noted in the introduction to this chapter, you should pledge enough property to cover the loan, but not more.) Next, describe the item you're pledging.

Samples

> 20xx Ford Ranger, license number A2345678, Vehicle Identification Number JKLM1234567890.

> Three Acme natural-gas-powered heat lamps, serial numbers: 1234567890; 2234567890; and 3234567890.

Some kinds of assets—often those that are licensed by the state, such as cars and boats— require the lender to take a security interest in the property by listing its name on the certificate of title instead of filing the conventional UCC Financing Statement discussed above. Contact the appropriate state agency for the procedure and forms to accomplish this.

3. Security for Promissory Note

Fill in the date of the promissory note, the amount borrowed under the promissory note, and the interest rate. There's no need to list the payment schedule.

4. Financing Statement

You don't need to insert anything in this paragraph. It confirms that the lender will file a financing statement—a Uniform Commercial Code form (called Form UCC-1) that's filed with a governmental agency to let the public know that the property the borrower is using in its business is subject to the lender's lien. Anyone checking the public records—a bank's loan department, for example—will learn that someone has a prior lien on the property described in the notice. This limits the borrower's ability to fraudulently sell the property to someone else or to offer it as collateral for another loan, pretending that it belongs 100% to the borrower.

All states accept a nationally standardized UCC-1 form, like the sample included below. Check your state's secretary of state website or call the office to obtain the proper form and learn the filing fees.

CAUTION

Remember to get a discharge. When you've paid off the loan, you're entitled to get a document from the lender verifying that there's no longer a security interest in the pledged property. If you forget to get this document and record it at the same office where the financing statement was filed, you can run into a snag when you go to sell the property or your entire business. That's because to a potential purchaser prudently doing a UCC search, it will appear that the property is still subject to the lender's lien.

5. Use and Care of the Secured Property

Nothing needs to be inserted here. This paragraph spells out the borrower's duty to safeguard the property so that the lender has something of value to sell in case the borrower defaults.

6. Borrower's Default

This paragraph says the borrower is in default— meaning that the lender can sue the borrower for repayment or return of the goods—if the borrower doesn't make required payments or doesn't promptly correct any violations of the requirements listed in the preceding paragraph.

In the first blank, fill in the number of days after which the borrower will be in default under the terms of the promissory note—that is, how long after the borrower has failed to make payments that the lender can sue the borrower for repayment. This should be the same number of days stated in the promissory note itself.

In the second blank, fill in the number of days the borrower has to correct a violation of the borrower's obligations regarding the use and care of the secured property—such as failing to maintain it in good repair—before the borrower is in default under the security agreement. Generally, a borrower might have anywhere from five to 60 days to correct a violation.

7. Lender's Rights

Fill in the name of the state where the property is located.

This paragraph summarizes the lender's rights under the Uniform Commercial Code if the borrower defaults on his or her obligations under this security agreement. Specifically, the lender is allowed to seize the secured property and sell, lease, or otherwise dispose of it.

8. Notice to Borrower

Fill in the location where the lender should send the borrower a notice if the borrower is in default and the lender plans to sell, lease, or otherwise dispose of the property. Note that the agreement provides that the lender must give the borrower at least ten days' notice before taking action with respect to the property. (This gives the borrower the chance to pay off the debt in full before the property is taken or turned over to someone else.)

Standard Clauses

The remainder of the agreement contains the standard clauses we discussed in Chapter 1. The only thing you'll need to fill in here is the name of the state whose law will apply to the contract in the paragraph called "Governing Law."

Signature

Fill in the required information. See Chapter 1 to read more about signing contracts.

Attachment to Security Agreement

If you check the first box under Paragraph 2 ("The tangible personal property owned by Borrower's business … as listed in attached Attachment 1"), you must fill in the attachment and attach it to the security agreement.

Sample UCC Financing Statement

UCC FINANCING STATEMENT
FOLLOW INSTRUCTIONS

A. NAME & PHONE OF CONTACT AT FILER (optional)
Edward Brown   555-123-5555

B. E-MAIL CONTACT AT FILER (optional)

C. SEND ACKNOWLEDGMENT TO: (Name and Address)

Olde Lighting, Inc.
123 Eastern Drive
Berkeley, CA 99999

THE ABOVE SPACE IS FOR FILING OFFICE USE ONLY

1. DEBTOR'S NAME: Provide only one Debtor name (1a or 1b) (use exact, full name; do not omit, modify, or abbreviate any part of the Debtor's name); if any part of the Individual Debtor's name will not fit in line 1b, leave all of item 1 blank, check here ☐ and provide the Individual Debtor information in item 10 of the Financing Statement Addendum (Form UCC1Ad)

1a. ORGANIZATION'S NAME			
Star Lighting, LLC			
1b. INDIVIDUAL'S SURNAME	FIRST PERSONAL NAME	ADDITIONAL NAME(S)/INITIAL(S)	SUFFIX

1c. MAILING ADDRESS	CITY	STATE	POSTAL CODE	COUNTRY
555 Jefferson Avenue	Berkeley	CA	99999	USA

2. DEBTOR'S NAME: Provide only one Debtor name (2a or 2b) (use exact, full name; do not omit, modify, or abbreviate any part of the Debtor's name); if any part of the Individual Debtor's name will not fit in line 2b, leave all of item 2 blank, check here ☐ and provide the Individual Debtor information in item 10 of the Financing Statement Addendum (Form UCC1Ad)

2a. ORGANIZATION'S NAME			
2b. INDIVIDUAL'S SURNAME	FIRST PERSONAL NAME	ADDITIONAL NAME(S)/INITIAL(S)	SUFFIX

2c. MAILING ADDRESS	CITY	STATE	POSTAL CODE	COUNTRY

3. SECURED PARTY'S NAME (or NAME of ASSIGNEE of ASSIGNOR SECURED PARTY): Provide only one Secured Party name (3a or 3b)

3a. ORGANIZATION'S NAME			
Olde Lighting, Inc.			
3b. INDIVIDUAL'S SURNAME	FIRST PERSONAL NAME	ADDITIONAL NAME(S)/INITIAL(S)	SUFFIX

3c. MAILING ADDRESS	CITY	STATE	POSTAL CODE	COUNTRY
123 Eastern Drive	Berkeley	CA	99999	USA

4. COLLATERAL: This financing statement covers the following collateral:

All furniture, fixtures, equipment, and inventory of Debtor. Also, any tangible personal property (including replacement inventory) that Debtor now owns or later acquires in connection with Debtor's business known as Star Lighting located at 555 Jefferson Ave., Berkeley, CA. Also the proceeds of all insurance policies that now or later cover the secured property.

5. Check only if applicable and check only one box: Collateral is ☐ held in a Trust (see UCC1Ad, item 17 and Instructions) ☐ being administered by a Decedent's Personal Representative

6a. Check only if applicable and check only one box:
☐ Public-Finance Transaction ☐ Manufactured-Home Transaction ☐ A Debtor is a Transmitting Utility

6b. Check only if applicable and check only one box:
☐ Agricultural Lien ☐ Non-UCC Filing

7. ALTERNATIVE DESIGNATION (if applicable): ☐ Lessee/Lessor ☐ Consignee/Consignor ☐ Seller/Buyer ☐ Bailee/Bailor ☐ Licensee/Licensor

8. OPTIONAL FILER REFERENCE DATA:

International Association of Commercial Administrators (IACA)

FILING OFFICE COPY — UCC FINANCING STATEMENT (Form UCC1) (Rev. 04/20/11)

1. Names

Insert the names of the borrower and the lender.

2. Terms of Attachment

Insert the date of the security agreement. Then list the tangible personal property that the borrower's business owns that is being pledged as security for repayment of the loan.

Sample

> All furniture, fixtures, and inventory of Borrower. Also any other tangible personal property that Borrower now owns in connection with Borrower's business known as Star Lighting located at 555 Jefferson Ave., Berkeley, CA. Also the proceeds of all insurance policies that now or later cover the secured property.

Buying a Business

 FORMS
To download the forms discussed in this chapter, go to this book's companion page on Nolo.com. See Appendix A for the link.

If you want to go into business, you have three basic choices:

- Start a business from scratch.
- Buy an existing business.
- Buy a franchise.

Buying an existing business can be a good middle course between the risk of starting a completely new enterprise and the high costs, forced uniformity, and other often-reported problems of operating a franchise. If you choose wisely, you have the opportunity to purchase a business that's already solidly profitable and has a chance to do even better with your infusion of new savvy and energy. Unfortunately, finding a profitable business that's not beset by hidden problems—at a price you can afford—isn't always easy.

RESOURCE

Chapter 10 of the *Legal Guide for Starting & Running a Small Business*, by Fred S. Steingold and David M. Steingold (Nolo), offers an extended discussion of the legal and practical issues of buying a business. It takes you through the purchase process step-by-step, including information on how to value the business and how to draft a solid purchase contract.

Once you locate a business that might be suitable for purchase, inquire about how the business is legally structured—the main alternatives being a sole proprietorship, a partnership, a corporation, or a limited liability company (LLC). The structure of the business will control what type of contract you use.

When you buy a business from a sole proprietorship, a partnership, or an LLC, you don't acquire the old legal structure, only the assets (and possibly the liabilities) of the business. Form 5A: Contract for Purchase of Assets From an Unincorporated Business is designed for such a purchase.

The situation can be different, however, when you buy a business that's being run as a corporation. In that situation, you can either buy the assets of the corporation or you can buy the corporation itself. This is known as an *entity* purchase. (Theoretically, it's also possible to buy a partnership entity or an LLC entity, but that hardly ever happens.) To purchase the corporation itself, including its name and all of its assets and liabilities, you buy the corporate stock from its existing shareholders.

In contrast, if you buy only a corporation's assets (and possibly take over some of its liabilities), the selling shareholders will still own the corporate shell minus the assets you've purchased. It's almost always better to buy the corporate assets rather than the corporate stock because, among other things, it helps you avoid the liabilities of the existing business and it can give you significant tax advantages. Form 5B: Contract for Purchase of Assets From a Corporation is designed for this purpose.

In some situations you might not be able to swing a deal in which you buy only corporate assets. This can occur, for example, if the seller insists on a stock sale—perhaps because he or she believes there's a tax advantage in going this route. And in a few instances, you might actually prefer to buy the corporation rather than its assets. This can occur, for example, if the corporation has a valuable long-term lease that can't be transferred (assigned) to another tenant, such as a new corporation you plan to form. If you buy the corporate stock, the existing corporation will be able to continue on as a tenant, enabling you to enjoy the benefits of the lease. If you agree to buy the stock of a corporation, however, you'll need to conduct an in-depth investigation of the corporation's financial affairs. You should be aware that in the real world, this second method is used quite infrequently. Form 5D: Contract for Purchase of Corporate Stock is designed for such situations.

Before a corporation or most of its assets are purchased, its shareholders and directors need to approve the sale. Use Form 5C: Corporate Resolution Authorizing Sale of Assets for this purpose.

After you and the seller have signed a contract covering your purchase of business assets or stock, there will need to be a formal transfer of the ownership. Form 5E: Bill of Sale for Business Assets is used to transfer ownership of objects such as machinery, inventory, supplies, and office equipment, (called tangible personal property). In some states, vehicle ownership can be transferred through a bill of sale, but in many states you must fill out an official form from the department or registry of motor vehicles to put the vehicle title in the name of the new owner. Real estate (land and buildings) is not included in a bill of sale, nor are intangible assets, such as accounts receivable, patents, or contracts. Instead, title to real property is transferred by a deed, which you file at a designated county office to make it a matter of public record. Intangible assets are transferred through various legal documents—the most common being an assignment.

If the seller asserts that all creditors have been paid, use the Form 5F: Seller's Affidavit—No Creditors to get this assurance in writing and under penalty of perjury. This will probably be the case unless you are buying the stock of a corporation.

CAUTION

Don't use Form 5F if the business still owes money. If the business you purchase will still have unpaid debts after the closing, Form 5F: Seller's Affidavit—No Creditors won't work. You'll have to rework the part of the purchase contract dealing with ongoing debts of the business. Also, if you live in California or Maryland, your state has a creditor notification law (called the bulk sales law), and more paperwork will be required; creditors will have to be notified of a sale. You'll either need to do some research (see "What Are Bulk Sales Laws?" below) or hire a lawyer to help you.

Finally, in buying any business, it's rare to pay the full purchase price up front. Most often, the buyer agrees to pay only a portion of the total at closing, relying on the seller to finance the rest. You might, for example, agree to buy a business for $150,000 by paying the seller $30,000 as down payment and the balance of $120,000 in monthly installments over a five-year period.

What Are Bulk Sales Laws?

Creditor notification or bulk sales laws swept the country at the end of the 19th century. But a hundred years later, legislators started having second thoughts. Today, these laws remain on the books in only two states: California and Maryland.

The bulk sales laws were created to deal with a scam in which a business owner would order lots of goods on credit—and then unload the business on an unsuspecting buyer. The original owner would pocket the money (leaving the bills unpaid), and then disappear. Where bulk sales laws are still in effect, they require that creditors be notified before business assets are transferred to a new owner. These laws apply to transfers where a major part of the seller's assets consists of materials, supplies, merchandise, or other inventory. Generally, they don't apply to transfers where the seller's business consists primarily of selling personal services.

Typically, a seller covered under a bulk sales law must give the buyer a list (sworn to under penalty of perjury) of all recent business creditors and the amount each is owed, if any. Then, several days before the sale is closed—the exact number of days is specified in the state law—the buyer must either send a notice to creditors so they know the business is changing hands and can arrange to have their claims paid at or before closing (Maryland) or publish and record a notice (California). If a proper notice is sent or published, the buyer hopes that, after the closing, purchased goods are free from old claims by the seller's creditors.

Although bulk sales notices are not conceptually difficult, you must prepare, send, and publish them in compliance with fussy state laws. The details differ in California and Maryland, so you'll need to get your rules and forms locally. Check with a law library, or a newspaper that publishes legal notices.

Whenever a portion of the sales price will be paid in the future, the seller will expect you to sign a promissory note for the balance of the purchase price (see Forms 4A, 4B, and 4C in Chapter 4). In addition, until the purchase price is paid in full, the seller will no doubt want to retain a security interest, or lien, in the assets you're purchasing. This is similar to the mortgage that a bank holds on a homeowner's home—if the homeowner defaults on a number of payments, the bank can foreclose on the home. Similarly, in the sale of a business, if you don't make the promised payments, the seller can take back the business assets, if you have signed Form 5G: Security Agreement for Buying Business Assets.

CAUTION

Environmental concerns. If you're the buyer and the assets you're buying include real estate—either vacant land or a building—you want to make sure that you're not going to run up against environmental protection laws. For more information on this subject, see Chapter 7.

Form 5A: Contract for Purchase of Assets From an Unincorporated Business

As explained in the beginning of this chapter, most small businesses are purchased by buying the assets rather than the entity. You can use Form 5A when you're buying the assets of a sole proprietorship, a partnership, or a limited liability company (LLC).

From a legal standpoint, buying a business from a sole proprietor or a single-member LLC is relatively simple because you're dealing with only one person. Buying from a partnership or an LLC with more than one owner is a bit more complex—mainly because you'll usually be dealing with two or more people whose interests will never be exactly the same. For this reason, it's wise to insist that all the partners or LLC members—not just those who own a majority stake—sign all the documents involved.

CAUTION

Both spouses must sign in community property states. Nine states follow the community property system: Arizona, California, Idaho, Louisiana, Nevada, New Mexico, Texas, Washington, and Wisconsin. In those states, absent a marriage contract providing otherwise, a married couple's property accumulated after marriage is community (jointly owned) property regardless of the name in which it's held (exceptions include property received by inheritance or gift). Community property normally includes an interest in a business (even one that was owned by one spouse prior to marriage).

Generally, in a community property state, if a spouse plays no role in running the business you're buying and you pay a fair price, the law doesn't absolutely require you to get the spouse's written consent. But because of the likelihood that the business is jointly owned, a better approach is to always obtain the signature of the spouse of the owners who are selling you the business. That way, you avoid the possibility that a later dispute between the spouses could threaten to affect your purchase.

Instructions for Form 5A: Contract for Purchase of Assets From an Unincorporated Business

All the forms in this book are provided in Appendix B and are downloadable on the Nolo website, using the link provided in Appendix A. As you read the instructions for Form 5A, you might want to refer to the form in Appendix B or open the downloadable form on your computer so you can follow along. (Before you use the form in Appendix B, be sure to photocopy it so you'll have a clean copy to use later.)

1. Names

Insert the names of the seller and buyer. The seller will be the sole proprietorship, the partnership, or the limited liability company (LLC) that is selling its assets to you.

If the seller is a sole proprietorship, insert the seller's own name. If the seller is a partnership, insert the name of the partnership. If the seller is an LLC, insert the name of the LLC. Consult the chart in Chapter 1 for more information about how to identify a business.

FORM

The different formats for the names clause are in the downloadable form Names.rtf.

Only the name of the sole proprietor, partnership, or LLC is inserted in the seller's slot even though others having some relationship to the company could be signing the contract. As discussed in Chapter 1, these additional signers can include, for example, a sole proprietor's spouse (in a community property state), the individual partners in a partnership, or the individual members of an LLC. Technically, they are not the sellers but are signing to agree to the terms of the contract. These people's names will appear at the end of the contract in the signature area.

2. Sale of Business Assets

In the first blank, insert the name that the seller's business uses. In the second blank, fill in the business's address. Include the street address, city, and state.

Sample

> Seller is selling to Buyer and Buyer is buying from Seller the assets of the business known as Red's Rite Spot, located at 123 Main Street, Fresno, California.

If the business is a sole proprietorship and it does not use a trade name or fictitious name, in the first blank you should enter a simple description of the seller's services, along with the seller's name.

Samples

> ... the refrigerator repair business of Andrea Quentin

> ... the editorial services firm of Jason Frederick

If the business has several locations and you're buying the assets used at more than one location, list all of the locations.

Sample

> Seller is selling to Buyer and Buyer is buying from Seller the assets of the business known as Bagels & Baguettes, located at 456 State Street and 789 North Liberty, Atlanta, Georgia.

3. Assets Being Sold

Specify exactly what you're buying by checking all the boxes that apply to your purchase. Unless you fill this in completely, you may be in for costly disagreements later on. If you're using the downloadable forms, delete the paragraphs that don't apply to your purchase and reletter the options, if necessary.

Check Box A if you'll be acquiring the inventory of the business. The inventory includes any goods the seller sells at retail. Paragraph 5 asks for more information about the inventory.

Check Box B if you're buying furniture, fixtures, and equipment from the seller. You will list the specific items on a separate page, Schedule A.

Check Box C if you're going to continue to occupy the same leased business premises. Fill in the required information about the seller's current lease. Before buying a business, you should always ask for copies of all leases. You should understand how much the rent is, how long the lease runs, and all other key terms before you agree to take over (and pay for) any existing leases.

You should also make sure that the seller can legally assign the leases. Many real estate leases contain clauses prohibiting the tenant from assigning the lease—that is, letting a new tenant take over the new space—without the landlord's permission. Whether a provision requiring the other party's consent to assign the lease is present or not, to avoid any unpleasant surprises it's best if the buyer asks the seller to get the landlord's written consent to taking over the lease before buying a business. Paragraph 13 gives you the option of including language in your purchase contract that requires this.

Check Box D if you will be taking over any other of the seller's contracts (except for real estate leases, which were covered above). For instance, you might want to take over existing equipment leases the seller had. This could include contracts for phone systems, copiers, computers, warehouse equipment (such as forklifts), vehicles, and large outdoor trash containers. You will list the specific contracts on a separate page, Schedule B.

You should always ask for copies of any contract you want to assume so that you understand the key terms. Also, you will want to be sure that the seller can legally assign the contracts. Many business contracts prohibit one party from assigning the contract to someone else without consent. To avoid unpleasant surprises, it's best if you ask the seller to get the other party's written consent to the assignment of any contract before buying the business. Paragraph 13 gives you the option of including language in your purchase contract that requires this.

Check Box E if you are purchasing the goodwill of the business. Goodwill is not a physical asset of the business; instead, it's the reputation, customer relationships, and business name of an existing business. If the business has not been successful, and you are purchasing the business for its physical assets only, you don't need to select this option.

If the business name is a particularly valuable asset, you should verify that the name has been properly protected as a trademark before purchasing it. If it hasn't been registered as a trademark,

another business might already have the right to use it, which could reduce its value to the buyer. You might want to search the registered trademark database of the U.S. Patent and Trademark Office (USPTO) to find out if the seller has registered the name. You can search this database for free at www.uspto.gov. Additionally, the seller may have registered the trademark with the state or states in which the seller does business. Check with the state agency in charge of registering trademarks—usually the secretary or department of state.

RESOURCE

Learn more about protecting business names. For information on legal protection for business names, see *Trademark: Legal Care for Your Business & Product Name,* by Stephen Fishman (Nolo).

Use Box F to list any assets not already clearly defined, including things like proprietary software or a patent, trademark, or copyright. Do not include accounts receivable here. If you want to purchase some or all of the seller's accounts receivable, you can record this in Paragraph 6.

Samples

All rights to the StarCo trademark.

All rights to the proprietary accounting software developed for the seller.

CAUTION

A covenant not to compete is not an asset of the business. If, as part of the sale, the seller will give you a covenant not to compete—an agreement by the seller not to compete against the buyer after the sale, which the buyer pays the seller for—you might be tempted to list it here. Don't. A noncompete agreement isn't considered a business asset; that's why Paragraph 16 covers this issue separately.

4. Purchase Price

In the first blank, insert the total purchase price. Your task, in order to take maximum advantage of favorable tax depreciation rules (see "Allocate Your Purchase Dollars to Get Tax Benefits," below), is to allocate the purchase price among the various items you're buying rather than simply stating a lump sum, since doing this can have favorable tax consequences. Fill in the various amounts. Do not include inventory, accounts receivable, or a covenant not to compete.

Sample

> The purchase price is $42,000, allocated as follows:
>
> A. Furniture, fixtures, and equipment $ 30,000
> B. Assignment of lease $ 4,000
> C. Assignment of contracts $ 0
> D. Goodwill $ 8,000
> E. Other: _____ $ 0

Make sure the amount of money you allocate to each asset adds up to the total purchase price. (Generally, anything the buyer pays for the business over and above the fair market value of the assets is allocated to goodwill.)

CAUTION

Consider having a professional appraisal done. Though not required by the IRS, it can make sense to obtain a professional appraisal of the business assets being purchased, especially for businesses purchased for over $100,000. If either the buyer or seller is ever audited by the IRS, the IRS might question the asset allocations, and can ignore and recalculate any allocations that it finds unreasonable. Having a professional appraiser's report to back up your allocations can help if you ever get audited.

RESOURCE

Learn more about allocating your purchase price. Chapter 10 of the *Legal Guide for Starting & Running a Small Business*, by Fred S. Steingold and David M. Steingold (Nolo), contains a more thorough discussion of the best legal and tax-saving strategies for allocating your purchase price. Also consider having your plan reviewed by a tax pro.

There are two other checkboxes at the end of this paragraph. First, the buyer and the seller will probably want to split monthly costs, such as rent, taxes, insurance premiums, utility costs, and security deposits. You can do this by prorating the expenses. For instance, if the sale of the business closes on the 15th of the month, but the seller has prepaid the rent for the entire month, the seller might want to adjust the purchase price upward to reflect the portion of the rent attributable to the buyer during that month. Check this box if you elect to prorate these amounts; you and the seller will tally them up at the closing, or just before, and make adjustments to the purchase price then.

Second, it's customary to provide that a physical count of the inventory will be taken just before closing, and a price will be set at that time. This is covered in Paragraph 5. Check this box if you will be buying inventory.

5. Price of Inventory (Optional)

This is an optional paragraph. If you're going to be buying the seller's current inventory of merchandise, check the box (if you're using the downloadable form and you won't be buying the inventory, delete the whole paragraph and renumber all that follow). Your contract provides that you will pay the seller what the seller paid for the goods (usually the invoiced amount).

Allocate Your Purchase Dollars to Get Tax Benefits

Generally, as the buyer, you will receive more favorable tax treatment by allocating as much of the purchase price as possible to assets that can be written off quickly (within the first few years of the purchase) and as little as possible to assets that must be deducted or written off over a longer period of time (such as 15 years). The price you pay for inventory, for example, can be written off as merchandise is sold. Tangible assets like furniture, fixtures, and equipment can be written off over five to seven years, so this is a category to which you will want to assign as much of the purchase price as possible. The amounts you pay for a trade name or goodwill, however, must be written off over 15 years; the same is true for the seller's covenant not to compete. You will probably want to allocate as little of the purchase price as possible to these kinds of assets.

To allocate a portion of the purchase price to a lease for business premises, you and the seller might want to consult a realtor or other real estate expert. The value you can allocate to a lease varies widely depending on its length and the location of the premises. For instance, a long-term lease with low rent in a prime location might be worth a lot of money, though rare. More common might be a long-term lease with high rent in a not-so-great location or one with particularly onerous terms—such a lease would obviously be less valuable.

As to other types of contracts being taken over, in general, contracts are worth money if they give the buyer a right to purchase or lease equipment at a price that's below current fair market value.

For example, if the seller was able to negotiate a long-term, low-cost lease for expensive equipment, the contract might be worth the difference between the rental price in the contract and the price the buyer would have to pay in today's rental market. On the other hand, a long-term contract to buy supplies at a price the buyer could easily get on the market today would not be as valuable.

Keep in mind that, to avoid problems with the IRS, the portion of purchase price allocated to a certain asset should correspond roughly to the asset's fair market value. After the sale, you and the seller each need to complete IRS Form 8594, *Asset Acquisition Statement*, and file it with your tax returns for the year in which the sale took place. You and the seller should agree on the allocation of the purchase price among the assets so that your numbers match up on the IRS forms. Better yet, you and the seller should fill out the form together and file duplicate copies of the form. If your numbers don't match, the IRS may audit you, the seller, or both, and come up with its own allocation of the purchase price, a result both parties want to avoid. For help filling out Form 8594, see *Tax Savvy for Small Business*, by Frederick W. Daily (Nolo).

Allocating the purchase price to the various assets being purchased can affect the amount of taxes you and the seller will have to pay each year for the next several years. To get the most tax advantage from your allocations, it's wise to consult a tax lawyer or a CPA who is knowledgeable about buying and selling businesses before you sign your contract.

The amount of inventory could fluctuate between the time the buyer and seller sign the contract and the time that the sale closes. As a result, someone must conduct a physical count of the inventory before the sale closes and then determine the price. If you and the seller are going to physically count the merchandise yourselves, check the box before the words "Seller and Buyer." If you plan to hire an inventory service company to do it, check the next box instead.

Then, insert the number of days before the closing when the merchandise will be physically counted. Ideally, this should occur as close to the closing date as possible—certainly not longer than a week before.

You might want to put a cap on the amount you'll have to pay for the inventory of the business. If so, check the last box and fill in the agreed-on amount.

> **CAUTION**
>
> **Don't pay full price for damaged or obsolete inventory.** Some inventory might not be readily saleable and the parties might want to add exceptions to what the buyer will accept—or place limits on what the buyer will pay for goods that are damaged, obsolete, or otherwise not worth what the seller paid for them. You might want to add such an exception or limit at the end of this paragraph.

Samples

> Buyer will pay seller the actual invoiced cost of any current (20xx) model year inventory, plus 50% of the actual invoiced cost of any of last year's model inventory. Buyer will not pay for any inventory for model years earlier than last year.

> Buyer will pay Seller only for unopened and undamaged goods.

If you add nothing here, you will purchase all of the inventory the seller has on hand at the closing, regardless of its condition (up to a maximum price, if you have agreed on one).

Incidentally, if you have any doubts about whether the seller has really paid for the inventory, you should ask for proof of payment, such as a canceled check—even if the seller gives you Form 5F, stating under oath that there are no creditors.

6. Accounts Receivable

When buying a business, it's usually best to agree that money already owed to the business (accounts receivable) will remain the seller's property. Otherwise, the buyer might be purchasing trouble—it's hard for the buyer to know whether a given account can be easily collected (because the buyer lacks experience with the customers who owe money) and thus it can be impossible to assign accounts receivable a realistic value. By contrast, the seller knows the customers and has experience getting them to pay up. From the buyer's point of view, it's usually better to leave the accounts receivable—and the headaches of collection—in the seller's hands.

Check the first box if you won't buy the seller's accounts receivable. You must send the seller any checks or money you receive from the seller's customers within ten days of receiving it.

Check the second box if, for some reason, you're willing to acquire the seller's accounts receivable (perhaps the seller has substantially discounted them or you've assured yourself that most accounts will be paid on time). Fill in the age of the accounts you're acquiring. It's more likely that you will be able to collect on a current account (one that's less than 30 days past due) than on one that's 90 days past due. For this reason, a buyer will usually purchase only accounts receivable that haven't been outstanding too long; for instance, it's unlikely a buyer would want to purchase accounts receivable that are more than 90 days old.

But even for current accounts receivable, it's sensible to pay a discounted amount. After all, you'll probably expend some effort in collecting the accounts, and even with a well-run business, a small percentage won't be collectable. There is no hard and fast rule about how much accounts receivable should be discounted; you will need to research your ability to collect on these accounts and negotiate a reasonable discount.

7. Deposit

The seller will usually expect you to pay a deposit (in legal jargon, an earnest money deposit) to bind the deal. You will pay this amount to the seller when you and the seller sign the purchase contract.

If your purchase falls through because the seller can't deliver as promised or a contingency can't be satisfied (for example, the landlord won't consent to assigning the lease to you as called for in the contract), you get this money back. If you back out without a good reason, the seller keeps the money. If, as expected, the deal proceeds, the money is applied toward the purchase price.

Fill in the amount of the deposit you're giving the seller to bind the deal. Obviously, from your point of view, the lower the amount, the better.

8. Payments at Closing

In this paragraph, you can check more than one box. Check the first box and insert the down payment you'll be paying the seller at closing (remember, this does not include the amounts payable for the inventory and the accounts receivable). The down payment will be significantly larger than the earnest money deposit. This cash amount, plus the deposit and the amount of the promissory note, should equal the total purchase price.

Also, check the second box if you're buying the business's inventory, and check the third box if you're buying the business's accounts receivable. If you have checked all three boxes, the check you give the seller at the closing should include payment for three things:

- the cash portion of the purchase price

- the amount you will pay for the accounts receivable, and
- the amount you will pay for the inventory.

9. Promissory Note (Optional)

In more than 90% of business purchases, the buyer makes a down payment at closing and pays the balance in installments over a number of years. If you are using a promissory note, check this box.

 RELATED TOPIC
Forms for promissory notes are covered in Chapter 4.

In the first section, you'll see three boxes mentioning sole proprietor, partnership, and corporation or LLC. These boxes state who will sign or cosign the contract for the buyer to personally guarantee payment of the purchase price.

CAUTION
If two people sign a promissory note, each is 100% responsible for paying the loan. In legalese, it's said that both signers of the promissory note are "jointly and individually liable," or "jointly and severally liable," for all payments. If the buyer defaults, the seller can sue and collect the full amount from either signer. See also Chapter 1.

Follow these instructions:

Buyer Is a Sole Proprietor and a Cosigner Will Personally Guarantee Payment. If you're buying the business as a sole proprietor and you alone will be responsible for the payments on the promissory note, you needn't check any of the boxes in Paragraph 9 of the contract. However, if you're buying the business as a sole proprietor and you've agreed to have your spouse or another person be fully responsible (along with you) for payment, check the first box and insert the name of the other person. Since the buyer is a sole proprietor, the seller might want the buyer's spouse to sign the promissory note as an additional assurance that payments will be made. The cosigner should sign this purchase contract.

Buyer Is a Partnership. If you're buying the business as a partnership, check the second box. Partners are automatically personally liable for all contracts entered into by the partnership. However, all partners of the buying company are required to sign this purchase contract to confirm that they are personally responsible for the buyer's payments on the promissory note.

Buyer Is a Corporation or an LLC and the Owners Will Personally Guarantee Payment. One advantage of forming a corporation or an LLC is that shareholders and LLC members are not ordinarily personally liable for business debts (in legalese, they enjoy limited liability). This means that, unless you and the other shareholders or members personally sign the promissory note, you won't be personally liable for making the payments. Unfortunately, in the real world, the seller is unlikely to agree to let your corporation or LLC be solely responsible for payments, but will instead insist that some or all of the corporate shareholders or LLC members personally guarantee payment of the promissory note (that is, waive their limited liability status by signing personally). If so, check the third box and insert the names of the people who are agreeing to be personally responsible for payment. These owners should sign this purchase contract.

Promissory Note Terms. The second section deals with the terms of the promissory note. Follow these instructions:

A. Fill in the annual interest rate.

B. Insert the amount of your monthly payment and the day of the month this payment is due. This contract assumes you'll make the same payment each month, as most people do with a home mortgage. To determine the amount of the monthly payment, you can consult an amortization calculator or schedule. You can find amortization calculators online, or you can use *Quicken*. If you don't have immediate access to the Internet or computer software to calculate the amortization, the chart in the instructions for Form 4A: Promissory Note (Amortized Monthly or Annual Payments) can help you determine what amount needs to be paid each month to pay off a loan over time.

C. Insert the date by which the entire balance is to be paid off. This may involve a big payment at the final payoff date. For example, you could use a 15-year amortization schedule to figure out the monthly amounts, but agree to pay off the balance within five years with the remaining balance to be paid in one big balloon payment.

D. Nothing needs to be filled in. (See the instructions for Form 4A, Paragraph 5, for an explanation of how payments are applied.)

E. Nothing needs to be filled in. (See the instructions for Form 4A, Paragraph 6, for an explanation of prepayment penalties.)

F. Insert how many days the buyer has before the seller can declare that the entire balance is due on a late payment. (See the instructions for Form 4A, Paragraph 7, for an explanation of loan acceleration.)

10. Security for Payment

If you're a homeowner, you probably signed a mortgage when you bought your house, giving the lender a security (ownership) interest in the real property until the loan is paid off. If you don't pay the principal or interest on schedule, or if you fall behind in paying property taxes or let the house insurance lapse, the lender has the legal right to foreclose and sell the property. Similarly, whoever is selling you a business will probably want to retain an ownership or security interest in the assets you're buying until you've made your last payment. If, in the meantime, you default on making installment payments, the security interest allows the seller to take back the assets.

By checking the first box, you agree to sign Form 5G: Security Agreement for Buying Business Assets giving the seller a security interest in the assets. You also acknowledge that the seller will be preparing a document called a Uniform Commercial Code (UCC) Financing Statement, which is filed (recorded) at a public office to let third parties such as lenders or purchasers know about the security interest. All states now accept a nationally standardized UCC-1 form. Check your state's secretary of state website or call the office to obtain the proper UCC form and filing fees. A good place to start is www.statelocalgov.net, a directory of state and local government websites.

CAUTION

Think twice before using your house as security. If you're buying a small business, especially one that primarily sells services and doesn't own much property, there might not be many tangible business assets to pledge as security for the portion of the purchase price you borrow from the seller. In that situation, the seller could suggest that you pledge some nonbusiness asset as security—your car or boat, perhaps. Fair enough. But if the seller asks for a mortgage on—or a deed of trust to—your house, think long and hard about it. Putting your house at risk for a business debt is often a poor choice, if for no other reason than that, if the business has a few slow months, your anxiety level will rise sky high.

If the existing lease is being assigned to you as part of the purchase price, the seller might want to take back a property or security interest in the lease so as to be eligible to become the tenant again and resume business at the same location if you default on your obligations. If the seller wants that kind of protection, check the second box.

11. Seller's Debts

This paragraph makes it clear that the seller will pay all business debts that could affect or be tied to the assets you're purchasing. For good measure, this paragraph requires the seller, at closing, to sign an affidavit (a statement under oath) confirming that all debts and liabilities of the business have been paid. Use Form 5F: Seller's Affidavit—No Creditors for this purpose.

CAUTION

Make sure preexisting business debts get paid. Sometimes a seller will need to use the money you pay at closing to take care of all business debts and liabilities. Fine, as long as you don't leave anything to chance. To make sure outstanding bills really do get paid, one good approach is to pay them yourself at closing—out of the seller's proceeds; then when you're sure there are no more, give the seller a check for the amount that's left over.

In some instances, the buyer could be tempted to pick up a business at a very reasonable price and take over some debts of the seller. Buyers should be wary of this, and in California and Maryland buyers should understand the full extent of the debts and know the technical details of their state's bulk sales law, which requires creditors to be notified of a business sale. Bulk sales laws are designed to prevent sellers from ordering large amounts of goods on credit, selling the business, and leaving the buyer—and the creditors—holding the bag. (See "What Are Bulk Sales Laws?" above, for more information about these laws.)

SEE AN EXPERT

See a lawyer if you're worried the seller could have unpaid debts. Because creditors come in many shapes and sizes, no one tactic will completely protect you against all of them. For further protection from undisclosed creditors, you might want to consider including a contract provision that allows you to hold back a chunk of the purchase price for 90 days to cover any unanticipated debts. If you want to create this kind of special arrangement, or just want help reviewing a seller's debts to make sure they get paid, help from a lawyer who specializes in small business issues can be worth the money.

12. Closing

At a closing, you meet with the seller to sign and exchange all the documents needed to complete the purchase. You pay whatever money and sign any promissory note required for the ownership of the assets to be transferred to you; the seller then signs over the assets to you.

Insert the date, time, and location of the closing.

Sample

> The closing will take place:
> Date: <u>Wednesday, May 2, 20xx</u>
> Time: <u>1:00 p.m.</u>
> Location: <u>123 Washington Street, Ethic, New York</u>.

13. Documents for Transferring Assets

Check all appropriate boxes (users of downloadable forms should delete the language that does not apply).

Check A if you're buying tangible assets—for example, furniture, equipment, or inventory.

Check B if you're taking over an existing lease of business space.

Check C if you're taking over any other contracts.

Check D if you're acquiring any trademarks, patents, or copyrights.

14. Seller's Representations

In this paragraph, you get the seller's written promise (warranty) as to various conditions affecting the assets you're buying so that you can have legal recourse against the seller if problems later arise. You also receive the seller's representations—factual statements you can rely on. In combination, these legal guarantees give you a broad basis for taking legal action against the seller if key promises are not honored or statements the seller has made as part of your purchase contract turn out to be untrue. If, for example, the seller states in writing that he or she has given you accurate information about the business's earnings but the information turns out to be inaccurate, you can use this representation as a basis for getting your money back or reducing the purchase price to offset losses caused by the misstatement.

In F, you might want to add additional items to fit your transaction.

Sample

> Seller will have the compressor in the 15-foot Polar Bear freezer (Serial No. 17411) replaced with an equivalent new model before closing and warrants that it will remain in good operating condition for 24 months following closing. Seller will be responsible for all parts and labor needed to repair the freezer if it fails to operate properly during the 24-month period.

TIP

Get a certificate of good standing before you buy a business. If you're buying a business from an LLC, a corporation, or even a partnership, you can usually get something called a certificate of good standing for the seller's business from your state's secretary of state's office or the agency that monitors business entities. A certificate of good standing can help you verify that the seller has met his or her filing responsibilities, and in some cases will even tell you whether the seller has paid the requisite state taxes. (In some states, you might have to check with the state treasury department to verify that a business has paid its taxes.) Obtaining a good standing certificate is fairly inexpensive and is one way of making sure you're buying a reputable business.

15. Buyer's Representations

It's important for a buyer to thoroughly examine the property and list any assets that appear to have problems. By doing so, you reserve the right to require the seller to fix the problem later. If you're not satisfied with the condition of some tangible assets, in Paragraph A, insert the appropriate language. If you're satisfied, insert "Not applicable."

Sample

> ... except for the Polar Bear freezer (serial no.17411), which Seller has agreed to repair.

If you're not paying the full price for the assets at the closing, but are giving the seller a promissory note for the unpaid balance, the seller will want to know if you're creditworthy and will probably ask you for a financial statement or other information about your financial situation. In Paragraph B, you promise that any information given was accurate.

16. Covenant Not to Compete

You might not want to buy a business unless its owners agree not to compete with you for a certain period after the sale. A covenant not to compete, also known as a noncompete agreement, usually requires the owners of the business being sold to refrain from competing against the buyer for one to three years—in the geographic area where the buyer conducts business. Without a covenant not to compete, the buyer takes the risk that the former owners will pocket the buyer's money and open up a competing business down the street, significantly reducing the value of the buyer's purchase.

A buyer probably shouldn't agree to buy a business unless the owners of the business being sold agree not to compete with the buyer for a certain period of time after the sale. If the owners are wary about agreeing not to compete, the terms of the agreement can always be negotiated in the seller's favor. For instance, the covenant not to compete can be limited to six months, allowing the buyer time to get the new business off the ground, and the owners can be well compensated for agreeing not to compete during that period of time.

It's usually reasonable for the buyer to require that every owner of the business being sold agree to a short covenant not to compete, and because spouses of business owners often work in the business and have business know-how, it can make sense to require them to agree to the covenant not to compete, too.

Noncompete agreements are not foolproof. They can, and often do, become the subject of legal disputes. This could happen if the seller receives a financially attractive offer to compete against the buyer after the sale, and the buyer has to bring the seller to court to stop the competition.

The seller could challenge the agreement's validity, claiming it's unreasonably restrictive— for instance, that it's too long, that it covers too many kinds of businesses, or includes too wide a geographic area. Fortunately, when a noncompete agreement is tied to the sale of a business, a court is unlikely to invalidate it, because the seller was (presumably) adequately compensated for agreeing not to compete. (When noncompete agreements are made between employers and employees, courts have often invalidated or modified the agreements because they unreasonably limited the employee's right to earn a living.) But to help ensure enforcement by a court if necessary, it's prudent for the buyer to ask only for those restrictions that are absolutely necessary to protect the buyer's business interests.

In the first blank, enter the number of years or months and choose "years" or "months." Ordinarily, the buyer will want the seller to agree not to compete for at least one year. Restricting the seller's ability to compete for up to three years is common, but anything more than that is likely to be invalidated by a court unless it's truly necessary to protect the buyer's business, which will be hard to prove.

The noncompete clause in this contract applies only to businesses that are similar to the one the buyer is purchasing. A noncompete agreement should be broad enough to include logical extensions of the existing business, but not so extensive that the person is restricted from opening a business in a different field. For example, if the buyer is buying a business that helps companies set up and maintain internal computer networks or intranets, there is no need to use noncompete language that's so broad it prevents the person from operating a business that helps design websites for selling products directly to the public. In addition, your contract limits the former owner's ability to compete only in areas where the buyer actually conducts business. This reasonable geographic scope should maximize your chances of creating an enforceable agreement.

In the second blank, you assign a value to each person's covenant not to compete. This will help the buyer if any of the owners of the business being sold or those owners' spouses later try to challenge the noncompete agreement in court. It's also important to assign a value to the noncompete agreement for tax purposes. You will pay these amounts at the closing.

17. Risk of Loss

It's possible, but not likely, that the business assets may become damaged or destroyed between the time the buyer and seller sign the purchase contract and the date they select to transfer the assets (the closing). This paragraph provides that the buyer may cancel the contract and receive a refund of any deposit if this happens. Nothing needs to be inserted here.

18. Disputes

See Chapter 1 for more information about dispute resolution clauses.

19. Additional Agreements

Insert any other terms that apply to your purchase.

Standard Clauses

The remainder of the agreement contains the standard clauses we discussed in Chapter 1. The only thing you'll need to fill in here is the name of the state whose law will apply to the contract, in the paragraph called "Governing Law."

Signatures

If the seller is a sole proprietor, the sole proprietor should sign the contract, and if the sole proprietor is married, the spouse should sign the agreement as well. See the beginning of this section for a discussion of getting a spouse's signature in the nine community property states.

If the seller is a partnership or an LLC, have all of the partners or LLC members sign the contract. If any of the partners or members are married, the spouses should sign the agreement as well. See the beginning of this section for a discussion of getting a spouse's signature in the nine community property states. (If you are including a covenant not to compete (see Paragraph 16, above), and if a spouse of a partner or member works in the business or has business know-how, that spouse should sign the contract to agree to the covenant not to compete, too.)

RELATED TOPIC

For more on signing contracts, see Chapter 1.

Schedules

If you are buying furniture, fixtures, and equipment (and selected that option in Paragraph 3), you need to list these items on a separate piece of paper labeled Schedule A. (Make sure the letter of the schedule matches the letter listed in Paragraph 3.)

Sample

5	48-inch round maple tables
5	42-inch square maple tables
5	42x30-inch maple tables
50	maple chairs
1	Acme convection oven, serial number 554444
1	Ultra-Freeze reach-in freezer, serial number 66332

When the parties sign the contract, each party should initial each page of the schedule.

If you are buying contracts (and selected that option in Paragraph 3), you need to list these contracts on a separate piece of paper labeled Schedule B. (Make sure the letter of the schedule matches the letter listed in Paragraph 3.) It's helpful to provide the date of the contract as well so there's no confusion over which contract it is.

Sample

> Equipment Lease between Seller and Tractors 'R' Us dated September 1, 20xx.
>
> Equipment Lease between Seller and Acme Machining, Inc., dated October 15, 20xx.
>
> Supply Agreement between Seller and Widgets of the World, dated May 11, 20xx.

The parties should initial each page of the schedule when they sign the contract.

Form 5B: Contract for Purchase of Assets From a Corporation

As discussed in the introduction to this chapter, there are two ways to structure the purchase of a corporation: You can purchase the corporation itself or you can buy only its assets. It's almost always better to buy the corporate assets rather than the corporate stock because, among other things, it helps you avoid the liabilities of the existing business and it gives you significant tax advantages. You can do this with Form 5B: Contract for Purchase of Assets From a Corporation.

CAUTION

Spouses of shareholders must sign in community property states. Nine states follow the community property system: Arizona, California, Idaho, Louisiana, Nevada, New Mexico, Texas, Washington, and Wisconsin. In those states, absent a marriage contract providing otherwise, a married couple's property accumulated after marriage is community (jointly owned) property regardless of the name in which it's held (exceptions include property received by inheritance or gift). Community property normally includes an interest in a business (even one that was owned by one spouse prior to marriage).

Generally, in a community property state, if a spouse plays no role in running the business you're buying and you pay a fair price, the law doesn't absolutely require you to get the spouse's written consent. But because of the likelihood that the business is jointly owned by the spouse, a better approach is to always obtain the signatures of the shareholders' spouses. That way, you avoid the possibility that a later dispute between the spouses could threaten to affect your purchase.

Get the Consent of All Shareholders

A corporation is a separate legal entity from its owners—the shareholders—and the corporation's bylaws, buy-sell agreement, or shareholders' agreement could permit the sale of its assets with the consent of a majority of the shareholders. However, it's legally safer to insist that all shareholders agree with the sale of the corporation's assets to avoid the possibility of having to deal with disgruntled minority owners after the fact. Get this consent in writing by following a two-step process:

1. Ask that all of the corporation's shareholders and directors sign and give you a copy of an official Corporate Resolution Authorizing Sale of Assets (Form 5C).

2. Require that all shareholders sign the Contract for Purchase of Assets From a Corporation (Form 5B).

A big bonus for insisting that all shareholders sign the contract is that it makes them personally liable for the warranties and representations in the contract. Without their signatures, should things go wrong, your only recourse would be against the corporation, which by that time would probably be without funds.

Instructions for Form 5B: Contract for Purchase of Assets From a Corporation

All the forms in this book are provided in Appendix B and on the Nolo website, using the link provided in Appendix A. As you read the instructions for Form 5B, you might want to refer to the form in Appendix B or open the downloadable form on your computer so you can follow along. (Before you use the form in Appendix B, be sure to photocopy it so you'll have a clean copy to use later.)

1. Names

Insert the name of the corporation that's selling the assets you're buying and the state in which it's incorporated. Then insert the buyer's name. See Chapter 1 for a discussion of how to identify the parties in legal forms.

Only the name of the corporation should be inserted in the seller's slot even though shareholders or shareholders' spouses might also be signing the contract. These people's names will be inserted at the end of the contract in the signature area.

2. Sale of Business Assets

In the first blank, insert the name that the seller's business actually uses. In the second blank, fill in the business's address. Include the street address, city, and state.

Sample

> Seller is selling to Buyer and Buyer is buying from Seller the assets of the business known as <u>Red's Rite Spot</u>, located at <u>123 Main Street, Sacramento, California</u>.

 TIP

Find out if the business and corporate names are different. A business might actually use a different name than that of the corporation. For example, a corporation called Rite Spot, Inc., could operate a restaurant called Red's Rite Spot. You'll use the corporation's name in the first paragraph and the business's day-to-day name here.

If the business has several locations and you're buying the assets used at more than one location, list all of the locations.

Sample

> Seller is selling to Buyer and Buyer is buying from Seller the assets of the business known as <u>Bagels & Baguettes</u>, located at <u>456 State Street and 789 North Liberty, Atlanta, Georgia</u>.

3. Assets Being Sold

See instructions for Paragraph 3 of Form 5A.

4. Purchase Price

See instructions for Paragraph 4 of Form 5A.

5. Price of Inventory (Optional)

See instructions for Paragraph 5 of Form 5A.

6. Accounts Receivable

See instructions for Paragraph 6 of Form 5A.

7. Deposit

See instructions for Paragraph 7 of Form 5A.

8. Payments at Closing

See instructions for Paragraph 8 of Form 5A.

9. Promissory Note (Optional)

See instructions for Paragraph 9 of Form 5A.

10. Security for Payment

See instructions for Paragraph 10 of Form 5A.

11. Seller's Debts

See instructions for Paragraph 11 of Form 5A.

12. Closing

See instructions for Paragraph 12 of Form 5A.

13. Documents for Transferring Assets

See instructions for Paragraph 13 of Form 5A.

14. Seller's Representations

See instructions for Paragraph 14 of Form 5A.

15. Buyer's Representations

See instructions for Paragraph 15 of Form 5A.

16. Covenant Not to Compete

See instructions for Paragraph 16 of Form 5A.

17. Risk of Loss

Nothing needs to be inserted here. See instructions for Paragraph 17 of Form 5A for an explanation of this paragraph.

18. Disputes

See Chapter 1 for more information about dispute resolution clauses.

19. Additional Agreements

Insert any other terms that apply to your purchase.

Standard Clauses

The remainder of the agreement contains the standard clauses we discussed in Chapter 1. The only thing you'll need to fill in here is the name of the state whose law will apply to the contract in the paragraph called "Governing Law."

Signatures

Have all of the shareholders sign the contract. If any of the shareholders are married, the spouses should sign the agreement as well. See the beginning of this section for a discussion of getting a spouse's signature in the nine community property states. (If you are including a covenant not to compete (see Paragraph 16, above), and if a spouse of a shareholder works in the business or has business know-how, that spouse should sign the contract to agree to the covenant not to compete, too.)

 RELATED TOPIC
For more on signing contracts, see Chapter 1.

Schedules

See "Schedules" in the instructions of Form 5A.

Form 5C: Corporate Resolution Authorizing Sale of Assets

Corporate bylaws often require the written consent of shareholders and directors before the corporation may sell all or substantially all of its assets. Traditionally, corporations have acted by having in-person meetings of shareholders or directors at which votes are taken and recorded in the form of resolutions, which are part of the minutes of the meetings. However, these days, shareholders of many corporations act by recording resolutions in a written consent, such as Form 5C, because it is more convenient than meeting and writing up minutes and just as legal. To be valid, these consents must be signed by shareholders or directors with a majority (or, if required by corporate documents, a supermajority) of the voting power of the corporation.

If you're buying the assets of a corporation (using Form 5B: Contract for Purchase of Assets From a Corporation), it makes sense to have all the shareholders and directors approve the sale of assets, even if unanimous consent isn't required under either the corporation's bylaws or state law. Use Form 5C: Corporate Resolution Authorizing Sale of Assets to do this.

Although this resolution can be prepared at any time, it makes sense for the shareholders and directors of the corporation being sold to wait until the parties have hammered out the details of the purchase agreement before signing the resolution and authorizing the sale. Usually, the shareholders and directors will sign the resolution shortly before or at the closing (the day specified in the purchase agreement for the parties to meet to exchange transfer documents and finalize the sale).

Instructions for Form 5C: Corporate Resolution Authorizing Sale of Assets

All the forms in this book are provided in Appendix B and on the Nolo website, using the link provided in Appendix A. As you read the instructions for Form 5C, you might want to refer to the form in Appendix B or open the downloadable form on your computer so you can follow along. (Before you use the form in Appendix B, be sure to photocopy it so you'll have a clean copy to use later.)

In the first blank on the resolution, insert the name of the corporation. In the second blank, insert the state in which it's incorporated. (See Chapter 1 for a discussion of how to identify the parties in legal forms.) Finally, after each shareholder and director has reviewed the purchase agreement to make sure that the terms of the purchase are acceptable, insert the date and have all of the shareholders and directors sign the

resolution. In many smaller corporations, the shareholders will also be the directors. If someone is both a shareholder and a director, have that person enter and sign his or her name twice—once under "Shareholders" and again under "Directors."

Form 5D: Contract for Purchase of Corporate Stock

As noted in the beginning of this chapter, when you buy a business from a corporation, it's almost always better to buy the corporate assets rather than the corporate stock. Use Form 5B: Contract for Purchase of Assets From a Corporation to do this. But in some situations (for example, the seller offers you a significantly better price), you might wish to deviate from this general rule and buy corporate stock. Use Form 5D: Contract for Purchase of Corporate Stock to accomplish this.

CAUTION
Watch for "change of control" provisions in the corporation's leases and contracts. Even when you're buying the stock of a corporation, you might need to get permission to take over a lease or other contracts to which the corporation is a party. This is because many savvy landlords and businesspeople have put so-called "change of control" provisions in their leases and contracts. These provisions provide that if the corporation sells more than a certain percentage of its stock, this transfer is really an assignment of the lease or contract—and requires the landlord's or other party's consent before the buyer can assume the seller's or the tenant's rights and benefits. To make sure your new business will benefit from these leases and contracts, ask to see copies of these documents. And if you discover one of these change of control provisions, ask the seller to get the landlord's or other party's permission to assign the lease or the contract before you buy the business.

⊘ CAUTION

Spouses of shareholders must sign in community property states. Nine states follow the community property system: Arizona, California, Idaho, Louisiana, Nevada, New Mexico, Texas, Washington, and Wisconsin. In those states, absent a marriage contract providing otherwise, a married couple's property accumulated after marriage is community (jointly owned) property regardless of the name in which it's held (exceptions include property received by inheritance or gift). Community property normally includes an interest in a business (even one that was owned by one spouse prior to marriage).

Generally, in a community property state, if a spouse plays no role in running the business you're buying and you pay a fair price, the law doesn't absolutely require you to get the spouse's written consent. But because of the likelihood that the business is jointly owned by the spouse, a better approach is to always obtain the signatures of the shareholders' spouses. That way, you avoid the possibility that a later dispute between the spouses could threaten to affect your purchase.

Instructions for Form 5D: Contract for Purchase of Corporate Stock

All the forms in this book are provided in Appendix B and on the Nolo website. As you read the instructions for Form 5D, you might want to refer to the form in Appendix B or open the downloadable form on your computer so you can follow along. (Before you use the form in Appendix B, be sure to photocopy it so you'll have a clean copy to use later.)

1. Names

Under "Seller," insert the names of the shareholders who are selling their stock to you. For you to fully own the business, you'll need to buy the shares of all existing shareholders, so be sure to list all of their names. (If you can't convince all of the existing shareholders to sell their stock, you should probably look for another business to buy.) Under "Buyer," insert the name of the buyer who is buying the stock from the present shareholder(s). (See Chapter 1 for a discussion of how to identify the parties in legal forms.)

2. Sale of Corporate Stock

In the first and second blanks, fill in the name of the corporation and the state of incorporation.

Sample

> Tried and True, Inc., a New Jersey corporation.

In the third blank, fill in the total number of shares the corporation has issued. In the remaining blanks, fill in the name of each shareholder and the number of shares of stock that the shareholder owns. Most small corporations issue only common stock to their shareholders, and your agreement assumes that this is the situation here. If the corporation you are purchasing has issued any shares of preferred stock, you should consult with an experienced business attorney to assist you with that more complicated transaction.

Also note that this paragraph calls for the corporate assets to be listed on an attached schedule labeled Schedule A. Instructions for adding this schedule can be found at the end of these instructions.

3. Purchase Price

In the first blank, fill in the price you are paying for each share of stock. In the second blank, fill in the total amount you are paying for all of the stock of the corporation. In actuality, the buyer and seller usually agree on a price for the business based on its value and then divide that by the number of outstanding shares of stock to arrive at a stock price. For help on determining a fair price for the business, see *Legal Guide for Starting & Running a Small Business*, by Fred S. Steingold and David M. Steingold (Nolo).

4. Provision for Payment of Undisclosed or Unpaid Liabilities (Optional)

If undisclosed liabilities or unpaid taxes surface after the purchase, the buyer might lose a significant sum of money if the buyer can't obtain reimbursement from the seller for these liabilities. To avoid this, you and the seller can agree that a portion of the purchase price will be placed in escrow or withheld by you for 90 days to pay any unlisted debts that surface during that time. If you and the seller have agreed on this, check the appropriate box.

Check Box A if you and the seller agree that a part of the purchase price will be placed in escrow with an outside person for 90 days to cover undetermined debts and tax liabilities of the corporation. You can then either fill in the name of the escrow agent or check the box indicating that you'll agree on an escrow agent later.

Check Box B if you and the seller agree that you'll simply withhold money for 90 days instead of placing this money with an escrow agent.

Whatever method you choose, we recommend that you write up a separate escrow agreement, as shown in the example below.

RELATED TOPIC

The proration and payment of utility bills is covered in the instructions for Form 5F in this chapter.

Escrow Agreement

Abigail Bernstein (Seller and sole shareholder of Abby's Cafe, Inc.), Carlos Diaz (Buyer), and Annette Miller (Escrow Agent) agree as follows:

1. As provided in Paragraph 3 of the Contract to Purchase Corporate Stock between Buyer and Seller, dated May 31, 20xx, Buyer is depositing $10,000 of the purchase price for the stock of Abby's Cafe, Inc., with Escrow Agent.

2. Escrow Agent acknowledges receipt of these funds and agrees to use the funds to pay any undisclosed or unpaid debts and liabilities of Abby's Cafe, Inc., incurred during the period ending May 31, 20xx.

3. After 90 days from the date of this agreement, Escrow Agent will return any excess funds to Seller.

_____
Date

_____
Abigail Bernstein, Seller

_____
Annette Miller, Escrow Agent

_____
Carlos Diaz, Buyer

---

5. Closing

At a closing, you meet with the seller to sign and exchange all the documents needed to complete the purchase. You pay (in the form of a cashier's check) whatever money is required for the ownership of the stock to be transferred to you and you receive stock certificates and other corporate documents.

Insert the date, time, and location of the closing.

Sample

> The closing will take place:
>
> Date: <u>Thursday, May 2, 20xx</u>
>
> Time: <u>1:00 p.m.</u>
>
> Location: <u>123 Washington Street, Essex, New York</u>

6. Documents for Buyer

This paragraph assures that you'll get the documents you need in order to take full charge of the business you're buying. As to stock certificates, the share-holders must provide you with the original stock certificates. On the back of most stock certificates there is preprinted language the shareholder can fill out to complete the transfer of the shares to the buyer. Alternatively, the shareholders or the buyer can prepare a separate stock transfer document, called a stock power or assignment separate from certificate, which legally transfers the stock to a buyer, by copying the language on the back of the stock certificate.

7. Sellers' Representations

See the instructions for Paragraph 14 of Form 5A.

Also, Paragraphs 7B and 7C call for the seller to attach schedules listing the corporation's assets (Schedule A) and its debts and liabilities (Schedule B). Instructions for adding these schedules can be found at the end of these instructions.

8. Covenant Not to Compete

See instructions for Paragraph 16 of Form 5A.

9. Risk of Loss

See instructions for Paragraph 17 of Form 5A.

10. Disputes

See Chapter 1 for more information about dispute resolution clauses.

11. Additional Agreements

Insert any other items that apply to your purchase.

12. Required Signatures

Insert the name of the corporation whose shares you're buying. All shareholders of the corporation must sign the contract.

Standard Clauses

The remainder of the agreement contains the standard clauses we discussed in Chapter 1. The only thing you'll need to fill in here is the name of the state whose law will apply to the contract in the paragraph called "Governing Law."

Signatures

Have all of the shareholders sign the contract. If any of the shareholders are married, the spouses should sign the agreement as well. See the beginning of this section for a discussion of getting a spouse's signature in the nine community property states. (If you are including a covenant not to compete (see Paragraph 8, above), and if a spouse of a shareholder works in the business or has business know-how, that spouse should sign the contract to agree to the covenant not to compete, too.)

 RELATED TOPIC
For more on signing contracts, see Chapter 1.

Schedules

Although it might seem tedious and time-consuming, the seller needs to list the corporate assets on a separate piece of paper labeled Schedule A. (Make sure the letter of the schedule matches the letter listed in Paragraphs 2 and 7B.) Taking an inventory of the corporation's assets lets you know exactly what you're getting, and it will also help you arrive at a fair price for the company. This list should include all tangible assets (such as equipment) and intangible assets of the business (such as intellectual property—copyrights, patents, and trademarks).

Sample

5	48-inch round maple tables
5	42-inch square maple tables
5	42x30-inch maple tables
50	maple chairs
1	Acme convection oven, serial number 554444
1	Ultra-Freeze reach-in freezer, serial number 66332

When the parties sign the contract, each party should initial each page of the schedule.

The seller must also list the corporation's debts and liabilities on a separate piece of paper labeled Schedule B. (Make sure the letter of the schedule matches the letter listed in Paragraph 7C.) Debts and liabilities should include outstanding promissory notes, unpaid creditors, tax problems, environmental concerns, and even pending or potential litigation. Don't worry about using legal or technical language; a simple description in plain English should be enough.

The parties should initial each page of the schedule when they sign the contract.

> **TIP**
> **It's your show now.** As the new owner of all shares, you'll want to immediately take legal charge by choosing a new board of directors. The new directors will then elect new officers. For guidance, see *The Corporate Records Handbook: Meetings, Minutes & Resolutions*, by Anthony Mancuso (Nolo), a book that explains how to handle most details of small corporation governance and provides all the forms necessary to accomplish the job.

Form 5E: Bill of Sale for Business Assets

When you purchase business assets from a sole proprietor, partnership, or limited liability company (Form 5A: Contract for Purchase of Assets From an Unincorporated Business) or from a corporation (Form 5B: Contract for Purchase of Assets From a Corporation), you'll want the seller to give you a bill of sale—a document that transfers the title to the business's tangible personal property. Usually, this will consist of the furniture, fixtures, and equipment and, in some cases, the inventory of goods sold. The seller should give you the bill of sale at closing.

As noted in the beginning of this chapter, some business assets you may be buying cannot be transferred through a bill of sale, but will require other documents instead. This includes land and buildings, which must be transferred by a deed that you record (file) at a designated county office to make it a matter of public record. It also includes intangible assets such as accounts receivable, contracts, trademarks, copyrights, and patents, which must be transferred using various legal documents—the most common being an assignment. The seller might or might not use a bill of sale to transfer ownership of any vehicles included in the sale, depending on the custom and laws in your state. In some states, the seller can simply sign the title to the vehicle authorizing the title to be changed to the new owner—a process you're likely familiar with if you've ever sold a car.

If you're buying the stock of a corporation rather than its assets (Form 5D: Contract for Purchase of Corporate Stock), you won't need a bill of sale. The corporation itself will continue to own the business assets. By buying the stock of the corporation, you'll automatically own the corporation and all its assets.

Instructions for Form 5E: Bill of Sale for Business Assets

All the forms in this book are provided in Appendix B and on the Nolo website using the link provided in Appendix A. As you read the instructions for Form 5E, you might want to refer to the form in Appendix B or open the downloadable form on your computer so you can follow along. (Before you use the form in Appendix B, be sure to photocopy it so you'll have a clean copy to use later.)

1. Names

Insert the name of the business that's selling the assets you're buying. Then insert the buyer's name. Make sure the names appear exactly as they appear on the purchase contract. (See Chapter 1 for a discussion of how to identify the parties in legal forms.)

2. Acknowledgment of Payment

If you're paying for the business assets in a single, lump-sum payment, check the first box.

If—as is more likely—you'll be making installment payments, check the second box. With an installment payment plan, the buyer will give the seller a cashier's check in the amount of an agreed-upon deposit or down payment and will sign a promissory note for the remainder of the purchase price. In addition, because the buyer hasn't yet paid for the assets in full, the seller will take a security interest in some or all of the assets, just in case the buyer fails to make payments as agreed. See the instructions to Form 5G: Security Agreement for Buying Business Assets for more information.

3. Warranty of Ownership

This paragraph contains a warranty (guarantee) that the seller owns the assets you're buying. This assures the buyer that no one else has any rights, such as a partial ownership interest or a security interest, in the assets the seller is transferring. If it later turns out that another person or company does have rights in the property, the buyer can sue the seller for breaching the warranty and can collect money for any damages the buyer suffers as a result.

Check the first box if you're paying the purchase price in full at closing.

Check the second box if you'll pay for the assets in part by a promissory note payable to the seller, with the seller retaining a security interest in the assets.

Signatures

The buyer does not have to sign the bill of sale. Only the owners of the business being sold, and perhaps their spouses, must sign it. In the first signature blank, insert either the sole proprietor's name, or if the company has more than one owner, the signing representative's name.

If the business being sold has more than one owner, all of the individual owners should sign the bill of sale as well, under "Personal Responsibility for Warranty," to personally accept responsibility for the warranty of ownership. If it turns out that the prior owners of the business sold were not in fact free to transfer the business assets—for instance, a creditor of the business had a security interest in its assets—the prior owners will be personally liable for any damages the buyer suffers. This is true even if the business is a corporation or a limited liability company that would otherwise offer limited personal liability for business debts. (For more on signing contracts, see Chapter 1.)

If the spouses of any owners signed the purchase contract, they should sign this bill of sale as well, in the "spouse" area.

Attachment to Bill of Sale

Insert the names of the seller and buyer exactly as they appear in the bill of sale. Next, clearly describe the property the seller is transferring to you. Your description of the assets should be as detailed as possible. It should include:

- the make, model, and serial number of any furniture, fixtures, or equipment
- the amount of and detailed description of any inventory, and
- a full description of any other tangible assets the seller is transferring to the buyer.

Sample descriptions of the business assets of a small restaurant

> 1 15-foot Polar Bear walk-in freezer, serial no. 8526422
>
> 1 Polar Bear reach-in freezer, serial no. 44986743
>
> 1 15-foot Polar Bear walk-in refrigerator, serial no. 883390E
>
> 1 Viking gas range, serial no. JUVS4590222
>
> 2 Cutlets Select meat slicers, serial nos. JCR0882 and JCR0883

Make sure both the buyer and seller initial the attachment to the bill of sale.

To make sure the property hasn't deteriorated between the time the parties sign the purchase agreement and the time of closing, the buyer should consider making a final inspection of the property just before closing the sale.

Form 5F: Seller's Affidavit— No Creditors

Use Form 5F: Seller's Affidavit—No Creditors if you're buying business assets (Form 5A: Contract for Purchase of Assets From an Unincorporated Business or Form 5B: Contract for Purchase of Assets From a Corporation). In this form, the seller promises under oath that as of the date of the closing there are no outstanding business debts or liabilities.

RELATED TOPIC
See the beginning of this chapter for a discussion of bulk sales requirements.

As noted earlier, only California and Maryland still have bulk sales laws. There's some variation in these states regarding the degree of formality

that's needed when a seller verifies in writing at the closing that all debts and liabilities of the business have been paid. It's safest to get the statement in the form of an affidavit—a written statement signed under oath in the presence of a notary public.

If the business will still owe money after the closing, the seller should not sign this form and the buyer and seller should research how they must comply with their state's bulk sales law.

Instructions for Form 5F: Seller's Affidavit—No Creditors

All the forms in this book are provided in Appendix B and on the Nolo website. As you read the instructions for Form 5F, you might want to refer to the form in Appendix B or open the downloadable form on your computer so you can follow along. (Before you use the form in Appendix B, be sure to photocopy it so you'll have a clean copy to use later.)

Introduction

At the beginning of the form, fill in the state and county where it will be signed and the name of the person who will sign it:

- If the seller is a sole proprietor, insert his or her name in the next blank.
- If the seller is a partnership, insert all partners' names in the blank.
- If the seller is a limited liability company, insert all members' names in the blank.
- If the seller is a corporation, insert all shareholders' names in the blank.

1. Entity Selling Assets

Check the box that describes whether the seller is a sole proprietor, a partnership, a limited liability company, or a corporation, and fill in the name of the business, if applicable.

Finally, fill in the name of the buyer.

2. No Security Interests

Nothing needs to be inserted here. The seller is affirming that the assets you're buying are not subject to any security interests or other liens.

3. No Creditors

Nothing needs to be inserted here. The seller is affirming that all debts and liabilities of the business have been paid and the business owners have no debts or liabilities that affect the assets or the right of the seller to transfer the assets.

Escrow Agreement

Abigail Bernstein, Seller, Carlos Diaz, Buyer, and Annette Miller, Escrow Agent agree as follows:

1. Seller is depositing $200 with Escrow Agent.
2. Escrow Agent acknowledges receipt of these funds and agrees to use the funds to pay the telephone and other utility charges for Abby's Cafe for the period ending May 31, 20xx.
3. After 60 days from the date of this Agreement, Escrow Agent will return any excess funds to Seller.

June 1, 20xx
Date

Abigail Bernstein
Abigail Bernstein, Seller

Annette Miller
Annette Miller, Escrow Agent

Carlos Diaz
Carlos Diaz, Buyer

💡 **TIP**

Arrange for payment of utility bills. At closing, the seller won't have an up-to-the minute phone bill and probably won't have final bills for gas, electricity,

or water either. Although lawyers can endlessly debate whether these undetermined utility bills do or do not amount to a debt or liability of the business, there's almost always a commonsense, practical way to deal with the issue. For example, if a third party, such as a lawyer, accountant, or title company representative, is assisting with the closing, you and the seller can agree that the seller will leave a few hundred dollars with the third party to pay the utility bills. In legal jargon, the money is left in escrow and the third party who's helping out is the escrow agent. Put your agreement in writing.

If there's no third party to take care of paying the bills, the seller should be willing to let you keep a few hundred dollars of the seller's money to pay the bills, with the understanding that you'll refund any excess within an agreed-upon amount of time. The important point here is that the undetermined final utility bills needn't trigger the cumbersome notice requirements of your state's bulk sales law.

4. No Claims

Nothing needs to be inserted here. The seller is affirming that there are no claims against the seller, the assets, or the business owners that affect the assets.

5. Indemnification

If the statements in the affidavit prove to be inaccurate, this clause binds the seller to make sure you won't suffer any loss.

Signature

All of the individual owners of the business being sold should sign this affidavit, using the proper signature format for the type of business (sole proprietorship, partnership, LLC, or corporation), as discussed in Chapter 1. The signers should sign the affidavit in the presence of a notary public who is authorized to notarize documents in the seller's state. (The seller should not sign the document before taking it to the notary; the notary must watch the seller's representatives sign it.)

Notarization

The seller or seller's representatives should sign this form in front of a notary public. The notary will want proof of each person's identity, such as a driver's license or passport. After the seller's representatives sign the document, the notary public will complete and attach a notarial certificate that usually includes the notary's signature and an official stamp.

Finding a notary public shouldn't be a problem; many advertise online and in the yellow pages. Banks, real estate offices, title companies, copy shops, and mailbox stores often have notary services. The notary's fee is usually modest—about $10 in most places.

> **TIP**
>
> **Notarization isn't always required.** In a number of states, the seller can simply sign this document "under penalty of perjury" and it will be the same as if notarized. The exact wording can vary.

Sample

> I certify (or declare) under penalty of perjury that the foregoing is true and correct.
>
> _____
> Signature
>
> _____
> Date and Place

Source: *California Code of Civil Procedure* Section 2015.5.

Form 5G: Security Agreement for Buying Business Assets

If you're buying business assets (Form 5A: Contract for Purchase of Assets From an Unincorporated Business or Form 5B: Contract for Purchase of Assets From a Corporation) and not paying the purchase price in full at closing, the seller will want you to sign a promissory note for the unpaid balance. (See Chapter 4 for examples and explanations of promissory notes.)

Along with the promissory note, the seller will no doubt want you to sign a security agreement that gives the seller what amounts to a continuing ownership interest in the property until you have made the final payment. If you don't keep up your payments, this security agreement allows the seller to take back the business assets. If you do make all the payments, the security agreement will end and the seller will no longer have a lien (security interest) on the property. As noted below, if you've signed a UCC Financing Statement in addition to a security agreement, when you've fully paid the debt, remember to have the seller sign a discharge that you can record at the proper public office to officially cancel the security interest.

> **CAUTION**
>
> **Be careful about putting nonbusiness assets at risk.** As noted in the instructions to Form 5A, if you're buying a service business, the seller may seek to secure payment of the promissory note by getting a mortgage or a deed of trust on your house. Putting your house at risk to buy a business is usually a poor idea.

Instructions for Form 5G: Security Agreement for Buying Business Assets

All the forms in this book are provided in Appendix B and on the Nolo website using the link provided in Appendix A. As you read the instructions for Form 5G, you might want to refer to the form in Appendix B or open the downloadable form on your computer so you can follow along. (Before you use the form in Appendix B, be sure to photocopy it so you'll have a clean copy to use later.)

1. Names

Insert the name of the buyer and the name of the business that's selling the assets. Make sure the names appear exactly as they appear on the purchase contract. (See Chapter 1 for a discussion of how to identify the parties in legal forms.)

Check the first box, which refers to the property you're buying. This is probably the same list the seller used for the bill of sale (see Attachment 1 to Form 5E).

Check the second box as well if you agree to give the seller a security interest in any property you add to the business, such as replacement inventory. This will give the seller a security interest in any property that you later acquire in connection with the business.

2. Security for Promissory Note

Fill in the date of the promissory note, the amount owed, and the interest rate, so that it's clear which promissory note the security agreement refers to. There's no need to list the payment schedule.

3. Financing Statement

The seller will prepare a financing statement, which is recorded (filed) at a public office to let third parties, such as lenders or purchasers, know that the property is subject to the seller's lien. That way, anyone checking the public records—for example, a bank's loan department—will learn that the seller has a prior lien, and thus an ownership interest, in the property described in the financing statement.

The form that is filed is a Uniform Commercial Code form called Form UCC-1. Check your state's secretary of state website or call the office to obtain the appropriate UCC form and learn the filing fees.

Once the UCC Financing Statement has been filed, anyone who buys the business assets from you will buy them subject to the lien of the person you're buying from—whether or not this new buyer actually looked at public records. This doesn't apply, however, to ordinary customers who buy items from an inventory of sale goods; they can buy merchandise without having to worry about a lien because the seller's lien only applies to the inventory as a whole—not to individual items you sell in the normal course of doing business.

Nothing needs to be inserted here.

> **CAUTION**
> **Remember to get a discharge when you've paid off the debt.** Once you've paid for the business assets, there's no longer a need for the seller to retain a security interest in them. You're entitled to receive a signed discharge form from the seller verifying that the lien is no longer in effect. You should then record (file) the discharge form at the same state or county office where the seller has recorded the UCC Financing Statement that you originally signed. If you forget to obtain a discharge and record it at the appropriate office, you could hit snags if you later try to sell the property.

4. Use and Care of the Secured Property

Check all appropriate boxes (downloadable form users should delete the language they don't want to include). This paragraph spells out the buyer's duty to safeguard the property so that the seller has something of value to take back if the buyer defaults.

5. Buyer's Default

Nothing needs to be filled in here. This paragraph says the buyer will be in default—meaning that the seller would be able to sue the buyer for repayment or return of the assets—if the buyer doesn't make required payments or doesn't promptly correct any violations of the requirements listed in the preceding paragraph.

For instance, if the buyer is late in making a payment and does not pay within ten days after the seller sends written notice of the late payment to the buyer, the buyer is in default. Or, if the buyer violates an obligation regarding the use and care of the secured property—such as failing to maintain it in good repair—and does not correct the violation within ten days of receiving written notice from the seller, the buyer will be in default.

6. Seller's Rights

This summarizes the seller's rights under the Uniform Commercial Code if you default on your obligations under this security agreement. Fill in the name of the state where the property is located. Specifically, the seller is allowed to seize the secured property and sell, lease, or otherwise dispose of it. But this agreement requires the seller to give notice to the buyer before taking back the property, and state law will probably prohibit the seller from forcing his or her way onto the buyer's private business space or house if the buyer tells the seller to keep out.

A seller who makes a mistake in seizing property could have to answer to civil charges of trespass or wrongful entry or criminal charges of breaking and entering or theft—and if the buyer resists, even assault.

7. Notice to Buyer

Fill in the location where the seller should send you a notice if you've defaulted and the seller is going to sell, lease, or otherwise dispose of the property. The seller must give the buyer ten days' notice before taking action with respect to the property. (This gives the buyer the chance to pay off the debt in full before the property is taken or turned over to someone else.)

Standard Clauses

The remainder of the agreement contains the standard clauses we discussed in Chapter 1. The only thing you'll need to fill in here is the name of the state whose law will apply to the contract, in the paragraph called "Governing Law."

Signatures

Both parties should sign, and the contract should be dated. See Chapter 1 for instructions on signing contracts.

Attachment to Security Agreement

Insert the names of the buyer and seller exactly as they appear in the security agreement. Next, clearly describe the property in which the seller will have a security interest. Your description of the assets should be as detailed as possible.

Sample

> 1 15-foot Polar Bear walk-in freezer, serial no. 8526422
>
> 1 Polar Bear reach-in freezer, serial no. 44986743
>
> 1 15-foot Polar Bear walk-in refrigerator, serial no. 883390E
>
> 1 Viking gas range, serial no. JUVS4590222
>
> 2 Cutlets Select meat slicers, serial nos. JCR0882 and JCR0883

Make sure both the buyer and seller sign the attachment to the security agreement.

Leasing Space

 FORMS

To download the forms discussed in this chapter, go to this book's companion page on Nolo.com. See Appendix A for the link.

Commercial leases are usually long and complicated—and often tilted heavily in favor of the landlord. By contrast, the leases in this chapter are comparatively short and simple, and more balanced from both the landlord's and tenant's points of view. But if you're a tenant and intend to use one of our forms, be forewarned: Most landlords (or their brokers or lawyers) have developed their own leases and usually insist that you use their forms. Still, especially with a smaller landlord—someone who owns only a single building or two, for example—you might have a shot at having the landlord agree to use one of these lease forms.

Even where landlords insist on using the twenty-page, fine-print monsters that they have paid law firms big bucks to tilt in their favor, a careful reading of this chapter should equip you to spot unfair clauses and insist on reasonable modifications. Especially when market conditions are tenant-friendly, it's key to understand that everything is negotiable (and in many instances, landlords present biased clauses precisely because they expect tenants to negotiate).

RESOURCE

Learn more about commercial leases. Chapter 13 of the *Legal Guide for Starting & Running a Small Business*, by Fred S. Steingold and David M. Steingold (Nolo), contains more information on negotiating a favorable lease and the basic law that applies to leases. For extensive information, we recommend the downloadable book *Negotiate the Best Lease for Your Business*, by Janet Portman (Nolo).

This chapter contains three leases—and seven additional forms associated with the leasing process. Using Form 6A: Gross Lease, you make one, all-inclusive rental payment each month, and it's up to the landlord to pay all property-related expenses, including taxes and insurance. However, in many real estate markets, especially for newer buildings, it's more common to use a net lease—one in which the tenant pays a fixed rent

but also has to pay for some or all of the building's operating expenses, such as real estate taxes, building maintenance, and landlord's insurance. In that case, use either Form 6B: Net Lease for Entire Building or Form 6C: Net Lease for Part of Building.

Sometimes you need to add to your lease information that doesn't fit within a prepared form or that doesn't adapt easily to word processing—a diagram, for example. You can add this material by using Form 6J: Attachment to Lease.

If conditions change during the life of your lease, you and the landlord can mutually agree to change the terms. You can accomplish this with the Form 6I: Amendment to Lease.

After you've leased space for your business, you might discover at some point that you can't or don't want to occupy the space—or some part of it—for the full term. Depending on the circumstances, the process of transferring occupancy rights to another tenant is referred to in legal jargon as subletting or assigning your lease.

If you transfer just some of your leased space to another tenant, or if you transfer all of the space for only part of your lease period, it's called a sublease. Typically, with a sublease the subtenant pays rent to you and you continue to pay the landlord under the terms of your lease. Use Form 6D: Sublease for this purpose. If your lease, like most leases, requires you to obtain the landlord's consent to a subletting of your space, use Form 6E: Landlord's Consent to Sublease.

By contrast, an assignment occurs if you transfer all of the space to someone else for the entire remaining term of the lease. In this situation, the new tenant deals directly with (pays rent to) the landlord. You can use Form 6F: Assignment of Lease to assign your space.

It's common to negotiate a lease with an option to extend the lease beyond its original duration. For example, you could have a three-year lease that gives you the option to extend the lease for another three years. Generally, a lease with an option to

Net Leases vs. Gross Leases

With a net lease, you pay rent plus additional amounts for operating expenses—typically, utilities, insurance, real property taxes, common area maintenance, janitorial services, snow removal, and lawn care. With a gross lease, you pay one monthly rent check to the landlord, who in turn takes care of these other expenses.

Will a gross lease or a net lease benefit you more? First, be aware that you might not have the opportunity to choose between the two—in most situations, the landlord will simply insist on one method rather than the other.

Given a choice, you probably care more which type of lease will be cheaper in the long run than who actually pays for taxes and insurance. As a general rule, you can expect the initial monthly rent on a net lease plus the extra charges for such things as insurance and taxes to come to less than the rent on a gross lease for the same space. That's because in agreeing to a gross lease, the landlord will often want to charge a little extra to protect against possible increases in property taxes, insurance, and other operating costs that could occur during the lease term (unless the lease calls for annual rent increases). Reasoning backward, while a net lease might be cheaper at the start (even after you pay all the extra items), with a net lease you, rather than the landlord, bear the risk of increases in taxes, insurance, and maintenance bills during the lease term.

The length of the lease is a key factor in determining whether a cheaper net lease or a more expensive gross lease is better. The shorter the lease period, the more likely you are to prefer a cheaper net lease, because costs will have less time to go up. If a lease is for more than three years—and certainly if it's for more than five years—a net lease, where you bear the risk of tax, insurance, and maintenance cost increases, becomes less attractive, even if it's slightly cheaper at the beginning.

---

renew requires the tenant to notify the landlord in writing when the tenant decides to extend the lease (exercise the option). Form 6G: Notice of Exercise of Lease Option allows you to do this.

> **CAUTION**
>
> **You might still be on the hook.** Don't assume that because you've sublet part or all of your space, or assigned the entire lease to another tenant, you're relieved of your responsibility to pay rent and meet other obligations in the lease. On the contrary, in most states, under either arrangement, you're still responsible for making good on any unpaid rent the subtenant or assignee fails to pay. You are free of future financial obligations only if the landlord explicitly releases you in an assignment of a lease. The landlord might be willing to do this if you're able to find a substitute tenant who's financially strong and willing to pay a higher rent. (See the instructions for Paragraph 9 of Form 6F, below.)

If your lease doesn't include an option to extend it, you and the landlord may still agree to an extension at any time before the original lease term runs out. Form 6H: Extension of Lease allows you and the landlord to lengthen the lease with perhaps a few modifications, without starting from scratch.

Form 6A: Gross Lease

As discussed in the beginning of this chapter, in a gross lease you pay the landlord a fixed monthly rent and it's up to the landlord to pay for all expenses of operating the building, including real estate taxes, real estate insurance, building maintenance, repairs, and utilities—except for any utilities that are separately metered and for which you agree to pay. If you've ever rented a house or an apartment unit, you probably signed what amounts to a gross lease, even though it didn't carry that name.

Instructions for Form 6A: Gross Lease

All the forms in this book are provided in Appendix B and on the Nolo website. To access the downloadable forms online, use the link provided in Appendix A. As you read the instructions for Form 6A, you might want to refer to the form in Appendix B or open the downloadable form on your computer so you can follow along. (Before you use the form in Appendix B, be sure to photocopy it so you'll have a clean copy to use later.)

1. Names

Insert the landlord's name and the name of your business. See Chapter 1 for a discussion of how to identify your business in legal documents.

2. Premises Being Leased

Fill in the address of the property you're leasing.

Sample

> 320 North Main Street, Ann Arbor, Michigan

If you're renting only part of a building, check the first box and then insert a description of the space you're leasing.

Sample

> The west 3,000 square feet of the second floor of the building.

If you will be sharing some facilities with other tenants, check the second box (before the words "Shared Facilities") and then check the items that apply. If necessary, specify in the blanks which facilities you have access to. Here are some examples of descriptions you might insert:

Parking Spaces. If your lease will give you the right to park in an adjacent parking lot that's shared with other tenants, specify whether you're entitled to a general area or a certain number of specific, reserved spaces.

Make Sure You Know How the Landlord Is Measuring the Space

Instead of stating the rent as an inclusive figure for the entire commercial space you're considering (for example, $2,000 a month for the first floor of the building), it's common for a landlord to quote a rate based on square footage. If the landlord uses the square-footage method, be sure you understand how the square footage will be computed. In the world of commercial leases, some landlords begin their measurements at the center of exterior walls and others even start at the outside of the walls. In either of these situations, you'll be paying for a good deal of unusable space.

To be sure you are really leasing the space you need, physically measure the interior space. This will allow you to determine how much the landlord will be charging you per square foot of usable space. For example, if it turns out that the landlord is measuring from the outside of the walls, the $12 per square foot per year price he quotes you may actually translate into $14 per square foot of usable space. That's not necessarily bad if your total monthly rent bill is competitive with the rent you'd pay for comparable space elsewhere. The point is that you can't make valid comparisons unless you know all the facts.

Be aware that another typical landlord practice—especially in an office building—is for the landlord to charge you rent for a percentage of the building's common areas even though you don't enjoy exclusive use of those areas. So, for example, if you rent 10% of the office space in a building, the landlord may add in 10% of the common area space in determining the square footage you're renting.

Samples

> The entire 400-square-foot parking lot on the north side of the building

> Spaces 14 through 32 in the adjacent parking lot

> Ten spaces in the parking lot on the corner of Fourth Street and Ash

Restroom Facilities. If you have access to only certain facilities in the building, describe them carefully.

Samples

> The men's and women's restrooms in the lobby and on the fourth floor

> The men's and women's restrooms in the main lobby and the unisex restroom in the west wing

In a building where all tenants, clients, and customers have access to all restroom facilities, you can simply enter:

> All restroom facilities in the building

Storage Areas. Insert the amount of space you're entitled to.

Samples

> The right half of the storage closet on the first floor

> The upper set of shelves in the garage

> One-half of the storage room (east half)

Hallways, Stairways, and Elevators. If you have access to only certain passages and elevators, describe them here. If you have access to any and all halls, stairs, and elevators in the building, say so.

Samples

> The front steps and first-floor hallways, but not the upper hallways or the back staircase

> All hallways, stairs, and elevators, including the freight elevator and loading dock

Conference Rooms. Describe your access to common meeting rooms and, if they will be available on a limited basis, explain the rules.

Samples

> The third-floor conference room, between 8 a.m. and noon only

> Room 5 on a first-come, first-served basis, but advance sign-up is required

If the broad categories listed on our form are not sufficiently specific, check "Other" and describe the extra facility you have access to, such as a shared kitchen. It's important to clearly describe all shared facilities in your lease, to preserve your rights and to avoid charges for janitorial or repair services associated with facilities you haven't been given access to.

3. Term of Lease

Fill in the dates the lease starts and ends. Understand that the date that the lease starts is not the same as the date that parties sign the lease (assuming you sign before the term begins). The date you sign the document is the date when you become obligated to the terms and conditions of the lease.

4. Rent

In the first blank, insert the day of the month on which rent is due, such as "the first." In the second blank, enter the date you will pay your first month's (or partial month's) rent. This date does not have to match the day of the month you will regularly pay rent each month thereafter. For instance, if you will move into the premises and start paying rent on December 15, enter that date here, even if you will pay rent on the first of every month from then on.

In the third blank, enter the amount of the first month's rent payment. If your first rent payment is for less than a full month (which will happen if your lease begins midmonth or your landlord is giving you a period of free rent), enter that figure. If not, enter the regular monthly rent here. Finally, in the fourth blank, enter the amount of the regular monthly rent.

> **TIP**
>
> **Ask for free rent.** It's common for a commercial landlord to give a tenant a few weeks or even months of free rent at the beginning of the lease term to cushion the tenant's moving costs. If you have expensive moving costs or expect a few slow months at the beginning of your lease as customers and clients become accustomed to your new location, you'll appreciate not having to pay rent. If the landlord will extend a period of free rent, it's a good idea to spell out your understanding in Paragraph 22, "Additional Agreements." If the landlord will not offer free rent, ask the landlord to reimburse you for all or part of your moving costs.

Next, check the first box if the lease will not provide for increases in rent. Check the second box if the lease *will* provide for systematic rent increases. Because the landlord pays the expenses on a gross lease, if expenses go up yearly, your landlord does less well financially. To buffer the impact of future increases in operating expenses, a landlord might want to provide that the rental amount you are obligated to pay will step up periodically. Assuming you have negotiated a favorable rental in the first place and the step-up is modest, you could find this acceptable.

If your industry or entire region hits an economic downturn, rents in your area might actually drop. In this case, a set dollar or percentage rent increase wouldn't be fair. There are two ways to work around this: The first is to provide that if certain expenses, such as property taxes, go up during the lease term, you must pay them, or at least some fraction of them. For example, if the property tax starts out at $3,000 and then jumps to $3,300, you'd be responsible for the additional $300. Another popular method uses increases in the Consumer Price Index or other inflation-sensitive indicator. If the landlord will provide for some type of rent increase, fill in the blank, following the samples below.

Samples

> Rent will increase $500 each year.

> Rent will be adjusted annually according to any increase in property taxes for the premises, measured against the taxes paid for the calendar year of the lease's starting date. Tenant will pay as additional rent one-half of any such increase.

> Rent will be adjusted annually based on any increase in the Consumer Price Index of the Bureau of Labor Statistics (All-Items Index or All Urban Consumers, U.S. City Average, 1982-1984=100) or any replacement index. The adjusted rent for the lease year following any adjustment (payable in monthly installments) will be the product arrived at by multiplying the rent for the previous year by a fraction, the numerator of which will be the index number for the month immediately preceding the adjustment and the denominator of which will be the index number for the month used in the numerator of the previous adjustment. In no event, however, will the rent increase exceed 5% per year.

TIP

Bargain for no rent increase for at least the first two years. Before you sign on the bottom line is the time when you have maximum bargaining power. Simply say no to a landlord who proposes raising the rent after only one year. To incorporate this into your lease, add the phrase "On the second anniversary of the beginning of the lease term" to your rent increase clause.

5. Option to Extend Lease

An option to extend the lease past its ending date can save you both time and money if, at the end of your lease term, you decide that you'd like to stay. If you have an option clause that you properly exercise, the landlord cannot offer the space to another tenant as long as you have not violated important provisions of your lease (meaning that you must be current in your rent and other responsibilities, such as maintaining your insurance and keeping your space in good repair).

If your landlord is granting you an option to extend the lease, check the first box. Insert the number of additional years you will gain by exercising the option. Next, enter the amount that the landlord will charge you for this option right. Landlords charge tenants when they grant option rights because an option ties their hands (they can't freely market the property as they wish, and have to go along if you properly exercise the right). And, you would have trouble enforcing this right if you couldn't prove to a judge that you paid for it (otherwise, a court might see the "right" as a mere gift, which may be rescinded). The clause describes this option right as "additional rent," which means that you will pay it as part of your first rent payment. Understand that if you secure a first and second option right, you'll need to pay for both of them when you make your first full month's rent payment.

Next, enter the date by which you must give the landlord notice that you intend to extend the lease. A date 60 days before the expiration of the original lease would be reasonable, but the landlord might bargain for a longer notice period of somewhere between 90 and 180 days. In the third blank,

describe any changed conditions for the new lease terms (including increased rent).

Samples

> During the extension period, the rent will be $3,200 per month.

> During the extension period, the rent will be $3,200 per month for the first year and $3,400 per month for the second year.

If you're able to negotiate an additional option period that will kick in after the first option period ends, check the second box, before the words "Second Option," and fill in the blanks as you did with the original option period. You'll need to pay for this second option right, too.

CAUTION

Rent for an option period should not be open-ended. Avoid saying that the rent for the option period will be negotiated later on. While this method defers the sometimes difficult task of determining what will constitute a reasonable rent in the future, accepting it means you run the obvious risk that the landlord will demand an unaffordable increase, making your option useless to you. Instead, either the same amount of rent you paid for the original lease term, a precise new rental amount, or an amount readily established by an objective mechanism ("current rent plus an increase based on the Consumer Price Index," as shown in the sample above, for example).

6. Security Deposit

It's common for residential landlords to require one or two months' rent as a security deposit, but commercial leases have no legal limit on the amount the landlord can charge. Insert the amount of any security deposit that you and the landlord have agreed on.

7. Improvements by Landlord

Your landlord might agree to modify the space to suit your needs—for example, by painting, installing flooring, removing or adding walls, or customizing electrical and plumbing systems. But while the landlord might agree to do some remodeling for you, it's an unusual landlord who will offer to do extensive remodeling without some form of compensation. Understand that if you're not charged directly, you invariably pay for extensive improvements by paying a higher rent.

If your landlord will make any improvements for you, check the first box. Then prepare a separate sheet called Attachment 1 (see Form 6J: Attachment to Lease) to describe the repairs and improvements (often called buildouts) the landlord will make. Before you rent the space, you might want to hire an experienced contractor to help you decide what changes are needed. If the repairs and improvements will be extensive, also consider having an architect or a contractor prepare detailed specifications so that they can be added to your attachment. If, instead, you're taking the premises as is, check the second box.

> **TIP**
>
> **Don't be shy about asking for improvements.** When leasing space for at least three or five years, landlords routinely agree to upgrade it to meet your needs. Realize that for their own tax and borrowing reasons, many landlords are more willing to spend money providing tenant-requested improvements than they are cutting the rent by the same amount. The extent of the improvements (or buildouts) is, of course, a matter of negotiation and depends on many factors, including how much rent you've agreed to pay.

8. Improvements by Tenant

It might be cheaper in the long run to do improvement or remodeling work yourself, rather than having the landlord do it, if the landlord will allow it. (Your landlord will want to know about and approve any alterations to the structure that you'd like to make during your tenancy.) However, this paragraph provides that the landlord will not unreasonably withhold consent to any improvements and alterations you want to make (this means that the landlord is not allowed to make arbitrary denials of your requests). Some landlords will even help with the cost, by giving the tenant a certain amount of money, called a tenant improvement allowance (TIA). If your landlord will do this, record your agreement in Paragraph 22, "Additional Agreements."

Whether you can remove improvements or built-in equipment paid for by you is often subject to negotiation between you and your landlord. This paragraph provides that you may remove any of your alterations and improvements at any time, as long as you repair any damage caused by attaching or removing improvements to the property. Of course, when your lease ends, the landlord might be willing to pay you for improvements you have made if they add value to the property, assuming you are willing to leave them.

Nothing needs to be inserted in this paragraph.

9. Tenant's Use of Premises

Describe your anticipated use of the space in sufficiently broad terms to cover all anticipated uses.

Samples

> Sale of office supplies. Sale, leasing, and servicing of office equipment.

> Servicing and repair of electrical appliances and electronic equipment.

This lease restricts you to your stated use for these reasons:

- **Zoning Compliance.** The lease includes the landlord's promise that, at the outset, the property is properly zoned for the business activities you specify here.

- **Code Compliance.** The landlord promises in the lease that the building will be up to code for your stated use.
- **Building Capacity.** The landlord needs assurance that your activities won't strain or damage the building's structure or systems. For example, the landlord will want to know if you're bringing in heavy equipment, in case the floor cannot support it.

10. Landlord's Representations

Nothing needs to be inserted here. This paragraph states that when your lease starts, the space will be properly zoned for your use and that the building will comply with all applicable laws and regulations. This last representation can be especially helpful if the government or an individual later claims that the building doesn't meet the requirements of the Americans with Disabilities Act—or a similar state law—and as a result extensive changes must be made. This paragraph also assures you that there are no known problems concerning toxic or hazardous substances.

11. Utilities and Services

Check the utilities and services that the landlord will furnish. Under the terms of a gross lease, the landlord will normally pay for all utilities and services in this list. You will be responsible for any utilities that aren't checked.

12. Maintenance and Repairs

Nothing need be filled in here. This section spells out the landlord's responsibilities and yours for maintenance and repairs. The landlord promises to maintain and repair the structure (roof, exterior, and common interior walls), common areas (such as the lobby and hallways), and the electrical, heating, plumbing, ventilating, and air-conditioning systems.

Sometimes it's difficult to know whether a maintenance job falls within the tenant's purview (as maintenance) or the landlord's (as replacement).

For more information on how to fairly allocate responsibilities, see the downloadable book *Negotiate the Best Lease for Your Business*, by Janet Portman (Nolo).

13. Insurance

Subparagraph A requires the landlord to carry and pay for property insurance for the building (this is commonly called fire and extended insurance). This insurance will not, however, cover the loss of your personal belongings, such as your inventory or business equipment. You'll need your own insurance policy for these items.

Subparagraph B requires you to carry public liability insurance. This insurance protects you if there is a claim filed against you or the landlord by someone who claims to have been injured on your rented premises or whose property is damaged there. Public liability insurance will cover you up to the limits of your policy. Typical limits are $100,000 per occurrence and no more than $300,000 in any one year. Depending on the nature of your business, your landlord might require higher limits. Enter the limits required by the landlord in Subparagraph B.

Subparagraph C contains a "mutual waiver of subrogation." This protects you against lawsuits filed by the landlord's insurance company over damage you have caused. This means, for example, that if your employee starts a fire that damages the building, the landlord's insurance company won't sue you to recoup the money it pays the landlord to repair the structure, even if your employee carelessly started the fire. The principle works the other way, too—if your business equipment is damaged due to the carelessness of the landlord, your insurer won't try to collect from the landlord after it pays your claim.

Subparagraph D requires you to supply proof that you have taken out and maintained the insurance you've promised to buy. This proof is known as a certificate of insurance, which you can obtain from your insurance company.

14. Taxes

Nothing needs to be filled in here. This paragraph obligates the landlord to pay all property taxes levied against the property. You, on the other hand, promise to pay all taxes levied against your personal property, such as your business inventory and vehicles. Note that even under a gross lease—where you're not responsible for insurance or taxes on the landlord's building—you'll be responsible for any personal property taxes your state or local government imposes on your furniture, fixtures, and equipment.

15. Subletting and Assignment

Nothing needs to be filled in here. In spite of your best efforts to negotiate a lease term that will suit your business needs, you could find in the future that you want to leave early or lease some of your space to another tenant. This lease provides that you may not assign your space (rent out your space to someone else permanently) or sublet it (rent out part of your space or all of it temporarily) without the landlord's consent. However, the landlord agrees in the lease to be reasonable when evaluating your request.

16. Damage to Premises

Nothing needs to be filled in here. This paragraph protects you if the premises are damaged by a flood or fire, for example. If your rented space is damaged through no fault of your own, you won't owe rent if the damage substantially interferes with your ability to carry on your business. If the interruption extends beyond 90 days, you'll have the option of terminating the lease.

17. Notice of Default

This paragraph gives you a chance to correct a default on the lease, such as nonpayment of rent. The landlord can't evict you until you've had the opportunity to take corrective action—the lease requires the landlord to give you ten days' notice before taking legal action.

18. Quiet Enjoyment

Nothing needs to be filled in here. The landlord assures you that you'll be able to peacefully occupy the space as long as you do what's required under the lease.

19. Eminent Domain

Nothing needs to be filled in here. Eminent domain is the procedure by which a government agency takes private property for a public purpose, such as a road or school. For example, a portion of a structure may be taken and torn down to make room for a municipal parking lot. When the government takes property, it will pay for its value, including the value of your lease. Your lease provides that if this happens to your building or leased premises, your lease will end and you will be entitled to share in the award, to the extent that it includes the value of your lease and your moving expenses.

20. Holding Over

Nothing needs to be filled in here. It's not unusual for tenants to stay in commercial space after the lease ends, with or without the landlord's permission (this is called holding over). This lease provides that if you hold over with the landlord's consent, your tenancy will continue under the same terms and conditions as your original lease, but will become month to month. However, the landlord will be able to terminate the tenancy with the proper amount of notice, 30 days in most states. Of course, if the landlord has made it clear that you should leave at the end of the term and you fail to do so, the landlord can begin eviction proceedings as soon as allowable under state law.

21. Disputes

See Chapter 1 for more information about dispute resolution clauses. Note that the landlord isn't required to participate in alternative methods of dispute resolution unless you've paid your rent to the landlord or placed it in escrow.

22. Additional Agreements

Fill in any other terms that you and the landlord have agreed to, such as the landlord's giving you one month's free rent, paying part of the cost of some approved remodeling work that you will do yourself, or providing other small services.

Samples

> Landlord will provide janitorial services three times a week.

> Landlord will add Tenant's name to the directory of building tenants.

> Landlord will rent no other space in the building to a retail food business.

CAUTION

Think about how you get access if the building is closed. If you're renting space in a building that you enter through a door, or lobby, entryway, or elevator that are also used by other tenants, make sure you'll have access to your space at all times you need it, even if the building is otherwise closed. If this might be a problem, add language to your lease specifying how you can get in when you need to, with specific reference to days and hours. Also, make sure you can control the lights, heating, and cooling and any other essential systems when the building is normally closed.

Standard Clauses

The remainder of the lease contains the standard clauses we discussed in Chapter 1. The only thing you'll need to fill in here is the name of the state whose law will apply to the contract in the paragraph called "Governing Law." Normally, landlords and tenants choose the state where the property is located.

Signatures

The landlord and tenant or tenant's representative should sign the lease. For more on signing contracts, see Chapter 1.

Guarantor

Landlords often want someone to personally guarantee the rent and any other sums due under the lease. Demanding a personal guarantee is particularly common when the tenant is an LLC or a corporation, where the business owners would not normally be personally liable for the rent. Corporation and limited liability company owners should think very carefully about personally guaranteeing a lease.

A personal guarantee means that your personal assets are at risk if the rent is not paid. Because the primary purpose of forming an LLC or a corporation is to limit the owners' personal liability for business debts, owners should understand that they are giving up this limited liability if they sign a personal guarantee. On the other hand, most commercial landlords will not lease to new or small corporations or LLCs without a personal guarantee. Giving up limited personal liability might be the only way to get the rental.

All guarantors must sign the lease and provide their addresses so that the landlord can contact them if the tenant fails to pay the rent or other sums due.

Form 6B: Net Lease for Entire Building

As discussed in the beginning of this chapter, in a net lease the tenant not only pays for the space but also for some or all of the building's operating costs—property taxes, property insurance, and maintenance. In the lingo of the real estate business, a lease that requires the tenant to pay for all of these costs is referred to as a "triple net lease" (or just a net lease). Form 6B is a triple net lease for use when you're leasing an entire building, while Form 6C is for leasing just a portion of a building.

Instructions for Form 6B: Net Lease for Entire Building

All the forms in this book are provided in Appendix B and on the Nolo website. To access the downloadable forms online, use the link provided in Appendix A. As you read the instructions for Form 6B, you might want to refer to the form in Appendix B or open the downloadable form so you can follow along. (Before you use the form in Appendix B, be sure to photocopy it so you'll have a clean copy to use later.)

1. Names

Insert the landlord's name and the name of your business. See Chapter 1 for a discussion of how to identify your business in legal documents.

2. Premises Being Leased

Fill in the address of the property you're leasing.

Sample

> 320 North Main Street, Ann Arbor, Michigan

3. Term of Lease

Fill in the dates the lease starts and ends.

4. Rent

See the instructions for Paragraph 4 of Form 6A for filling in the first four blanks. After you have filled in the four blanks, you'll need to indicate whether your lease will provide for rent increases by checking the appropriate box. This is where your instructions differ from those for Form 6A.

Under a net lease for an entire building, the tenant pays for all utilities and services, which typically go up over time (see the instructions for Paragraph 11, below). By contrast, in a gross lease the landlord pays for these expenses, which is why landlords using gross leases often provide for systematic rent increases. But even in a net lease, the landlord might still ask for a rent increase in order to capture the increasing value of the space alone. For example, if the landlord thinks the building and neighborhood will become increasingly desirable, the rent for the space (per square foot or however you've measured your space) will rise at specified times and for a specified amount during the lease term. If you agree to such an arrangement, remember that you will continue to be responsible for any increases in the cost of utilities.

Check the first box if the lease *will not* provide for increases in rent. Check the second box if the lease *will* provide systematic rent increases for the space alone.

5. Option to Extend Lease

See the instructions for Paragraph 5 of Form 6A.

6. Security Deposit

See the instructions for Paragraph 6 of Form 6A.

7. Improvements by Landlord

See the instructions for Paragraph 7 of Form 6A.

8. Improvements by Tenant

See the instructions for Paragraph 8 of Form 6A.

9. Tenant's Use of Premises

See the instructions for Paragraph 9 of Form 6A.

10. Landlord's Representations

See the instructions for Paragraph 10 of Form 6A.

11. Utilities and Services

Nothing needs to be inserted here. Under a net lease for an entire building, a tenant pays for all utilities and services, such as water, electricity, and gas, including the electricity or gas needed to run the heating and air-conditioning systems.

SEE AN EXPERT

Consider getting help on the details of net leases. In all lease negotiations, you and the landlord will jockey for position regarding who will bear the cost of any future increases in the cost of property taxes, insurance, maintenance, utilities, and janitorial service. You can negotiate with the landlord to modify Form 6B to change the allocation of any operating cost. For example, you could have the tenant be responsible for maintenance but not for taxes and insurance, or you can negotiate to place a cap on the amount you're obligated to pay. If you make lots of changes, the wording might get to be a bit of a challenge. So if you are new to the commercial real estate world, and especially if your lease is long and the rent is expensive, it makes sense to have a real estate or small business expert (or an attorney) review your work and perhaps even do some or all of the negotiating for you.

12. Maintenance and Repairs

Nothing needs to be filled in here. As the tenant, you are responsible for all structural maintenance and repairs, including the roof, exterior and interior walls, and other structural elements such as the elevators. You must also clean and maintain parking areas, yards, and the exterior of the building. (Maintenance includes snow removal.)

13. Insurance

See the instructions for Paragraph 13 of Form 6A.

14. Taxes

Nothing needs to be filled in here. This lease obligates you to pay the yearly property taxes that are levied to support recurring government expenses, such as maintaining the roads and paying for law enforcement. The lease excludes special taxes that are assessed (imposed) for specific local improvements, such as a one-time sewer project. However, if your lease is quite long, such as ten years or more, your landlord might want you to

pay for these assessed taxes, too. Note that you'll be responsible for both the real estate taxes and your own personal property taxes—the taxes on your furniture and equipment—if your state or local government imposes a tax on such property.

15. Subletting and Assignment

See the instructions for Paragraph 15 of Form 6A.

16. Notice of Default

See the instructions for Paragraph 17 of Form 6A.

17. Quiet Enjoyment

See the instructions for Paragraph 18 of Form 6A.

18. Eminent Domain

See the instructions for Paragraph 19 of Form 6A.

19. Holding Over

See the instructions for Paragraph 20 of Form 6A.

20. Disputes

See Chapter 1 for more information about dispute resolution clauses. Note that the landlord isn't required to participate in alternative methods of dispute resolution unless you've paid your rent to the landlord or placed it in escrow.

21. Additional Agreements

Fill in any other terms that you and the landlord have agreed to. For examples of language, see the instructions for Paragraph 22 of Form 6A.

Standard Clauses

The remainder of the lease contains the standard clauses we discussed in Chapter 1. The only thing you'll need to fill in here is the name of the state whose law will apply to the contract in the paragraph called "Governing Law" (usually the state where the property is located).

Signatures

The landlord and tenant or tenant's representative should sign the lease. For more on signing contracts, see Chapter 1.

Guarantor

See the explanation of the Guarantor clause for Form 6A.

Form 6C: Net Lease for Part of Building

As discussed in the beginning of this chapter, in a net lease, the tenant not only pays rent but also pays for some or all of the building's operating costs—property taxes, property insurance, and maintenance. In the lingo of the real estate business, a lease that requires the tenant to pay for all of these costs is referred to as a triple net lease. Form 6C is a net lease for use when you're leasing just a portion of a building, in a multi-tenant situation (each tenant contributes to the various costs).

Instructions for Form 6C: Net Lease for Part of Building

All the forms in this book are provided in Appendix B and on the Nolo website. To access the downloadable forms online, use the link provided in Appendix A. As you read the instructions for Form 6C, you might want refer the form in Appendix B or open the form on your computer so you can follow along. (Before you use the form in Appendix B, be sure to photocopy it so you'll have a clean copy to use later.)

1. Names

Insert the landlord's name and the name of your business. See Chapter 1 for a discussion of how to identify your business in legal documents.

2. Premises Being Leased

Fill in the address of the property you're leasing.

Sample

> 320 North Main Street, Ann Arbor, Michigan

Then insert a description of the space in the building that you're leasing.

Sample

> the west 3,000 square feet of the second floor of the building.

If you will be sharing some facilities with other tenants, check the box before the words "Shared Facilities" and then check the items that apply. If necessary, specify in the blanks which facilities you have access to. Here are some examples of descriptions you might insert:

Parking Spaces. If your lease will give you the right to park in an adjacent parking lot that's shared with other tenants, specify whether you're entitled to a general area or a certain number of specific, reserved spaces.

Samples

> The entire 400-square-foot parking lot on the north side of the building

> Spaces 14 through 32 in the adjacent parking lot

> Ten spaces in the parking lot on the corner of Fourth Street and Ash

Restroom Facilities. If you have access to only certain facilities in the building, describe them carefully.

Samples

> The men's and women's restrooms in the lobby and on the fourth floor

> The men's and women's restrooms in the main lobby and the unisex restroom in the west wing

In a building where all tenants, clients, and customers have access to all restroom facilities, you can simply enter:

> All restroom facilities in the building

Storage Areas. Insert the amount of space you're entitled to.

Samples

> The right half of the storage closet on the first floor

> The upper set of shelves in the garage

> One-half of the storage room (east half)

Hallways, Stairways, and Elevators. If you have access to only certain passages and elevators, describe them here. If you have access to any and all halls, stairs, and elevators in the building, say so.

Samples

> Tenant may use the front steps and first-floor hallways, but not the upper hallways or the back staircase.

> Tenant may use all hallways, stairs, and elevators, including the freight elevator and loading dock.

Conference Rooms. Describe your access to common meeting rooms and, if they will be available on a limited basis, explain the rules.

Samples

> The third-floor conference room, between 8 a.m. and noon only

> Room 5 on a first-come, first-served basis, but advance sign-up is required

If the broad categories listed on our form are not sufficiently specific, check "Other" and describe the extra facility you have access to, such as a shared kitchen. It's important to clearly describe all shared facilities in your lease, to preserve your rights and to avoid charges for janitorial or repair services associated with facilities to which you don't have access.

3. Term of Lease

Fill in the dates the lease starts and ends.

4. Rent

See the instructions for Paragraph 4 of Form 6A for filling in the first four blanks. After you have filled in the four blanks, you'll need to indicate whether your lease will provide for rent increases by checking the appropriate box. This is where your instructions differ from those for Form 6A.

Under a net lease for part of a building, the tenants are billed separately for utilities and services, which typically go up over time (see the instructions for Paragraph 11, below). By contrast, in a gross lease, the landlord pays forthese expenses, which is why landlords using gross leases often provide for systematic rent increases. But even in a net lease such as this one, the landlord may still ask for a rent increase in order to capture the increasing value of the space alone. For example, if the landlord thinks the building and neighborhood will become increasingly desirable, the rent for the space (per square foot or however you've measured your space) will rise at specified times and by a specified amount during the lease term. If you agree to such an arrangement, remember that you will continue to be responsible for any increases in the cost of utilities.

Check the first box if the lease *will not* provide for increases in rent. Check the second box if the lease *will* provide systematic rent increases for the space alone.

5. Option to Extend Lease

See the instructions for Paragraph 5 of Form 6A.

6. Security Deposit

See the instructions for Paragraph 6 of Form 6A.

7. Improvements by Landlord

See the instructions for Paragraph 7 of Form 6A.

8. Improvements by Tenant

See the instructions for Paragraph 8 of Form 6A.

9. Tenant's Use of Premises

See the instructions for Paragraph 9 of Form 6A. If you're a retailer or food business sharing space in a building with other similar businesses, the landlord might propose limiting what you can sell so your activities won't directly compete with those of other tenants. For example, if you're leasing space for a bookstore in a building where other space is occupied by a sandwich shop, the landlord might insist on a clause saying you can't sell food or even coffee drinks. Or, if you're leasing space for your art gallery in a shopping mall where other space is occupied by a jeweler, the landlord might want language prohibiting you from selling jewelry.

TIP

Getting protection from competitors or incompatible businesses. If you're a doctor or dentist renting space in a professional building, you understandably might want to protect your image by having the landlord agree to rent retail space only to compatible tenants, such as a pharmacy, eyeglass store, or medical equipment rental service. Or, if you're renting space for a computer repair business, you might want language in your lease prohibiting the landlord from allowing other tenants from offering the same services. If so, you'll need to bargain for it and add your understanding to Paragraph 23, "Additional Agreements."

Sample

> In all other leases or written rental agreements executed after the date that the parties sign this lease, covering space in the building at 456 University Avenue, Sarasota, Florida, Landlord will prohibit the tenant or any subtenant from operating a computer repair business.

10. Landlord's Representations

See the instructions for Paragraph 10 of Form 6A.

11. Utilities and Services

You may be billed separately for some services—for example, garbage pickup—while sharing some utility costs with other tenants in the building. If possible, try to arrange for separate metering or billing for all of your utilities and services. This has the obvious advantage of allowing you to pay for precisely the amount of utility or service you use. There might, however, be an advantage to sharing with others if the utility or service provider will give you a better rate based on volume.

In Subparagraph A, check any utilities and services that are separately metered or billed for the space you're leasing. If there are other services you will pay for alone, check "Other" and enter them.

Samples

> Placement and upkeep of plants in the lobby area opposite its entryway

> Cost of cable service

In Subparagraph B, fill in the percentage you'll pay for utility and service charges that are not separately metered or billed. Usually the percentage is based on a ratio of how many square feet you're renting as compared to how many rentable square feet the building contains. Thus, if you're renting 5,000 square feet in a building that contains 50,000 square feet of rentable space, you'll likely be paying 10% of the utilities.

Next, check the utilities or services for which you will share the cost. If the building has services not listed that you will share, check "Other" and enter them.

Samples

> Placement and upkeep of plants in the lobby area opposite the main entryway

> Security surveillance service

Finally, fill in the day that you will pay these charges and fill in the frequency with which the landlord must show you the actual bills. Anywhere between two months and six months seems reasonable.

12. Maintenance and Repair of Common Areas

Common area maintenance, also known as CAM, is typically performed by the landlord but paid for by the tenants (in proportion to the amount of space they rent). Check the boxes for those parts of the common areas the landlord will maintain and repair. (Landlords usually maintain all common areas.) If the building has areas not listed that the landlord will be responsible for repairing, check "Other" and enter them.

Sample

> Basement workout room and showers

Fill in the percentage of the costs you'll pay —probably the same percentage you used in Paragraph 11—and the day of the month you'll pay it.

Security Measures

Your lease requires the landlord to keep common areas "safe and free of trash." In years past, the question of safety was tied to conditions that would lead to accidents. Nowadays, however, this promise includes a commitment to provide reasonable security from criminal intrusions. For example, a promise to maintain hallways, stairs, and entryways means that the landlord must provide an adequate level of locks, lighting, intercom systems, or even security guards.

It can be difficult to know how much security is called for in your building. Factors to consider include the history of the building (have criminal incidents occurred there in the past?), the nature of the neighborhood, the attractiveness of the goods inside, and the practical ability to install security measures. Be sure to discuss these needs frankly with your landlord.

If your landlord will provide special security measures, such as hiring a night guard, you might want to record your understandings either in Paragraph 23, "Additional Agreements," or in an attachment to your lease. (You can use Form 6J: Attachment to Lease for this purpose.)

13. Maintenance and Repair of Leased Premises

The landlord will be responsible for maintaining and replacing structural elements of the building that have outlived their useful life. These expenses, also known as capital expenditures, are ordinarily not passed through to the tenants as CAM costs. For example, tenants would not normally be responsible for paying for replacing a heating system.

If the landlord will maintain a significant structural element of the building that is not listed here, check "Other" and enter it.

Sample

> Building risers (electrical and communications pathways)

You will be responsible for keeping your rented space clean and in good repair.

14. Insurance

Subparagraph A requires the landlord to carry property insurance for the building (commonly called fire and extended insurance). Fill in the percentage of the landlord's insurance costs you'll pay—probably the same percentage you used in Paragraph 11. This insurance will not cover the loss of your personal belongings, such as your inventory or business equipment. You'll need your own insurance policy for these items.

Subparagraph B requires you to carry public liability insurance. This insurance protects you if there is a claim filed against you or the landlord by someone who claims to have been injured on your rented premises or whose property is damaged there. Public liability insurance will cover you up to the limits of your policy. Typical limits are $100,000 per occurrence and no more than $300,000 in any one year. Depending on the nature of your business, your landlord may require higher limits. Enter the limits required by the landlord in Subparagraph B.

Subparagraph C contains a "mutual waiver of subrogation." This protects you against lawsuits filed by the landlord's insurance company over damage you might have caused. This means, for example, that if your employee starts a fire that damages the building, the landlord's insurance company won't sue you to recoup the money it pays the landlord to repair the structure, even if your employee carelessly started the fire. The principle works the other way, too—if your business equipment is damaged due to the carelessness of the landlord, your insurer won't try to collect from the landlord after it pays your claim.

Subparagraph D requires you to supply proof that you have taken out and maintained the insurance you've promised to buy. This proof is known as a certificate of insurance, which you can obtain from your insurance company.

15. Taxes

Your lease will obligate you to pay a part of the yearly property taxes that are used to support recurring government expenses, such as maintaining the roads and paying law enforcement. Most of the time, tenants pay their share of the property taxes based on their square footage, but not always. If one tenant's business has greatly improved the property, resulting in a higher tax bill, you might have an argument for placing a greater property tax burden on that tenant. Fill in the percentage of the landlord's real estate taxes you'll pay—in most cases, the same percentage you used in Paragraph 11.

> **CAUTION**
>
> **A tax rise could be imminent.** Especially when you're renting space in a newly remodeled building, an upwards reassessment of property taxes might be imminent. Of course, many other factors can trigger a new tax assessment. It's always a good idea to check with the municipality to find out what to expect. And as with other open-ended obligations in a lease, it can make sense to bargain for a cap.

16. Subletting and Assignment

See the instructions for Paragraph 15 of Form 6A.

17. Damage to Premises

See the instructions for Paragraph 16 of Form 6A.

18. Notice of Default

See the instructions for Paragraph 17 of Form 6A.

19. Quiet Enjoyment

See the instructions for Paragraph 18 of Form 6A.

20. Eminent Domain

See the instructions for Paragraph 19 of Form 6A.

21. Holding Over

See the instructions for Paragraph 20 of Form 6A.

22. Disputes

See Chapter 1 for more information about dispute resolution clauses. Note that the landlord isn't required to participate in alternative methods of dispute resolution unless you've paid your rent to the landlord or placed it in escrow.

23. Additional Agreements

Fill in any other terms that you and the landlord have agreed to. For examples of language, see the instructions for Paragraph 22 of Form 6A.

Standard Clauses

The remainder of the lease contains the standard clauses we discussed in Chapter 1. The only thing you'll need to fill in here is the name of the state whose law will apply to the contract in the paragraph called "Governing Law" (usually the state where the property is located).

Signatures

The landlord and tenant or tenant's representative should sign the lease. For more on signing contracts, see Chapter 1.

Guarantor

See the explanation of the Guarantor clause for Form 6A.

Form 6D: Sublease

If you sublet your space, you become a landlord—or, more precisely, a sublandlord—as far as your subtenant is concerned. The subtenant will pay you the rent you charge and you, in turn, will remain responsible for paying your landlord the full rent called for by the original lease and honoring all the other terms of the lease.

Use this form if you would like to turn over part of your space to another tenant, or if you want to lease out all of your space for a while but return to the space during the term of your original lease.

Even if you sublease all of your space and move out, you remain obligated to all of the terms and conditions of your own lease with the landlord. Even if you haven't received rent from the subtenant, you must still pay the entire rent to the landlord. You will also be responsible for any damage the subtenant causes. These are good reasons to collect an adequate security deposit from your subtenant, which you'll be able to set up in this sublease. Both you and your subtenant must comply with all of the terms of the original lease.

If you intend to completely move away from this location and do not plan to return during the term of your lease, you should assign your lease rather than sublet the space. This could allow you to avoid potential financial responsibilities to the landlord (explained below). To assign your lease, use Form 6F: Assignment of Lease instead of this sublease.

If your lease doesn't mention subleasing, the laws of most states give you the right to sublet your space or assign the lease to another tenant, whether or not the landlord approves. But finding yourself in this situation is unusual. Most leases, like the ones in this book, say that a tenant can't sublet or assign without the written consent of the landlord. If you have a lease of this latter type, you'll need to get the landlord's permission before your sublease will be legally enforceable. Use Form 6E: Landlord's Consent to Sublease to get the landlord's written consent.

Check your original lease carefully for any restrictions your landlord placed on your ability to sublet. Some leases state that the landlord may use his or her sole discretion when evaluating the subtenant, which means that the landlord can reject a potential subtenant without grounds. If you're fortunate, your lease will say that the landlord will not be unreasonable when evaluating your proposed subtenant, which means that only good, objective business reasons will support the landlord's decision to reject a subtenant.

> **SEE AN EXPERT**
>
> **If the landlord arbitrarily rejects your sub-tenant, you might be able to walk away from the lease.** Suppose your lease requires the landlord's consent for you to sublet space or assign the lease. You approach the landlord with a creditworthy subtenant who runs a reasonably quiet business that doesn't interfere with other tenants' businesses, but the landlord arbitrarily refuses to consent to your subleasing to that business. Chances are you're in a strong legal position to end the lease with no further obligation to pay rent, because the landlord seems to be unreasonably withholding consent for you to sublet. But because this is a tricky legal area, and especially when a lot of money is at stake, if you're in this situation we recommend you consult a local lawyer who specializes in commercial real estate law.

Instructions for Form 6D: Sublease

All the forms in this book are provided in Appendix B and on the Nolo website. To access the downloadable forms online, use the link provided in Appendix A. As you read the instructions for Form 6D, you might want to refer to the form in Appendix B or open the form on your computer so you can follow along.

(Before you use the form in Appendix B, be sure to photocopy it so you'll have a clean copy to use later.)

These instructions assume that you're the sub-landlord and are preparing the sublease form.

1. Names

Insert the names of the sublandlord (you) and subtenant. See Chapter 1 for a discussion of how to identify businesses in legal documents.

2. Property Subleased

Choose one of the two options. Check the first box if you're subleasing all of the space covered by your lease. Then fill in the location exactly as it appears in your lease.

Sample

> 320 North Main Street, Ann Arbor, Michigan

Check the second box if you're subleasing just part of the space covered by your lease. Then fill in the location and describe the part of the space you're subleasing.

Sample

> The following part of the premises at 320 North Main Street, Ann Arbor, Michigan. Specifically, Subtenant is leasing the west 3,000 square feet of the second floor of the building.

3. Original Lease

In the first blank, insert the beginning date of the original lease. The beginning date is not necessarily the date of your first rent payment, though it often is. In the next two blanks, insert the name of your landlord and then your name.

In the last blank in this paragraph, insert any-thing that will be different from the terms of the original lease. The subtenant will always be subject to the same restrictions as you are under the original lease, but you may impose additional restrictions or obligations on the subtenant that are not present or in conflict with your original lease. For instance, you might want the subtenant to perform maintenance chores for you or pay part of your utilities, or you could agree to limited signage or the subtenant's use of certain entrances or storage areas but not others.

Sample

> In addition to paying rent, Subtenant will reimburse Sublandlord for one-half of the electric and water bills; Subtenant will make such reimbursement within ten days after receiving a copy of the bills from Sublandlord.

Unless you state differently here, the subtenant will be entitled to all of your rights contained in the original lease. For example, the parking places that come with the original lease will, unless you specify otherwise, be available to the subtenant. But you might decide that your subtenant will have fewer rights than you do under the original lease. For example, your lease might allow you to stay open until 8 p.m., but you could want your subtenant to close up shop at 6 p.m. As long as your additional restrictions do not negatively affect the landlord or other tenants in the building, you may restrict the subtenant's rights.

Samples

> Subtenant may use the subleased space only between the hours of 9 a.m. to 5 p.m., Monday through Friday.

> Subtenant may not use the parking spots that Sublandlord has leased from Landlord.

TIP

It's okay to keep some information private. The subtenant needs to know most of the terms of the original lease to avoid inadvertently violating those terms. But there's no legal requirement that you reveal the details of your financial arrangements with your landlord. Although we generally think a policy of full disclosure is best in the long run, if you prefer to keep these details confidential, simply black out the financial terms on the copy of the original lease you attach to the sublease.

4. Term of Sublease

Fill in the date the sublease starts and the date it ends. Understand that the date that the sublease starts is not the same as the date that parties sign the lease (assuming you sign before the term begins). The date you sign the document is the date when you become obligated to the terms and conditions of the sublease.

5. Rent

In the first blank, insert the day of the month on which rent is due, such as the first. In the second blank, enter the date your subtenant will pay the first month's (or partial month's) rent. This date does not have to match the day of the month the subtenant will regularly pay rent each month thereafter. For instance, if the subtenant will move into the premises and start paying rent on December 15, enter that date here, even if the subtenant will pay rent on the first of every month from then on.

In the third blank, enter the amount of the first month's rent payment. If the subtenant's first rent payment is for less than a full month (which could happen if the subtenant's lease begins midmonth) enter that figure. If not, enter the regular monthly rent here. Finally, in the fourth blank, enter the amount of the regular monthly rent.

Next, check the first box if the lease *will not* provide for increases in rent. Check the second box if the lease *will* provide for systematic rent increases. When the original lease contains provisions for the rent to go up, based on cost-of-living increases or a fixed amount, it's appropriate for the subtenant to pay some or all of the increases. You can use the same language as is in your original lease.

Samples

> Rent will increase $500 each year.

> Rent will be adjusted annually according to any increase in property taxes for the premises, measured against the taxes paid for the calendar year of the lease's starting date. Subtenant will pay as additional rent one-half of any such increase.

> Rent will be adjusted annually based on any increase in the Consumer Price Index of the Bureau of Labor Statistics (All-Items Index or All Urban Consumers, U.S. City Average, 1982-1984=100) or any replacement index. The adjusted rent for the lease year following any adjustment (payable in monthly installments) will be the product arrived at by multiplying the rent for the previous year by a fraction, the numerator of which will be the index number for the month immediately preceding the adjustment and the denominator of which will be the index number for the month used in the numerator of the previous adjustment. In no event, however, will the rent increase exceed 5% per year.

TIP

Consider getting the rent early. It's often a good idea to have the subtenant pay you the rent a few days before you have to pay the landlord. Otherwise, if the subtenant is a day or two late, you'll have to pay the landlord out of your own funds. For example, if you have to pay rent on the first day of each month, it makes sense to provide that the subtenant's rent will be due on the 25th day of the preceding month.

6. Option to Extend Sublease

An option gives the subtenant the choice of staying in the space beyond the original term of the sublease. Before granting an option to the subtenant, remember that you can't give the subtenant any rights that you don't have. Make sure that your lease lasts at a minimum as long as the option period.

Insert the number of additional years for which the subtenant will extend the sublease by exercising the option, and the amount you will charge for the option (see the instructions for Clause 5 in Form 6A: Gross Lease). Then, enter the date by which the subtenant must give you notice of his or her intent to extend the sublease. A date 60 days before the expiration of the sublease is reasonable. If the option in the sublease will extend the sublease beyond the original term of the original lease, the deadline for exercising the option should obviously be earlier than your deadline to exercise the option in the original lease. The ability of the subtenant to extend the sublease should be conditioned on your having extended your lease first.

> **EXAMPLE:** Al has a five-year original lease with an option to extend for another five years. After two years, Al subleases to Martha for the remaining three years of the lease with an option to extend the subtenancy for an additional five years, but only if Al has exercised his own option to extend. Obviously, Martha's deadline for notifying Al that she's extending the subtenancy must be earlier than Al's deadline for notifying his landlord that he's exercising his option to extend the original lease. Al and Martha insert a date for renewing that sublease that's 60 days earlier than the date in Al's original lease for exercising his option.

In the third blank, describe any changed conditions for the new lease terms (including increased rent).

Sample

> During the extension period, the rent will be $1,500 per month.

7. Security Deposit

Insert the amount of the security deposit that you will require. Make sure the amount is at least as much as what you have given to the landlord. One or two months' rent is a typical security deposit.

8. Notices From Landlord

Nothing needs to be filled in here. This clause is designed to lessen the chance that any noncompliance on the part of the sublandlord or the subtenant will result in the landlord declaring that the sublandlord is in default under the lease. The clause requires the subtenant to immediately notify the sublandlord if it receives a notice of noncompliance from the landlord (this gives the sublandlord the opportunity to cure the problem). Similarly, if the landlord notifies the sublandlord of a breach by the subtenant, the sublandlord will immediately notify the subtenant, giving it a chance to make matters right.

9. Subletting and Assignment

Nothing needs to be filled in here. Both you and the landlord need to consent before the subtenant can sublet the space to someone else or assign the sublease.

10. Insurance

Subparagraph A contains a "mutual waiver of subrogation." Here you promise that your insurance company won't sue the subtenant to recoup any money it pays you for damage caused by the subtenant. The principle works the other way, too—if the subtenant's business equipment is damaged due to your carelessness, the subtenant's insurer won't try to collect from you after it pays the claim.

Subparagraph B requires the subtenant to carry public liability insurance. Typical limits are $100,000 per occurrence and no more than $300,000 in any one year. Depending on the nature of the subtenant's business, you might want to require higher limits. Enter the required limits in subparagraph B. The subparagraph also requires the subtenant to add you and the landlord to its liability insurance policy as additional insureds. This means that you and the landlord will be covered under the policy if an injured person sues either one of you. Most of the time, insurance companies will include additional insureds at no cost or a minimal cost.

Subparagraph C requires the subtenant to supply proof of having taken out and maintaining the required insurance. This proof is known as a certificate of insurance, which the subtenant can obtain from his or her insurance company.

11. Condition of Premises

You might agree to modify the rented space to suit your subtenant's needs—for example, by painting, installing flooring, removing or adding walls, or customizing electrical and plumbing systems. For example, let's say that the owners of a gourmet market (who lease their market space) realize that their customers want a selection of fine baked goods. Not wanting to go into the bakery business, the owners sublease a corner of the market to a successful bakery whose products are made offsite. The market owners (the sublandlords) enter the following clause in their sublease:

> Sublandlord will install counter space, lighting, and a display case for Subtenant.

If you will modify the space for your subtenant, check the first box and describe the modification. But if you are subletting to someone whose business activities are similar to yours, there might be no reason to modify the space. In this event, check the second box that the subtenant accepts the space "as is."

Remember that you cannot extend any rights or privileges to the subtenant that you do not have yourself under your original lease. If the original lease forbids modifications without the landlord's written consent (as is common in many leases), you'll need the landlord's okay before you can promise improvements for your subtenant. If you promise a modification without clearing it first with your landlord, you might not be able to deliver—and you might even be headed for a legal tangle with the frustrated subtenant.

12. Landlord's Consent

Nothing needs to be filled in here. This paragraph states that your landlord consents to the sublease; there is a place at the end of the lease for your landlord to sign. You can also get the landlord's written consent by using Form 6E: Landlord's Consent to Sublease.

13. Disputes

See Chapter 1 for more information about dispute resolution clauses. Note that you are not required to participate in alternative methods of dispute resolution unless the subtenant is up-to-date in rent payments or has placed the rent in escrow.

14. Additional Agreements

Fill in any other terms that you and the subtenant have agreed to.

Standard Clauses

The remainder of the sublease contains the standard clauses we discussed in Chapter 1. The only thing you'll need to fill in here is the name of the state whose law will apply to the contract in the paragraph called "Governing Law" (usually the state where the property is located).

Signatures

You, the subtenant, and the landlord should sign the lease. For more on signing contracts, see Chapter 1.

Is the Guarantor's Consent Needed?

A guarantor is someone who signed the original lease promising to make good on your financial obligations under the lease if you fail to do so. As long as you and the landlord don't make substantial changes to the original lease—such as changing the amount of the rent or the way it is calculated—the guarantor remains on the hook for the duration of the lease.

And, assuming your original lease does not prohibit subleasing outright, the guarantor remains financially obligated to the landlord even after you sublease the space. This is because the guarantor was on notice that a sublease might happen, as long as the original lease does one of the following:

- states that the landlord will not unreasonably withhold consent to sublet the space
- specifies that the landlord may use his or her sole discretion in evaluating a subtenant
- specifies that the tenant may sublease the property without the landlord's consent, or
- is completely silent on the issue of subleasing.

However, if the original lease flatly prohibits subleasing, but the landlord changes his or her mind and consents to your sublease, the guarantor would probably be released from his or her obligations (because this would constitute a substantial change to the terms of the original lease). A release would be likely when the sublease extends to the end of the original lease term.

Form 6E: Landlord's Consent to Sublease

Leases usually require the landlord's written consent before a sublease becomes legally enforceable. Form 6E accomplishes that. If a guarantor signed the original lease, you might need to get the guarantor to sign the sublease as well. You can read more about whether a guarantor's consent will be required in "Is the Guarantor's Consent Needed?" above.

Instructions for Form 6E: Landlord's Consent to Sublease

All the forms in this book are provided in Appendix B and on the Nolo website. To access the downloadable forms online, use the link provided in Appendix A. As you read the instructions for Form 6E, you might want to refer to the form in Appendix B or open the form on your computer so you can follow along. (Before you use the form in Appendix B, be sure to photocopy it so you'll have a clean copy to use later.)

1. Names

Insert the names of the landlord, tenant, and subtenant.

2. Consent to Sublease

First, fill in the date the sublease (Form 6D) between the sublandlord (the original tenant) and the subtenant was signed. If the sublease will be signed the same day the landlord signs the consent form, enter that day's date here. Attach a copy of the sublease to this consent form.

Then, fill in a description of what is being sub-leased. If you're subleasing all the space covered by the original lease, simply use the description in the lease here. Otherwise, you'll need to create a new description.

RELATED TOPIC

For examples of descriptions, see the instructions for Paragraph 2 of Form 6D: Sublease.

3. Status of Original Lease

You don't need to insert anything here. This para-graph includes several statements concerning your performance of your original lease obligations. First, it states that the original lease you signed with the landlord is in full effect, which means that there have been no changes other than those that you've attached to (or made on) the original lease. Next, it states that you are currently not in default under the lease you signed with the landlord, which means that you are current in your rent and have complied with other terms and conditions of the lease. Finally, the consent form includes a promise by both you and the landlord that the original lease will not be modified without the subtenant's written consent, which means that any extensions or amendments of the underlying lease must have the subtenant's signature as well as yours and the landlord's.

4. Notice of Default

This paragraph makes sure that both you and the subtenant will get notice if the landlord thinks there's a default, so you can have an opportunity to correct the problem. Without such a clause, if you or the subtenant fails to meet a financial obligation under the original lease, the landlord could immediately dip into your security deposit—and then demand that you bring the deposit back up to its original amount. Under some leases, a landlord may have the option of declaring the original lease breached (violated) instead, which opens the way for the landlord to terminate the lease. Carefully read the underlying lease to be sure you understand the landlord's rights if you or the subtenant fail to pay rent or meet another financial obligation.

Because breaches of financial and other lease obligations—such as the duty to maintain the rented space or comply with use restrictions—can often be corrected, you'll want a generous notice and cure period. This clause states that the landlord will notify you of a lease violation in writing and that you and the subtenant are allowed to fix the problem within the number of days that you specify here (this is called a cure provision). If you or the subtenant fail to correct the problem, the landlord may terminate the tenancy.

The cure provision in this form is compatible with the leases contained in this book. (The leases do not specify a cure period; you and the landlord are simply adding one here to the consent form.)

However, you might be working with a lease from another source that provides for a different cure period. If your original lease does specify a different cure period, it's a good idea to raise the issue with the landlord and the subtenant so that there is no uncertainty as to what the cure period will be. In most cases, if there is a conflict between provisions in an original lease and provisions in this sublease consent form, the more recent document—the consent form—will control, meaning that the cure period in the consent form will be used. In any case, insert the number of days that you and the subtenant will have to cure any default (correct the violation under the lease) before the landlord can take action against you or the subtenant.

Signatures

You, the subtenant, and the landlord should sign the sublease. For more on signing contracts, see Chapter 1.

Form 6F: Assignment of Lease

An assignment of a lease is used where all of the leased space is being turned over to another business for the entire balance of the lease term, as would be appropriate if the original tenant goes out of business, sells the business, or moves permanently. Use this form if you intend to move out of your leased location completely and do not plan to return.

If, on the other hand, you would like to turn over part of your space to another tenant while you occupy the rest, or if you want to lease out all of your space for a while and return later, you'll be subleasing the space, not assigning it. In that case, use Form 6D: Sublease instead.

In an assignment, the original tenant (in legal jargon, the assignor) transfers the lease to a new tenant (the assignee). The new tenant usually pays the rent directly to the landlord, but the original tenant nevertheless remains responsible to the landlord for the rent and possibly other monetary obligations if the new tenant doesn't pay. However,

with a financially strong new tenant, the landlord might be willing to release the original tenant from lingering responsibilities under the lease. This form contains a release (Paragraph 9) that you can use for this purpose. If the landlord does not release you from your financial obligations under the lease, you'll be like a guarantor, or cosigner, for the new tenant in case the new tenant fails to pay rent or honor other monetary obligations.

Most leases require the landlord's written consent before an assignment of a lease becomes enforceable. Check your lease carefully for any restrictions your landlord might have placed on your ability to assign the lease. Your lease might specify that the landlord can use sole discretion when evaluating the new tenant, which means that the landlord can reject your proposed tenant without grounds.

Your assignment form will include a provision that states that your landlord consents to the sublease, and it will have a place at the end for your landlord to sign. By signing this form, your landlord gives you the written consent you need to turn over your lease to a new tenant.

Instructions for Form 6F: Assignment of Lease

All the forms in this book are provided in Appendix B and on the Nolo website. To access the downloadable forms online, use the link provided in Appendix A. As you read the instructions for Form 6F, you might want to refer to the form in Appendix B or open the form on your computer so you can follow along. (Before you use the form in Appendix B, be sure to photocopy it so you'll have a clean copy to use later.)

1. Names

Insert the names of the original tenant, the new tenant (the person taking over the lease), and the landlord. See Chapter 1 for a discussion of how to identify businesses in legal documents.

2. Assignment

In the first blank, insert the beginning date of the original lease between the landlord and the original tenant.

Next, you'll indicate the location of the space covered by the lease. Choose one of the two options. Check the first box if you're assigning an entire building to the new tenant. Then fill in the location exactly as it appears in your lease.

Sample

> 320 North Main Street, Ann Arbor, Michigan

Check the second box if you're assigning part of a building. Then fill in the location and go on to describe the part of the building you're assigning.

Sample

> The following part of the premises at 320 North Main Street, Ann Arbor, Michigan. Specifically, New Tenant is leasing the west 3,000 square feet of the second floor of the building.

3. Effective Date

Fill in the date the assignment takes effect. As of that date, the new tenant will be responsible for paying rent and complying with all of the other obligations under the lease. In addition, you will no longer be entitled to continue to use the property. If you need time to pack up and arrange for a move, be sure to factor that in.

4. Acceptance

Nothing needs to be filled in here. The new tenant agrees to take over the lease and be bound by its terms.

5. Condition of Premises

Nothing needs to be filled in here. This paragraph states that the new tenant has inspected the rented premises and accepts them as is. This statement protects you from any future claim by the new tenant that you promised but failed to provide improvements or alterations. If the new tenant wants to modify the space, the new tenant must take this up with the landlord.

6. Landlord's Certification

In Subparagraph A, fill in the date through which you've paid rent. The new tenant will be responsible for rent after this date. In Subparagraph B, fill in the amount of any security deposit that the landlord is holding.

7. Reimbursement

As part of a lease assignment, the new tenant typically reimburses the original tenant for the security deposit that's been left with the landlord. Also, typically, the new tenant reimburses the original tenant for any rent and other items (such as taxes, insurance, or maintenance) paid in advance. Check the applicable boxes.

> **EXAMPLE:** On June 1, Rodrigo Portaformo & Associates paid rent for the entire month of June. The new tenant, Z-Pop, Inc., is to take over the space on June 16. Z-Pop will reimburse Rodrigo for rent Rodrigo paid for the last half of June, so the second box is checked.

8. Landlord's Consent

This paragraph specifies that the landlord consents to the assignment; there is a place at the end of the lease for your landlord to sign. You don't need to fill in anything.

If a guarantor signed the original lease, you might need to get the guarantor to sign the sublease as well. You can read more about whether or not a guarantor's consent will be required in "Is the Guarantor's Consent Needed?" above.

9. Release

Check the box if the landlord is willing to relieve you of any further responsibility to the landlord under the lease, once the assignment takes effect. Obviously, it's to your advantage to convince the landlord to cut you free when the new tenant takes over. Your best argument will be to point to the financial stability and good business record of the new tenant, which will make it unlikely that the landlord would ever have to call on you to bail out the new tenant.

Standard Clauses

The remainder of the assignment contains the standard clauses we discussed in Chapter 1. The only thing you'll need to fill in here is the name of the state whose law will apply to the contract in the paragraph called "Governing Law" (usually the state where the property is located).

Signatures

You, the new tenant, and the landlord should sign the lease. For more on signing contracts, see Chapter 1.

Form 6G: Notice of Exercise of Lease Option

Many leases give the tenant the option to extend the lease beyond its original term. You can use this form to notify your landlord that you are choosing to exercise the option. Landlords commonly give tenants a short window of time in which to exercise an option, as far in advance of the lease ending date as possible. This gives landlords plenty of time to put the space on the market before your lease is up if you decide not to exercise your option.

Check your original lease or option agreement carefully to determine when and how you must exercise the option. Also check for any specific instructions on how to communicate your decision to exercise the option. *Follow those instructions if they differ from the process and form presented here.*

When you secured the option to extend your original lease, you might have negotiated for changed terms for the new lease period, such as extended use of the facilities in a shared building. Any new understandings recorded in your original lease will take effect when the new lease term begins. Your original lease will continue to be your lease agreement after you exercise this option—you don't have to fill out a new lease agreement, unless you are making substantial changes to the terms of your lease.

If you would like to change other terms or conditions of the lease, besides the ending date, use Form 6I: Amendment to Lease to amend the original lease, or just create a brand-new lease. If your changes are numerous or complicated, we suggest that you create a brand-new lease. Doing so will help you avoid confusion about the terms of your extended lease.

You might be able to extend or renew your lease even if you didn't secure a formal option when you signed the original lease—all it takes is an agreement between you and the landlord that you'll stay on for a set period of time. If you are extending your lease without an option, use Form 6H: Extension of Lease instead of this notice.

Instructions for Form 6G: Notice of Exercise of Lease Option

All the forms in this book are provided in Appendix B and on the Nolo website. To access the downloadable forms online, use the link provided in Appendix A. As you read the instructions for Form 6G, you might want to refer to the form in Appendix B or open the form on your computer so you can follow along. (Before you use the form in Appendix B, be sure to photocopy it so you'll have a clean copy to use later.)

Introduction

Chances are, this is the first time you are extending your lease; if this is the case, this will be Extension 1, and you do not need to change anything. If it happens to be your second extension, change the number "1" to the number "2."

At the top of the form—in the first blank space—fill in the landlord's name.

1. Exercise of Lease Option

Put your name or the name of your business (according to the convention in the lease) in the first blank. Then insert the date through which you're extending the lease. Your landlord might have given you the option to extend your lease by a period of years—such as "three additional years"— or until a specific ending date. If you agreed upon an additional amount of time, convert that period to a calendar date and enter it here. Using a date helps to avoid any confusion about exactly when your lease ends. If your original option specified a new ending date, be sure to enter that date here.

Finally, insert the description of the premises— the same description that's in the original lease.

2. Notice to Landlord

Insert the beginning and ending dates of the original lease. The beginning date is usually the date of your first rent payment—you can usually find it at the end of the lease with the signatures.

Signature

Date and sign the notice (the landlord need not sign). For more on signing contracts, see Chapter 1.

Guarantor

Many landlords insist that tenants supply a guarantor—a person whom the landlord can look to in case the tenant fails to pay the rent or to meet other monetary obligations under the lease. Examine your original lease to see whether you see signatures, in addition to those of the landlord and tenant, that are identified as guarantors'

signatures. Guarantors sometimes record their obligation on an attachment to the lease instead of the lease itself. *Extending the term of your lease will not automatically extend the obligation period for any existing guarantors.* In fact, unless your existing guarantors sign this extension notice, their responsibility will end on the original ending date of the lease.

If one or more existing guarantors will agree to guarantee payments for the extended lease period, enter their names here. Each guarantor must sign the lease and provide an address so that the landlord can contact the guarantor. The landlord will contact the guarantor and ask for the rent if the tenant fails to pay it.

Even if your original lease did not have guarantors, your landlord can insist that guarantors sign this notice to extend the lease, which binds them to the terms and conditions of the original lease, up to the new ending date.

Form 6H: Extension of Lease

Even if you've signed a lease that doesn't include an option for the tenant to extend the lease, you and the landlord may nevertheless agree to a lease extension. As long as the lease terms will remain basically the same during the extension period, you don't have to prepare a whole new lease. Your original lease will continue to be your lease agreement after you sign this extension.

When you create this extension agreement, you'll have a chance to note any changes that you want to make to the original lease and that you want to apply to the new lease period.

TIP
It's sometimes best to do a completely new document. If your changes are numerous or complicated, we suggest that you create a brand-new lease. Doing so will help you avoid confusion about the terms of your lease. In the new lease, specifically state that it replaces the earlier one.

If your original lease contained an option to extend the lease or you have since bargained with the landlord for an option, use Form 6G: Notice of Exercise of Lease Option instead of this form.

Instructions for Form 6H: Extension of Lease

All the forms in this book are provided in Appendix B and on the Nolo website. To access the downloadable forms online, use the link provided in Appendix A. As you read the instructions for Form 6H, you might want to refer to the form in Appendix B or open the form on your computer so you can follow along. (Before you use the form in Appendix B, be sure to photocopy it so you'll have a clean copy to use later.)

Introduction

Chances are, this is the first time you are extending your lease—if this is the case, this will be Extension 1, and you do not need to change anything. If it happens to be your second extension, change the number "1" to the number "2."

1. Names

Insert the landlord's name and the name of your business. See Chapter 1 for a discussion of how to identify your business in legal documents.

2. New Lease Term

In the first two blanks, insert the beginning and ending dates of the original lease. The beginning date is usually the date of your first rent payment; you can normally find it at the end of the lease with the signatures.

In the next two blanks, fill in a description of the premises, which should be the same as the premises described in the original lease, and then fill in the date through which the lease is extended.

3. Modifications to Lease

Insert any new terms and conditions that will apply during the extension period. Identify each paragraph that you're amending by its number, as shown in the examples below. And keep in mind that if your changes are lengthy, it might be better to start over with a new lease form.

Samples

> Paragraph 4: The rent will be $2,000.00 per month.

> Paragraph 3: Tenant will have access to the basement exercise facility as of January 1, 20xx.

> Paragraph 22: As of the ending date in Paragraph 2, tenant must vacate the premises entirely.

> Paragraph 11: Landlord will not pay for water as of May 1, 20xx.

If you have no modifications, insert the word "None."

Signatures

Both the landlord and tenant need to sign the lease. For more on signing contracts, see Chapter 1.

Guarantor

Many landlords insist that tenants supply a guarantor—a person whom the landlord can look to in case the tenant fails to pay the rent or to meet other monetary obligations under the lease. Examine your original lease to see whether you see signatures, in addition to those of the landlord and tenant, that are identified as guarantors' signatures. Guarantors sometimes record their obligation on an attachment to the lease instead of the lease itself. *Extending the term of your lease will not automatically extend the obligation period for any existing guarantors.* In fact, unless your existing guarantors sign this extension notice, their responsibility will end on the original ending date of the lease.

If one or more existing guarantors will agree to guarantee payments for the extended lease period, enter their names here. Each guarantor must sign the lease and provide an address so that the landlord can contact the guarantor. The landlord will contact the guarantor and ask for the rent if the tenant fails to pay it.

Even if your original lease did not have guarantors, your landlord can insist that guarantors sign this extension of lease form, which binds them to the terms and conditions of the original lease, up to the new ending date.

Form 6I: Amendment to Lease

Suppose that while your lease is still in effect, you and the landlord agree to make some changes. You don't have to redo the entire lease, which might even risk opening up a wide range of issues best left alone. Instead, you can simply prepare and sign an amendment. For more on amending contracts, see Chapter 1.

If you'll make more than a few changes, it's often best to redo the whole lease so that you don't get confused about what's in and what's out.

Instructions for Form 6I: Amendment to Lease

All the forms in this book are provided in Appendix B and on the Nolo website. To access the downloadable forms online, use the link provided in Appendix A. As you read the instructions for Form 6I, you might want to refer to the form in Appendix B or open the form on your computer so you can follow along. (Before you use the form in Appendix B, be sure to photocopy it so you'll have a clean copy to use later.)

Amendment Number

At the top, fill in the number of the Amendment. If you have made no previous amendments, fill in "1"; number subsequent amendments successively.

1. Names

Insert the landlord's name and the name of your business. See Chapter 1 for a discussion of how to identify your business in legal documents.

2. Terms Amended

In the first two blanks, fill in the date of the original lease and the location of the premises.

Then, in plain English, put in the amended terms. You can change a paragraph or provision in the original lease or remove it altogether. If possible, identify each paragraph that you're amending by its number, as shown in most of the examples below. Then describe in detail the changes you'd like to make to it.

Samples

> Paragraph 3: Tenant will have access to the basement exercise facility as of June 1, 20xx.

> By September 1, 20xx, Landlord will reduce Tenant's space by moving the north wall of the space ten feet to the south. Beginning September 1, 20xx, and for the balance of the lease term, the rent will be reduced to $1,500 per month.

> Paragraph 9: Tenant may engage in retail activities as well as wholesale.

> Paragraph 16 of the original lease is deleted in its entirety.

It's a good idea to attach a copy of all amendments to each copy of the original lease so that the lease terms are all in one place.

3. Effective Date

Fill in the date the amendment takes effect. The date that your amendment becomes effective need not be the date that you and the landlord sign the amendment. The date you sign the amendment is simply the date that you both become bound to its terms, which will often include a change or addition to your lease that will take effect sometime in the future.

4. Other Terms of Lease

Nothing needs to be filled in here. This paragraph states that all other terms of your original lease will remain in effect, and that if there is any disagreement between what the original lease states and what the amendment states, the terms of the amendment will control.

Signatures

All parties to the original lease should sign the amendment, and the amendment should be dated.

Guarantor

Many landlords insist that tenants supply a guarantor—a person whom the landlord can look to in case the tenant fails to pay the rent or to meet other monetary obligations under the lease. Examine your original lease to see whether you see signatures, in addition to those of the landlord and tenant, that are identified as guarantors' signatures. Guarantors sometimes record their obligation on an attachment to the lease instead of the lease itself. All guarantors to the original lease must sign the amendment.

Each guarantor must sign the lease and provide an address so that the landlord can contact the guarantor. The landlord will contact the guarantor and ask for the rent if the tenant fails to pay it.

Even if your original lease did not have guarantors, if your amendment increases your financial responsibility, your landlord can insist that you find new guarantors to sign the lease who did not guarantee the original lease.

Form 6J: Attachment to Lease

You might need to include lengthy information in a commercial lease—perhaps a detailed list of improvements the landlord will make to the property—that would make the lease too long and difficult to read. One simple way to deal with this problem is to create an attachment to the lease, which legally is a part of it. Attachments are discussed in general in Chapter 1.

Some examples of material that might go into an attachment:

- a drawing showing the exact location of the leased space within a building
- plans and specifications for improvements to be installed in the leased space by you or the landlord, or
- a list of new equipment that the landlord will provide within the leased space.

TIP
You can make an attachment out of an existing document. When the material to be attached to the lease already exists as a document (for example, a sketch of the leased space or a list of improvements to be made), you can easily make it into an attachment by adding the following at the beginning of the document:

> Attachment to the lease dated [*fill in the date*] covering the premises at [*fill in the address*].

Fill in the appropriate number, date, and location. If you and the landlord then initial the attachment, its contents will become a part of the lease.

Instructions for Form 6J: Attachment to Lease

All the forms in this book are provided in Appendix B and on the Nolo website. To access the downloadable forms online, use the link provided in Appendix A. As you read the instructions for

Form 6J, you might want to refer to the form in Appendix B or open the form on your computer so you can follow along. (Before you use form in Appendix B, be sure to photocopy it so you'll have a clean copy to use later.)

Attachment Number

At the top, fill in the number of the attachment. If you have made no previous attachment, fill in "1"; number subsequent attachments successively. You should refer to the attachment by number in the main body of the lease.

1.   Names

Insert the landlord's name and the name of your business. See Chapter 1 for a discussion of how to identify your business in legal documents.

2.   Terms of Attachment

In the first two blanks, fill in the date of the original lease and the location of the premises.

Then, in the third blank, describe in detail the information you want to add to your lease. Your description will usually be a long list of items or a detailed legal description that doesn't easily fit into the original lease. For instance, if the landlord agrees to fix up the space for you, you'll want to specifically list the improvements that you have bargained for.

Sample

> Before Tenant's move-in date, Landlord will complete the following improvements to the property at Landlord's expense:
> - replace the front door with Arco Model #4590
> - partition the back office into three rooms by means of additional floor to ceiling walls
> - paint lines for Tenant's parking spaces in adjacent lot
> - paint all office walls with Hammet & Jones Color #230, Ecru Spice
> - paint kitchen walls with Hammet & Jones Color #509, Mayonnaise
> - install three additional electrical outlets in main reception area
> - install five GFI electrical outlets in kitchen, and
> - install three GFI electrical outlets in bathroom.

If you're adding information to an existing lease clause, identify the paragraph by its number.

Sample

> Paragraph 11. Landlord agrees to pay membership dues on Tenant's behalf in the Piedmont Merchants' Association for calendar year 20xx. Tenant agrees to pay dues for succeeding years up to and including the year in which Tenant's occupancy will end.

Signatures

All parties who signed the original lease should sign the attachment, and the attachment should be dated.

Purchasing Real Estate

 FORMS

To download the forms discussed in this chapter, go to this book's companion page on Nolo.com. See Appendix A for the link.

This chapter includes a variety of forms related to purchasing and renovating commercial real estate.

Buying or Leasing—Which Makes More Financial Sense?

In theory, there can be financial advantages to owning your own building. Income tax laws, for example, encourage real estate ownership by allowing you to deduct depreciation, interest, and property taxes. And, assuming you pay a reasonable price and purchase a building in a desirable location, chances are you'll realize a decent profit when you eventually sell. Finally, if you buy a building that's larger than you need, you might be able to rent out the remaining space for enough money to cover a good portion of your mortgage, taxes, and other operational costs.

But buying a building isn't the best thing for every small business. Money is a scarce resource. You might be better served using it to develop your core business. If you operate a recreational fishing business, for example, it might make more sense for you to buy two more boats than a building. Or if you own a successful instant print shop, it might be better to rent and open another well-equipped location than to place a bet on the future of the local real estate market by purchasing the building you currently occupy.

If you're fortunate enough to have found a building you want to buy, and have already negotiated the purchase terms with the seller, you'll want to use Form 7A: Contract to Purchase Building.

Most purchases aren't so straightforward, though. For example, perhaps you've located an attractive building and reached agreement with the owner on the price, but you want time to do some additional investigating before you fully commit.

To keep it from being purchased by someone else while you make a final decision, you need to negotiate—and likely pay for—an option to buy the building at a set price for a stated period of time. You can use Form 7B: Option to Purchase Building to formalize your option agreement.

If you plan to build your own building, use Form 7C: Contract to Purchase Vacant Land to enter a binding agreement to buy the land to build it on. If you aren't ready to commit but want to secure your right to purchase for a period of time, you can use Form 7D: Option to Purchase Vacant Land to buy yourself some time.

If you've obtained an option to purchase real estate and have decided to go ahead with the purchase, use Form 7I: Exercise of Option to Purchase Real Estate, to let the owner know that you're going to proceed.

No matter what type of property you want to buy or the details of the purchase contract you use, you might want to add material—such as a site plan, survey, or lengthy legal description—to the contract. You can customize Form 7E: Attachment to Contract, and use it to add such supplemental material to the purchase contract.

It's common for a real estate buyer to state in the purchase contract that the deal is contingent on a number of things happening. Two of the most common contingencies are obtaining adequate financing and receiving a favorable inspection report from a professional inspector. Typically, the contract provides that all contingencies must be removed in writing before closing. You can use Form 7G: Removal of Contingency, to remove contingencies either all at once or one by one as each is satisfied.

To extend the time for removing a contingency, use Form 7H: Extension of Time to Remove Contingencies.

After the signing of a contract to purchase real estate, you and the seller might agree to change one or more of its terms. All changes to the contract—even minor ones—should be in writing and signed by every person or entity that signed the original contract. Customize Form 7F: Amendment of Contract to reflect any changes you and the seller agree to make.

TIP

Do a new contract if changes are extensive. Amending an existing contract usually works fine for one or two minor changes. But multiple amendments can become confusing, especially if you need to change an amendment. When you're faced with more than a few edits (or even one significant one), it's far less confusing to create a new contract. Simply rewrite the paragraphs that are being changed and state in the first sentence of the revised contract that it replaces the earlier version.

Beware of Possible Environmental Problems

Before you buy real estate, you should research any possible environmental problems with the property. Purchasing contaminated property can lead to a number of headaches. For one thing, even though you didn't cause the contamination, you might get stuck with a huge bill for site cleanup under the federal Comprehensive Environmental Response Compensation and Liability Act (also called CERCLA, or Superfund) and similar laws. Additionally, lending institutions balk at lending money to buy or remediate contaminated property. And you might face lawsuits from neighboring property owners whose property is affected by contamination originating from the site.

Contamination can be a particular problem if the property you're buying is—or was—home to a manufacturing business, dry cleaner, or gas station. Surface activity or faulty underground storage tanks at these types of businesses can cause chemicals to leach into the soil. So before you make a binding commitment to buy real estate, perform appropriate due diligence so you know exactly what you're getting into—and have a viable plan for environmental cleanup, if necessary.

The purchase contracts in this chapter allow you to make your purchase contingent on an environmental inspection. Once you've entered into an option agreement, you can perform whatever investigations you want before you're committed to buy.

If you have any suspicion at all that the property is contaminated, you need to get a Phase I Environmental Site Assessment (often simply called a Phase I ESA) performed by an experienced consultant. The purpose of a Phase I ESA is to research the history of the property and identify any potential environmental risks that might have resulted. If the Phase I ESA indicates that there could be a problem on the property, you'll need to dig even deeper by getting a Phase II ESA, during which actual tests for contamination are performed. Because environmental law is so complex and your legal exposure is potentially enormous, you should consult an experienced environmental lawyer if the Phase I ESA shows a possible problem. You might also want to get legal help before that point if environmental contamination is of special concern to you.

A positive result from a Phase II ESA can lead to further testing and evaluations to determine the full extent of what's going on, the cost to clean up the site, and ways to prevent further contamination. This in-depth testing and, of course, the cleanup, can be very expensive. Before ordering a Phase II ESA, small businesses with limited budgets should seriously evaluate whether moving forward is a financially wise decision.

There are two kinds of protective clauses you can include in your contract or option, if the seller is willing:

Warranties and Representations. The seller promises (warrants and represents) that there is no environmental contamination on the site and that the site complies with all environmental laws and regulations.

Indemnification. The seller agrees to indemnify you for cleanup costs and related expenses if an environmental condition that existed while the seller owned the property comes to light while you own the property. If you have a deep-pocket seller—or at least one who's likely to be solvent in the future—this enables you to recoup all or part of your losses if you later have to clean up the site.

Legal Ownership: Whose Name Should Go on the Deed?

To complete the transfer of the property, you will need to create a deed—the legal document that officially transfers the property to the buyer. Every deed is filed with the county clerk or recorder. Check with a local real estate attorney or your county land records office about the rules for transferring property in your area.

If your business is a sole proprietorship (you and the business are the same legal entity), you'll most likely take title in your own name or jointly with your spouse. With other types of business entities, the decision as to whose name you put on the deed as legal owner requires more extensive analysis.

If your business is a partnership, a corporation, or an LLC, one choice is for the business itself to own the real estate—in which case, the name of the business would appear on the deed. Alternatively, one or more of the business owners can personally own the real estate and lease it to the business, using much the same type of written lease you'd use with an outside tenant. This can be a useful arrangement if some of the business owners don't want the business to invest in real estate. And for a regular, or C, corporation (not an S corporation), some tax advisers see an advantage if the business owners personally own the real estate and lease it to the corporation, since this avoids the possibility of double taxation, which can occur if the corporation owns real estate.

> **EXAMPLE:** Enterprise Corporation buys a building for $100,000. Two years later, Enterprise sells the building for $200,000. The corporation must pay tax on the $100,000 gain. Then, when the money is distributed to the shareholders, they must also pay tax on the money they receive. By contrast, if the corporation's shareholders buy the building, keep the title in their own names, and lease it to the corporation, there's only one tax to pay when they sell the building.

SEE AN EXPERT

Consult a professional. To help you decide whether legal title to real estate should be taken in the name of your business or in the name of one or more individuals who own the business, it's wise to consult a lawyer or CPA who is knowledgeable about taxes and business planning.

RESOURCE

Finding a good lawyer. When you need a lawyer, asking someone you trust for a referral is a good place to start. You can also try one of these excellent and free resources:

- **Nolo's Lawyer Directory.** Nolo has an easy-to-use online directory of lawyers, organized by location and area of expertise. You can find the directory and its comprehensive profiles at www.nolo.com/lawyers.

- **Lawyers.com.** At Lawyers.com you'll find a user-friendly search tool that allows you to tailor results by area of law and geography. You can also search for attorneys by name. Attorney profiles prominently display contact information, list topics of expertise, and show ratings—by both clients and other legal professionals.

- **Martindale.com.** Martindale.com offers an advanced search option that allows you to sort not only by practice area and location, but also by criteria like law school. Whether you look for lawyers by name or expertise, you'll find listings with detailed background information, peer and client ratings, and even profile visibility.

Form 7A: Contract to Purchase Building

Use this contract if you're buying an existing building. Many of the items in this contract are negotiable between you and the seller.

Instructions for Form 7A: Contract to Purchase Building

All the forms in this book are provided in Appendix B and on the Nolo website. To access the downloadable forms online, use the link provided in Appendix A. As you read the instructions for Form 7A, you might want to refer to the form in Appendix B or open the form on your computer so you can follow along. (Before you use the form in Appendix B, be sure to photocopy it so you'll have a clean copy to use later.)

1. Names

Insert the names of the seller and buyer. Consult the chart in Chapter 1 for more information about how to identify a business.

2. Purchase of Real Estate

Though not legally necessary, it's helpful to identify the property by a common, easily recognizable name. For example, if the property is an office building, it might go by a name such as "The Cathcart Towers." If the property has a common name, enter it in the first blank. If not, write "N/A" in the blank (if you're using the downloadable form, delete the language).

You must insert the property address whether or not you inserted a common name for the property. In addition to the mailing address, the address you enter here should include the county in which the

property is located. That is the county in which the deed will be filed.

On the next line, you must provide a detailed legal description of the property. You can find the legal description on the seller's deed or on the seller's title insurance policy.

Legal descriptions can be short ("Lot 50 of Georgetown Subdivision in the City of Detroit, Wayne County, Michigan") or can run on for several paragraphs or even pages. If the legal description is short, enter it directly on the lines provided. If it's long, it's a good idea to put the description in an attachment (you can use Form 7E: Attachment to Contract) and check the box indicating that it's attached.

When creating the attachment, it's important to copy the legal description carefully. Check (and double-check) to make sure you've copied it correctly, because an incorrect legal description can cause headaches later.

Attachment 1

to the Contract to Purchase Building dated March 1, 20xx, between Fred Langley and ABC Realty, Inc., a California corporation

Commencing at the Southeast corner of "4th" Street SE° SW°; thence N 00°36'30" E along the West line of said SE° SW°, a distance of 651.30 feet; thence N 88°10' E, a distance of 57.00 feet to the True Point of Beginning; thence continuing N 88°10' E, a distance of 213.56 feet to the westerly line of "F" Street; thence N 00°42'32" W along said last westerly line, a distance of 67.50 feet; thence S 88°10' W, a distance of 95.75 feet; thence S 00°36'30" E, a distance of 67.50 feet to the True Point of Beginning.

3. Purchase Price

Enter the full purchase price the buyer and seller have agreed on in the first blank. In the second blank, enter the amount the buyer will put down as a deposit. In the third blank, fill in the name of the escrow company, the title company, or the escrow agent or other third party who will hold the deposit. Be aware that institutional escrow agents have additional forms for the buyer and the seller to sign to define the escrow agent's responsibilities when handling deposits. Subtract the deposit from the full price and insert the balance in the last blank.

TIP

Keep the deposit as low as possible. A real estate broker or experienced lawyer can tell you what constitutes a typical deposit in your community, but in the final analysis, the amount is always negotiable. If things go wrong, you'll be glad if you negotiated to keep it as low as possible. That way, the amount that will be subject to forfeiture will be small if you find yourself needing to cancel the purchase at some point for a reason that's not squarely allowed by the contract language.

4. Financing Contingency

Chances are you'll be borrowing part of the purchase price from a bank or other lender. By including a financing contingency, you can back out of the deal (and get your deposit back) if you can't get financing. But the contract does obligate you to apply promptly for the financing and pursue the application in good faith.

TIP

It can pay to prequalify. Find out how much you can borrow from a bank or other lender before you sign a purchase contract. Most lenders are willing to look over your financial statement and give you at least a tentative loan commitment even before you find

the right building. By knowing in advance how much you'll be able to borrow, you won't waste time trying to buy a building you can't afford. You can also use proof of preapproval to assure the seller that you have the financial capacity to close the deal.

Fill in the amount you'll need to borrow. When determining this amount, don't forget closing costs, the expense of moving, and outlays that might be needed for repairs, renovation, and decorating. Next, specify the number of days you'll have in which to apply for the loan.

Finally, insert a date by which you agree to remove the financing contingency. After this date, you will no longer be allowed to cancel the deal and get your deposit back should your financing fall through. Call a few lenders to see how long the mortgage process is currently taking before you set the date: Most of the time, the lender needs at least 30 to 45 days to process and approve your application.

Your contract contains a clause (Paragraph 18) that makes the contract voidable by either party if the financing contingency is not removed by the required date. This means that if the buyer can't finalize financing for the property by that date, either party can cancel the contract and the seller will return the buyer's deposit.

5. Inclusions

Personal property that's attached to the building (called a fixture) is included in the sale, even if it's not listed in the contract. Personal property that isn't attached to the building normally remains the property of the seller unless the contract specifies that it will be transferred to the buyer. The legal line between fixtures that go with the building and personal property that doesn't is not always clear. For example, shelving and display cases might be attached (in which case they are fixtures) or free-standing (in which case they are likely personal property). Usually, if removing an item from the building would cause any damage, the item is a fixture.

Financing a Real Estate Purchase

There are many ways to finance a real estate purchase.

Pay Cash

If you have liquid funds, paying cash for the property is one option. This approach normally makes sense only if you don't need capital to build your business.

Borrow the Purchase Money From a Commercial Lender

Many entrepreneurs finance the purchase, borrowing from a bank or other commercial lender. The lender will want you to have some money of your own in the deal—perhaps 30% or 40% of the purchase price. In addition, you'll need to secure the loan by giving the lender a mortgage or deed of trust on the building.

If a mortgage is used as security for the loan, three basic documents are typically involved:

- **Deed:** The seller signs a legal form entitled a deed transferring the legal ownership of the property to you.
- **Promissory Note:** With a mortgage, you agree in writing to make specified payments to the lender until the loan has been fully paid off.
- **Mortgage/Deed of Trust:** With a mortgage, you sign a legal form giving the lender the right to take the property and sell it to pay off the loan balance if you don't make your loan payments as promised. The lender can, if necessary, file a lawsuit against you to enforce its right to sell the property. If a deed of trust procedure is instead used as security for the loan, you give the trustee (often a title company) the right to sell your property solely at the instruction of the lender—the lender doesn't have to get a court order.

Borrow From the Seller Instead of a Bank

Sellers who don't need all of the money from the sale immediately might be willing to self-finance the deal. As with outside financing, the seller will deed the property to you, and you'll give the seller a down payment plus a promissory note and either a mortgage or deed of trust to secure payment of the balance.

In many states, seller financing can also be accomplished by a land contract—an installment purchase agreement in which you promise to pay off the balance of the purchase price by making specified payments to the seller. If you don't keep up the payments, the seller can take back full ownership of the property through procedures called forfeiture or foreclosure.

It's also possible to work out a combination of commercial and seller financing. You might, for example, borrow part of the purchase money from a bank, giving the lender a first mortgage or first deed of trust as security for the loan. Then, the seller might agree to accept a note for part of the balance, in return for your granting a second mortgage or second deed of trust. Using this procedure, you could buy a $200,000 building this way:

Down payment from savings	$ 20,000
Loan from bank secured by first mortgage	100,000
Note to seller secured by second mortgage	80,000
Total Package	$200,000

In the first blank, list any personal property you will purchase from the seller. If you aren't sure whether a certain item of property qualifies as a fixture, it's best to list it here if you intend to purchase it. As long as an item is clearly made part of the deal, it will transfer to the buyer, regardless of whether it's personal property or a fixture. If no additional personal property is to be included, insert "None."

In the second blank, indicate whether any personal property will be transferred to you subject to any taxes, liens, or encumbrances. For example, if the seller purchased a commercial refrigerator on an installment plan, and you plan to take over payments on it, note it here.

At closing, the seller should give the buyer a bill of sale for the listed personal property. You can use Form 8C: Bill of Sale for Goods for this purpose.

6. Exclusions

The seller might want to exclude some items that would otherwise be included in the sale, such as a fancy light fixture, a built-in trophy case, or some cabinetry or machinery that's bolted to the building. List any exclusions here. If the seller does not want to exclude any particular items, insert "None."

7. Condition of Equipment

Here, the seller promises (warrants) that the equipment included in the sale will be in good working condition when you take over the building, with the exception of anything listed here.

The effect of this warranty is that the seller will have to pay to repair anything that isn't in good working condition when you take possession of the building. For example, if the air conditioner isn't working when you move in , the seller must pay to fix it. If it's beyond repair, the seller will have to replace it with a comparable unit. However, if the air conditioner is working when you move in but breaks down a week later, it's your responsibility (unless you have proof that the seller misrepresented the unit's condition while you were under contract).

List any equipment that the seller is not guaranteeing to be in good working condition. Be as specific as possible. For example, list the serial number, brand name, and location of each item whenever feasible. Write "No exceptions" if the seller is guaranteeing that all of the equipment will be in good working condition.

8. Physical Problems With Property

When you purchase a building, you accept it in as-is condition, with one exception: Sellers are legally obligated to disclose any hidden or latent defects they have actual knowledge of. For example, a seller who has seen the roof leak after multiple storms must let the buyer know about the problem, even if the buyer's inspection didn't reveal the leak (perhaps because the inspection was done during a dry season). Sellers don't have to investigate or test for issues, and aren't liable for any issues they never knew about.

Both you and the seller benefit from the seller's disclosure obligation. If the seller lists a hidden defect, you can take steps to learn about how serious it is. Armed with this knowledge, you could perhaps negotiate a lower price to account for the anticipated costs of repair, or even walk away from the deal if the issue is beyond the scope of what you're willing to take on.

It's also in the seller's best interest to be transparent about any issues with the property. Once the Contract to Purchase Building is signed by both parties (and is therefore binding), the seller is released from any responsibility for or liability arising from the problems disclosed in this section.

If the seller discloses multiple physical problems, you might want to list and describe them in a separate attachment (use Form 7E: Attachment to Contract). If the seller agrees to fix any issues before the sale closes, you can describe the seller's commitment to make repairs in Paragraph 22 of the contract, "Additional Agreements."

Sample

> Before closing, Seller will replace, at the Seller's expense, the roof. Seller will use a licensed, competent contractor to perform all work. The new roof shall consist of new materials similar in style and warranty to those currently at the Property. The Seller shall ensure that all necessary permits, inspections, and approvals are obtained.

Insert the words "No exceptions" if the seller doesn't know of any hidden or hard-to-find physical problems with the building that wouldn't be apparent through an inspection.

TIP

Make your purchase contingent on receiving a satisfactory inspection. Don't forego your opportunity to investigate every nook and cranny of the property—a thorough inspection can save you huge sums of money in the long run. We'll cover contingencies below in the discussion of Paragraph 17 of the contract.

9. Cleaning of Premises

Nothing needs to be inserted here. This paragraph requires the seller to clean up the building before closing so you don't walk into a trash heap.

10. Special Assessments

Nothing needs to be inserted here. This paragraph specifies whether you or the seller will pay for charges assessed for public improvements, such as streets and sidewalks, depending on when these charges become a lien on the property. Your state's law or your county's municipal code will determine when and whether a special assessment becomes a lien. In many areas, as soon as a special assessment or a portion of a special assessment becomes due, it becomes a lien on the property. If it has become a lien, you need to be sure it will be paid, because these liens can affect your ability to sell the property or use the property as collateral for a loan. And if a lien remains unpaid long enough, the county can foreclose on the property to pay the lien.

To determine if an assessment has become a lien, you should do a title search on the property. In Paragraph 17, "Additional Contingencies," you can make the purchase contingent on your satisfaction with the title search.

11. Other Government Charges

Nothing needs to be inserted here. This paragraph specifies who pays for other municipal charges that might not be classified as special assessments. The seller will pay all charges made against the property by any government authority for installation or extension of water, sanitary, or sewer service, if such charges arise before or on the date of closing. The buyer will pay for any such charges incurred after the date of closing.

12. Real Estate Taxes

This paragraph allocates the real estate taxes between you and the seller. Normally, nothing needs to be filled in or added here.

Allocating real estate taxes between the buyer and the seller is called tax proration. It can seem confusing if you've never done it before. Although there are many local methods for prorating taxes, the formula in this contract is one of the simplest and fairest. It's also the most common.

The formula is as follows: If the seller pays a real estate tax prior to the closing date, the tax is treated as if it applies to the entire year following the date the tax is paid. Then the tax is divided up based on the amount of time the seller owns the property during the year following payment of the tax and the amount of time the buyer owns the property.

The buyer reimburses the seller for tax paid on months the seller does not own the property. For simplicity's sake, each month in that year is treated as having 30 days.

EXAMPLE: Suppose the seller pays a real estate tax of $1,200 that's due on July 1, 2022. The buyer and the seller then close the purchase a month and a half later, on August 15, 2022. Applying the language of the contract, the July 1 tax is treated as covering the year from July 1, 2022 through June 30, 2023. Because the seller paid taxes for a period of time when the seller won't own the property (August 15, 2022 to June 30, 2023), the buyer will reimburse the seller for 10.5 months of the real estate tax ($1,050) at closing.

13. Other Prorations

There might be other costs or income associated with the property that will need to be prorated between you and the seller at closing. Consider what expenses the seller might prepay (pay for in advance), such as insurance and garbage services. You'll also need to prorate income the seller might receive in advance, such as rent. For example, if there's a tenant in place when you buy the property, the tenant might pay rent for the entire month of September on September 1. If you close mid-September, the month's rent must be divided appropriately between you and the seller at closing.

Write the prorations that will need to be made at closing on the line provided.

14. Closing and Possession

Your closing date is the day you pay the money to the seller for the property and receive the deed in return. Insert the closing date here.

This contract specifies that the buyer will receive physical possession of the building at closing—usually, this is the simplest procedure. If the seller needs to remain in the property after closing, consider consulting an attorney to draw up an agreement detailing your post-closing arrangements.

15. Transfer of Title

Nothing needs to be inserted here. At the closing, the seller will deliver the property's title to the buyer with a document called a warranty deed. By transferring title to the buyer with this kind of deed, the seller guarantees (warrants) that the buyer is receiving (marketable) title. In other words, that the seller identified in the contract has full ownership and power to sell the property, and is transferring it unencumbered by any liens. If the buyer later discovers that the title is not clear (due to something like unpaid taxes or a mechanic's lien), the buyer can sue the seller for damages, and possibly pursue a title insurance claim.

Generally, state and local transfer taxes are the seller's responsibility. Your contract provides that the seller will pay them.

16. Title Insurance

A title insurance policy insures against "clouds" on title, such as liens, litigation, and debts. If you discover a cloud on title after closing—for example, someone comes forward and claims she owns the property—you can make a claim on your title insurance. So long as the problem isn't one that is excepted from coverage under your policy, the insurer is obligated to investigate the matter, take steps to clear the title, and possibly pay you for any losses you incur.

Who pays for the insurance policy depends on the custom in your area. For example, in Los Angeles, California, the seller pays for the title insurance policy, while in San Francisco, the buyer pays for the policy. In some places, the buyer and seller split the cost of the title insurance equally. In other areas, the buyer and seller might negotiate who's going to pay the title insurance premiums. Call a local real estate lawyer or title insurance company to find out what the custom is in your area, and check the appropriate box.

17. Additional Contingencies

Contingencies are conditions that must be met or resolved by a date set out in the contract. If the conditions aren't satisfied, the buyer can cancel the contract. The buyer imposes contingencies before fully committing to the purchase to ensure that there aren't problems with the property or issues that might prevent the buyer from using it as planned.

How Title Insurance Works

Title insurance can involve three distinct but related documents: a title insurance commitment, an owner's title insurance policy, and a lender's insurance policy.

Title Insurance Commitment. A few weeks before closing, the title insurance company issues a title insurance commitment—a written promise to provide a title insurance policy—to the buyer. This lets the buyer know ahead of time what the insurer is willing to insure against and what it won't cover when it issues the final policy at closing.

Title policies often list specific exceptions—meaning the insurer won't pay for damages that arise from certain matters. For example, most policies except from coverage anything that relates to an easement known about at the time of closing. For this reason, the buyer should obtain, or ask a lawyer to obtain, copies of all significant legal documents relating to the property—such as building and use restrictions and easement agreements—so that the buyer or the buyer's lawyer can personally review them and advise the buyer about the probability of future issues.

In effect, a commitment letter might say, "We'll guarantee clear title in the buyer's name if the seller gives the buyer a warranty deed and pays off the existing mortgage at or before closing. The title will, however, be subject to all building and use restrictions as well as easements."

Because the commitment letter will be written in legal jargon, if there are significant conditions or exceptions to what the title company will cover—for instance, if the title insurance company won't cover any problems with unknown easements or requires the removal of a large mortgage that the buyer is worried the seller won't pay off—the buyer should have an experienced local property lawyer review the letter. (See "Standard Exceptions to Title Insurance Coverage," below, for examples of what the title insurance might not cover.)

Owner's Title Insurance Policy. The owner's insurance policy insures that the buyer will own clear legal title to the building, subject to any lender's lien. Under this policy, the title insurance company must reimburse the new owner for any losses due to a problem with the title. When the sale closes, the title company makes sure that all of its requirements have been met for issuing the owner's insurance policy to the buyer; typically, it will be a few weeks before the actual policy is prepared and mailed to the buyer.

Lender's Insurance Policy. If the buyer is financing the purchase through an outside lender, the buyer will pay for a separate insurance policy—one that guarantees that the buyer's bank or other lender has a valid first lien on or security interest in the building. In other words, the insurance guarantees that the lender won't be left holding the bag if it turns out someone else already has a mortgage or lien that would interfere with the lender's ability to foreclose on the property. Although the buyer will pay for it, this second policy is solely for the lender's protection and is entirely separate from the owner's title insurance policy issued to the buyer.

Standard Exceptions to Title Insurance Coverage. In many parts of the country, the owner's title insurance policy will be issued with what the title company calls standard exceptions. This means that the title insurance doesn't cover certain potential problems. The title company will list these standard exceptions in the title insurance commitment letter. The most common problems that typically aren't covered are boundary disputes and construction liens resulting from recent work on the building.

Fortunately, it's almost always possible to have the title insurance company issue the title insurance policy without standard exceptions for a minimal additional charge, which means that the buyer gets broader coverage. To issue this broader coverage, the title insurance company likely will require two things:

- a land survey, which the buyer might already have: Many lenders order a physical survey of the land and its boundaries (in real estate jargon, a surveyor's "mortgage report"), and
- a written statement from the seller that there has been no recent work on the building or that any recent work has been paid for—a guarantee that any reasonable seller should be able to provide.

This paragraph is called "Additional Contingencies" because there is an earlier contingency in this contract—the financing contingency (Paragraph 4).

Contingencies ensure that the buyer receives and has the opportunity to review important information about the property before going ahead with the purchase.

Although you don't have to have any contingencies in your contract, we recommend including the following if they are relevant to your situation.

Contractor's Inspection. An inspection by a contractor reveals what condition the building is in and whether the buyer is likely to face any expensive repairs. For the buyer, a lot of money can ride on a good building inspection, so it's worth the investment to hire an experienced inspector with a reputation for attention to detail. The buyer should also consider having experts perform separate inspections of electrical, plumbing, heating, and other specialized systems. If the inspectors find problems, the buyer can propose to the seller a list of things that need fixing.

Architect's Inspection. An architect's inspection can help the buyer determine the feasibility and cost of potential renovations or remodeling.

Environmental Inspection. An environmental inspection will let the buyer know if there is soil contamination or other environmental hazards, as well as how much potential mitigation is likely to cost.

Review of Building and Use Requirements. A review of planning and zoning rules will alert the buyer to any restrictions on what the building can be used for, as well as any requirements relating to remodeling.

Survey. A survey of the property will disclose any boundary problems, such as a neighboring building or fence that encroaches on the property, and will also let the buyer know if part of the building is on someone else's property.

Title Insurance Commitment Review. Including a review of the commitment letter from the title insurance company as a contingency enables the buyer to cancel the deal if either the buyer or the buyer's lawyer isn't satisfied with the commitment the title insurance company is willing to make. As noted earlier, the buyer will want to hire a lawyer if the title insurance commitment contains significant exceptions. If the title insurance commitment is relatively straightforward or the buyer is experienced in real estate matters, the buyer might feel comfortable approving the commitment without a lawyer's involvement.

Even if the buyer does not impose the insurance commitment review contingency, the contract requires that the buyer receive a policy commitment letter before closing; the buyer just won't have the option of canceling the deal without penalty before the closing if the buyer isn't satisfied with the title insurance commitment.

Appraisal. The appraisal contingency states that the buyer will purchase the property only if its professionally appraised value is at least as much as the amount the buyer has contracted to pay for it. A lender will likely require an appraisal. Even if you're paying cash for the property, consider getting an appraisal performed to ensure you don't overpay.

Review of Common Interest Community Documents. If the property is part of an owners' association or common interest community, the buyer will likely be required to become a member of the association and abide by its rules. These rules are laid out in various documents, such as declarations and bylaws. The buyer will want to find out as much as possible about what is required to join and the specifics of the rules the buyer must adhere to. For this reason, the buyer will want to check the box for this contingency, which requires the seller to provide all community documents and gives the buyer time to review them. If you don't like what you see, you can cancel the contract.

Check the box for each contingency you want to include and fill in a date by which the contingency must be removed. When selecting the date, keep in mind how long the inspection or review process is likely to take. For instance, an architect's inspection might not take more than a week or two, but it could take a while to conduct an environmental inspection and review an environmental report. If you selected the title insurance commitment review contingency, you should enter the number of days the buyer has to review the document after receiving it (rather than entering a specific date).

18. Removal of Contingencies

Nothing needs to be filled in here. This paragraph tells what happens if a contingency isn't removed by the specified date: The contract becomes voidable—that is, it may be canceled—by either party. If either party chooses to cancel the contract because a contingency has not been removed, the seller will return the buyer's deposit.

To remove a contingency, the buyer notifies the seller (in writing) that the buyer is satisfied that a particular requirement has been met. (You can use Form 7G: Removal of Contingency for that purpose.) Once a contingency has been removed, the buyer cannot fail to complete the sale because of a problem with that particular issue without penalty.

19. Loss Before Closing

Nothing needs to be filled in here. If the building burns down before closing, that's the seller's problem —not yours. Since the risk of loss falls on the seller, the seller is obligated either to rebuild or repair the building at the seller's expense and then honor the purchase contract. If that's not feasible, the parties might decide to reduce the purchase price so the buyer pays for the land only or they might decide to scrap the whole contract.

20. Default

Nothing needs to be filled in here. This paragraph tells what happens if you back out of the deal without a legally proper reason. (A legal reason would be not being able to remove the financing contingency because you don't qualify for a loan.) If you default, the seller can sue you for money damages, which normally is the difference between the fair market value of the building (say, $300,000) and what you agreed to pay (say, $325,000). Or you and the seller can agree that if you default without a good reason, the seller can simply keep your deposit without having to show an actual monetary loss—a remedy known as liquidated damages.

This paragraph also covers what happens if the seller refuses to proceed with the sale without a valid reason. If the seller defaults, you can enforce the contract by asking a judge to order the seller to deed the building to you (upon payment of the purchase price, of course). This is known as specific performance. Or, if you don't want to enforce the contract, you can sue for money damages—again, normally it's the difference between what you agreed to pay (say, $290,000) and the fair market value of the building (say, $300,000). Or you can skip the hassles and just get back your deposit.

21. Disputes

See the discussion of dispute resolution clauses in Chapter 1.

22. Additional Agreements

Insert any additional agreements between you and the seller. Be as specific and clear as possible. Consider hiring a real estate attorney to assist in drafting any complex terms.

Standard Clauses

The remainder of the agreement contains the standard clauses we discussed in Chapter 1. The only thing you'll need to fill in here is the name of the state whose law will apply to the contract in the paragraph called "Governing Law."

Signatures

Both parties should sign, and the contract should be dated. See Chapter 1 for instructions on signing contracts.

Attachment

If you checked the second box in Paragraph 2, include an attachment describing the property. You can use Form 7E: Attachment to Contract to create an attachment. When preparing two or more attachments, number them consecutively: Attachment Number 1, Attachment Number 2, and so on.

Form 7B: Option to Purchase Building

When you execute this option contract with a seller, the seller agrees not to sell the property to anyone else during the period of time you agree on. Usually, buyers pay an agreed-upon price to obtain an option. During the option period, you have the opportunity to investigate the condition of the building—and address any other concerns you might have—before you commit to proceed with the purchase. Buyers also purchase options when they're considering more than one property but aren't ready to make a firm offer on one.

Depending on how your contract is worded, if you decide not to purchase the property, the seller keeps the option fee. If you go ahead with the purchase, the fee will often, but not always, be applied to your down payment.

Even though the option contract doesn't commit you to buying the property, it includes many of the details of the potential sale. That way, if you decide to purchase the property, many of the details you'll need for Form 7A: Contract to Purchase Building will have already been decided or addressed. You might even want to attach Form 7A to this form (by using Paragraph 21 Additional Agreements) so that everyone knows what to expect if you exercise your option.

If you choose to exercise the option, you will need a deed to complete the transfer of the property. Check with a local real estate attorney or your county land records office about the rules for transferring property in your area.

Instructions for Form 7B: Option to Purchase Building

All the forms in this book are provided in Appendix B and on the Nolo website. To access the downloadable forms online, use the link provided in Appendix A. As you read the instructions for Form 7B, you might want to refer to the form in Appendix B or open the form on your computer so you can follow along. (Before you use the form in Appendix B, be sure to photocopy it so you'll have a clean copy to use later.)

1. Names

Insert the names of the seller and purchaser. Consult the chart in Chapter 1 for more information about how to identify a business.

2. Option to Purchase Building

The buyer will pay the seller a fee in exchange for the seller's agreement not to sell the property during the option period. The buyer will pay this money to the seller at the time the parties sign the option contract.

Insert the amount of the option fee.

To complete the rest of this paragraph, refer to the instructions for Paragraph 2 of Form 7A.

3. Exercise of Option

Insert the date by which you must exercise the option. Negotiate for enough time to perform all the investigations you need in order to feel comfortable with your decision—whether you decide to exercise the option or not.

Select one or both of the methods by which you'll deliver written notice to the seller if you decide to exercise the option. If you hand-deliver the notice, require the seller to sign a second copy acknowledging receipt and noting the date and time the notice was received. If you send the notice to the seller's office, it must be sent by certified mail or private overnight mail service. The contract provides that the notice will be treated as delivered when you place it in the possession of the U.S. Postal Service or a private carrier. This timing is important if you're running up against the option deadline or if there is a dispute about when you sent the notice to the seller.

4. Purchase Price

Put the full purchase price in the first blank. Then indicate whether the option fee stated in Paragraph 2 will be applied toward the purchase price if you elect to exercise the option. It's customary to apply the option fee toward the purchase price, but this could be a point for negotiation.

5. Inclusions

See instructions for Paragraph 5 of Form 7A.

6. Exclusions

See instructions for Paragraph 6 of Form 7A.

7. Condition of Equipment

See instructions for Paragraph 7 of Form 7A.

8. Access to Property

During the option period, the contract allows you to bring experts into the building and onto the surrounding land for inspections and surveys. The buyer must give the seller reasonable notice before conducting an inspection. It's the buyer's responsibility to pay for the inspectors' services.

Each of the following inspections will help the buyer make an intelligent decision about whether to buy the building.

Contractor's Inspection. A contractor who fully examines the structure can tell you what condition it's in, what maintenance it requires, and whether it needs repairs.

Architect's Inspection. If you're thinking of doing any renovation or remodeling work, it's essential to have an architect inspect the building to determine whether your plans are feasible and within your budget.

Environmental Inspection. It's critical to conduct an environmental inspection before buying a commercial building. The inspection will determine whether there's contamination or other environmental hazards that pose a health risk or could require a costly cleanup effort.

Survey. A survey of the property will disclose any boundary problems, such as a neighboring building or fence that encroaches on the property, and will also let the buyer know if part of the building is on someone else's property.

9. Physical Problems With Property

See instructions for Paragraph 8 of Form 7A.

10. Cleaning of Premises

Nothing needs to be inserted here. This paragraph requires the seller to clean up the building before closing so you don't walk into a trash heap.

11. Special Assessments

Nothing needs to be filled in here. See instructions for Paragraph 10 of Form 7A for a discussion of this paragraph.

12. Other Government Charges

Nothing needs to be filled in here. See instructions for Paragraph 11 of Form 7A for a discussion of this paragraph.

13. Real Estate Taxes

Nothing needs to be filled in here. See instructions for Paragraph 12 of Form 7A for a discussion of this paragraph.

14. Other Prorations

See instructions for Paragraph 13 of Form 7A for a discussion of this paragraph.

15. Closing and Possession

See instructions for Paragraph 14 of Form 7A.

16. Transfer of Title

Nothing needs to be inserted here. See instructions for Paragraph 15 of Form 7A for a discussion of this paragraph.

17. Title Insurance

A. To complete Section A, see the instructions for Paragraph 16 of Form 7A.
B. Contingencies are conditions that the buyer imposes on the seller or the property. The sale is contingent on these conditions being met. If these conditions aren't satisfied, the buyer can cancel the contract, even if the buyer has already given the seller notice of the buyer's intention to exercise the option to purchase.

Although you don't have to include these contingencies in your contract, we strongly recommend that you do so. They ensure that you receive and can review important information about the property before going ahead with the purchase. Here are some of the reasons you might want to include the listed contingencies in your contract:

Survey. A survey of the property will disclose any boundary problems, such as a neighboring building or fence that encroaches on the property, and will also let the buyer know if part of the building is on someone else's property.

Title Insurance Commitment Review. Review "How Title Insurance Works," above. Including a review of the commitment letter from the title insurance company as a contingency enables you to cancel the deal if either you or your lawyer isn't satisfied with the commitment the title insurance company is willing to make. As noted in "How Title Insurance Works," a buyer will want to hire a lawyer if the title insurance commitment contains significant exceptions. If the title insurance commitment is relatively straightforward or you are experienced in real estate matters, you might feel comfortable approving the commitment without a lawyer's involvement.

Even if you do not impose the insurance commitment review contingency, the contract requires that you receive a policy commitment letter before closing. If you have already given the seller notice of your intention to exercise the option to purchase, you just won't have the option of canceling the deal without penalty.

If you check a box to include either of these contingencies, you must receive the related documents (the title insurance commitment and/or a survey report) by a mutually agreed-upon date so that you have adequate time to review the documents. Insert the date in the first blank. Also, insert the number of days you will have to review these documents after receiving them before you must remove the contingency. When selecting the number of days you have to review the documents after receiving them, keep in mind how long it will take to review each document and investigate any problems.

To remove a contingency, you notify the seller (in writing) that you are satisfied that a particular requirement has been met. (You can use Form 7G: Removal of Contingency.) Once you remove a contingency, you cannot fail to complete the sale because of a problem with that particular issue without penalty.

Your contract provides that the contract becomes voidable—that is, it may be canceled—by either party if a contingency isn't removed by the specified date for removal. If either party chooses to cancel the contract because a contingency has not been removed, the seller will return your deposit.

18. Loss Before Closing

Nothing needs to be filled in here. See instructions for Paragraph 19 of Form 7A for a discussion of this paragraph.

19. Default

Nothing needs to be filled in here. See instructions for Paragraph 20 of Form 7A for a discussion of this paragraph.

20. Disputes

See the discussion of dispute resolution clauses in Chapter 1.

21. Additional Agreements

Insert any additional agreements between you and the seller. Be as specific and clear as possible. Consider hiring a real estate attorney to assist in drafting any complex terms. Also, you might want to use this section to refer to and incorporate a copy of the purchase agreement (such as Form 7A: Contract to Purchase Building) that you plan to use in the event you exercise your option.

Standard Clauses

The remainder of the contract contains the standard clauses we discussed in Chapter 1. The only thing you'll need to fill in here is the name of the state whose law will apply to the contract in the paragraph called "Governing Law."

Signatures

Both parties should sign, and the contract should be dated. See Chapter 1 for instructions on signing contracts.

Attachment

If you checked the second box in Paragraph 2, include an attachment describing the property. You can use Form 7E: Attachment to Contract to create an attachment.

Form 7C: Contract to Purchase Vacant Land

Buying land is a bit less involved than buying a building—mostly because there's no building or equipment to inspect. But you still have plenty of homework to finish before you complete your purchase. It's critical that you find out whether local zoning ordinances and building codes allow you to proceed with the type of use and construction you envision for the site. If you discover that current ordinances prohibit your planned use, you'll want the contract to be contingent on the ability to get the land rezoned to permit your desired use or to get an appropriate zoning variance from a local appeals board before you're obligated to close on the deal. And you also need to investigate the status of utilities to make sure you'll have all the services your business needs. Outside of urban areas where there might not be municipal utilities, you'll want to find out if the land can be served by an on-site well and septic system.

Another major concern is whether the land has ever been used as a dump site for toxic substances. To protect yourself from surprise cleanup costs and other liabilities, make the contract contingent on your receiving a satisfactory report from an environmental expert hired by you to inspect the site.

SEE AN EXPERT

Get help from professionals. Building on undeveloped land can be complicated. If you've never bought land before, it's important to seek the advice of engineers, architects, contractors, and possibly lawyers to make sure you'll be able to put the land to your intended use.

Instructions for Form 7C: Contract to Purchase Vacant Land

All the forms in this book are provided in Appendix B and on the Nolo website. To access the downloadable forms online, use the link provided in Appendix A. As you read the instructions for Form 7C, you might want to refer to the form in Appendix B or open the form on your computer so you can follow along. (Before you use the form in Appendix B, be sure to photocopy it so you'll have a clean copy to use later.)

1. Names

Insert the names of the seller and the purchaser. Consult the chart in Chapter 1 for more information about how to identify a business.

2. Purchase of Real Estate

See the instructions for Paragraph 2 of Form 7A.

3. Purchase Price

See the instructions for Paragraph 3 of Form 7A.

4. Financing Contingency

See the instructions for Paragraph 4 of Form 7A.

5. Special Assessments

See the instructions for Paragraph 10 of Form 7A.

6. Other Government Charges

See the instructions for Paragraph 11 of Form 7A. Be aware that streets, sidewalks, water, and sewer lines might need to be extended to the land to make it usable. Working with all the appropriate agencies—such as city and county governments and utility providers—can be extremely challenging and possibly prohibitively expensive. Check with the local authorities on what to expect.

7. Real Estate Taxes

Nothing needs to be filled in here. See the instructions for Paragraph 12 of Form 7A for a discussion of this paragraph.

8. Closing and Possession

See the instructions for Paragraph 14 of Form 7A.

9. Transfer of Title

Nothing needs to be inserted here. See the instructions for Paragraph 15 of Form 7A for a discussion of this paragraph.

10. Title Insurance

See the instructions for Paragraph 16 of Form 7A.

11. Additional Contingencies

See the instructions for Paragraph 17 of Form 7A. Make sure you have a chance to make all necessary investigations about your ability to develop the land.

12. Removal of Contingencies

Nothing needs to be filled in here. See the instructions for Paragraph 18 of Form 7A for a discussion of this paragraph.

13. Default

Nothing needs to be filled in here. See the instructions for Paragraph 20 of Form 7A for a discussion of this paragraph.

14. Disputes

See the discussion of dispute resolution in Chapter 1.

15. Additional Agreements and Amendments

Insert any additional agreements between you and the seller. Be as specific and clear as possible. Consider hiring a real estate attorney to assist in drafting any complex terms.

Signatures

Both parties should sign, and the contract should be dated. See Chapter 1 for instructions on signing contracts.

Attachment

If you checked the second box in Paragraph 2, include an attachment describing the property. You can use Form 7E: Attachment to Contract to create an attachment.

Form 7D: Option to Purchase Vacant Land

This option contract allows you to tie up vacant land while you decide whether to buy it. You might use this contract if you're considering several pieces of land and aren't ready to make a firm offer on one.

This option contract gives you a chance to investigate the land—and any concerns you have—before committing to move forward with the purchase. Among other things, you'll want to be sure that the land is free from environmental contamination, that you can build the type of building you want to build on it, that the utility services you need are or can be available at an affordable price, and that the type of business you plan to operate will comply with local zoning ordinances. (It's critical that you find out whether local zoning ordinances and building codes permit you to proceed with the type of use and construction you envision for the site. If not, you'll want the contract to be contingent on the ability to get the land rezoned to permit your desired use or to get an appropriate zoning variance from a local appeals board before you're obligated to close on the deal. And you need to be sure that utility services are available—or, outside of urban areas where utilities might not be available, that the land can be served by an on-site well and septic system.)

If you find problems with any of these items or if you can't arrange for needed financing, you can drop the deal entirely (assuming you ask for these contingencies in the contract). By contrast, if everything checks out and you exercise this option, you commit yourself to proceeding with the purchase.

Because granting you an option to purchase prevents the seller from selling the property to someone else during the option period, the seller will undoubtedly ask you to pay a fee. Depending on how your contract is worded, if you don't proceed with the deal, the seller keeps the option fee. If you go ahead with the purchase, the fee will often, but not always, be applied to your down payment.

Even though the option contract doesn't commit you to buying the property, it includes many of the details of the potential sale. That way, if you decide to purchase the property, many of the details you'll need for Form 7C: Contract to Purchase Vacant Land will have already been decided or addressed. You might even want to attach Form 7C to this form (by using Paragraph 14 Additional Agreements) so that everyone knows what to expect if you exercise your option.

If you choose to exercise the option, you will need a deed to complete the transfer of the property. A deed is a legal document you'll file with the county recorder that officially transfers the property to the buyer. Check with a local real estate attorney or your county land records office about the rules for transferring property in your area.

Instructions for Form 7D: Option to Purchase Vacant Land

All the forms in this book are provided in Appendix B and on the Nolo website. To access the downloadable forms online, use the link provided in Appendix A. As you read the instructions for Form 7D, you might want to refer to the form in Appendix B or open the form on your computer so you can follow along. (If you use the form in Appendix B, be sure to photocopy it first so you'll have a clean copy to use later.)

1. Names

Insert the names of the seller and the purchaser. Consult the chart in Chapter 1 for more information about how to identify a business.

2. Option to Purchase Vacant Land

See the instructions for Paragraph 2 of Form 7B.

3. Exercise of Option

See the instructions for Paragraph 3 of Form 7B.

4. Purchase Price

See the instructions for Paragraph 4 of Form 7B.

5. Access to Property

This paragraph allows you to have experts go on the land to make inspections or do a survey to determine the true boundaries. You must give the seller reasonable notice before conducting an inspection. It's your responsibility to pay for the inspectors' services. Each of the following inspections will help you make an informed decision about whether to buy the property:

- **Contractor's Inspection.** An inspection by a contractor lets you find out about the cost of building on the land—and any possible construction problems.
- **Architect's Inspection.** If you're interested in constructing a building, an architect's inspection can help you decide if the land is a feasible site for the type of building you'd like to erect.
- **Environmental Inspection.** As we discussed in more detail at the beginning of this chapter, it's critical that you conduct an environmental inspection of the property before you buy it. This will let you know if there's any soil contamination or other environmental hazard that could involve you in a costly cleanup effort.
- **Survey.** A survey of the property will disclose any boundary problems—such as a neighboring building or fence that occupies part of the property you're buying—and will also let you know if you have enough room to build on the site.

6. Special Assessments

See the instructions for Paragraph 10 of Form 7A.

7. Other Government Charges

See the instructions for Paragraph 11 of Form 7A.

8. Real Estate Taxes

Nothing needs to be filled in here. See the instructions for Paragraph 12 of Form 7A for a discussion of this paragraph.

9. Closing and Possession

See the instructions for Paragraph 14 of Form 7A for a discussion of this paragraph.

10. Transfer of Title

Nothing needs to be inserted here. See the instructions for Paragraph 15 of Form 7A.

11. Title Insurance

See the instructions for Paragraph 16 of Form 7B.

12. Default

Nothing needs to be filled in here. See the instructions for Paragraph 20 of Form 7A.

13. Disputes

See the discussion of dispute resolution clauses in Chapter 1.

14. Additional Agreements

Insert any additional agreements between you and the seller. Be as specific and clear as possible. Consider hiring a real estate attorney to assist in drafting any complex terms. Also, you might want to use this section to refer to and incorporate a copy of the purchase agreement (such as Form 7C: Contract to Purchase Vacant Land) that you plan to use in the event you exercise your option.

Standard Clauses

The remainder of the contract contains the standard clauses we discussed in Chapter 1. The only thing you'll need to fill in here is the name of the state whose law will apply to the contract in the paragraph called "Governing Law."

Signatures

Both parties should sign, and the contract should be dated. See Chapter 1 for instructions on signing contracts.

Attachment

If you checked the second box in Paragraph 2, include an attachment describing the property. You can use Form 7E: Attachment to Contract to create an attachment.

Form 7E: Attachment to Contract

Often when you prepare a real estate contract, there are some details or conditions that are so wordy they don't fit neatly into the main form. You can deal with this problem by creating an attachment—a separate page or pages of material tacked on the end of the contract that becomes a part of it.

Some items that might go into an attachment include:

- the legal description of the property
- plans and specifications for improvements to be made by the seller before the closing, and

Sample

> Before closing, Seller will complete the following improvements to the property at Seller's expense: [*List the specifics, including detailed drawings and materials to be used.*]

- any agreements relating to the seller's continuing use of premises.

Sample

> For 30 days following the closing, Seller will have the right to store the following equipment in the basement storage area at no charge:
> [*Insert list of equipment to be stored.*]
> While Seller's equipment is stored there, Buyer will keep the access door to the basement locked, but will open it on request of Seller.

Instructions for Form 7E: Attachment to Contract

All the forms in this book are provided in Appendix B and on the Nolo website. To access the downloadable forms online, use the link provided in Appendix A. As you read the instructions for Form 7E, you might want to refer to the form in Appendix B or open the form on your computer so you can follow along. (Before you use the form in Appendix B, be sure to photocopy it so you'll have a clean copy to use later.)

When preparing two or more attachments, number them consecutively: Attachment 1, Attachment 2, and so on.

Begin by inserting the full title of the contract you are attaching this form to. For example, if you're drafting an attachment to Form 7C, you would title this form "Attachment 1 to Contract to Purchase Vacant Land."

1. Names

List the full names of parties exactly as they appear in the main contract.

2. Terms of Attachment

On the first blank, state the full title of the contract the attachment is part of. Then, in the next blank, enter the date of the main contract. In the third blank, insert the property address or common name.

Finally, in the last blank, describe in detail the information you want to include in your attachment. This is usually something like a legal description or a list of improvements.

Sample

> Legal Description:
> Commencing at the Southeast corner of "4th" Street SE° SW°; thence N 00°36'30"E along the West line of said SE° SW°, a distance of 651.30 feet; thence N 88°10' E, a distance of 57.00 feet to the True Point of Beginning; thence continuing N 88°10' E, a distance of 213.56 feet to the westerly line of "F" Street; thence N 00°42'32" W along said last westerly line, a distance of 67.50 feet; thence S 88°10' W, a distance of 95.75 feet; thence S 00°36'30" E, a distance of 67.50 feet to the True Point of Beginning.

Signatures

All parties who signed the purchase contract should sign and date the attachment.

Form 7F: Amendment of Contract

Sellers and buyers often agree to make changes to the terms of the real estate purchase contract before closing. There's no need to redo the entire contract for small changes. Instead, you can simply prepare and sign an amendment.

What can you put in an amendment? The possibilities are virtually unlimited. A price reduction might be appropriate, for example, if your contractor's inspection has disclosed several expensive problems with the building. In this situation, unless the seller is willing to pay a contractor directly to accomplish the needed work, the two of you might agree on a reduced purchase price as a condition of your removing the contingency requiring a satisfactory contractor's report.

Sample

> Paragraph 3 is amended to reduce the purchase price from $500,000 to $450,000. Paragraph 17 is amended by removing the contingency requiring a satisfactory contractor's report.

Or you and the seller might agree to split the cost of replacing an item that your inspector found to be in questionable condition.

Sample

> Paragraph 7 is amended by the addition of the following: Before closing, Seller will arrange to have the air-conditioning unit replaced with a new one of the same brand and capacity. Seller and Buyer will share equally the cost of the new unit and its installation. Paragraph 17 is amended by removing the contingency requiring a satisfactory contractor's report.

If the seller or a current tenant needs additional time to move out of the building, making the scheduled closing date impractical, you and the seller might agree to an amendment extending the time for closing.

Sample

> Paragraph 14 is amended to move the time for closing and delivery of possession from May 15, 20xx, to June 1, 20xx.

A change like this might also be appropriate if you learn your lender can't put together the necessary paperwork by the original closing date.

Or suppose you've signed a contract to buy a building in a research park with the idea that you'll be doing some light manufacturing in addition to research and office usage. You then receive the covenants, conditions, and restrictions for the building and learn that manufacturing is permitted only by permission of managers of the research park association. You and the seller might agree to amend the contract to give you a chance to address this issue rather than simply cancel the deal and face a possible fight over whether you're entitled to get your deposit back.

Sample

> The following clause is added to Paragraph 17: Buyer will apply promptly to the research park association for permission to use the building for light manufacturing. The closing will be moved from September 1, 20xx, to October 1, 20xx, to allow Buyer enough time to accomplish this. The parties agree that if such permission is not granted by the new closing date, the contract will be canceled and Seller will return Buyer's deposit.

Instructions for Form 7F: Amendment of Contract

All the forms in this book are provided in Appendix B and on the Nolo website. To access the downloadable forms online, use the link provided in Appendix A. As you read the instructions for Form 7F, you might want to refer to the form in Appendix B or open the form on your computer so you can follow along. (Before you use the form in Appendix B, be sure to photocopy it so you'll have a clean copy to use later.)

Number amendments consecutively, and attach a copy of each to the original contract.

Begin by inserting the full title of the contract you are amending. For example, if you're amending Form 7C, you would title this form "Amendment 1 of Contract to Purchase Vacant Land."

1. Names

List the full names of parties exactly as they appear in the main contract.

2. Terms of Amendment

In the first blank, enter the full title of the contract you're amending. In the next blank, enter the date of the contract being amended. In the third blank, insert the property address or common name.

Finally, in the last blank, describe in detail the information you want to include in your amendment. Include the changes you are making to the contract and a paragraph or provision number, if possible. For example, if you are deleting a paragraph or clause in your agreement, your amendment might read "Paragraph 16 of the original contract is deleted in its entirety." If you are changing a portion of an agreement—for instance, you are moving the closing date—your amendment might read "Paragraph 14 is amended to move the time for closing and delivery of possession from May 15, 20xx, to June 1, 20xx." See above for more examples.

Signatures

All parties who signed the contract you're amending should sign and date the amendment.

Form 7G: Removal of Contingency

Once you clear up a contingency—for example, obtain financing or a satisfactory inspection report—you can use this form to let the seller know that the contingency is being removed and that, assuming there are no other contingencies, the sale can go forward.

Instructions for Form 7G: Removal of Contingency

All the forms in this book are provided in Appendix B and on the Nolo website. To access the downloadable forms online, use the link provided in Appendix A. As you read the instructions for Form 7G, you might want to refer to the form in Appendix B or open the form on your computer so you can follow along. (Before you use the form in Appendix B, be sure to photocopy it so you'll have a clean copy to use later.)

Introduction

Insert the full title of the contract containing the contingency you're removing. Then, in the blanks provided, enter the date of the main contract, the address of the property, and the names of the parties as they appear in the purchase contract.

Contingencies

Check a box for each contingency that you're removing and fill in the paragraph number in which it appeared in the purchase contract. If you and the other party agreed on a nonstandard contingency that's specific to your deal, check "Other:" and fill in a description. For instance, you and the seller might have agreed that you must be able to get a neighboring property owner to grant an easement over her land before committing to buy the property. Here's an example of how to describe it:

Sample

> Contingency regarding an easement across the southwestern corner of the neighboring property owned by Eileen Ames (contract Paragraph # 14).

Signature

Only you, as buyer, need to sign and date this removal form.

 TIP

You might want to remove contingencies one by one. It's common for your purchase contract to have different deadlines for removing different contingencies. For example, you might have only ten days to remove the contingency for a satisfactory contractor's inspection, but 30 days to remove the contingency for arranging financing. In that situation, you'll have to give the seller more than one Removal of Contingency form. But even if the purchase contract has just one deadline that applies to all the contingencies, you might still want to remove the contingencies one by one as you're able to do so; doing this reassures the seller that you're serious about going forward with the deal.

Form 7H: Extension of Time to Remove Contingencies

You might find that, despite your best efforts, you need more time before you can confidently remove a contingency. The lender, for example, might be taking longer than expected to review your loan application or you might need to have an additional inspection made of the property. In most situations, the seller will likely agree to extend the time for you to remove one or more contingencies. You can use Form 7H: Extension of Time to Remove Contingencies to document this agreement.

Instructions for Form 7H: Extension of Time to Remove Contingencies

All the forms in this book are provided in Appendix B and on the Nolo website. To access the downloadable forms online, use the link provided in Appendix A. As you read the instructions for Form 7H, you might want to refer to the form in Appendix B or open the form on your computer so you can follow along. (Before you use the form in Appendix B, be sure to photocopy it so you'll have a clean copy to use later.)

Introduction

Insert the full title of the contract containing the contingency for which you need an extension. Then, in the lines provided, enter the date of the main contract, the address of the property, and the parties' names exactly as they appear in the original contract.

Contingencies

Check a box for each contingency for which the removal date is being extended, fill in the paragraph number in which the original deadline appeared in the purchase contract, and fill in the new deadline date. If you and the other party agreed on a nonstandard contingency that's specific to your deal, check "Other:" and fill in a description. For instance, you and the seller might have agreed that you must be able to get a neighboring property owner to grant an easement over her land before committing to buy the property. Here's an example of how to describe it:

> Contingency regarding an easement across the southwestern corner of the neighboring property owned by Eileen Ames (Contract Paragraph #14) is extended to February 13, 20xx.

Signatures

Both seller and buyer need to sign and date this extension form.

Form 7I: Exercise of Option to Purchase Real Estate

Use this form if you've signed an option contract, such as Form 7B: Option to Purchase Building or Form 7D: Option to Purchase Vacant Land, and you decide to exercise your option.

When you properly deliver this form to the seller using one of the methods called for in the option contract, you've got a firm deal—subject to the satisfaction of contingencies.

Instructions for Form 7I: Exercise of Option to Purchase Real Estate

All the forms in this book are provided in Appendix B and on the Nolo website. To access the downloadable forms online, use the link provided in Appendix A. As you read the instructions for Form 7I, you might want to refer to the form in Appendix B or open the form on your computer so you can follow along. (Before you use the form in Appendix B, be sure to photocopy it so you'll have a clean copy to use later.)

Insert the name of the seller and your name exactly as they appeared in the option contract.

Fill in the description of the property you're purchasing (the address or common name).

Enter the full name of and date of the option contract.

Only you, the buyer, need to date and sign the document.

Buying, Selling, Manufacturing, Renting, and Storing Goods

 FORMS

   To download the forms discussed in this chapter, go to this book's companion page on Nolo.com. See Appendix A for the link.

If your business sells goods at retail and customers pay you in full at the time of sale, you'll rarely need to worry about purchase contracts. When a sale is completed on the spot, there are relatively few loose ends. On the other hand, if your business buys or sells goods for later delivery, you'll likely want to record the deal with Form 8A: Sales Contract (Lump-Sum Payment) or Form 8B: Sales Contract (Installment Payments).

RESOURCE

For more information on laws affecting sales transactions, see the *Legal Guide for Starting & Running a Small Business,* **by Fred S. Steingold and David M. Steingold (Nolo).** It covers the legal requirements for dealing with customers; legal issues involved with receiving cash, checks, and credit cards; and the issues of extending credit and getting paid.

Use Form 8C: Bill of Sale for Goods to document the transfer of ownership of goods from a seller to a buyer. It may be used be in conjunction with a sales contract, such as Form 8A or Form 8B. In a typical sale, however, delivery to the buyer together with a receipt signed by the buyer is sufficient legal evidence that ownership has been transferred. In the real world of starting or running a small business, you'd be most likely to use a bill of sale in the following situations:

- **Purchase of a Business.** To document the transfer of ownership of inventory, furniture, and equipment to someone who's buying all the assets of a business. (Use Form 5E: Bill of Sale for Business Assets for this purpose.)
- **Purchase of a Building.** To document the transfer of ownership of furniture and equipment presently in a building to someone who's buying that building.
- **Transfers to or From Business Owners.** To document the transfer of ownership of property between a company and its owners. For example, to document the transfer of ownership from shareholders who are transferring tangible property they own (computers, furniture, and so on) to their corporation, or the transfer of ownership of property from a partnership to individual partners upon breakup of the partnership.
- **Sale of Expensive Items.** To document the transfer of ownership of costly and possibly unique equipment (a customized alarm system, a packaging device, or a work of art, for example), especially when the buyer anticipates that ownership might need to be proven at a later time.

When the purchase price is going to be paid over time and the sale involves valuable items, the seller will no doubt want the right to take back the goods or equipment if the buyer doesn't make payments. The seller does this by retaining an ownership interest (in legal jargon, a security interest) in the property. This can be accomplished using Form 8D: Security Agreement for Buying Goods in which the buyer acknowledges the seller's right to repossess if timely payments aren't made.

If your goods will be custom manufactured, both the manufacturer and the customer have a real need to prepare and sign a written contract detailing the terms of the transaction, such as Form 8E: Contract for Manufacture of Goods. Doing so will help avoid later disputes about whether the exact specifications of the goods and the payment terms have been met.

To record terms and details, you'll also want to prepare a written contract if you're:

- renting equipment (Form 8F: Equipment Rental Contract)
- storing items (Form 8G: Storage Contract), or
- accepting items on consignment or consigning items (Form 8H: Consignment Contract).

Form 8A: Sales Contract (Lump-Sum Payment)

This form assumes that the buyer will pay the purchase price, minus any down payment, in one lump sum—most likely when the seller delivers the items to the buyer. For example, you're planning to open a restaurant and have agreed to buy seven tables and 28 chairs from a restaurant across town that is closing in a month. To avoid the possibility of confusion about what you bought, when you can expect delivery, and when you'll pay for the tables and chairs, you need a written sales contract setting forth all key terms of your deal. When you sign the contract, you will give the seller a down payment for 10% of the purchase price; when the seller delivers the furniture to you, you will pay the entire balance of the agreed price.

Or perhaps you're selling your present computer system to another business to make room for your new improved setup, which is scheduled to arrive soon. In addition to recording the basic facts of the transaction, such as what you're selling, the purchase price, and the down payment amount, you might want to tie the delivery date of your existing system to the arrival of your new one. You could also use this form to spell out the extent of your obligation to install the old system at the buyer's business place.

Instructions for Form 8A: Sales Contract (Lump-Sum Payment)

All the forms in this book are provided in Appendix B and on the Nolo website. To access the downloadable forms online, use the link provided in Appendix A. As you read the instructions for Form 8A, you might want to refer to the form in Appendix B or open the form on your computer so you can follow along. (Before you use the form in Appendix B, be sure to photocopy it so you'll have a clean copy to use later.)

SKIP AHEAD

Paying in installments. If you want to create a sales contract where the buyer will pay for goods or equipment in installments, rather than in one lump-sum payment, do not use this form. Instead, use Form 8B: Sales Contract (Installment Payments).

1. Names

Insert the names of the seller and the buyer. See Chapter 1 for a discussion of how to identify the parties in legal forms.

2. Property Being Sold

Describe the items you're buying or selling. Be as specific as is necessary to clearly identify the items, using a serial number if there is one.

Samples

> The ten-year-old, 16-foot-long Star Town refrigerated display case (serial #1875) presently used at Sunflower Bakery

> Canon color copier, serial #1234, together with stand and ten reams of 20-pound laser-grade bond paper

> 2,000 men's 100% cotton T-shirts manufactured by Fruit of the Loom in assorted sizes and colors

3. Condition of Property

If some of the property being sold is new, check the first box.

If some of the property being sold is used, you will need to check either the second or the third box to indicate whether the buyer will accept the property in as-is condition or whether the seller will be modifying the property before delivery, in which case the details should be inserted.

Sample

> Seller will replace, at Seller's expense, the broken handle on the refrigerated display case.

You may check more than one box.

If there are problems with the goods that the seller can't or does not want to fix, the seller should disclose them to the buyer, especially if the property is a car or another vehicle. Disclosing defects reduces the possibility that a buyer can later argue successfully that there was fraud or misrepresentation in the sale. The seller should disclose defects or problems with the property that the buyer wouldn't likely discover through a casual inspection. In the last blank in this section, describe any defects in as much detail as possible.

Samples

> Third shelf on refrigerated display case is slightly uneven, causing condensation to collect on the right-hand side of the shelf.

> The light indicator for the on-off switch on the Canon copier does not work.

> The left sleeve on each Fruit of the Loom T-shirt is shorter than the right by 1/8".

To make sure the property hasn't deteriorated between the time the parties sign the contract and the time of delivery, the buyer should consider making a final inspection of the property just before accepting and paying for the delivered goods.

4. Purchase Price

Insert the price, including any down payment.

5. Down Payment

If the buyer is making a down payment on the goods, check the first box and insert the amount. Otherwise, check the second box.

If the buyer makes a down payment, the buyer will pay this amount when the contract is signed and will pay the balance when the goods are delivered or on another specified date.

TIP

Tip for buyers: Keep the down payment as low as possible. If you're the buyer and things go wrong, you'll be glad if you negotiated to keep the down payment as small as possible. That way, if you need to cancel the purchase, you've minimized the amount you will lose.

6. Time of Payment

Check the first box if the balance of the purchase price will be due on delivery of the goods or equipment.

Check the second box if the balance of the purchase price will be due in one lump sum at some time other than delivery, and insert the agreed-upon date.

7. Method of Payment (Optional)

Check the box that indicates the method of payment.

If the buyer is using a credit card, the seller will need to obtain the buyer's credit card number and the card's expiration date, and otherwise comply with the processing bank's rules.

8. Delivery

Fill in the date and location of delivery. The seller can either make the goods available at the seller's place of business or deliver the goods directly to the buyer, or the parties can agree on another delivery location.

9. Ownership

Nothing needs to be inserted here.

The seller is guaranteeing the buyer that the seller is the legal owner of the property and that the seller is therefore free to transfer it to the buyer. (In other words, no one else has any rights in the property being sold, such as a partial ownership interest or a security interest or lien on the property.)

If it later turns out that there is a security interest or money owed on the property, the buyer has the right to sue the seller for any damages the buyer suffers as a result.

Buyers' Remedies for Defective or Damaged Goods

Whether you're buying or selling goods, it's important to understand how warranties, and warranty disclaimers, operate.

A warranty is a promise or guarantee that a seller of goods makes to a buyer about the quality of the goods being sold. In general, a warranty gives the buyer recourse to sue the seller for damages if the goods fail to live up to promises the seller made to the buyer. In legal lingo, some warranties are expressed and others are implied.

Express Warranties. An expressed, or express, warranty is a statement that guarantees a product to work in a certain way or for a certain amount of time. Most express warranties state something like, "This product is warranted against defects in materials or workmanship for three years from date of sale." Your sales contract does not contain any express warranties, but the seller should still be cautious about making verbal express warranties, to which the buyer might try to hold the seller.

In most states, a sales contract can deny, or disclaim, any express warranties that the seller might have previously made verbally. But this sales contract does not disclaim any previously made warranties.

Implied Warranties. Unlike express warranties, which need to be stated, the law automatically implies two kinds of warranties regardless of whether the seller actually promises anything to the buyer. In other words, these warranties apply to sales regardless of whether they are stated in a contract. These two implied warranties come with almost everything that is bought and sold.

The implied warranty of merchantability is an assurance that a new item will work if the buyer uses it for its ordinary purpose or that a used item will work as expected, given its age and condition.

The implied warranty of fitness of purpose applies when a buyer purchases an item with a specific purpose in mind. If a seller has reason to know that the buyer has a particular purpose in mind for the goods, the seller guarantees that the property is fit for that purpose. For instance, let's say a customer asks a retailer to recommend the best sleeping bag for subzero temperatures. The customer later discovers that the sleeping bag barely keeps him warm in 50-degree weather. Because the retailer knew about the buyer's intended purpose, the buyer would have the right to sue the retailer for violating the implied warranty of fitness for a particular purpose.

Because, by law, implied warranties apply to most products, they are difficult to deny, or disclaim. This sales contract does not disclaim any implied warranties.

Denying, or Disclaiming, Warranties. Some sellers want to disclaim warranties for a variety of reasons. However, not all states allow sellers to disclaim warranties, especially implied warranties. And even if disclaiming warranties is allowed in your state, such disclaimers are not popular with judges—a judge could determine that it would be unfair to enforce a disclaimer of implied warranties against the buyer.

If you are the seller and want to disclaim warranties, you might want to consult a small business attorney to help you determine whether you can legally do so in your state and to create a disclaimer clause that complies with your state law requirements.

If you are the buyer and the seller wants to include a warranty disclaimer in your contract, make sure you thoroughly inspect the goods and, if necessary, ask a knowledgeable dealer or a repair person to inspect the goods before you buy so you know what you're getting.

RESOURCE

For more information about warranties, disclaimers, and tips on dealing with consumers, see Chapter 17 of *Legal Guide for Starting & Running a Small Business,* **by Fred S. Steingold and David M. Steingold (Nolo).**

10. Transfer of Ownership

The seller needs to legally transfer ownership of the property with a document in addition to this sales contract. Proper documentation allows the buyer to prove—for example, if challenged by the seller or other person in a lawsuit—that the buyer has obtained legal ownership of the property.

Check the appropriate box: "a receipt," "a bill of sale," or "such documents as may be required by the state of."

To transfer cars, trucks, boats, and planes, which are registered with the state government, many states require you to use an official state transfer of title form. Your secretary of state's office or department of vehicle registration can tell you if the type of property being transferred requires a state transfer of title form and can provide you with the needed form. If you will use a state form, fill in the name of your state.

You'll probably need to use a bill of sale only if you are buying or selling expensive items or unique goods or equipment—for example, a work of art or a customized alarm system—or if the buyer anticipates that ownership of the property will need to be proved at a later time. To accomplish this, use Form 8C: Bill of Sale for Goods.

11. Other Terms and Conditions

Here you can describe any additional agreements you've reached that aren't already included in the contract.

Samples

> Buyer will arrange for transporting the 16-foot Star Town refrigerated display case (serial #1875) from the Sunflower Bakery to Buyer's place of business and will pay for that transportation.

> If the Canon copier (serial #96810) needs repair within 30 days of delivery to Buyer, Seller will pay the repair cost. During the next 60 days after the initial 30-day period, Seller and Buyer will share any needed repair costs equally. After 90 days from delivery, Buyer is 100% responsible for any repair costs.

Standard Clauses

The remainder of the contract contains the standard clauses we discussed in Chapter 1. The only thing you'll need to fill in here is the name of the state whose law will apply to the contract in the paragraph called "Governing Law."

Signatures

Both the buyer and seller should sign the contract. See Chapter 1 for instructions on signing contracts.

Form 8B: Sales Contract (Installment Payments)

As with Form 8A: Sales Contract (Lump-Sum Payment), this form is designed for situations where you agree to buy or sell goods or equipment to be delivered in the future. But instead of requiring the entire purchase price to be paid on delivery, Form 8B: Sales Contract (Installment Payments) provides for the buyer to pay for the items over a period of months or years.

Instructions for Form 8B: Sales Contract (Installment Payments)

All the forms in this book are provided in Appendix B and on the Nolo website. To access the downloadable forms online, use the link provided in Appendix A. As you read the instructions for Form 8B, you might want to refer to the form in

Tip for Buyers: It's Wise to Do a Lien Check

It's possible that the seller previously gave someone else a lien on the property you're buying—perhaps because the seller hadn't fully paid off the property or had used the property as collateral for a loan. Less frequently (but equally important), personal property may be subject to something called a judgment lien. This is a lien the state imposes against someone's property when he or she loses a lawsuit, so that the property can be taken to pay the judgment.

If there is a lien on the property, the third party holding the lien has a legal ownership interest in the property unless the seller pays off what's owed. Since selling property that's subject to a lien usually triggers the lienholder's right to seize the property, the lienholder could repossess the property from you. If that happens, you could sue the seller for incorrectly asserting that there were no liens on the property, but that could be both inconvenient and expensive—and might yield nothing if the seller has already spent your money.

To avoid this possibility, you should find out whether any liens have been filed against a particular item of property. You should conduct a lien check in any state in which the seller or the property was ever located, and use every possible name the seller might have used, including a business name. Lien checks usually cost a few dollars, but it's money well spent to be sure no one else has a claim on the property. Here's where you'll need to go to perform a lien check:

Lien Checks for Vehicles, Boats, and Planes. For these, a lien will usually be on file with the state agency that handles registrations and transfers (often the department of motor vehicles). After locating the proper office, the buyer should ask how to look at or order a copy of the lien record for the item.

Lien Checks for Other Property. For other personal property, the lien will be recorded in a Uniform Commercial Code Financing Statement, or UCC-1, filed with a state or county office. To learn whether property is subject to a UCC Financing Statement, you should start by contacting the secretary of state's office for information about where UCC and other liens are recorded. Then you should inquire specifically about whether there's a lien on the property you are purchasing.

Appendix B or open the form on your computer so you can follow along. (Before you use the form in Appendix B, be sure to photocopy it so you'll have a clean copy to use later.)

TIP

Paying in one lump sum. If you want to create a sales contract where the buyer will pay for goods or equipment all at once, rather than in installments, do not use this form. Instead, use Form 8A: Sales Contract (Lump-Sum Payment).

1. Names

Insert the names of the seller and the buyer. See Chapter 1 for a discussion of how to identify the parties in legal forms.

2. Property Being Sold

See instructions for Paragraph 2 of Form 8A.

3. Condition of Property

See instructions for Paragraph 3 of Form 8A.

4. Purchase Price

Insert the price, including any down payment.

5. Down Payment

See the instructions for Paragraph 5 of Form 8A.

6. Time of Payment

Specify how the balance of the purchase price will be paid. You can create any installment schedule that meets your needs. When specifying the schedule, you may also want to indicate how the installment payments will be made—for instance, by personal check, or cashier's check. You can also tie installment payments to the dates of partial deliveries of the goods, as shown in the third sample below.

Samples

> Buyer will pay the purchase price in two installments of $3,000 each. The first will be due on July 1, 20xx; the second will be due on September 1, 20xx. Payments will be made by cashier's check.

> Buyer will pay the purchase price, less the $500 down payment, in 36 monthly installments of $300 each to be paid on the first day of each month beginning July 1, 20xx.

> Seller agrees to deliver 25 wrought-iron figurines on the first day of each month for four months, beginning January 1, 20xx. Buyer will pay the purchase price in four installments of $250 each. The first payment will be due on January 1, 20xx; the second will be due on February 1, 20xx; the third on March 1, 20xx; and the fourth on April 1, 20xx.

7.   Method of Payment (Optional)

Check the box that indicates the method of payment.

If the buyer is using a credit card, the seller will need to obtain the buyer's credit card number and the card's expiration date, and otherwise comply with the processing bank's rules.

8.   Delivery

If the seller will make a full delivery of the goods on one date, enter the date the seller will deliver the goods, or make the goods available, to the buyer. Also enter the location of delivery. The seller can either make the goods available at the seller's place of business or deliver the goods directly to the buyer, or the parties can agree on another delivery location.

In some instances, however, the buyer and seller might want to tie the timing of the buyer's installment payments to partial deliveries of the goods by the seller. For instance, suppose the buyer is agreeing to buy 40 bookcases over a period of four months. The seller agrees to deliver ten bookcases on the first day of each month for four months. The buyer agrees to pay the seller one-quarter of the purchase price (minus any down payment) on each of those dates. They use the following installment schedule in the "Time of Payment" paragraph (see instructions for Paragraph 6, above):

Sample

> Seller agrees to deliver ten bookcases on the first day of each month for four months, beginning July 1, 20xx. Buyer will pay the balance of the purchase price in four installments of $900 each. The first payment will be due on July 1, 20xx; the second will be due on August 1, 20xx; the third on September 1, 20xx; and the fourth on October 1, 20xx.

If you wish to tie the delivery of goods to the installment payments, leave the delivery date in this paragraph blank, or write in, "See 'Time of Payment,' above." Fill in the location of delivery. Again, the seller can either make the goods available at the seller's place of business or deliver the goods directly to the buyer, or the parties can agree on another delivery location.

9.   Ownership

Nothing needs to be inserted here. See the instructions for Paragraph 9 of Form 8A.

10. Transfer of Ownership

See the instructions for Paragraph 10 of Form 8A.

Tip for Sellers: Alternatives to Charging Interest

When the buyer takes full delivery of the goods up front, the seller might want to charge the buyer interest on the unpaid balance of the purchase price—because the seller is essentially lending the buyer funds to purchase the goods and take delivery right away.

However, charging interest can require the seller to comply with some complicated legal rules that apply to installment sales. To keep matters simple, the seller and the buyer can agree to a higher purchase price (and thus higher installment payments) instead of dealing with the details of interest, finance charges, and late fees—all of which are regulated by often complex laws that can vary widely from state to state.

You can use either an amortization chart or a financial calculator to help you calculate what a monthly payment (principal and interest) would be using a certain interest rate. Then use this monthly payment amount as the installment payment in your sales contract, without mentioning a rate of interest and subjecting the transaction to financing regulations. To calculate these monthly payments, you can use the free calculators at www.nolo.com/legal-calculators.

> **EXAMPLE:** Roger is selling goods to a buyer for $25,000 over three years—this comes out to an installment payment of $694.44 per month. The buyer is willing to pay a little more to receive the goods up front. To calculate the higher monthly payment, Roger goes to www.nolo.com/legal-calculators and selects the "How much will my loan payments be?" calculator. He enters the purchase amount as $25,000, the loan term as three years, and the interest rate as 7%. The calculator tells him that the monthly payment at that interest rate would be $771.93 per month. He offers to provide the goods up front at that higher rate.

If, however, you're a seller and prefer to charge interest on the purchase price, you'll need to familiarize yourself with the laws in your state covering installment purchases. Your state chamber of commerce or a trade association serving your industry is a good starting point for getting this information.

11. Security Interest

When selling expensive goods or equipment, the seller will probably want to retain a security interest in the goods being sold until the buyer has made the last payment for the goods. That way, if the buyer doesn't make installment payments as promised, the security interest allows the seller to take back the goods.

If you select the second box, the buyer agrees to sign a security agreement giving the seller a security interest in the goods. After you have completed this contract, you need to complete Form 8D: Security Agreement for Buying Goods. The buyer also acknowledges that the seller will file a Uniform Commercial Code Financing Statement at a public office to let third parties such as lenders or purchasers know about the security interest. This document is explained further in the instructions for the security agreement.

12. Other Terms and Conditions

Fill in any other terms you've agreed to. See the instructions for Paragraph 11 of Form 8A.

Standard Clauses

The remainder of the contract contains the standard clauses we discussed in Chapter 1. The only thing you'll need to fill in here is the name of the state whose law will apply to the contract in the paragraph called "Governing Law."

Signatures

Both the buyer and seller should sign the contract. See Chapter 1 for instructions on signing contracts.

Form 8C: Bill of Sale for Goods

When you buy or sell personal property you'll often need a bill of sale to document the transfer of the property. In many sales, however, including those handled regularly by a retail seller, having the buyer sign a receipt at the time the property is delivered is sufficient legal evidence that ownership of the property has been transferred.

Most likely, you'll need to use this bill of sale only if you are buying or selling expensive items or unique goods or equipment—for example, a work of art or a customized alarm system. In addition, a buyer should insist that the seller sign a bill of sale any time the buyer anticipates that ownership could need to be proved at a later time.

Note that a sales contract doesn't take the place of a bill of sale. A sales contract sets out the terms of the sale—for example, the amount and type of goods the buyer is purchasing, and the sales price—but the bill of sale is the document that completes the legal transfer of the property to the buyer. The bill of sale proves that property has been legally transferred to the buyer and that the seller has received full payment for the property (except in the case of installment payments). The seller should give the buyer a bill of sale at the close of the transaction.

Do not use this bill of sale in the following situations:

- **Sale of Personal Property That Is Required to Be Registered With the State.** Some states require you to use official transfer of title forms when selling vehicles, boats, or planes. The secretary of state's office or department of vehicle registration can tell you whether the type of property you want to transfer requires a state transfer of title form and can provide you with the form you need.
- **Sale of Real Estate.** If the seller is transferring real estate, the buyer must complete a deed and record it with the county in which the property is located.
- **Sale of Assets of a Business.** If you want to transfer all of the assets of a business, use Form 5E: Bill of Sale for Business Assets instead.
- **Sale of Intellectual Property.** If the seller is transferring intellectual property, such as a trademark, patent, or copyright, the seller must use a separate document called an

assignment. For an assignment of trademark form, see *Trademark: Legal Care for Your Business & Product Name*, by Stephen Fishman (Nolo). For forms you can use to assign a copyright, see *The Copyright Handbook: What Every Writer Needs to Know*, by Stephen Fishman (Nolo). For forms for assigning a patent, see *Patent It Yourself*, by David Pressman (Nolo).

Instructions for Form 8C: Bill of Sale for Goods

All the forms in this book are provided in Appendix B and on the Nolo website. To access the downloadable forms online, use the link provided in Appendix A. As you read the instructions for Form 8C, you might want to refer to the form in Appendix B or open the form on your computer so you can follow along. (Before you use the form in Appendix B, be sure to photocopy it so you'll have a clean copy to use later.)

1. Names

Insert the names of the seller and the buyer. See Chapter 1 for a discussion of how to identify the parties in legal forms.

2. Transfer of Ownership

Describe the property being sold. You can usually use the same description you've used in Paragraph 2 of the sales contract. To make sure the property hasn't deteriorated between the time the parties sign the purchase agreement and the time of closing, the buyer should consider making a final inspection of the property just before closing the sale.

In the second paragraph, check the first box if the seller has received payment in full. Fill in the amount of the purchase price. Check the second box if the buyer will make payments to the seller. Fill in the amount of the down payment and the balance of the purchase price still owed. Fill in the date of the sales contract that sets out the payment plan.

3. Condition of Property

Check the first box if the property is new. Check the second box if the property is used. You may check both boxes.

4. Warranty of Ownership

Nothing needs to be inserted here. See "Tip for Buyers: It's Wise to Do a Lien Check," above, which describes how a buyer can check for any liens on the property being purchased.

Signature

Only the seller needs to sign. See Chapter 1 for instructions on signing contracts.

Form 8D: Security Agreement for Buying Goods

When the purchase price is going to be paid over time and the sale involves valuable items, the seller will no doubt want the right to take back the goods or equipment if the buyer doesn't make payments. The seller does this by retaining an ownership interest (in legal jargon, a security interest) in the property. This can be accomplished using Form 8D: Security Agreement for Buying Goods in which the buyer acknowledges the seller's right to repossess the goods if timely payments aren't made.

This form would typically be used in conjunction with Form 8B: Sales Contract (Installment Payments) to give the seller the legal right to take back the property if the buyer doesn't make payments when they come due.

Instructions for Form 8D: Security Agreement for Buying Goods

All the forms in this book are provided in Appendix B and on the Nolo website. To access the downloadable forms online, use the link provided in Appendix A. As you read the instructions for Form 8D, you might want to refer to the form in Appendix B or open the form on your computer so you can follow along. (Before you use the form in Appendix B, be sure to photocopy it so you'll have a clean copy to use later.)

1. Names

Insert the names of the seller and the buyer. See Chapter 1 for a discussion of how to identify the parties in legal forms.

2. Grant of Security Interest

Describe the property—use the same description you used in the sales contract. (See instructions for Paragraph 2 of Form 8A.)

3. Installment Payments

In the first blank, enter the date of the sales contract. This is usually the date the contract was signed. You can usually find this information in the first paragraph of the sales contract or at the end of the contract with the signatures.

Next, on the blank line, list the amounts of the installment payments and when they're due. Make sure the payment schedule matches the schedule described in your sales contract.

Samples

> Buyer will pay the purchase price in two installments of $3,000 each. The first will be due on July 1, 20xx; the second will be due on September 1, 20xx. Payments will be made by cashier's check.

> 36 monthly installments of $300 each to be paid on the first day of each month beginning July 1, 20xx.

4. Financing Statement

The buyer must also sign a financing statement, which is recorded (filed) at a public office to let third parties such as lenders or purchasers know that the property is subject to the seller's lien. That way, anyone checking the public records—for example, a bank's loan department—will learn that the seller has a prior lien, and thus an ownership interest, in the property described in the financing statement.

The form that the buyer must sign and file is a Uniform Commercial Code form called Form UCC-1. Check your state's secretary of state website or call the office to obtain the appropriate UCC form and learn the filing fees. A good place to start is www.statelocalgov.net, a directory of state and local government websites.

When the buyer has made all installment payments, the buyer needs to remember to get a discharge of the security interest. This is a document issued by the seller verifying that the seller no longer holds a security interest in the property. If the buyer forgets to obtain a discharge and record it at the same office where the financing statement was filed, the buyer may hit snags if he or she later tries to sell the property.

Nothing needs to be inserted here.

> **CAUTION**
>
> **Sellers: File the UCC Financing Statement promptly.** It's essential that you file the financing statement with the appropriate governmental office as soon as possible. Otherwise, without your knowing it, someone else might beat you to the punch and file a financing statement signed by the same buyer and covering the same property. If that happens, the first filer will have first dibs on the secured property—probably leaving nothing for you to seize if the buyer fails to pay you.

5. Use and Care of the Secured Property

Nothing needs to be inserted here. This paragraph spells out the buyer's duty to safeguard the property so that the seller has something of value to take back if the buyer defaults.

6. Default of Buyer

Nothing needs to be inserted here. This paragraph says the buyer is in default—meaning that the seller can sue the buyer for repayment or return of the goods—if the buyer doesn't make required payments or doesn't promptly correct any violations of the requirements listed in the preceding paragraph. For instance, if the buyer is late in making a payment and does not pay within ten days after the seller sends written notice of the late payment to the buyer, the buyer is in default. Or, if the buyer violates an obligation regarding the use and care of the secured property—such as failing to maintain it in good repair—and does not correct the violation within ten days of receiving written notice from the seller, the buyer is in default.

7. Rights of Seller

Insert the name of the state where the property is located. This paragraph summarizes the seller's rights under the Uniform Commercial Code if the buyer defaults on his or her obligations under this security agreement. Specifically, the seller is allowed to seize the secured property and sell, lease, or otherwise dispose of it.

> **CAUTION**
>
> **See a lawyer before seizing property.** Suppose you're the seller and the buyer hasn't kept up payments on the property you've sold. Recovering the property covered by the security agreement can be as simple as walking into the building where the property is located and taking it. But this agreement requires that you notify the buyer before you take back the property, and state law will probably prohibit you from forcing your way onto the buyer's private business space or house if the buyer tells you to keep out.
>
> In short, if you make a mistake in seizing property, you could have to answer to civil charges of trespass or wrongful entry or criminal charges of breaking and

entering or theft—and if someone resists your taking the property, even assault. So before you bravely try to exercise your rights under a security agreement, get advice from an experienced business lawyer. Specifically, ask whether it's lawful to simply take the property if you can get to it by peaceful means or if you'll need to obtain a court order.

RESOURCE

Finding a good lawyer. When you need a lawyer, asking someone you trust for a referral is a good place to start. You can also try one of these excellent and free resources:

- **Nolo's Lawyer Directory.** Nolo has an easy-to-use online directory of lawyers, organized by location and area of expertise. You can find the directory and its comprehensive profiles at www.nolo.com/lawyers.
- **Lawyers.com.** At Lawyers.com you'll find a user-friendly search tool that allows you to tailor results by area of law and geography. You can also search for attorneys by name. Attorney profiles prominently display contact information, list topics of expertise, and show ratings—by both clients and other legal professionals.
- **Martindale.com.** Martindale.com offers an advanced search option that allows you to sort not only by practice area and location, but also by criteria like law school. Whether you look for lawyers by name or expertise, you'll find listings with detailed background information, peer and client ratings, and even profile visibility.

8. Notice to Buyer

Fill in the location where the seller should send the buyer a notice if the buyer is in default and the seller plans to sell, lease, or otherwise dispose of the property. Note that the agreement provides that the seller must give the buyer at least five days' notice before taking action with respect to the property. (This gives the buyer the chance to pay off the debt in full before the property is taken or turned over to someone else.)

Standard Clauses

The remainder of the agreement contains the standard clauses we discussed in Chapter 1. The only thing you'll need to fill in here is the name of the state whose law will apply to the contract in the paragraph called "Governing Law."

Signatures

Both parties must sign. See Chapter 1 for instructions on signing contracts.

Form 8E: Contract for Manufacture of Goods

Sometimes, the goods the buyer wants to purchase don't exist yet or, if they do exist, must be modified or customized to meet the buyer's specifications. Use this form when a seller agrees to make or customize goods for a buyer.

Instructions for Form 8E: Contract for Manufacture of Goods

All the forms in this book are provided in Appendix B and on the Nolo website. To access the downloadable forms online, use the link provided in Appendix A. As you read the instructions for Form 8E, you might want to refer to the form in Appendix B or open the form on your computer so you can follow along. (Before you use the form in Appendix B, be sure to photocopy it so you'll have a clean copy to use later.)

1. Names

Insert the names of the seller and the buyer. See Chapter 1 for a discussion of how to identify the parties in legal forms.

2. Property Description

Check the box that indicates whether the property will be manufactured or merely customized.

Next, describe the property.

Samples

> Four modular computer workstations.

> A portable exhibit unit for use at trade shows based on Model 600 shown in Seller's current catalog.

> One thousand red and blue baseball hats (catalog #27) printed with Buyer's name and logo on the front.

TIP

Use an attachment if you need to include specifications. To avoid disputes over exactly what is being ordered, you need to describe the goods carefully. One of the best ways to do this is to include a contract attachment (Form 1A) with detailed plans, drawings, parts lists, or whatever else it takes to define exactly what the contract covers. If you need to include a drawing in your specifications, such as a graphic of your company logo or a CAD technical drawing, you can add it to the attachment. See Chapter 1 for more about adding attachments.

If you will add an attachment, check the box in this paragraph.

3. Purchase Price

Insert the purchase price. See "Tip for Sellers: Alternatives to Charging Interest," above, which describes how to charge a fair price without invoking the legal rules surrounding the collection of interest.

4. Down Payment

If the buyer will make a down payment, check the first box and insert the amount. Otherwise, check the second box.

5. Time of Payment

Check the first box if the purchase price (less any down payment) is due upon delivery.

Check the second box if the purchase price will be due at a time other than that of delivery, and describe when it is due.

Check the third box if payment will be due in installments; then prepare an attachment containing the payment schedule. If you will attach specifications as Attachment 1, then your payment schedule will be Attachment 2. If not, it will be Attachment 1. Insert the appropriate number in the blank. See Chapter 1 on adding attachments.

6. Method of Payment

See the instructions for Paragraph 7 of Form 8A.

7. Delivery

If the seller will make a full delivery of the goods on one date, fill in the date and location of delivery. The seller can either make the goods available at the seller's place of business or deliver the goods directly to the buyer, or the parties can agree on another delivery location.

In some instances, however, the buyer and seller might want to tie the timing of the buyer's installment payments to partial deliveries of the goods by the seller. For instance, suppose the buyer is agreeing to buy 40 bookcases over a period of four months. The seller agrees to deliver ten bookcases on the first day of each month for four months. The buyer agrees to pay the seller one-quarter of the purchase price (minus any down payment) on each of those dates. They use the following installment schedule:

Sample

> Seller agrees to deliver ten bookcases on the first day of each month for four months, beginning July 1, 20xx. Buyer will pay the balance of the purchase price in four installments of $900 each. The first payment will be due on July 1, 20xx; the second will be due on August 1, 20xx; the third on September 1, 20xx; and the fourth on October 1, 20xx.

If you wish to tie the delivery of goods to the installment payments, you must use an attachment to spell out the installment and delivery schedule (see instructions for Paragraph 5, above). Leave the delivery date in this paragraph blank, or write in, "See 'Time of Payment,' above." Fill in the location of delivery. Again, the seller can either make the goods available at the seller's place of business or deliver the goods directly to the buyer, or the parties can agree on another delivery location.

8. Ownership

Nothing needs to be inserted here. See the instructions for Paragraph 9 of Form 8A.

9. Transfer of Ownership

Nothing needs to be inserted here. A bill of sale allows the buyer to easily prove—if challenged in a lawsuit, for example—that legal ownership of the property has been transferred. To accomplish this, use Form 8C: Bill of Sale for Goods.

10. Security Interest

See the instructions for Paragraph 11 of Form 8B.

11. Other Terms and Conditions

Fill in any other terms you've agreed to.

Sample

> Seller will be responsible for transporting the workstations to Buyer's place of business and installing them there.

Standard Clauses

The remainder of the contract contains the standard clauses we discussed in Chapter 1. The only thing you'll need to fill in here is the name of the state whose law will apply to the contract in the paragraph called "Governing Law."

Signatures

Both parties need to sign. See Chapter 1 for instructions on signing contracts.

Attachments

Be sure to add any attachments that are needed (for example, see instructions for Paragraphs 2 and 5, above). See Chapter 1 for more about adding attachments.

Form 8F: Equipment Rental Contract

This contract can be used if you rent, rather than sell, equipment to customers.

Instructions for Form 8F: Equipment Rental Contract

All the forms in this book are provided in Appendix B and on the Nolo website. To access the downloadable forms online, use the link provided in Appendix A. As you read the instructions for Form 8F, you might want to refer to the form in Appendix B or open the form on your computer so you can follow along. (Before you use the form in Appendix B, be sure to photocopy it so you'll have a clean copy to use later.)

1. Names

Insert the names of the owner of the equipment and the renter (the person or company paying to rent the equipment). See Chapter 1 on identifying the parties to a contract.

2. Equipment Being Rented

Provide a detailed description of the property to be rented. When describing an item, be concise, but use enough detail to identify it.

Samples

> The following two portable space heaters: SunRay Model R, serial No. 1234, and SunRay Model R, serial No. 1235

> One 16-foot heavy-duty Reliance Electric extension cord

3. Duration of Rental Period

Insert the times and dates the rental period will begin and end.

Sample

> The rental will begin at <u>5:00 p.m.</u> on <u>December 1, 20xx</u> and will end at <u>5:00 p.m.</u> on <u>January 31, 20xx</u>.

4. Rental Amount

Specify the rental rate. Then check the period covered by the rate—daily, weekly, or monthly.

5. Payment

Indicate the amount the renter has agreed to pay up front for the stated rental period.

If the owner requires a security deposit, check this box and enter the amount of the deposit. A security deposit will protect the owner if the equipment is lost, stolen, or damaged. It is the renter's responsibility to pay for lost, stolen, or damaged equipment, up to the current value of the equipment. A security deposit can also be put toward any late fees owed on the equipment. The owner will return any unused portion of the security deposit to the renter when the equipment is returned.

Many rental businesses, for example, require a cash deposit to cover rental and security deposit charges. The cash deposit is returned to the renter

when he or she returns the equipment in good condition and pays the rent amount owed. Or if the renter uses a credit card, the rental shop puts a hold on the card for the rental and security deposit, but then only charges the rent amount when the equipment is returned in good condition. (If you are using the electronic version of this form, you can delete the optional language about the security deposit, if you don't wish to include it.).

TIP

Benefit from the experience of others. If equipment rental is a major part of your business, contact an industry trade association for workable ideas on how to minimize your losses stemming from lost or damaged items. Also, focus on how to cope with the predictable problem that some property will be returned late.

6. Delivery

Specify the delivery date—probably the date the rental begins. Then check the box that indicates where delivery will be made. The owner can either make the equipment available at the owner's place of business or deliver the equipment directly to the renter, or the parties can agree on another delivery location.

7. Late Return

It is not unusual for a renter to continue to use rented equipment after the rental period ends, with or without notifying the owner. This rental contract provides that if the renter does not return the equipment by the end of the stated rental period, the owner can charge a fee for each day that the equipment is late. Enter the daily amount the renter must pay if the returned equipment comes back late. To encourage timely return of rented items, the owner might want to consider charging a higher daily rent for the property after the stated rental period ends.

The renter will be charged the late fee for each day or partial day (a period less than 24 hours) that the equipment is not returned beyond the end of the rental period. If the renter put down a security deposit, the owner may subtract these late charges from it.

8. Damage or Loss

Because the renter is responsible for any damage to the equipment, the renter should carefully inspect all equipment before accepting it and make sure any defects are listed here. Unless defects to the equipment are noted in the contract, the rented equipment is assumed to be in good condition.

Describe any defects in the equipment.

Samples

> There is a dent on the top of the air-conditioning unit.

> The power washer is missing a side panel.

> The quarter-inch drill bit is missing from the drill bit collection.

9. Value of Equipment

Fill in the total current value of the rented property. This figure will help establish what the renter owes if the property is lost, stolen, or damaged. If the equipment is damaged while in the renter's possession, the renter will be responsible for the cost of repair, up to the current value of the equipment. If the equipment is lost or stolen while in the renter's possession, the renter must pay the owner its current value.

TIP

Be conservative. To minimize the possibility of future court hassles, make sure the equipment's value is not overestimated. You wouldn't want to pay for the value of new goods if the lost or damaged equipment was several years old when you rented it. A used lawn mower, for example, will obviously have a value that's lower than a brand-new one.

10. Use of Equipment

This clause is optional. If you rent equipment that could be dangerous if used improperly, such as jet-skis or lawn mowers, you might want to consider including this clause to protect your business from liability if someone is injured (through no fault of yours) while using your equipment. If this box is checked, the renter agrees to take responsibility for injury to him- or herself and others, and to use the equipment safely and only in the manner for which it is intended to be used. The renter also agrees to indemnify the owner for any injuries or damage arising out of the renter's misuse of the equipment. This means that if the renter's misuse of the equipment injures anyone or damages property— for example, the renter hits a swimmer while carelessly riding on a jet-ski—the renter has to pay the costs for defending the owner in a lawsuit as well as any damages (financial compensation) the owner owes as a result of the lawsuit.

Including the renter's liability clause in your contract won't guarantee that the owner will be protected from all liability for injuries and damage. First, if the owner's actions contribute to an injury or property damage—for instance, the owner fails to regularly tighten the screws on a lawn mower blade and it severs a gas line—the owner will be liable for the damages caused by the equipment.

Second, many judges don't like contracts that attempt to disclaim liability, so the renter's liability clause might not be enforceable in all courts. So, even when including this clause, the owner should always take reasonable safety precautions. This includes properly maintaining the equipment to ensure it's in safe condition and providing renters with instructions and warnings regarding equipment use. For further protection, owners should maintain adequate liability insurance.

RESOURCE

Obtaining the right insurance is essential if you want to protect your business. If you want to know more about buying insurance for your small business, Chapter 12 of the *Legal Guide for Starting & Running a Small Business*, by Fred S. Steingold and David M. Steingold (Nolo), contains invaluable information about researching, buying, and negotiating a business insurance policy.

Standard Clauses

The remainder of the contract contains the standard clauses we discussed in Chapter 1. The only thing you'll need to fill in here is the name of the state whose law will apply to the contract in the paragraph called "Governing Law."

Signatures

Both the owner and the renter should sign the contract. See Chapter 1 for instructions on signing contracts.

Form 8G: Storage Contract

Use Form 8G: Storage Contract when a business will take temporary possession of and store goods or equipment owned by an individual or another business. If you are storing goods with an established storage facility, however, that business will require you to use its standard contract.

Instructions for Form 8G: Storage Contract

All the forms in this book are provided in Appendix B and on the Nolo website. To access the downloadable forms online, use the link provided in Appendix A. As you read the instructions for Form 8G, you might want to refer to the form in Appendix B or open the form on your computer so you can follow along. (Before you use the form in Appendix B, be sure to photocopy it so you'll have a clean copy to use later.)

1. Names

Insert the names of the customer (the owner of the goods or equipment to be stored) and the storer (the person or business that will hold on to the property). See Chapter 1 for a discussion of how to identify the parties in legal forms.

2. Property Being Stored

Describe what's being stored. When describing an item, be concise, but use enough detail to identify it.

Bailing Out of Archaic Language

You might come across a storage contract that uses the archaic legal terms bailment, bailor, or bailee. This jargon reflects the fact that historically and technically, storage contracts are part of something called bailment law.

A bailment was created whenever one person turned over tangible personal property (goods and equipment) to another person for safekeeping. The person who turned over the property was called a bailor; the person who received the property was called a bailee. Over the centuries, judges created a web of rules covering the bailment relationship—including fine distinctions between whether the bailee is just doing the bailor a favor by accepting the goods (a gratuitous bailment) or is getting paid (a bailment for hire).

Today, there's no legal reason to use these old-fashioned terms, which have been dropped from the law in many states. A storage contract written in plain English that spells out the responsibilities of each person is perfectly legal. If there's a dispute that winds up in court, the judge will be guided by your contract language—not by the centuries-old rules concerning bailment.

Samples

three Andover halogen desk lamps and a Dell computer system, serial #1234, including hard drive, monitor, and printer

one four-foot by six-foot teak office desk (Scandi brand)

3. Storage Period

Identify the storage period beginning and ending dates.

4. Storage Fees

Specify the amount the customer is paying for storage.

5. Additional Fees

It's not unusual for customers to keep their property in storage after the storage period ends, with or without notifying the storer. Additional fees will be charged if the customer does not take back the property by the end of the storage period listed in the contract and the storer is willing to continue to store the property. The additional fee must be paid as soon as the initial storage period ends, if not before.

Insert the charge that will be due if the customer leaves the property in storage after the storage period ends, and check whether it will be daily, weekly, or monthly.

6. Refunds

Nothing needs to be inserted here. The customer may end the storage agreement at any time by taking the property out of storage. Storage fees paid by the customer are nonrefundable, however, unless the storer terminates the storage contract.

7. End of Storage

This storage contract provides that if the customer does not take back the property by the end of the stated storage period, the storer can either continue to store the property (and charge additional fees) until the customer takes it back or the storer can terminate the storage agreement.

The storer may terminate the storage agreement by sending written notice to the customer. Insert the number of days' notice the customer must receive before the storer ends the storage contract.

If the storer ends the storage contract and sells the stored property, he or she must do so in a commercially reasonable manner. What's reasonable for different types of property can vary (you would probably sell a horse differently than a computer, for example), but generally the storer should advertise the property for sale in an appropriate place or sell it at public auction.

8. Storage Location

Fill in the location where the property will be stored. The storer is required to keep the property at the address you enter here and to use reasonable care to protect it.

9. Value of Property

This clause is optional. Because it's possible that the stored property will get lost or damaged as a result of the storer's actions or negligence, it's wise for the customer and storer to agree in advance on its replacement value. If the storer is at fault for damage to or loss of the property, the storer must pay the replacement value of the property to the customer (if you're using the downloadable form and you don't want to include this option, delete it and renumber the paragraphs that follow).

TIP

A storer should take precautions. If you're a storer and accept used goods or equipment for storage, you'll want to insert a dollar amount for replacement should the goods be damaged or destroyed that reflects the age and actual condition of the items being stored. You wouldn't want to pay for new goods if the item lost was several years old. Also, if storing goods is a routine part of your business, check with an insurance broker or agent to see what coverage is available to pay for damage and losses.

CAUTION

A customer should maintain insurance. If you're a customer leaving goods or equipment with a storage company, you can be reasonably confident that the company carries insurance on stored items. This insurance, however, may not cover theft, fire, or flood. Especially if you're leaving extremely valuable items for storage, you'll want to make sure you have insurance of your own to cover damage or loss by theft, fire, flood, and other causes that are normally beyond the control of the storer.

10. Condition of Property

Because the storer is responsible for any loss or damage it causes through its own actions or negligence, the storer should carefully inspect all property before accepting it for storage. Unless defects to the property are noted in the contract, the stored property is assumed to be in good condition. List any defects in the property; for example:

Samples

> There is a large dent in the side of the refrigerator.

> The surface of the writing desk has a foot-long scratch.

11. Reasonable Care

Nothing needs to be inserted here. In general, a storer is legally obligated to use reasonable care in looking after stored property. This wording reflects that general principle of law. As noted above, the customer is responsible for loss or damage to the stored property caused by events beyond the storer's control—so the customer should maintain adequate insurance coverage.

12. Other Terms and Conditions

Fill in any other terms.

Sample

> Storer will keep the property in a cool and dry place at all times.

Standard Clauses

The remainder of the contract contains the standard clauses we discussed in Chapter 1. The only thing you'll need to fill in here is the name of the state whose law will apply to the contract in the paragraph called "Governing Law."

Signatures

Both the customer and the storer should sign the contract. See Chapter 1 for instructions on signing contracts.

Form 8H: Consignment Contract

In a consignment agreement, the owner of goods (in legal jargon, the consignor) puts the goods in the hands of a consignee (another person or a business—usually a retailer), who then attempts to sell them. In our contract, we call the owner of the goods the customer.

If the goods are sold, the consignee receives a fee, which is usually a percentage of the purchase price, with the rest of the money being sent to the customer. A sculptor (the customer), for example, might place his or her work for sale at an art gallery (as consignee) with the understanding that if the artwork sells, the gallery keeps 50% of the sale price. Or a homeowner, as customer, might leave old furniture with a resale shop as consignee, which might keep one-third of the proceeds if the item sells. Typically, the customer remains the owner of the goods until the consignee sells the goods.

Instructions for Form 8H: Consignment Contract

All the forms in this book are provided in Appendix B and on the Nolo website. To access the downloadable forms online, use the link provided in Appendix A. As you read the instructions for Form 8H, you might want to refer to the form in Appendix B or open the form on your computer so you can follow along. (Before you use the form in Appendix B, be sure to photo-copy it so you'll have a clean copy to use later.)

1. Names

Insert the names of the customer and the consignee (the business that will market the goods to the public). See Chapter 1 for a discussion of how to identify the parties in legal forms.

2. Property Consigned

Check the appropriate box to indicate whether the goods have been delivered or will be delivered to the consignee.

Next, list the goods and the prices at which they'll be offered for sale. When describing an item, be concise, but use enough detail to identify it.

Sample

> Vera Wang wedding dress, style #3124

The consignee often sets the price, but the customer and consignee should mutually agree on a sales price before entering it into the contract.

3. Efforts to Sell

Nothing needs to be inserted here. This paragraph requires the consignee to display the goods and attempt to sell them at or above the prices listed in the contract. The consignee must obtain the written consent of the customer before selling an item at a lower price than the price entered here.

4. Proceeds of Sale

Insert the percentage of the sale price that the consignee will receive if the goods are sold.

The commission percentage to be paid to the consignee varies depending on the type of goods being consigned. For instance, consignees often receive 20% to 40% commissions on the sale of clothes. For artwork, the consignee may receive as much as 40% to 50% of the sales price. For automobiles, the commission percentage may be much lower, such as 5%.

5. Ownership Before Sale

Nothing needs to be inserted here. This sentence recognizes that the customer isn't giving up owner-ship of the goods.

6. Risk of Loss

Nothing needs to be inserted here. If the goods are damaged or lost while in the consignee's possession, this contract requires the consignee to pay the customer the selling price as listed in the contract minus the sales commission listed in the contract. If you're leaving goods on consignment and are concerned about the consignee's ability to pay you if the goods are lost or stolen, ask to see a copy of the consignee's insurance policy. When very valuable items are being consigned, it's often appropriate to ask to be named as a coinsured so that you can receive a share of the insurance proceeds if a loss occurs.

CAUTION

If you're a consignee, check your insurance coverage. Before you accept the risk of loss or theft, make sure your business insurance policy covers you for loss of "personal property of others" left in your possession—and that the amount of coverage is adequate. Getting full reimbursement for the selling price of consigned goods could require an added endorsement (supplement) to your insurance policy. Check with your insurance agent or broker.

7. Termination of Consignment

Either party may terminate this contract at any time. In case of termination, the consignee can either return the goods to the customer's address, make them available at the consignee's place of business for the customer to pick up, or deliver them to another location. Check the box indicating where the goods will be returned to the customer, and enter the address.

8. Other Terms and Conditions

Insert any other agreed-upon terms.

Sample

> Consignee in its discretion may reduce the sale price of an item by 10% to facilitate a sale. Consignee's commission will be computed based on the actual sale price.

Standard Clauses

The remainder of the contract contains the standard clauses we discussed in Chapter 1. The only thing you'll need to fill in here is the name of the state whose law will apply to the contract in the paragraph called "Governing Law."

Signatures

Both the customer and the consignee should sign the contract. See Chapter 1 for instructions on signing contracts.

Hiring Employees and Independent Contractors

FORMS

To download the forms discussed in this chapter, go to this book's companion page on Nolo.com. See Appendix A for the link.

Hiring, managing, and firing employees can expose you to a number of legal pitfalls. If something goes amiss, you could become involved in a nasty lawsuit by a rejected job applicant or a fired employee—or might find yourself involved in an enforcement action by a federal or state agency. Unfortunately, hiring independent contractors rather than employees doesn't necessarily improve things—if you manage workers carelessly, you can face a plethora of worker-related legal problems. The IRS, for example, could severely penalize you if you improperly classify an employee as an independent contractor.

To fully understand how best to use the forms in this chapter and reduce the likelihood of costly legal entanglements, become familiar with the basic legal principles involved in hiring both employees and independent contractors. The books recommended below offer the guidance you need.

RESOURCE

Learn more about hiring or working as an employee or independent contractor. Chapter 15 of the *Legal Guide for Starting & Running a Small Business,* by Fred S. Steingold and David M. Steingold (Nolo), contains a thorough survey of the legal principles that govern the hiring of workers and considerable useful advice on how to stay out of hot water.

For even greater depth on the legal side of hiring, managing, and firing workers, see *The Employer's Legal Handbook,* by Fred S. Steingold (Nolo).

Working With Independent Contractors, by Stephen Fishman (Nolo), will help you decide if you can hire a worker as an independent contractor without violating IRS and other government regulations and help you retain ownership of your intellectual property when hiring independent contractors.

Working for Yourself: Law & Taxes for Independent Contractors, Freelancers & Gig Workers of All Types, by Stephen Fishman (Nolo), contains a wealth of information and forms for independent contractors who run their own business.

You can also find plenty of free legal information about working as an independent contractor on Nolo.com at www.nolo.com/legal-encyclopedia/consultants-contractors.

One peril you face in the hiring process is that your job application form could violate laws that protect applicants from discrimination—for example, because of age, gender, race, ethnicity, or disability. Another legal pitfall is that you might invade the applicant's privacy by seeking information about personal matters unrelated to the applicant's job qualifications—for example, inquiring about the applicant's marital history or political beliefs. Form 9A: Employment Application helps you focus on legitimate information you are legally entitled to solicit from the applicant while helping you avoid getting into the many sensitive areas that can land you in legal hot water.

Of course, it pays to follow up on information the applicant gives you to be sure it's accurate and hasn't been shaded to paint an overly favorable picture. Specifically, you'll probably want to check with the applicant's prior employers and, if academic credentials are important to you, with the schools attended by the applicant. To avoid claims that you've invaded the applicant's privacy by seeking information without express permission, have the applicant sign Form 9B: Authorization to Release Information. When you present this to prior employers or schools, you have a better chance of gaining their cooperation.

An employer and an employee can differ in recalling the terms of employment that were offered at the beginning of the employment relationship. Putting the terms in writing by using Form 9C: Offer Letter can head off potential misunderstandings about the scope and length of employment, especially as to whether a job was guaranteed for any time period.

In some types of work, there's the possibility that an employee can harm your business in at least two ways: The employee might misuse confidential information while working for you or later begin a business that competes with yours using information gained while working for you. Whether you should worry about this depends on a number of factors, including the type of business you're in and the level of skill and trust the employee's work will entail. If you're concerned about a key employee being able

Checklist for Hiring Workers

Consider if you need to hire employees or if independent contractors will suffice:

☐ Familiarize yourself with the difference between independent contractors and employees. (See Form 9F: Contract With Independent Contractor, below.)

☐ If hiring an independent contractor, use a written independent contractor agreement. (See Form 9F.)

Complete the following procedures before hiring employees:

☐ If you haven't yet already, obtain a federal employer identification number by filing IRS Form SS-4 (the IRS requires one for all employers). (This form is included with this book.) Or, to receive your EIN immediately, you can apply online at www.irs.gov.

☐ Register with your state's labor department or similar agency for payment of unemployment compensation taxes—these payments go to your unemployment compensation fund, which provides short-term relief to workers who are laid off. To find the proper agency, go to www.dol.gov/whd/contacts/state_of.htm.

☐ Be prepared to file IRS Form 940 to report your federal unemployment tax each year. (This form is included with this book.) You must file this form in any year in which you:

- paid wages of $1,500 or more in any quarter of the current or prior year, or
- had one or more employees for at least part of a day in any 20 or more different weeks of the current or prior year. Count all full-time, part-time, and temporary employees, but don't count partners if your business is a partnership. Form 940 is available from the IRS website at www.irs.gov.

☐ Set up a payroll system for withholding taxes and making payroll tax payments to the IRS. (You'll need to withhold a portion of each employee's income and deposit it with the IRS, and also make Social Security and Medicare tax payments to the IRS.) Obtain IRS Publication 15, Circular E, *Employer's Tax Guide*. You can get this publication from the IRS website at www.irs.gov.

☐ Get workers' compensation insurance—this is mandatory in all states except Texas, unless your employees fall within an exemption. You'll need this coverage in case a worker suffers an on-the-job injury, because such injuries aren't covered by normal liability insurance. (In addition, you must notify new hires of their rights to workers' compensation benefits.) For more information on workers' compensation laws, see *The Manager's Legal Handbook*, by Lisa Guerin and Sachi Barreiro (Nolo).

☐ Familiarize yourself with Occupational Safety and Health Administration (OSHA) requirements and prepare an Injury and Illness Prevention (IIP) Program. For information on compliance with OSHA regulations, including creating an IIP Program, go to the OSHA website at www.osha.gov. For more information on health and safety in the workplace, see *The Employer's Legal Handbook*, by Fred S. Steingold (Nolo).

☐ Contact the federal Department of Labor and your state labor department for information on notices you must post in the workplace. For information on federal posters, go to the Department of Labor website at www.dol.gov. Use their online "Poster Advisor" to determine which posters you must display in your workplace. In addition, you must comply with your state department of labor's poster requirements. Find a list of state departments of labor at www.dol.gov/whd/contacts/state_of.htm.

☐ Create an employment application for each type of position you will fill. (See Form 9A: Employment Application, below.)

☐ Create an employee handbook. Although not required, it can be an excellent idea to have a handbook describing your business's employee policies and making it clear that employment is at will unless an employee has signed a written employment contract. Make sure every employee is given a copy as part of your job offer. A great resource is *Create Your Own Employee Handbook: A Legal & Practical Guide for Employers*, by Amy DelPo and Lisa Guerin (Nolo).

☐ Create a sign-up procedure for employee benefits. If your business has established employee benefit programs, such as health insurance or a 401(k) plan, you'll need a sign-up procedure so employees can name their dependents and select options.

Complete the following tasks each time you hire a new employee:

☐ Report the employee to your state's new-hire reporting agency for child support purposes. For information on the new-hire reporting program, which requires employers to report information on employees for the purpose of locating parents who owe child support, go to the Administration for Children & Families website at www.acf.hhs.gov/css/employers/employer-responsibilities/new-hire-reporting. This website provides a link to state-by-state reporting information. Note that the new hire reporting agency in your state might or might not be your state's labor department.

☐ Fill out Form I-9, *Employment Eligibility Verification*, from the U.S. Citizenship and Immigration Services (USCIS) to verify the employee's eligibility to work in the United States. The employee completes Section 1 of the form; you complete Section 2. For full details, go to the USCIS website, www.uscis.gov, and click on I-9 Central under the Verification heading at the bottom of the page. The form need not be filed with the USCIS, but it must be kept in your files either for three years after the date of hire or for one year after employment is terminated, whichever is later, and made available for inspection by officials of the USCIS. (As of press time, the USCIS was instructing employers to continue using the form with the August 31, 2019 expiration date until further notice. This form is included with this book. Before using it, though, be sure to check the USCIS website for a new version of the form.)

☐ Have the employee fill out IRS Form W-4, *Employee's Withholding Allowance Certificate*. This form does not need to be filed with the IRS, but it tells you how many allowances an employee is claiming for tax purposes, so that you can withhold the correct amount of tax from his or her paycheck. (This form is included with this book.)

to harm your business in the future, you can get a measure of legal protection by having the employee sign Form 9D: Confidentiality Agreement and Form 9E: Covenant Not to Compete (if your state enforces this type of contract).

When hiring independent contractors, it is always a good idea to use a written contract, both to avoid misunderstandings about your agreement and to help you in the event of a government audit. Form 9F: Contract With Independent Contractor contains all of the provisions you'll need to formalize your agreement.

Form 9A: Employment Application

You can reduce some of the legal risks of hiring employees well before you ask an applicant to fill out an employment application. Start by writing a job description for each position. In listing job duties, stick to absolute essentials. That way, you'll reduce your chances of violating antidiscrimination laws or the Americans with Disabilities Act (ADA), which prohibits you from excluding an applicant who's able to perform the essential job functions but whose disability might make it impossible to perform a marginal duty.

EXAMPLE: Moonbeam Manufacturing Company needs a file clerk to file and retrieve various sales documents. Other employees usually answer the phone. Because answering the phone isn't an essential file clerk job duty, Moonbeam should not list it as a requirement in the job description. If Moonbeam did list answering the phone in the description, it could needlessly discourage an applicant whose hearing is impaired and has trouble with phone calls.

Also, in writing a job description, be realistic in listing the education and experience requirements. If, for example, you require a college degree for a job that can easily be done by someone with a high school education, you might exclude a disproportionate number of applicants in your area who are members of minority groups, in violation of antidiscrimination laws.

When you begin advertising for applicants, avoid any nuances that can be interpreted as evidence that you discriminate on the basis of sex, age, marital status, or any other illegal category. For example, use "salesperson" instead of "salesman," "energetic" instead of "young," and "two-person job" instead of "married couple."

In the job application and during interviews, tightly focus on the applicant's skills and experience. Be careful about asking questions that may be used as evidence of discrimination. For example, it's a mistake to ask if a person is married (possible evidence of marital status discrimination), what language is spoken in the home (possible evidence of national origin discrimination), or whether the person has a health problem (possible evidence of disability or genetic information discrimination).

Form 9A: Employment Application is designed to avoid questions that might be viewed as discriminatory or that might unnecessarily invade the applicant's privacy. It focuses on the applicant's education and job experiences, but also gives the applicant a chance to state any other training, skills, or achievements that might be important.

Every individual applying for a particular position should fill out the same application. Otherwise, you leave yourself vulnerable to claims that you discriminated against some applicants by asking them questions that you didn't ask other applicants. To learn more about discrimination and the hiring process, including how to ask questions that will provide the information you need without landing you in legal trouble, see *The Employer's Legal Handbook*, by Fred S. Steingold (Nolo).

Instructions to Form 9A: Employment Application

All the forms in this book are provided in Appendix B and on the Nolo website. To access the downloadable forms online, use the link provided in Appendix A. As you read the instructions for Form 9A, you might want to refer to the form in Appendix B or open the form on your computer so you can follow along. (Before you use the form in Appendix B, be sure to photocopy it so you'll have a clean copy to use later.)

All blanks on this form are meant for the prospective employee to fill out; you need not fill in anything beforehand.

The application is divided into six sections, which we'll briefly discuss.

Background. You should never ask applicants where they are from or whether they are citizens of the United States. Ask only whether someone is legally authorized to work in this country.

CAUTION

It might be illegal to ask an applicant about prior felony convictions. Thirteen states and the District of Columbia have passed "ban-the-box" laws that bar most private employers from asking about criminal convictions on job applications. While the laws typically contain exemptions for jobs that require handling cash, entering people's homes, or working with children, minors, or vulnerable adults, you should proceed cautiously, even if the job meets these criteria. In some states, you can't reject an applicant who's been convicted unless the conviction is substantially related to a particular job or disqualifies the applicant from getting a required bond.

Education. When asking about education, think about the skills required for the job you are trying to fill. The more highly skilled the job, the more information you will need about the applicant's education. For example, if you are looking for a groundskeeper, then you probably don't need to know about any education beyond high school. If you are looking for a plumber, then asking about trade school is appropriate, but asking about college might not be. If you are hiring a doctor, then asking about all levels of education is appropriate.

Employment. When reviewing the employment history portion of the application, be sure to pay attention to the dates of employment. Note whether the individual tends to move around a lot or stick with a job for a significant period of time. If you want to hire someone for the long haul, this might be important information for you. Also pay attention to whether there are any gaps of time that aren't accounted for. Perhaps the applicant is hiding something by keeping a job off the list.

References. It's a good idea to call a few of the applicant's former employers to double-check the applicant's honesty and to get professional references for the applicant. Although some employers are reluctant to say much about a former employee, others are more than happy to tell you what they know. Even the most reluctant employers are willing to verify basic information, such as dates of employment, job title, and job duties. Also, you never know what sort of useful bits of information can come up when talking to a personal reference. Finding out how the reference and the applicant met can often give you some insight into the applicant's personality—and be good fodder for interview questions.

Additional Qualifications. Although it might seem like "fluff," an applicant's assessment of his or her own special qualifications and skills provides topics for interview questions, so be sure to read this section of the application carefully. There's much more to an applicant than simply educational background and employment history. This portion of the application gives you the opportunity to discover unique qualifications that might set one applicant apart from others.

Job Description. If you attach a job description to the application, you can ask the applicant to come to the interview prepared to discuss his or her abilities to handle each job duty. During the interview, refer to the job description and ask how the applicant plans to perform the job. This way, you'll learn about the applicant's qualifications and strengths. It also gives the applicant the opportunity to raise with you any needs he or she might have for reasonable accommodations. A reasonable accommodation is either something that you do for the applicant or equipment that you provide to the applicant that makes it possible to do the job despite a disability. If you attach a job description to the application, check the box to the left of the words "Job Description."

Form 9B: Authorization to Release Information

After taking an employment application from a potential employee and conducting an interview, you'll almost surely want to dig a bit deeper into the person's background by contacting former places of employment and verifying academic credentials.

Legally, academic records are confidential; they can't be released to you without the applicant's consent. Although no similar protection covers an applicant's employment history, some former employers are wary when asked to provide a reference, often because they fear a defamation claim if they speak candidly about a former employee's shortcomings. You can smooth out the process by asking the applicant to sign Form 9B: Authorization to Release Information. This form will let former employers or school record keepers know that they're on safe legal ground because the applicant has authorized them to release the information to you. Also, it will eliminate any invasion of privacy claim the applicant might otherwise try to assert against you for obtaining confidential information without permission.

> **TIP**
> **Be prepared for special forms that schools and colleges may prefer.** Schools and colleges, fearful of legal problems, might insist on the use of their release forms and might not accept a form such as the one included here. You can speed up the process by calling to see if they require you to use their own release and, if so, asking that one be emailed or mailed to you.

If you want to get an applicant's credit report, or you hire someone outside your company to conduct the investigation—for example, a background checking firm or a private investigator—then you must comply with a federal law called the Fair Credit Reporting Act (FCRA). This law requires you to get separate written consent and to give certain information to the applicant before requesting the credit report background check. To learn more about the FCRA and the legal rules on investigating applicants, see *The Employer's Legal Handbook,* by Fred S. Steingold (Nolo).

Instructions to Form 9B: Authorization to Release Information

All the forms in this book are provided in Appendix B and on the Nolo website. To access the downloadable forms online, use the link provided in Appendix A. As you read the instructions for Form 9B, you might want to refer to the form in Appendix B or open the form on your computer so you can follow along. (Before you use the form in Appendix B, be sure to photocopy it so you'll have a clean copy to use later.)

Insert the name of your business in the first blank line.

When you present the authorization to the applicant, truthfully explain what types of information you plan to seek and why. This is not the time to lie to an applicant (indeed, there is no good time to lie to an applicant), because you could invalidate the authorization if you get the applicant to sign it under false pretenses. After you explain what type of

information you will seek, ask the applicant to date and sign the authorization in the designated blanks.

After you fill out this form with the name of your business, you might want to make copies of it to keep on hand. Then, when you need to check an applicant's background, you can give the form to the applicant to read and sign.

Form 9C: Offer Letter

When you decide whom to hire for a particular position, it's a good idea to send the successful applicant an offer letter. The letter formally offers the job to the candidate, but it serves additional purposes as well. It explains the terms of the position—the start date, position title, and compensation—so you can make sure there's no confusion over these important details. You can also use an offer letter to preserve your company's right to terminate employment at will.

Unlike many legal terms, employment at will means just about what it sounds like: At-will employees are free to quit at any time and for any reason, and your company is free to fire them at any time, for any reason that isn't illegal. (You can't fire an employee for discriminatory reasons, for example, or to punish the employee for complaining of a health and safety violation.) In every state but Montana, employees are presumed to work at will unless they have a contract promising continued employment, either for a set term (for example, one year), or indefinitely (for example, unless the employee commits gross misconduct or the company is sold).

Even with this presumption on your side, however, it's a very good idea to bolster it with a written agreement, signed by the employee, acknowledging that employment is at will. This type of agreement protects you from claims that someone at your company entered into an oral contract with the employee promising continued employment or that such a contract could fairly be implied from statements made by your company and the circumstances of the job. And, it's a good idea to get this agreement at the very start of the job, before anyone at your company has a chance to make the kinds of statements that could otherwise be interpreted as a promise of job security.

Of course, there might be times when you want to offer an employee a contract for a set term. For example, if your company is starting a new venture, you might want to make sure that the person you promote to lead it sticks around at least long enough to get things off the ground. The offer letter below allows for this possibility as well: You can designate someone at your company who is authorized to create exceptions to the usual at-will policy and enter into written employment contracts.

Instructions to Form 9C: Offer Letter

All the forms in this book are provided in Appendix B and on the Nolo website. To access the downloadable forms online, use the link provided in Appendix A. As you read the instructions for Form 9C, you might want to refer to the form in Appendix B or open the form on your computer so you can follow along. (Before you use the form in Appendix B, be sure to photocopy it so you'll have a clean copy to use later.)

Salutation

At the top of the letter, fill in the date and the applicant's name and address.

First Paragraph

In the first paragraph, insert the name of the position and your company name. (For example, "I am pleased to offer you the position of customer service representative at BigBank, USA.")

Second Paragraph

In the second paragraph, fill in the applicant's start date and compensation, using the appropriate increment of time—that is, per hour, week, month, or year. If there are other job details you want to highlight, you may add them here. For example, if your company has more than one location or offers employees a choice of several work shifts, you might want to add information here about where and when the employee will work.

Third Paragraph

In the third paragraph, you'll need to add your company's name in the first three blanks. The final blank is where you can designate someone who is authorized to enter into employment contracts. It's a good idea to designate the person by position (CEO or Human Resources Director, for example) rather than by name, so you don't have to change your standard offer letter as people come and go. You'll want to name someone fairly high up in the company to take on this significant responsibility.

Fourth Paragraph

In the fourth paragraph, insert your company's name in the blank.

Signature

Enter the full name and title of the person who will sign and send the letter. Print out two copies of the agreement and have the representative sign both of them.

Acceptance of Offer of Employment

Mail both signed copies to the applicant, who must sign and date the acceptance portion of both letters if taking the job. Include a self-addressed, stamped envelope, so the applicant can sign and return one by mail and keep the other. That way, you'll both have a signed copy of the letter. Place the signed offer letter in your new employee's personnel file.

Form 9D: Confidentiality Agreement

Occasionally employees use confidential business information for their personal or financial advantage and might even disclose it to competitors.

To capture in writing the employee's commitment not to benefit personally from confidential information or improperly disclose it to others, use Form 9D: Confidentiality Agreement. Also called a nondisclosure agreement, a confidentiality agreement can prohibit an employee from disclosing a secret invention, design, an idea for a new product or website, or confidential financial information about your company.

If you enter into a confidentiality agreement with an employee and that employee later uses or discloses your trade secrets without your permission, you can ask a court to stop the employee from making any further disclosures. You can also sue the employee for your losses.

In your agreement, you can define the types of information you want kept secret—although you should not set out any actual secrets in the confidentiality agreement—and therefore reduce the chances of confusion over what is, and what isn't, a secret.

There is no need to have all of your employees sign such an agreement. Most workers aren't exposed to much truly confidential information. Reserve confidentiality agreements for only those employees who are likely to learn confidential information.

This agreement is for employees only. For confidentiality agreements you can use with independent contractors and vendors, see *Consultant and Independent Contractor Agreements*, by Stephen Fishman (Nolo).

Instructions to Form 9D: Confidentiality Agreement

All the forms in this book are provided in Appendix B and on the Nolo website. To access the downloadable forms online, use the link provided in Appendix A. As you read the instructions for Form 9D, you might want to refer to the form in Appendix B or open the form on your computer so you can follow along. (Before you use the form in Appendix B, be sure to photocopy it so you'll have a clean copy to use later.)

Introduction

In the first and second blanks, fill in the names of your company and the employee. (Consult the chart in Chapter 1 for more information about how to identify your business.)

In the third blank, insert the benefit the employee is receiving in exchange for signing this agreement. (To make your confidentiality agreement legally enforceable, you must give the employee who signs the agreement something of value in return for the employee's promise to keep your information secret. In legal terms, this thing of value is called consideration.)

If you ask the employee to sign the agreement at the beginning of the employment relationship, then the consideration can simply be the fact that you are providing the employee with a job. For example, if you ask a prospective employee to sign the agreement as a condition of receiving a job offer from you, then the thing of value that you are giving to the individual is employment.

If, however, you wait until the middle of your employment relationship with the employee before asking for a signature on a confidentiality agreement, then you must give the employee something else, such as a raise, to make sure your agreement is enforceable. For example, if you ask an employee who has been working for you for three months to sign a confidentiality agreement, the mere fact that you will continue to employ the individual is probably not sufficient consideration, because you've already given that benefit to the individual. Instead, you'll have to give the employee a raise, bonus, or promotion.

Here are some examples of how you might describe the benefit:

Samples

> ... employment as a sales representative

> ... a raise of $2,000 per year

> ... a promotion to the position of director of business development, with a pay increase of $10,000 per year

1. Agreement Not to Disclose Confidential Information

You don't need to insert anything here. This paragraph prevents your employee from disclosing your confidential information to third parties except when the employee is required to do so as part of the job or when required to do so by law. The employee agrees not to disclose trade secrets, sales and profits figures, customer lists, relationships with contractors, customers, or suppliers, or opportunities for new or developing business.

2. Return of Confidential Information

You don't need to insert anything here. You don't want a former employee to keep any documents, computer disks, or other materials containing your confidential information. This paragraph prohibits the employee from taking confidential information without permission, and it requires the employee to return any confidential information received from you if you demand the information back or if your employment relationship with the employee ends for any reason.

3. Right to an Injunction

You don't need to insert anything here. In this paragraph, the employee agrees that you should be able to obtain an injunction against the employee if the employee violates the agreement. An injunction is a ruling from a court ordering someone to stop doing something. In the case of a confidentiality agreement, the court would order an employee who is disclosing confidential information to stop doing so. Similarly, if you learn that the employee is about to disclose confidential information, you could ask the court to prevent the employee from doing so.

4. Reasonableness

You don't need to insert anything here. In this clause, your employee is acknowledging that the restrictions you've placed on the employee are reasonable. This helps prevent the employee from later claiming that the restrictions aren't really necessary to protect your business and can help convince a judge that it's fair to enforce the agreement against the employee.

5. Survivability

You don't need to insert anything here. Your agreement provides that the employee's obligations survive—that is, continue to bind the employee —even after the employee leaves. This ensures that the employee can't argue that the terms of the agreement applied only while the employee was working for you.

Standard Clauses

The remainder of the agreement contains the standard clauses we discussed in Chapter 1. The only thing you'll need to fill in here is the name of the state whose law will apply to the contract in the paragraph called "Governing Law."

Signatures

Only the employee needs to sign the agreement. The employee should sign two copies of the agreement. You should keep one of these originals and the employee should keep the other. Keep your copy in the employee's personnel file so you can refer to it quickly, if necessary.

> **CAUTION**
> **Take additional steps to maintain secrecy.** Merely listing a type of information in a confidentiality agreement is usually insufficient to give it confidential status in the eyes of the law. A court probably won't conclude that information is really confidential unless you actually limit access to it. For example, if you start

handing out a secret recipe to favored customers or make no effort to restrict access to your customer list, this sort of agreement is unlikely to be enforced if the employee later begins to make use of the information. Asking an employee to sign this agreement should be just one of the steps you take to protect your confidential information. As part of your general practice, you should have procedures in place that clearly identify all confidential materials as being confidential.

Form 9E: Covenant Not to Compete

Occasionally, employees quit and start a business that competes with a former employer or take a job with a competitor. If you want to prevent an employee from unfairly learning from you and then becoming a rival in the marketplace, use Form 9E: Covenant Not to Compete. A covenant not to compete is an agreement that requires an employee to refrain from competing against an employer by working for a competitor or opening a competing business.

You can prevent an employee from competing with your business for a certain length of time after departing—usually for up to two years—especially if that employee is privy to your trade secrets or has close relationships with your customers. Use this form selectively. There is no need to have all of your employees sign such an agreement. Most workers aren't exposed to much truly confidential information, and few employees have the practical ability to set up a competing shop or work for a competitor and lure away a significant number of your customers.

You should always have a good reason for asking an employee to sign a covenant not to compete. If you ever need to enforce it in court, a judge will enforce it only if you had a legitimate reason for making the agreement, since a covenant not to compete limits the employee's ability to earn a living. There are two main reasons a business might ask an employee to sign a covenant not to compete:

first, to protect its trade secrets, and second, to protect a valuable customer base.

A trade secret is confidential information one business has that gives it a competitive advantage over other businesses that don't have the information. Covenants not to compete protect your trade secrets by preventing a former employee from taking the information to a competitor. A covenant not to compete can also prevent the loss of valuable customers, because your former employee will be forbidden from luring them away.

Some States Won't Enforce Employee Noncompete Agreements

In most states, courts will require employees to honor their noncompete agreements—but not always to their full extent. And a few states ban any enforcement of these agreements.

California takes the strictest stance. A statute bans the enforcement of any contract that restrains a person from engaging in a lawful profession, trade, or business. North Dakota has a statute nearly as strict as California's.

Other states have statutes that somewhat limit the use of noncompete agreements. These limits can range from mild to severe. And in states that don't have such statutes, court decisions often impose similar limits. So before you ask an employee to sign a noncompete agreement, check with an employment lawyer in your state. You can find a useful chart summarizing the noncompetition rules of all 50 states at www. beckreedriden.com/50-state-noncompete-chart-2.

Courts treat confidentiality agreements differently. They generally will be fully enforced.

Used wisely, a covenant not to compete can be a valuable tool for protecting your business. However, covenants not to compete are not without their pitfalls. If you try to enforce the agreement against a former employee, he or she could argue that the agreement is unreasonably restrictive—for instance, that the time period during which the employee may not compete is too long, or that it covers too many kinds of businesses or too wide a geographic area. If your agreement isn't drafted properly, a court might side with the employee and let the employee go to work for the competition.

> EXAMPLE 1: The Tax Shop, a storefront business specializing in preparing tax returns, has its key employees agree in writing that for 18 months after leaving their jobs, they won't open a competing tax preparation business within three miles of The Tax Shop's office. The restriction appears reasonable and will likely withstand a legal challenge by an employee.

> EXAMPLE 2: Solution 1040, another tax preparation service, requires its employees to agree that for five years after leaving their jobs, they won't work anywhere in the state at a job that involves doing tax returns. The restriction appears to be overly broad and almost surely wouldn't be enforced by a court.

To help ensure the enforceability of your covenant not to compete, it's prudent to include only those restrictions that are absolutely necessary to protect your business interests. For example, our covenant not to compete applies only to businesses that are similar to the one the buyer is purchasing. In addition, your contract limits the former owner's ability to compete only in areas where the buyer actually conducts business. This reasonable geographic scope should maximize your chances of creating an enforceable agreement.

Finally, you, as employer, will choose the amount of time the employee will be prevented from competing against you. Restricting the seller's ability to compete for up to three years is common, but anything more than that is likely to be invalidated by a court unless it's truly necessary to protect your business, which will be hard to prove.

Instructions for Form 9E: Covenant Not to Compete

All the forms in this book are provided in Appendix B and on the Nolo website. To access the downloadable forms online, use the link provided in Appendix A. As you read the instructions for Form 9E, you might want to refer to the form in Appendix B or open the form on your computer so you can follow along. (Before you use the form in Appendix B, be sure to photocopy it so you'll have a clean copy to use later.)

Introduction

In the first and second blanks, fill in the name of your company and the employee's name. (Consult the chart in Chapter 1 for more information about how to identify your business.)

In the third blank, insert the benefit the employee is receiving in exchange for signing this agreement. (To make your covenant not to compete legally enforceable, you must give the employee who signs the agreement something of value in return for the employee's promise not to compete. In legal terms, this thing of value is called consideration.)

If you ask the employee to sign the agreement at the beginning of the employment relationship, then the consideration can simply be the fact that you are providing the employee with a job. For example, if you ask a prospective employee to sign the agreement as a condition of receiving a job offer from you, then the thing of value that you are giving to the individual is employment.

However, what if you wait until the middle of your employment relationship with the employee before asking for a signature on the agreement? In a majority of states, continuing to employ an existing at-will employee constitutes adequate consideration supporting a noncompete agreement. Nothing extra need be provided the employee in return for signing the agreement. For example, if you ask an employee who has been working for you for three months to sign the agreement, the fact that you will continue to employ the individual is sufficient consideration. In a minority of states, however, additional consideration must be provided to an existing employee for a noncompetition agreement to be valid—for example, you'll have to give the employee a raise, bonus, promotion, or extra vacation days. These states include Alaska, Kentucky, Massachusetts, Minnesota, Montana, North Carolina, Oregon, Pennsylvania, South Carolina, Texas, Washington, West Virginia, and Wyoming. Additional consideration is also required in all states where an existing employee is not an at-will employee—for example, he or she has signed an employee agreement for a set term or providing the employee may only be fired for cause.

Here are some examples of how you might describe the benefit:

Samples

> ... employment as a programmer analyst

> ... continued employment as a programmer analyst

> ... a raise of $1,000 per year

> ... a promotion to the position of Sales Manager, with a pay increase of $3,000 per year

1. Agreement Not to Compete

Insert the number of months or years after leaving your employment that the employee is not per-mitted to compete with your business. Here, the key is to be realistic—don't insert an unreasonable amount of time simply to punish your employee for leaving. As an employer, you need to evaluate and decide how long it's reasonable to ask a former employee not to compete against your business. The length of time may depend on a number of factors:

- how long the information the employee knows will be valuable to a competitor
- how long it will take your business to train and hire a replacement, and
- whether your state imposes any limits on the length of time an employee may agree not to compete.

Ordinarily, courts will enforce covenants not to compete that last anywhere from six months to two years. After that, they might not. South Dakota and Louisiana limit the time to two years by law. If you ask for anything longer than one or two years and you have to take a former employee to court, you risk a judge's refusing to enforce your agreement at all.

2. Right to an Injunction

See the instructions for Paragraph 3 of Form 9D.

3. Reasonableness

See the instructions for Paragraph 4 of Form 9D.

4. Survivability

See the instructions for Paragraph 5 of Form 9D.

Standard Clauses

The remainder of the agreement contains the standard clauses we discussed in Chapter 1. The only thing you'll need to fill in here is the name of the state whose law will apply to the contract in the paragraph called "Governing Law."

Signatures

Only the employee needs to sign the agreement. The employee should sign two copies of the agreement. You should keep one of these originals and the employee should keep the other. Keep your copy in the employee's personnel file so you can refer to it quickly if necessary.

Form 9F: Contract With Independent Contractor

Independent contractors are people who contract to work for others without having the legal status of an employee. If you hire a worker who qualifies under the law as an independent contractor, you don't have to pay the employer's share of the worker's Social Security and Medicare taxes, nor do you have to withhold the worker's share of those taxes or the worker's income taxes. The independent contractor is responsible for reporting and paying all Social Security, Medicare, and income taxes on his or her earnings. (You are, however, required to inform the IRS if you've paid an independent contractor $600 or more in one year.)

In addition to the reduced bookkeeping and financial obligations you have when you hire an independent contractor instead of an employee, you're not bound by many of the federal and state laws that normally govern the employer-employee relationship.

The IRS strongly prefers that workers be classified as employees and not as independent contractors. If you classify someone as an independent contractor, and that person should be classified as an employee, you can face IRS penalties. To withstand an IRS challenge to independent contractor classification, you must show that the worker will control both the outcome of the project and how the job gets done. It also helps if you can show that the worker has at least some control over how he or she charges for the job.

It's sometimes difficult to know whether the IRS will agree that you've correctly classified a worker as an independent contractor. The easy cases involve workers who clearly are in business for themselves, demonstrated by such characteristics as:

- The worker is available to perform services for many businesses.
- The worker has a fixed base of operations— a commercial or office location, perhaps, or a room at home—and ongoing business expenses.

- The worker lists the business in the phone book and also drums up business through newspaper ads, radio commercials, and circulars.
- The worker has a business website, and markets his or her services to the public through advertising and other means.

By contrast, people who work under your close supervision for fixed wages are almost certainly employees rather than independent contractors.

TIP

It's safest to deal with entities. To achieve a degree of assurance that you won't have IRS problems, consider asking the worker to incorporate or form an LLC. Then enter into a contract with the entity—not the individual. The IRS will almost always treat this as a valid arrangement and accept the fact the worker isn't your employee but instead is an employee of his or her own entity. Incidentally, you can form a one-person corporation or LLC in every state.

Unfortunately, some workers fall into an ambiguous area where the distinction between an employee and an independent contractor gets fuzzy. You might wish to get advice from a tax expert before classifying someone as an independent contractor. If you do decide to treat the worker as an independent contractor, having a written contract like Form 9F helps you establish that the classification is proper.

CAUTION

A contract by itself can't create an independent contractor relationship. A contract is useful to document the financial arrangements to which you and the worker agree and who has control over how the work is to be done. But a contract, by itself, can't magically convert someone who's an employee, as defined by IRS rules, into an independent contractor.

RESOURCE

Learn more about hiring independent contractors. *The Legal Guide for Starting & Running a Small Business*, by Fred S. Steingold and David M. Steingold (Nolo), explains the differences between employees and independent contractors and how you can avoid legal problems and penalties when you classify workers.

To read about the legal tests for independent contractor status, consult the IRS form SS-8 (and related instructions), *Determination of Worker Status for Purposes of Federal Employment Taxes and Income Tax Withholding* and IRS Publication 15 (Circular E) *Employer's Tax Guide*, both available at www.irs.gov.

For details on the legal and practical facets of engaging independent contractors and for a large variety of legal forms, see *Working With Independent Contractors*, by Stephen Fishman (Nolo).

If you are an independent contractor who is hired by others, see *Working for Yourself: Law & Taxes for Independent Contractors, Freelancers & Gig Workers of All Types*, by Stephen Fishman (Nolo).

Instructions for Form 9F: Contract With Independent Contractor

All the forms in this book are provided in Appendix B and on the Nolo website. To access the downloadable forms online, use the link provided in Appendix A. As you read the instructions for Form 9F, you might want to refer to the form in Appendix B or open the form on your computer so you can follow along. (Before you use the form in Appendix B, be sure to photocopy it so you'll have a clean copy to use later.)

1. Names

Insert your name (the client) and the name of the independent contractor who will be performing services for you. (Consult the chart in Chapter 1 for more information about how to identify your business and the independent contractor.)

2. Services to Be Performed

Describe the services that the independent contractor will be performing for you. Avoid giving the independent contractor specific instructions on how to do the work. You can give details about the results you want the independent contractor to achieve, but don't tell the contractor exactly how to accomplish the job. Here are examples of bad and good descriptions of independent contractor services.

Sample of a bad description:

> Contractor will landscape the green areas that surround the office building over the next three months. Contractor will start work promptly every morning at 9:00. Contractor will use only soil from Farm Fresh Soils on Market Avenue. Contractor will plant ten Monterey Pines along the front of the building and five Monterey Pines along each side. Between the Monterey Pines, contractor will plant sunflowers and lilac. Contractor will take three 15-minute breaks every day, plus one 30-minute break for lunch. Contractor will wear an orange safety vest at all times.

Sample of a good description:

> Contractor will landscape the green areas that surround the office building. Contractor will use drought-resistant California native plants.

3. Time for Performance

If the whole project must be completed by a specific date and there is no work due at intervals before that date, check the first box and fill in the date. This option is appropriate for work that can't be broken into pieces or phases. If, on the other hand, you would like the contractor to complete the project in a piecemeal manner, with each piece due on a different date, check the second box and insert the schedule. For example, if you are hiring a contractor to paint your office building, you might want the contractor to complete each floor of the building by a certain date. Or, if the contractor will landscape your outdoor area, you might want to break the work down into specific tasks.

Sample

> January 14, 20xx: Landscape design completed
>
> February 1, 20xx: Trees planted
>
> February 15, 20xx: Shrubs planted
>
> March 1, 20xx: Grasses planted
>
> March 15, 20xx: All work completed

4. Payment

Most firms pay independent contractors in one of two ways: by fixed fee or by unit of time. A fixed fee means that you pay the independent contractor one amount for the entire project—for example, $1,000 to landscape your office grounds. Paying by unit of time means that you pay the independent contractor for the time spent working—for example, $50 per hour to copyedit your corporate publications.

Generally speaking, it is better to pay an independent contractor by fixed fee rather than by unit of time. This is because government agencies tend to view a fixed fee as evidence that the worker is an independent contractor, not an employee. However, if the standard practice in your business community is to pay by unit of time—for example, most people pay copy editors by the hour—or if it truly is the best way for you to pay the worker, then you should feel free to use the unit of time method. The payment method alone will not make the worker an employee.

Samples of fixed fees:

> - Client will pay Contractor $400 for Phase I of the job and $600 for Phase II of the job.
> - Client will pay Contractor $1,500 on January 14, 20xx, and $1,500 on March 15, 20xx.

Samples of payments by unit of time:

> - Client will pay Contractor $15 an hour.
> - Client will pay Contractor $1,000 per week.

If you use the second method, consider putting a cap on the independent contractor's total compensation. The independent contractor then bears much of the risk of correctly estimating how much time it will take to do the job and how profitable the job will be.

Sample

> Client will pay Contractor $15 an hour up to $3,500 for the entire job.

Your agreement must also specify when you will pay the independent contractor. (You should always make your payment contingent on receiving an invoice from the contractor.) One simple option is to pay the independent contractor the full amount after the contractor has completed the work.

Sample

> When Contractor completes the project described in this agreement, Contractor will submit an invoice to the Client stating the total amount due. Client will have 30 days from the invoice date to make full payment.

If you're paying the contractor a fixed fee, the contractor might not want to wait until the end of a job to receive payment from you. This is particularly true in the case of work that the contractor will complete over a long period of time. You and the contractor can agree to divide the payment into two parts, with your paying a down payment at the beginning and the rest at the end.

Sample

> Client will pay Contractor 20% of the total fee after both parties have signed this agreement. When Contractor has completed the work described in this agreement, Contractor will give an invoice to Client reflecting the work that has been done and the remaining dollar amount due. Client will have 30 days from the invoice date to make the remaining payment.

If you are paying the contractor by the hour or by another unit of time, another simple option is to have the contractor send you an invoice every so often that states the amount due to date.

Sample

> Every 30 days, Contractor will submit an invoice to client describing the work contractor has done during the 30-day period and the current amount due. Client will pay invoices within 15 days of receipt.

If the contractor is working according to a performance schedule that you specified in Paragraph 3, you might want to make your payments to the contractor on the same schedule (but only after receiving periodic invoices). You can describe the payment schedule in the same terms as you described the performance schedule. Your description of the payment schedule will vary depending on whether you are paying the contractor a fixed fee or by unit of time.

Sample of a fixed fee:

> Contractor is performing the work described in this agreement in five parts, as described in Paragraph 3. Client is paying contractor a fixed fee of $5,000 for the total job. After Contractor completes each part of the performance schedule, Contractor will submit an invoice to Client for 1/5 of the total fee, or $1,000. Client will pay each invoice within 30 days of receipt.

Sample

> After Contractor completes each scheduled step of the project, Contractor will submit an invoice to Client detailing the work completed and the amount that Client owes Contractor for that step. Client will have 30 days to pay each invoice.

If paying by unit of time, be sure to include both the unit of time and the payment arrangements in this paragraph.

5. State and Federal Taxes

Nothing needs to be inserted here. For an employer, one of the advantages of hiring an independent contractor is that the employer does not have to pay or withhold Social Security or Medicare taxes, nor does the employer have to make unemployment contributions or workers' compensation contributions for the worker. This paragraph makes it clear that you will not be withholding money or paying taxes for the worker, and the worker promises to pay these taxes. By requiring the contractor to acknowledge this in writing, you are creating good evidence to a government agency that the worker is an independent contractor rather than an employee.

6. Fringe Benefits

Nothing needs to be inserted here. This paragraph provides that the independent contractor will not receive any benefits, such as health insurance, that you provide to your employees. Not having to provide benefits to the contractor makes it less expensive than an employee relationship. This is also good evidence to a government agency evaluating your relationship that the worker is not an employee.

7. Invoices

Nothing needs to be inserted here. The contractor should submit invoices to you that detail the work the contractor has performed and the amount due for those services. Keep these invoices for your records in case you are ever audited by a government agency; they provide good evidence of the independent contractor's status. (Employees do not usually submit invoices for work performed.)

8. Independent Contractor Status

Nothing needs to be inserted here. This paragraph explicitly states that you and the worker intend for your relationship to be an independent contractor relationship. Although this kind of statement is not a magic bullet, having a clause in your contract that clearly states the worker is an independent contractor can help you convince government agencies that you have classified the worker correctly, in case you are ever audited.

9. Other Clients

Nothing needs to be inserted here. This paragraph specifically allows the contractor to perform services for other clients while he or she is working for you. Unlike employees, who typically work for only one business, contractors may perform services for a number of different businesses. It's often good evidence of the contractor's nonemployee status for the contractor to provide services for another company. Contractors who perform services for just one business tend to look more like employees to government agencies.

10. Assistants

Nothing needs to be inserted here. This paragraph specifies that the contractor, rather than your business, will hire assistants to help perform the services. These people will be the contractor's responsibility; the contractor must pay for their services, as well as pay their employment taxes and other expenses. This type of provision is further evidence that the worker is a contractor rather than an employee. Employees typically do not have the right to hire assistants without your consent, and they don't usually pay assistants out of their own pocket.

11. Equipment and Supplies

A. Usually, the client does not provide equipment or supplies to an independent contractor. After all, the independent contractor is a separate business, and separate businesses usually factor in the costs of equipment and supplies when setting their fees. In addition, providing equipment or supplies to an independent contractor can make the relationship look more like an employee relationship than an independent contractor relationship. This might hurt your case if a government agency ever questions the worker's classification.

Sometimes, however, it is appropriate for the hiring firm to provide equipment or supplies to an independent contractor. For example, let's say you have hired an accountant to come to your office and audit your books. It would be reasonable for you to provide the accountant with a workspace in your office with the appropriate office supplies. Or maybe you've hired a janitorial service to clean your office every week. It would be reasonable for you to provide supplies such as mops and cleansers.

If the independent contractor will be providing all the necessary equipment, tools, and supplies to do the work, write the word "None" in the space provided. Otherwise, write in the equipment, tools, and supplies that you will provide.

B. Independent contractors incur a variety of expenses while performing their work, from postage fees to charges for long distance phone calls to travel costs. Usually, the client does not pay an independent contractor's expenses. The independent contractor is a separate business, and separate businesses usually factor in the cost of expenses when setting their fees. In addition, paying expenses can make the relationship look more like an employee relationship than an independent contractor relationship. This could cause trouble if a government agency questions the worker's classification.

Sometimes it is customary for employers to pay the expenses of certain types of independent contractors. For example, attorneys usually charge their clients an hourly fee plus expenses such as postage and photocopying. In such a situation, it is acceptable to pay the expenses without worrying too much about a worker being reclassified as an employee. If the independent contractor will be responsible for all expenses, write the word "None" in the space provided. Otherwise, write in the expenses for which you'll be responsible.

TIP

A worker's investment in tools and supplies helps show independence. Requiring the worker you're contracting with to provide all or most equipment, tools, and supplies and to pay all or most expenses can help establish the existence of a true independent contractor

relationship. It's evidence that the worker has a financial investment in the project that a typical employee wouldn't have.

12. Disputes

See the discussion of dispute resolution clauses in Chapter 1.

Standard Clauses

The remainder of the agreement contains the standard clauses we discussed in Chapter 1. The only thing you'll need to fill in here is the name of the state whose law will apply to the contract in the paragraph called "Governing Law."

Signatures

Both contractor and client need to sign. See Chapter 1 for instructions on signing contracts.

Extending Credit and Getting Paid

 FORMS

To download the forms discussed in this chapter, go to this book's companion page on Nolo.com. See Appendix A for the link.

Many customers prefer a choice when it comes to paying for the goods or services you sell to them. From your point of view, cash is the preferred method. But you'll unnecessarily deter customers if you make cash the only way they can pay you. You'll probably be willing to accept a check if the customer has acceptable ID—although there's always some risk that a check will bounce or that the customer has presented false ID. Fortunately, most people don't carry checks these days. Credit and debit cards avoid the risk of nonpayment; the downside is that you'll need to pay a modest fee for each transaction you process using one of these cards. Still, for most small businesses, accepting cash, checks, and credit cards or debit cards will generally ensure that your customers won't stiff you, and your customers will appreciate having a choice of payment methods.

Another option is to offer your customers credit directly. These days, it's less common—and less necessary—for a small business to extend credit to customers. But even so, you might decide that doing so will increase your bottom line. This chapter offers forms you can use if you choose to go that route.

RESOURCE

Learn more about extending credit. Federal and state laws regulate extending credit to customers—especially nonbusiness customers. Some of those laws are described below. For more information on these laws, as well as rules and tips for accepting cash, checks, and credit or debit cards, see *Legal Guide for Starting & Running a Small Business*, by Fred S. Steingold and David M. Steingold (Nolo).

If you do decide to extend credit to customers, it makes good business sense to have them complete a credit application so that you can evaluate whether they're good credit risks. Obviously, you don't want to offer credit to customers who have a history of not paying, or who have to be chased for the money.

For nonbusiness customers, you can use Form 10A: Credit Application for an Individual Customer. An individual customer is a person who wants to be billed for goods or services used primarily for personal, family, or household use.

You might decide to obtain a credit report to check on the creditworthiness of an individual customer. You can purchase a credit report on a customer from a national credit reporting agency such as TransUnion (www.transunion.com), Experian (www.experian.com), or Equifax (www.equifax.com). If you deny credit wholly or in part based on that applicant's credit report, you'll need to notify him or her in writing. To do this, you can use Form 10B: Adverse Action Letter.

When the credit applicant isn't an individual consumer, you can use Form 10C: Credit Application for a Business Customer. If you want to review a business's credit report, you can order one from Dun & Bradstreet (www.dnb.com).

Getting a credit application and doing a credit check won't always guarantee that the customer will pay you as agreed. You might have to coax money from the customer by phone calls or collection letters. If so, you can adapt forms 10D, 10E, and 10F to your needs. The first letter is a mild nudge. The second and third letters turn up the heat in reminding the customer of the need for payment.

Form 10A: Credit Application for an Individual Customer

You can use this form to help you decide whether to extend credit to a nonbusiness customer. The applicant provides contact information so that, if necessary, you can reach him or her by mail, phone, fax, or email. The applicant also provides employment information, credit references, and banking references. The terms of your credit arrangements are set out in the form so the applicant knows what to expect.

Federal Laws That Regulate Consumer Credit

If you sell goods or services to consumers on credit for personal, family, or household purposes, you must comply with several federal laws. States, too, have adopted consumer credit laws that typically mirror provisions of the federal law. Here's an introduction to the major federal laws that affect consumer credit.

The Truth in Lending Act

This law helps customers know their rights. It requires you to disclose your credit terms and regulates how you advertise consumer credit. Here is some of the information you must disclose to a consumer who buys on credit:

- the monthly finance charge
- the annual percentage rate (APR)
- when payments are due
- the total sale price (the cash price plus all other charges), and
- the amount of any late payment charges and when they'll be imposed.

The Equal Credit Opportunity Act

You cannot discriminate against an applicant on the basis of race, color, religion, national origin, age, sex, marital status, or public assistance status. You're free to consider legitimate factors in granting credit, such as the applicant's earnings, savings, and credit record. You can also reject a consumer who hasn't reached the legal age in your state for entering into contracts.

The Fair Credit Billing Act

This law tells you what to do if a customer claims you made a mistake in your billing. The law applies to open-end credit accounts only, such as credit cards, and revolving charge accounts. It does not cover installment contracts, which are loans or extensions of credit that the customer repays on a fixed schedule.

If you choose to offer open-end credit to your customers, you must also comply with certain notice and billing requirements. To learn more, check out the Federal Trade Commission's website at www.ftc.gov.

The customer must notify you within 60 days after you mailed the first bill containing the claimed error. You must respond within 30 days unless you've already resolved the dispute. You must also conduct a reasonable investigation and, within 90 days of getting the customer's letter, explain why your bill is correct or else correct the error.

During the investigation, you cannot report the disputed amount as delinquent to credit reporting agencies or other creditors, nor can you take any collection action. You may include the disputed amount on your monthly billing statement to the customer.

The Fair Credit Reporting Act

This law deals primarily with credit reporting agencies. It's intended to protect customers from having credit declined because of incomplete or misleading credit report information. The customer can get a copy of his or her credit report and ask that an inaccurate item be corrected or removed. The customer can also add a 100-word statement to the credit report explaining his or her side of the story.

The Fair Debt Collection Practices Act

This federal law addresses abusive methods used by third-party collectors—bill collectors you hire to collect overdue bills. Your small business is more likely affected by state laws that apply directly to collection methods used by a creditor. These state laws are discussed in the explanation of the first collection letter (Form 10D).

After the applicant completes the form, call or write his or her employer to confirm employment, as well as the credit references to learn about his or her payment history. Check with the banking reference to confirm the existence of the listed accounts. You might be asked to provide evidence that the applicant has consented to the disclosure of this information. If so, you can mail or fax the application itself, in which the applicant expressly authorizes the disclosure.

You can also order a credit report from a national credit reporting agency such as TransUnion (www. transunion.com), Experian (www.experian.com), or Equifax (www.equifax.com).

> ⓘ CAUTION
>
> **Guard against misuse of information on credit applications and in credit reports.** To prevent identity fraud and other illegal or improper use of consumer information, store credit applications and credit reports in a safe place, such as a locked cabinet. Use a secure password for information you keep online. When you no longer have a legitimate business need for this material, shred the physical documents and delete the online file.

Instructions for Form 10A: Credit Application for an Individual Customer

All the forms in this book are provided in Appendix B and on the Nolo website. To access the downloadable forms online, use the link provided in Appendix A. As you read the instructions for Form 10A, you might want to refer to the form in Appendix B or open the form on your computer so you can follow along. (Before you use the form in Appendix B, be sure to photocopy it so you'll have a clean copy to use later.)

The applicant will supply practically all of the information that the form requires. The only thing you'll need is the name of your business in the form's first blank space.

At the bottom of the form, we've provided some standard credit arrangement terms. Modify these as you see fit.

Form 10B: Adverse Action Letter

If you deny a customer's credit application, you must comply with notice requirements set forth by two federal laws—the Fair Credit Reporting Act (FCRA) and the Equal Credit Opportunity Act (ECOA). You can combine the requirements of both laws into one notice.

The Fair Credit Reporting Act law requires that if you deny credit to an applicant based wholly or partly on a credit report or on information from another source such as an employer or a credit reference, you must notify the applicant in writing. This is typically called an adverse action notice.

The adverse action notice must notify the applicant of your credit decision (for example, that you are denying credit or terminating existing credit), the name, address, and telephone number of the credit reporting agency (CRA) that provided the report on which you relied, and certain disclosures about the CRA. You must also notify the applicant if you took the adverse action, at least in part, because of the applicant's credit score. You must then provide the range of possible scores, the key factors affecting the applicant's score, the date the score was created, and the name of the agency that provided the score.

If you relied on an outside source other than a CRA, you must notify the applicant that he or she has the right to request, within 60 days, that you disclose the nature of this information.

Under the ECOA, if you deny a customer's application for credit or provide credit on terms less favorable than requested, you must notify the applicant of your decision, the name of the federal agency that oversees compliance (in most cases this will be the FTC), certain language about the ECOA, and either: the specific, principal reasons for that decision, or notice that the applicant has 60 days to request specific reasons.

The ECOA notice requirements do not apply if you are extending credit that is not a credit card account, is not subject to a finance charge, and is paid in four installments or less.

Keep a copy of each adverse action letter you send. It will be crucial if the applicant or a governmental agency later claims that you didn't comply with the law. To protect the applicant's privacy, keep your copy—along with the application —in a safe place, as recommended in the above instructions for Form 10A.

Instructions for Form 10B: Adverse Action Letter

All the forms in this book are provided in Appendix B and on the Nolo website. To access the downloadable forms online, use the link provided in Appendix A. As you read the instructions for Form 10B, you might want to refer to the form in Appendix B or open the form on your computer so you can follow along. (Before you use the form in Appendix B, be sure to photocopy it so you'll have a clean copy to use later.)

Opening Section

As with any business letter, you'll probably use your letterhead for this form. Your letterhead should include your business name, address, and phone number—and it might include additional information, such as a fax number and email address. Beneath the letterhead information, insert the current date.

Begin the letter with the applicant's name and address, and a salutation, such as "Dear Mr. Smith."

Reasons for Denying Credit

The next section of the letter lets you tell the applicant why you've denied credit. The most common reasons are listed here. If one or more applies, check the boxes. If the reason you denied credit is not listed, check the "Other" box and then clearly state the reason.

Sources of Information

If you've relied on a credit report or information from other sources, such as the applicant's employer

or credit reference, you can check the "Other Information" box. In the case of a credit report, check the "Consumer Reporting Agency" box and insert the name and contact information.

Here is the contact information for each of the three national reporting agencies:

Experian
888-397-3742
www.experian.com

TransUnion
800-916-8800
www.transunion.com

Equifax
888-548-7878
www.equifax.com

If you relied on a credit score in making your credit decision, check the "Credit Scoring Company" box and fill in the appropriate information.

Notice

The notice section near the end of the letter is required by the Federal Trade Commission.

Name and Title

At the end of the letter, just below the place where you'll sign it, insert your name and your title, such as Manager, President, Member, Partner, or Owner.

CAUTION

If you offer different credit terms to different customers, you'll need to provide additional notices. You must comply with additional notice requirements if you use a credit report to decide on APRs or other credit terms, and you charge a credit applicant a rate (or impose a term) less favorable than what you offer to 40% of your other applicants. This is called the risk-based pricing notice. The rules can be complicated, so if you offer different rates and terms to different credit applicants, be sure to read the law. You can find it by typing "16 CFR 640" into the Google search box.

Form 10C: Credit Application for a Business Customer

You can use this form when the applicant is a business. It works for any type of business customer —sole proprietorship, partnership, corporation, or limited liability company (LLC). The form asks for basic information similar to what an individual applicant would provide, but you need more than that for a business applicant. You need to know what type of entity the business is and who the individuals are who can speak for the business, so the form has places for the applicant to provide that information as well.

When the customer is a small corporation or an LLC, you want to make sure that you don't have to rely just on the business's cash flow or assets for payments. It's prudent to require that the individual signing the application personally guarantee payment of the account. Otherwise, your only source of payment could be a shaky or underfunded entity. In some businesses, however, it's against trade practices to ask for a personal guarantee. Learn the practices in your industry before asking for a personal guarantee. If you do ask for one, check with your state law to see if a signature on a credit application is sufficient. You might have to obtain a new guarantee each time you extend credit to the company.

If the business is owned by an individual who hasn't incorporated or formed an LLC, the owner's individual and business assets are available to satisfy the debt.

For general partnerships, you can go after the assets of the individual partners, so it's a good idea to get the names of the partners. A limited partnership consists of general and limited partners; only the assets of the general partners are available to satisfy the debt.

You might also want to ask for the personal guarantee of others if a credit applicant has weak financial status. This is often called cosigning.

After the applicant completes the form, call or write the listed credit references to learn about the business's payment history. You can also check with the banking reference to confirm the existence of the listed accounts. You might be asked to provide evidence that the business has consented to the disclosure of this information. If so, you can mail or fax the application itself, in which the signer expressly authorizes the disclosure.

If you want to review a business's credit report, you can order one from Dun & Bradstreet (www. dnb.com).

> **CAUTION**
>
> **If you deny business credit, be sure to comply with the ECOA.** The Equal Credit Opportunity Act (ECOA) sets forth certain notice requirements if you deny credit to a business. The nature of the notice depends on whether the business had gross revenues of more or less than $1 million in the previous year. To find out the notice requirements that apply, read the law; it's located in the Code of Federal Regulations at 12 C.F.R. 202.9. You can find the text by visiting the website of Cornell's Legal Information Institute at www.law.cornell.edu, clicking on "C.F.R.," and typing "12 CFR 202.9" into the search box (or type "12 CFR 202.9" into the Google search box).

Instructions for Form 10C: Credit Application for a Business Customer

All the forms in this book are provided in Appendix B and on the Nolo website. To access the downloadable forms online, use the link provided in Appendix A. As you read the instructions for Form 10C, you might want to refer to the form in Appendix B or open the form on your computer so you can follow along. (Before you use the form in Appendix B, be sure to photocopy it so you'll have a clean copy to use later.)

The applicant will supply practically all of the information that the form requires. The only thing you'll need to supply is the name of your business in the form's second blank space.

At the bottom of the form, we've provided some standard credit arrangement terms. Modify these as you see fit.

Form 10D: First Collection Letter

This letter is a gentle reminder to a customer who has not paid his or her bill. The assumption is that the customer is acting in good faith and has simply misplaced the bill or forgotten to send in the payment. Or maybe the customer has been ill, on vacation, or dealing with a family crisis. The letter gives the customer the benefit of the doubt. Still, it sends the clear message that prompt payment is expected.

Include a self-addressed envelope to nudge the customer into compliance. To make payment even easier for the customer, consider putting postage on the envelope.

> **CAUTION**
> **Avoid abusive collection practices.** Many states have laws that say that certain methods are out of bounds in attempting to collect a consumer debt. Your common sense will probably tell you what actions to avoid. Here's a partial list of practices that can get you in trouble:
> - threatening to use physical force to collect a debt
> - falsely threatening that the debtor's failure to pay will result in a criminal accusation
> - causing a phone to ring repeatedly or continuously to annoy a debtor
> - communicating with a debtor so often that it constitutes harassment, and
> - communicating with the debtor's employer about a debt, unless the debtor has consented in writing—though you can contact the employer to verify employment.

Instructions for Form 10D: First Collection Letter

All the forms in this book are provided in Appendix B and on the Nolo website. To access the downloadable forms online, use the link provided in Appendix A. As you read the instructions for Form 10D, you might want to refer to the form in Appendix B or open the form on your computer so you can follow along. (Before you use the form in Appendix B, be sure to photocopy it so you'll have a clean copy to use later.)

Opening Section

As with any business letter, you'll probably use your letterhead for this form. Your letterhead should include your business name, address, and phone number—and it might include additional information, such as a fax number and email address. Beneath the letterhead information, insert the current date.

Then insert the applicant's name and address, and a salutation, such as "Dear Mr. Smith."

Body of the Letter

Insert the amount the customer owes and the type of goods or services that the customer purchased from your business.

Name and Title

At the end of the letter, just below the place where you'll sign it, insert your name and your title, such as Manager, President, Member, Partner, or Owner.

Form 10E: Second Collection Letter

Consider using this letter if the customer has ignored your first letter (Form 10D). This letter is not as gentle as the first one. With this letter your business puts more pressure on the customer to pay up.

Instructions for Form 10E: Second Collection Letter

All the forms in this book are provided in Appendix B and on the Nolo website. To access the downloadable forms online, use the link provided in Appendix A. As you read the instructions for Form 10E, you might want to refer to the form in Appendix B or open the form on your computer so you can follow along. (Before you use the form in Appendix B, be sure to photocopy it so you'll have a clean copy to use later.)

Opening Section

As with any business letter, you'll probably use your letterhead for this form. Your letterhead should include your business name, address, and phone number—and it might include additional information, such as a fax number and email address. Beneath the letterhead information, insert the current date.

Then begin the letter with the applicant's name and address, and a salutation, such as "Dear Mr. Smith."

Body of the Letter

Insert the amount the customer owes and the type of goods or services that the customer purchased from your business. Then, put in the date that the purchase was made. This helps drive home the point that several months have elapsed since the customer received the goods or services.

Name and Title

At the end of the letter, just below the place where you'll sign it, insert your name and your title, such as Manager, President, Member, Partner, or Owner.

Form 10F: Third Collection Letter

This letter is tougher than the first two. It suggests that if the customer continues to delay payment, you'll take collection action. The type of action you might take isn't spelled out, but the customer will probably be concerned that you will turn the matter over to a collection agency or start a lawsuit. Be sure not to threaten any action that you don't intend to take, however. Some states prohibit this.

Instructions for Form 10F: Third Collection Letter

All the forms in this book are provided in Appendix B and on the Nolo website. To access the downloadable forms online, use the link provided in Appendix A. As you read the instructions for Form 10F, you might want to refer to the form in Appendix B or open the form on your computer so you can follow along. (Before you use the form in Appendix B, be sure to photocopy it so you'll have a clean copy to use later.)

Opening Section

As with any business letter, you'll probably use your letterhead for this form. Your letterhead should include your business name, address, and phone number—and it might include additional information, such as a fax number and email address. Beneath the letterhead information, insert the current date.

Then begin the letter with the applicant's name and address, and a salutation, such as "Dear Mr. Smith."

Body of the Letter

Insert the amount the customer owes and the type of goods or services that the customer purchased from your business. Then, put in the date that the purchase was made. As with the second collection letter—Form 10E—this emphasizes the fact that several months have elapsed since the customer received the goods or services.

Finally, insert a deadline that the customer must meet to avoid collection action.

Name and Title

At the end of the letter, just below the place where you'll sign it, insert your name and your title, such as Manager, President, Member, Partner, or Owner.

How to Use the Downloadable Forms on the Nolo Website

This book comes with electronic forms that you can download here:

www.nolo.com/back-of-book/RUNSF.html

To use the forms, your computer must have specific software programs installed. Here is a list of types of files provided by this book, as well as the software programs you'll need to access them:

- **RTF.** You can open, edit, print, and save these form files with most word processing programs such as Microsoft *Word*, Windows *WordPad*, and recent versions of *WordPerfect*.
- **PDF.** You can view these files with Adobe *Reader*, free software from www.adobe.com. Government PDFs are sometimes fillable using your computer, but some PDFs are designed to be printed out and completed by hand.

Editing RTFs

Here are some general instructions about editing RTF forms in your word processing program. Refer to the book's instructions for help about what should go in each blank.

- **Underlines.** Underlines indicate where to enter information. After filling in the needed text, delete the underline. In most word processing programs you can do this by highlighting the underlined portion and typing CTRL-U.

- **Bracketed and Italicized Text.** Bracketed and italicized text indicates instructions. Be sure to remove all instructional text before you finalize your document.
- **Optional Text.** Optional text gives you the choice to include or exclude text. Delete any optional text you don't want to use. Renumber numbered items, if necessary.
- **Alternative Text.** Alternative text gives you the choice between two or more text options. Delete those options you don't want to use. Renumber numbered items, if necessary.
- **Signature Lines.** Signature lines should appear on a page with at least some text from the document itself.

Every word processing program uses different commands to open, format, save, and print documents, so refer to your software's help documents for help using your program. Nolo cannot provide technical support for questions about how to use your computer or your software.

CAUTION

Nolo's forms are copyrighted. In accordance with U.S. copyright laws, the Nolo forms provided by this book are for your personal use only.

List of Forms

To download the following forms, go to: **www.nolo.com/back-of-book/RUNSF.html**

Form Title	File Name	Form Title	File Name
Dispute Resolution Clause	Disputes.rtf	Promissory Note (Interest-Only Payments)	Form4C.rtf
Formats for Names in Legal Forms	Names.rtf	Promissory Note (Lump-Sum Payment)	Form4D.rtf
Signature Formats	Signing.rtf	Security Agreement for Borrowing Money	Form4E.rtf
Personal Guarantee	Guarantee.rtf	Contract for Purchase of Assets From an Unincorporated Business	Form5A.rtf
Attachment	Form1A.rtf		
Amendment	Form1B.rtf	Contract for Purchase of Assets From a Corporation	Form5B.rtf
Checklist for Starting a Small Business	Form2A.rtf		
Partnership Agreement	Form2B.rtf	Corporate Resolution Authorizing Sale of Assets	Form5C.rtf
Preincorporation Agreement	Form2C.rtf		
Corporate Bylaws	Form2D.rtf	Contract for Purchase of Corporate Stock	Form5D.rtf
Stock Agreement	Form2E.rtf		
LLC Operating Agreement for Single-Member LLC	Form2F.rtf	Bill of Sale for Business Assets	Form5E.rtf
		Seller's Affidavit—No Creditors	Form5F.rtf
LLC Membership Certificate	Form2G.rtf	Security Agreement for Buying Business Assets	Form5G.rtf
Stock Certificate	Form2H.rtf		
Notice of Shareholders' Meeting	Form3A.rtf	Gross Lease	Form6A.rtf
Notice of Directors' Meeting	Form3B.rtf	Net Lease for Entire Building	Form6B.rtf
Shareholder Proxy	Form3C.rtf	Net Lease for Part of Building	Form6C.rtf
Minutes of Shareholders' Meeting	Form3D.rtf	Sublease	Form6D.rtf
Minutes of Directors' Meeting	Form3E.rtf	Landlord's Consent to Sublease	Form6E.rtf
Minutes of Telephone Conference Directors' Meeting	Form3F.rtf	Assignment of Lease	Form6F.rtf
		Notice of Exercise of Lease Option	Form6G.rtf
Consent of Shareholders	Form3G.rtf	Extension of Lease	Form6H.rtf
Consent of Directors	Form3H.rtf	Amendment to Lease	Form6I.rtf
Promissory Note (Amortized Monthly or Annual Payments)	Form4A.rtf	Attachment to Lease	Form6J.rtf
		Contract to Purchase Building	Form7A.rtf
Promissory Note (Balloon Payment)	Form4B.rtf	Option to Purchase Building	Form7B.rtf

Form Title	File Name	Form Title	File Name
Contract to Purchase Vacant Land	Form7C.rtf	Consignment Contract	Form8H.rtf
Option to Purchase Vacant Land	Form7D.rtf	Employment Application	Form9A.rtf
Attachment to Contract	Form7E.rtf	Authorization to Release Information	Form9B.rtf
Amendment of Contract	Form7F.rtf	Offer Letter	Form9C.rtf
Removal of Contingency	Form7G.rtf	Confidentiality Agreement	Form9D.rtf
Extension of Time to Remove Contingencies	Form7H.rtf	Covenant Not to Compete	Form9E.rtf
Exercise of Option to Purchase Real Estate	Form7I.rtf	Contract With Independent Contractor	Form9F.rtf
Sales Contract (Lump-Sum Payment)	Form8A.rtf	Credit Application for an Individual Customer	Form10A.rtf
Sales Contract (Installment Payments)	Form8B.rtf	Adverse Action Letter	Form10B.rtf
Bill of Sale for Goods	Form8C.rtf	Credit Application for a Business Customer	Form10C.rtf
Security Agreement for Buying Goods	Form8D.rtf	First Collection Letter	Form10D.rtf
Contract for Manufacture of Goods	Form8E.rtf	Second Collection Letter	Form10E.rtf
Equipment Rental Contract	Form8F.rtf	Third Collection Letter	Form10F.rtf
Storage Contract	Form8G.rtf		

The following are government forms in PDF format. Download them at:
www.nolo.com/back-of-book/RUNSF.html

Form Title	File Name
IRS Form SS-4—*Application for Employer Identification Number*	fss4.pdf
IRS Form W-4—*Employee's Withholding Allowance Certificate*	fw4.pdf
IRS Form 2553—*Election by a Small Business Corporation*	f2553.pdf
IRS Form 940—*Employer's Annual Federal Unemployment (FUTA) Tax Return*	f940.pdf
IRS Form 8594—*Asset Acquisition Statement Under Section 1060*	f8594.pdf
USCIS Form I-9—*Employment Eligibility Verification*	i-9.pdf

Forms

Contract Basics—Chapter 1

Form 1A: Attachment

Form 1B: Amendment

Forming Your Business—Chapter 2

Form 2A: Checklist for Starting a Small Business

Form 2B: Partnership Agreement

Form 2C: Preincorporation Agreement

Form 2D: Corporate Bylaws

Form 2E: Stock Agreement

Form 2F: LLC Operating Agreement for Single-Member LLC

Form 2G: LLC Membership Certificate

Form 2H: Stock Certificate

Running Your Corporation—Chapter 3

Form 3A: Notice of Shareholders' Meeting

Form 3B: Notice of Directors' Meeting

Form 3C: Shareholder Proxy

Form 3D: Minutes of Shareholders' Meeting

Form 3E: Minutes of Directors' Meeting

Form 3F: Minutes of Telephone Conference Directors' Meeting

Form 3G: Consent of Shareholders

Form 3H: Consent of Directors

Borrowing Money—Chapter 4

Form 4A: Promissory Note (Amortized Monthly or Annual Payments)

Form 4B: Promissory Note (Balloon Payment)

Form 4C: Promissory Note (Interest-Only Payments)

Form 4D: Promissory Note (Lump-Sum Payment)

Form 4E: Security Agreement for Borrowing Money

Attachment Number _____

1. **Names.** This attachment is made by _____
    _____ and _____
    _____ .

2. **Terms of Attachment.** We agree to the following attachment to the _____
    _____ dated _____ concerning:

    _____
    _____
    _____
    _____
    _____
    _____
    _____
    _____
    _____
    _____
    _____
    _____
    _____
    _____
    _____
    _____
    _____
    _____
    _____
    _____
    _____

Dated: _____

Name of business: _____

a _____

By: _____

Printed name: _____

Title: _____

Address: _____
_____

Name of business: _____

a _____

By: _____

Printed name: _____

Title: _____

Address: _____
_____

Amendment Number _____

1. **Names.** This amendment is made by _____

_____ and _____

_____ .

2. **Terms of Amendment.** We agree to the following amendment to the _____

_____ dated _____ concerning:

_____

_____

_____

_____

_____

_____

_____

_____

_____

_____

_____

_____

_____

_____

_____

_____

In all other respects, the terms of the original contract and any earlier amendments will remain in effect. If there is conflict between this amendment and the original contract or any earlier amendment, the terms of this amendment will prevail.

Dated: _____

Name of business: _____

a _____

By: _____

Printed name: _____

Title: _____

Address: _____

_____

Name of business: _____

a _____

By: _____

Printed name: _____

Title: _____

Address: _____

_____

Checklist for Starting a Small Business

Evaluate and Develop Your Business Idea

- ☐ Determine if the type of business suits you.
- ☐ Use a break-even analysis to determine if your idea can make money.
- ☐ Write a business plan, including a profit/loss forecast and a cash flow analysis.
- ☐ Investigate business financing.
- ☐ Set up a basic marketing plan.

Decide on a Legal Structure for Your Business

- ☐ Research the various types of ownership structures:
  - ☐ Sole proprietorship
  - ☐ Partnership
  - ☐ LLC
  - ☐ C corporation
  - ☐ S corporation
- ☐ Identify the factors involved in choosing a business structure:
  - ☐ The number of owners of your business
  - ☐ How much protection from personal liability you'll need, which depends on the risks involved in your business
  - ☐ How you'd like the business to be taxed
  - ☐ Whether your business would benefit from being able to sell stock
- ☐ Get more in-depth information from a self-help resource or a lawyer, if necessary, before you settle on a structure.

Choose a Name for Your Business

- ☐ Think of several business names that might suit your company and its products or services.
- ☐ Check the availability of your proposed business names:
  - ☐ If you will do business online, check if your proposed business names are available as domain names.
  - ☐ Check with your county clerk's office to see whether your proposed names are on the list of fictitious or assumed business names in your county.
  - ☐ For corporations and LLCs: Check the availability of your proposed names with the Secretary of State or other corporate filing office.
  - ☐ Do a federal or state trademark search of the proposed names still on your list. If a proposed name is being used as a trademark, eliminate it if your use of the name would confuse customers or if the name is already famous.

- [ ] Choose among the proposed names that are still on your list.
- [ ] Register your business name:
    - [ ] As a fictitious or assumed business name, if necessary
    - [ ] As a federal or state trademark (*if you'll do business regionally or nationally and will use your business name to identify a product or service*)
    - [ ] As a domain name (*if you'll use the name as a Web address too*)

Prepare Organizational Paperwork

- [ ] Sole proprietorship: N/A
- [ ] Partnership:
    - [ ] Partnership agreement (*This form is included in this book.*)
    - [ ] Buy-sell agreement
- [ ] LLC:
    - [ ] Articles of organization
    - [ ] Operating agreement (*This form is included in this book—for one-member LLCs only.*)
    - [ ] Buy-sell agreement
- [ ] C corporations:
    - [ ] Preincorporation agreement (*This form is included in this book.*)
    - [ ] Articles of incorporation
    - [ ] Corporate bylaws (*This form is included in this book.*)
    - [ ] Buy-sell agreement, a.k.a. Stock Agreement (*This form is included in this book.*)
- [ ] S corporations:
    - [ ] Articles of incorporation
    - [ ] Corporate bylaws (*This form is included in this book.*)
    - [ ] Buy-sell agreement, a.k.a. Stock Agreement (*This form is included in this book.*)
    - [ ] File IRS Form 2553, *Election by a Small Business Corporation* (*This form is included in this book.*)

Find a Business Location

- [ ] Identify the features and fixtures your business will need.
- [ ] Determine how much rent you can afford.
- [ ] Decide what neighborhoods would be best for your business and find out what the average rents are in those neighborhoods.
- [ ] Make sure any space you're considering is or can be properly zoned for your business. (If working from home, make sure your business activities won't violate any zoning restrictions on home offices.)
- [ ] Before signing a commercial lease, examine it carefully and negotiate the best deal.

File for Licenses and Permits

☐ Obtain a federal employment identification number by filing IRS Form SS-4 (unless you are a sole proprietorship or single-member limited liability company without employees). (*This form is included in this book.*)

☐ Obtain a seller's permit from your state if you will sell retail goods.

☐ Obtain state licenses, such as specialized vocation-related licenses or environmental permits, if necessary.

☐ Obtain a local tax registration certificate, a.k.a. business license.

☐ Obtain local permits, if required, such as a conditional use permit or zoning variance.

Obtain Insurance

☐ Determine what business property requires coverage.

☐ Contact an insurance agent or broker to answer questions and give you policy quotes.

☐ Obtain liability insurance on vehicles used in your business, including personal cars of employees used for business.

☐ Obtain liability insurance for your premises if customers or clients will be visiting.

☐ Obtain product liability insurance if you will manufacture hazardous products.

☐ If you will be working from your home, make sure your homeowners' insurance covers damage to or theft of your business assets as well as liability for business-related injuries.

Set Up Tax Reporting and Accounting

☐ Familiarize yourself with the general tax scheme for your business structure:

　☐ Sole proprietorship

　☐ Partnership

　☐ LLC

　☐ C corporation

　☐ S corporation

☐ Familiarize yourself with common business deductions and depreciation.

☐ Get the following information from the IRS:

　☐ IRS Publication 334, *Tax Guide for Small Business*

　☐ IRS Publication 583, *Starting a Business and Keeping Records*

　☐ *Tax Calendar for Small Businesses*

☐ Set up your books:

　☐ Decide whether to use the cash or accrual system of accounting.

　☐ Choose a fiscal year if your natural business cycle does not follow the calendar year (if your business qualifies).

☐ Set up a record-keeping system for all payments to and from your business.

☐ Consider hiring a bookkeeper or accountant to help you get set up; or purchase *Quicken Home and Business* (Quicken), *QuickBooks* (Quicken), or similar small business accounting software.

Hire Workers

☐ Consider if you need to hire employees or if independent contractors will suffice:

☐ Familiarize yourself with the difference between independent contractors and employees.

☐ If hiring an independent contractor, use a written independent contractor agreement. (*This form is included in this book.*)

☐ Register and prepare procedures before hiring employees:

☐ If you haven't yet, obtain a federal employment identification number by filing IRS Form SS-4. (*This form is included in this book.*)

☐ Register with your state's employment department or similar agency for payment of unemployment compensation taxes and be prepared to file IRS Form 940 to report your federal unemployment tax each year. (*This form is included in this book.*)

☐ Set up a payroll system for withholding taxes and making payroll tax payments to the IRS. Obtain IRS Publication 15, Circular E, *Employer's Tax Guide.*

☐ Get workers' compensation insurance. (In addition, you must notify new hires of their rights to workers' compensation benefits.)

☐ Familiarize yourself with Occupational Safety and Health Administration (OSHA) requirements and prepare an Injury and Illness Prevention Program.

☐ Contact the federal Department of Labor and your state labor department for information on notices you must post in the workplace.

☐ Create an employment application for each type of position you will fill. (*This form is included in this book.*)

☐ Create an employee handbook.

☐ Complete these tasks each time you hire a new employee:

☐ Report the employee to your state's new hire reporting agency for child support purposes.

☐ Fill out Form I-9, *Employment Eligibility Verification*, from the U.S. Citizenship and Immigration Services (USCIS). (*This form is available in this book, but check www.uscis.gov for a new version before using it.*)

☐ Have the employee fill out IRS Form W-4, *Employee's Withholding Allowance Certificate.* (*This form is available in this book.*)

Partnership Agreement

1. **Partners.**

   _____

   _____

   _____

   _____

   (the Partners), agree to the following terms and conditions.

2. **Partnership Name.** The Partners will do business as a partnership under the name of _____ _____ .

3. **Partnership Duration.** The partnership ☐ began ☐ will begin on _____ . It will continue

   ☐ indefinitely until it is ended by the terms of this agreement.

   ☐ until _____ , unless ended sooner by the terms of this agreement.

4. **Partnership Office.** The main office of the partnership will be at _____ _____ .

   The mailing address will be

       ☐ the above address.

       ☐ the following address: _____ _____ .

5. **Partnership Business.** The primary business of the partnership is _____ _____ .

6. **Capital Contributions.** The Partners will contribute the following capital to the partnership on or before _____ .

   ### A. Cash Contributions

Partner's Name	Amount
_____	$ _____
_____	$ _____
_____	$ _____
_____	$ _____
_____	$ _____
_____	$ _____

   ### B. Noncash Contributions

Partner's Name	Description of Property	Value
_____	_____	$ _____
_____	_____	$ _____
_____	_____	$ _____
_____	_____	$ _____
_____	_____	$ _____

7. **Capital Accounts.** The partnership will maintain a capital account for each Partner. The account will consist of the Partner's capital contribution plus the Partner's share of profits and less the Partner's share of losses and distributions to the Partner. A Partner may not remove capital from his or her account without the written consent of all Partners.

8. **Profits and Losses.**

   A. The net profits and losses of the partnership will be credited to or charged against the Partners' capital accounts

      ☐ in the same proportions as their capital contributions.

      ☐ as follows: _____ .

   B. The partnership will make distributions to the Partners only if all the Partners agree.

9. **Salaries.** No Partner will receive a salary for services to the partnership.

10. **Interest.** No interest will be paid on a Partner's capital account.

11. **Management.** Each Partner will have an equal say in managing the partnership.

    ☐ All significant partnership decisions will require the agreement of all the partners.

    ☐ Routine partnership decisions will require the agreement of a majority of the partners.

    ☐ The following partnership actions will require the agreement of all the Partners:

       ☐ borrowing or lending money

       ☐ signing a lease

       ☐ signing a contract to buy or sell real estate

       ☐ signing a security agreement or mortgage

       ☐ selling partnership assets except for goods sold in the regular course of business

       ☐ _____ .

12. **Partnership Funds.** Partnership funds will be kept in an account at _____
    _____ , unless all Partners agree to another financial institution.

    Partnership checks

    ☐ may be signed by any Partner.

    ☐ must be signed by all the Partners.

    ☐ must be signed by _____ Partners.

13. **Agreement to End Partnership.** The Partners may unanimously agree to end the partnership.

14. **Partner's Withdrawal.**

    ☐ The partnership will end if a Partner withdraws by giving written notice of such withdrawal to each of the other Partners.

    ☐ Upon the withdrawal of a Partner, the other Partners will, within 30 days, decide either to end the partnership or buy out the withdrawing Partner's interest and continue the partnership. A decision to buy out the withdrawing Partner's interest and continue the partnership requires the unanimous consent of the remaining Partners.

15. **Partner's Death.**

    ☐ The partnership will end if a Partner dies.

    ☐ Upon the death of a Partner, the other Partners will, within 30 days, decide either to end the partnership or buy out the deceased Partner's interest and continue the partnership. A decision to buy out the withdrawing Partner's interest and continue the partnership requires the unanimous consent of the remaining Partners.

16. **Buyout.** If the remaining Partners decide to buy the interest of a withdrawing or deceased Partner under Paragraph 14 or 15, the remaining Partners, within _____ days after that Partner's withdrawal or death, will pay the withdrawing Partner or the deceased Partner's estate

☐ the amount in the capital account of the withdrawing or deceased Partner as of the date of withdrawal or death.

☐ the fair market value of the interest of the withdrawing or deceased Partner as determined by the partnership's accountant.

☐ _____
_____.

17. **Entire Agreement.** This is the entire agreement between the parties. It replaces and supersedes any and all oral agreements between the parties, as well as any prior writings.

18. **Successors and Assignees.** This agreement binds and benefits the heirs, successors, and assignees of the parties.

19. **Notices.** All notices must be in writing. A notice may be delivered to a party at the address that follows a party's signature or to a new address that a party designates in writing. A notice may be delivered:

(1) in person

(2) by certified mail, or

(3) by overnight courier.

20. **Governing Law.** This agreement will be governed by and construed in accordance with the laws of the state of _____ .

21. **Counterparts.** This agreement may be signed by the parties in different counterparts and the signature pages combined will create a document binding on all parties.

22. **Modification.** This agreement may be modified only by a written agreement signed by all the parties.

23. **Waiver.** If one party waives any term or provision of this agreement at any time, that waiver will be effective only for the specific instance and specific purpose for which the waiver was given. If either party fails to exercise or delays exercising any of its rights or remedies under this agreement, that party retains the right to enforce that term or provision at a later time.

24. **Severability.** If any court determines that any provision of this agreement is invalid or unenforceable, any invalidity or unenforceability will affect only that provision and will not make any other provision of this agreement invalid or unenforceable and such provision shall be modified, amended, or limited only to the extent necessary to render it valid and enforceable.

Dated: _____

Signature: _____

Printed name: _____

Address: _____

_____

Dated: _____

Signature: _____

Printed name: _____

Address: _____

_____

Dated: _____

Signature: _____

Printed name: _____

Address: _____

_____

Dated: _____

Signature: _____

Printed name: _____

Address: _____

_____

Dated: _____

Signature: _____

Printed name: _____

Address: _____

Preincorporation Agreement

1. **Shareholders' Names.** _____
   _____
   _____
   _____

   (the Shareholders) agree to the following terms and conditions.

2. **Incorporation.** The Shareholders will form a corporation under _____
   law. The Shareholders will file the articles of incorporation as soon as possible after the execution of this
   agreement.

   ☐ _____ will sign the articles of incorporation
   as incorporator.

   ☐ All of the Shareholders will sign the articles of incorporation as incorporators.

3. **Corporate Name.** The corporation will be called _____ .

   ☐ The corporation may also do business under the assumed or fictitious name of _____
   _____ , which will be registered as required by law.

4. **Corporate Purpose.** The principal corporate purpose will be _____
   _____ .

5. **Corporate Stock.** The corporation will issue a total of _____ shares of common stock to the
   people listed in the next paragraph. All shares will have equal rights in voting on matters submitted to
   Shareholders. No additional shares will be authorized or issued unless all Shareholders agree in writing.

6. **Stock Subscriptions.** The Shareholders subscribe for the following shares of stock, at a price per share
   of $_____ :

Name	Shares	Total Price
_____	_____	$_____
_____	_____	$_____
_____	_____	$_____
_____	_____	$_____

   Payment is due upon incorporation. The corporation will issue a stock certificate to the
   Shareholder as evidence of stock ownership.

7. **Tax Status.** The shares will be issued under Section 1244 of the Internal Revenue Code.

   ☐ The corporation will elect S corporation status. Each Shareholder will sign the IRS election form
   consenting to such status.

8. **Board of Directors.** The Shareholders will constitute the initial Board of Directors.

9. **Officers.** The initial corporate officers will be:

   _____ , President
   _____ , Vice-President
   _____ , Secretary
   _____ , Treasurer

10. **Place of Business.** The corporation's main office will be at: _____
    _____ .

11. **Bylaws.** The Shareholders will create and adopt bylaws that include all of the terms contained in this agreement.

12. **Entire Agreement.** This is the entire agreement between the parties. It replaces and supersedes any and all oral agreements between the parties, as well as any prior writings.

13. **Successors and Assignees.** This agreement binds and benefits the heirs, successors, and assignees of the parties.

14. **Notices.** All notices must be in writing. A notice may be delivered to a party at the address that follows a party's signature or to a new address that a party designates in writing. A notice may be delivered:

    (1) in person

    (2) by certified mail, or

    (3) by overnight courier.

15. **Governing Law.** This agreement will be governed by and construed in accordance with the laws of the state of _____ .

16. **Counterparts.** This agreement may be signed by the parties in different counterparts and the signature pages combined will create a document binding on all parties.

17. **Modification.** This agreement may be modified only by a written agreement signed by all the parties.

18. **Waiver.** If one party waives any term or provision of this agreement at any time, that waiver will be effective only for the specific instance and specific purpose for which the waiver was given. If any party fails to exercise or delays exercising any of its rights or remedies under this agreement, that party retains the right to enforce that term or provision at a later time.

19. **Severability.** If any court determines that any provision of this agreement is invalid or unenforceable, any invalidity or unenforceability will affect only that provision and will not make any other provision of this agreement invalid or unenforceable and such provision shall be modified, amended, or limited only to the extent necessary to render it valid and enforceable.

Dated: _____

Signature: _____

Printed name: _____

Address: _____

_____

Dated: _____

Signature: _____

Printed name: _____

Address: _____

_____

Dated: _____

Signature: _____

Printed name: _____

Address: _____

_____

Corporate Bylaws

These are the bylaws of _____

_____ , a _____ corporation.

Article I: Meetings of Shareholders

1. The annual meeting of shareholders will be held on the _____ in
    _____ . The annual meeting of
    shareholders will begin at _____ and will take place at the principal office of the corporation.

2. At the annual meeting, the shareholders will elect a board of _____
    directors and may take any other shareholder action permitted by state law.

3. A special meeting of the shareholders may be called at any time by

    ☐ the president.

    ☐ _____ or more shareholders.

    ☐ _____ or more directors.

4. At least 15 days before an annual or special meeting, the secretary will send a notice of the meeting
    to each shareholder. The notice must be sent by first-class mail and must state the time and place of
    the meeting. For a special meeting, the notice must also include the purposes of the meeting; no action
    can be taken at a special meeting except as stated in the notice, unless all shareholders consent.

5. Shareholders may attend a meeting either in person or by proxy. A quorum of shareholders at
    any shareholders' meeting will consist of the owners of a majority of the shares outstanding. If a
    quorum is present, the shareholders may adjourn from day to day as they see fit, and no notice of
    such adjournment need be given. If a quorum is not present, the shareholders present in person or
    by proxy may adjourn to such future time as they agree upon; notice of such adjournment must be
    mailed to each shareholder at least 15 days before such adjourned meeting.

6. Each shareholder, whether represented in person or by proxy, is entitled to one vote for each share of
    stock standing in his or her name on the books of the company.

7. Proxies must be in writing.

8. All shareholders' actions require the assent of a majority of the corporate shares that have been
    issued, but if state law requires a greater number of votes, that law will prevail.

    ☐ Exception: _____
    requires the assent of _____ of the corporate shares that have been issued.

9. Shareholders may, by written consent, take any action required or permitted to be taken at an
    annual or special meeting of shareholders. Such action may be taken without prior notice to
    shareholders. The written consent must:

    • state the action taken, and

    • be signed and dated by the owners of shares having at least the number of votes that would be
      needed to take such action at a meeting.

    If the written consent is not signed by all shareholders, the secretary will within three days send a
    copy of the written consent to the shareholders who did not sign it.

Article II: Stock

1. Stock certificates must be signed by the president and secretary of the corporation.
2. The name of the person owning shares represented by a stock certificate, the number of shares owned, and the date of issue will be entered in the corporation's books.
3. All stock certificates transferred by endorsement must be surrendered for cancellation. New certificates will be issued to the purchaser or assignee.
4. Shares of stock can be transferred only on the books of the corporation and only by the secretary.

Article III: Board of Directors

1. The board of directors will manage the business of the corporation and will exercise all the powers that may be exercised by the corporation under the statutes of the State of _____ _____ , the articles of incorporation, or the corporate bylaws.
2. A vacancy on the board of directors by reason of death, resignation, or other causes may be filled by the remaining directors, or the board may leave the position unfilled, in which case it will be filled by a vote of the shareholders at a special meeting or at the next annual meeting. During periods when there is an unfilled vacancy on the board of directors, actions taken by the remaining directors will constitute actions of the board.
3. The board of directors will meet annually, immediately following the annual meeting of shareholders. The board of directors may also hold other regular meetings, at times and places to be fixed by unanimous agreement of the board. At annual or regular meetings, the board may take any actions allowed by law or these bylaws. Special meetings may be called by
   - ☐ the president
   - ☐ any director
   - ☐ _____ or more directors

   by giving _____ days' written notice to all directors.

   A notice of a special meeting must be sent by first-class mail and must state the time, place, and purposes of the meeting; no action can be taken at a special meeting of directors except as stated in the notice, unless all directors consent.
4. A quorum for a meeting will consist of _____ directors.
5. Directors will act only by
   - ☐ unanimous assent of the directors.
   - ☐ the assent of a majority of those directors present.
   - ☐ the assent of at least _____ directors.
6. The directors will not be compensated for serving as such. A director may, however, serve in other capacities with the corporation and receive compensation for such service.
7. Directors may, by written consent, take any action required or permitted to be taken at a directors' meeting. Such action may be taken without prior notice to the directors. The written consent must:
   - state the action taken, and
   - be signed and dated by at least the number of directors whose votes would be needed to take such action at a meeting.

   If the written consent is not signed by all directors, the secretary will within three days send a copy of the written consent to the directors who did not sign it.
8. Directors may meet or participate in meetings by telephone or other electronic means as long as all directors are continuously able to communicate with one another.

Article IV: Officers

1. The officers of the corporation will consist of a

   ☐ president

   ☐ vice-president

   ☐ secretary

   ☐ treasurer

   ☐ secretary-treasurer

   and such other officers as the board of directors may appoint.

2. The president will preside at all meetings of the directors and shareholders, and will have general charge of the business of the corporation, subject to approval of the board of directors.

3. In case of the death, disability, or absence of the president, the ☐ vice-president ☐ secretary will perform and be vested with all the duties and powers of the president.

4. The secretary will keep the corporate records, including minutes of shareholders' and directors' meetings and consent resolutions. The secretary will give notice, as required in these bylaws, of shareholders' and directors' meetings.

5. The treasurer will keep accounts of all moneys of the corporation received or disbursed, and will deposit all moneys and valuables in the name of the corporation in the banks and depositories that the directors designate. Checks against company accounts will be signed as directed by the board of directors.

6. The salaries of all officers will be fixed by the board of directors and may be changed from time to time by the board of directors.

Article V: Fiscal

1. The books of the corporation will be closed at a date to be selected by the directors prior to the filing of the first income tax return due from the corporation. The books will be kept on

   ☐ a cash basis.

   ☐ an accrual basis.

2. Within 75 days after the corporation's fiscal year ends, the treasurer will provide each shareholder with a financial statement for the corporation.

Article VI: Amendments

Any of these bylaws may be amended or repealed by a vote of the owners of a majority of the shares outstanding at any annual meeting or at any special meeting called for that purpose.

Adopted on: _____

By: _____

Printed name: _____

By: _____

Printed name: _____

By: _____

Printed name: _____

By: _____

Printed name: _____

By: _____

Printed name: _____

By: _____

Printed name: _____

Stock Agreement

1. **Names.** _____

   _____

   _____

   _____

   (Shareholders) and _____ (Corporation) agree to the following.

2. **Restrictions on Sale of Stock.** Shareholders will sell their stock in _____

   _____ only as stated in this agreement.

3. **Offer to Corporation.** A Shareholder who receives a good faith written offer to purchase all or part of his or her shares will offer the Corporation the opportunity to buy the shares on the same terms and will give the Corporation a copy of the offer he or she has received. The Corporation, through its board of directors, will have ten days from the time it receives written notice from a Shareholder to decide whether the Corporation will buy the shares.

4. **Offer to Shareholders.** If the Corporation does not buy the shares, the selling Shareholder will offer the remaining Shareholders (in writing and on a pro rata basis) the opportunity to buy the shares on the same terms and will give the remaining Shareholders a copy of the offer he or she has received. The remaining Shareholders will have ten days from the time they receive written notice from the selling Shareholder to decide whether to buy the shares on a pro rata basis or such other basis as the remaining Shareholders may agree upon.

5. **Remaining Shares.** If any shares are not bought by the Corporation or the remaining Shareholders, the selling Shareholder may sell those shares to the person who made the offer to purchase. The terms will be the same as those offered to the Corporation and other Shareholders. Any sale to the person who made the offer must take place within 30 days after the procedures described in Paragraphs 3 and 4 have been concluded, or such sale will be invalid.

6. **Continuing Effect.** Anyone who becomes an owner of shares of stock in the Corporation will be bound by this agreement. The following will be endorsed on all stock certificates:

   The transfer of shares represented by this certificate is subject to the terms of a stock agreement signed by the Shareholders and the Corporation, dated _____ . A copy is on file with the corporate secretary.

7. **Death of Shareholder.** *(Optional)*

   Upon the death of a Shareholder, the Corporation will, within 180 days, buy the deceased Shareholder's shares from the deceased Shareholder's estate. The amount to be paid will be

   ☐ the fair market value of the deceased Shareholder's shares as determined by the Corporation's accountant.

   ☐ _____ .

   The Corporation will buy and maintain insurance on the life of each Shareholder in an amount sufficient to pay for the shares of a Shareholder who dies. Life insurance proceeds that exceed the purchase price of the shares will belong to the Corporation.

8. **Entire Agreement.** This is the entire agreement between the parties. It replaces and supersedes any and all oral agreements between the parties, as well as any prior writings.

9. **Successors and Assignees.** This agreement binds and benefits the heirs, successors, and assignees of the parties.

10. **Notices.** All notices must be in writing. A notice may be delivered to a party at the address that follows a party's signature or to a new address that a party designates in writing. A notice may be delivered:

    (1) in person

    (2) by certified mail, or

    (3) by overnight courier.

11. **Governing Law.** This agreement will be governed by and construed in accordance with the laws of the state of _____ .

12. **Counterparts.** This agreement may be signed by the parties in different counterparts and the signature pages combined will create a document binding on all parties.

13. **Modification.** This agreement may be modified only by a written agreement signed by all the parties.

14. **Waiver.** If one party waives any term or provision of this agreement at any time, that waiver will be effective only for the specific instance and specific purpose for which the waiver was given. If any party fails to exercise or delays exercising any of its rights or remedies under this agreement, that party retains the right to enforce that term or provision at a later time.

15. **Severability.** If any court determines that any provision of this agreement is invalid or unenforceable, any invalidity or unenforceability will affect only that provision and will not make any other provision of this agreement invalid or unenforceable and such provision shall be modified, amended, or limited only to the extent necessary to render it valid and enforceable.

Shareholders

By: _____ Dated: _____

Printed name: _____

Address: _____

By: _____ Dated: _____

Printed name: _____

Address: _____

By: _____ Dated: _____

Printed name: _____

Address: _____

By: _____ Dated: _____

Printed name: _____

Address: _____

Corporation

Name of business: _____ ,

a _____

By: _____ Dated: _____

Printed name: _____

Title: _____

Address: _____

LLC Operating Agreement for Single-Member LLC

1. **Names.** This operating agreement is made by _____
   _____ , a limited liability
   company, the Company, and _____
   _____
   _____ , the Member.

2. **Formation.** The Company has been formed under the _____ statute
   authorizing the formation of limited liability companies. The purpose of the Company is stated in the
   articles of organization.

3. **Offices.** The Company will have one or more offices at places the Member designates. The initial
   registered office of the Company is located at _____
   _____ and the Member is the agent.

4. **Management.** The Member has the right to manage the Company's business. The Member may
   delegate to another person the authority to perform specified acts on behalf of the Company.

   ☐ If the Member dies or is unable to act, the Company will be managed by _____
   _____ or by the person the Member last designates
   in writing to manage the Company. That person will have full authority to manage the Company
   until the Member can do so.

5. **Liability and Indemnification.** Members will not be personally liable for the expenses, debts, or
   liabilities of the LLC. The LLC will indemnify the Member or manager for all acts and omissions
   related to the normal operations of the LLC if the person acted in good faith, without gross
   negligence. The LLC will indemnify the Member or any manager who is made a party to a threatened
   or pending lawsuit or other legal proceeding, whether civil or criminal. Indemnification includes
   expenses, attorneys' fees, judgments, penalties, fines, and amounts paid in settlement.

6. **Capital Contributions.** In exchange for the Member's interest in the Company, the Member will
   contribute to the Company
   ☐ $ _____ .
   ☐ the following property: _____
   _____ .

   The Member will not be paid interest on this capital contribution.

7. **Taxes.** For federal tax purposes, the Company will be taxed
   ☐ as a sole proprietorship, with profits and losses passing through to the Member.
   ☐ as a corporation.

8. **Tax Year and Accounting Method.** The tax year of this LLC ends on December 31. The LLC uses the
   ☐ cash method of accounting.
   ☐ accrual method of accounting.

9. **Funds.** The Member will determine the financial institution that will hold Company funds and will
   determine the authorized signatures on Company accounts.

10. **Additional Members.** The Company may admit one or more additional members upon such terms as are determined by the Company and the Member. If new members are admitted, the articles of organization and this operating agreement will be appropriately amended.

11. **Distributions.** The Member will determine when and how cash and other assets of the Company will be distributed.

12. **Dissolution and Termination of the LLC.** The duration of this LLC is perpetual. However, this LLC will terminate upon:

    ☐ The decision of the Member to dissolve the LLC.

    ☐ The entry of a decree of dissolution of the LLC under state law.

    If the LLC is to dissolve according to one of the above provisions, the Member will complete a dissolution of the LLC in accordance with state law.

    The death, retirement, or resignation of a member will not cause an automatic dissolution of the LLC.

Dated: _____

Name of business: _____ ,

a _____

By: _____

Printed name: _____

Title: _____

Address: _____

_____

LLC Membership Certificate

_____

Organized Under the Laws of _____

Certificate Number _____   Number of shares _____

This certifies that _____
is the owner of _____ membership units of _____
_____ . These membership units are transferable on the
books of the company in person or by the owner's attorney-in-fact upon surrender of this certificate
properly endorsed.

    Any sale or transfer of these membership units is subject to the terms of the company's operating
agreement dated _____ , 20_____ .

Signed on _____ , 20_____ .

_____
_____ , President

_____
_____ , Secretary

Stock Certificate

_____

Incorporated Under the Laws of _____

Certificate Number _____   Number of Shares _____

This certifies that _____

is the owner of _____ shares of the stock of _____

_____ . These shares are transferable on the books of the corporation

in person or by the owner's attorney-in-fact upon surrender of this certificate properly endorsed. Any sale

or transfer of these shares is subject to a stock agreement dated _____ ,

20_____ .

Signed on _____ , 20_____ .

_____

_____ , President

_____

_____ , Secretary

Notice of Shareholders' Meeting

To the shareholders of _____ :

☐ An annual   ☐ A regular   ☐ A special meeting of shareholders will be held as follows:

Date: _____

Time: _____

Place: _____

Purposes: _____

_____

_____

_____

_____ .

    ☐ To transact any other business that properly comes before the meeting.

☐ This special meeting has been called by:

    ☐ the president.

    ☐ an authorized officer: _____ .

    ☐ the following directors: _____

_____

_____

_____ .

    ☐ the following shareholders: _____

_____

_____

_____ .

Dated: _____

By: _____

Printed name of secretary: _____

Secretary of _____

Notice of Directors' Meeting

To the directors of _____ :

☐ An annual   ☐ A regular   ☐ A special   meeting of directors will be held as follows:

Date: _____

Time: _____

Place: _____

Purposes: _____

_____

_____

_____

_____ .

    ☐ To transact any other business that properly comes before the meeting.

☐ This special meeting has been called by:

    ☐ the president.

    ☐ an authorized officer: _____ .

    ☐ the following directors: _____

_____

_____

_____ .

Dated: _____

By: _____

Printed name of secretary: _____

Secretary of _____

Shareholder Proxy

I appoint _____

as my proxy to vote all of my shares of stock of _____

_____ at the ☐ annual ☐ regular ☐ special meeting of

shareholders to be held on _____ .

Dated: _____

Signature: _____

Printed name: _____

Address: _____

Minutes of Shareholders' Meeting

The shareholders of _____

held ☐ an annual   ☐ a regular   ☐ a special   meeting on _____ at

_____ .

The meeting began at _____ and ended at _____ .

Notice. Notice of the meeting was provided to the shareholders in accordance with the corporation's bylaws and state rules for proper notice.

    ☐ The meeting was called by _____ .

Quorum. The following persons, constituting a quorum, were present in person or by proxy:

_____

_____

_____

_____ .

Actions Taken.

    ☐ The minutes of the   ☐ annual   ☐ regular   ☐ special   shareholders' meeting held on

    _____ were approved.

    ☐ The shareholders took the following actions: _____

_____

_____

_____

_____

_____

_____

_____

_____

_____

_____

_____

_____

_____

_____

_____ .

Dated: _____

By: _____

Printed name of secretary: _____

Secretary of _____

©nolo **NOLO** www.nolo.com   **Form 3D: Minutes of Shareholders' Meeting**   Page 1 of 1

Minutes of Directors' Meeting

The directors of _____

held ☐ an annual ☐ a regular ☐ a special meeting on _____ at
_____ .

The meeting began at _____ and ended at _____ .

Notice. Notice of the meeting was provided to the directors in accordance with the corporation's bylaws and state rules for proper notice.

    ☐ The meeting was called by _____ .

Quorum. The following directors, constituting a quorum, were present: _____

_____

_____

_____

_____

Actions Taken. The directors took the following actions:

    ☐ The minutes of the   ☐ annual   ☐ regular   ☐ special   directors' meeting held on
    _____ were approved.

    ☐ The directors took the following actions: _____

_____

_____

_____

_____

_____

_____

_____

_____

_____

_____

_____

_____

_____

_____

_____

_____

Dated: _____

By: _____

Printed name of secretary: _____

Secretary of _____

Minutes of Telephone Conference Directors' Meeting

The directors of _____

held a meeting by telephone conference on _____ . The meeting began

at _____ and ended at _____ . Throughout the meeting,

the directors could remain in voice contact with one another.

Quorum. The following directors, constituting a quorum, participated in the telephone conference:

_____

_____

_____

_____ .

Actions Taken. The directors took the following actions:

_____

_____

_____

_____

_____

_____

_____

_____

_____

_____

_____

_____

_____

_____

_____

_____

_____

_____

_____

_____ .

Dated: _____

By: _____

Printed name of secretary: _____

Secretary of _____

Consent of Shareholders

The shareholders of _____

consent to the following: _____

_____

_____

_____

_____

_____

_____

_____

_____

_____

_____

_____

_____

_____

_____

_____

_____

_____

_____

_____

_____.

By: _____   Dated: _____

Printed name: _____

By: _____   Dated: _____

Printed name: _____

By: _____   Dated: _____

Printed name: _____

By: _____   Dated: _____

Printed name: _____

By: _____   Dated: _____

Printed name: _____

Consent of Directors

The directors of _____

consent to the following: _____

_____

_____

_____

_____

_____

_____

_____

_____

_____

_____

_____

_____

_____

_____

_____

_____

_____

_____

_____

_____ .

By: _____   Dated: _____

Printed name: _____

By: _____   Dated: _____

Printed name: _____

By: _____   Dated: _____

Printed name: _____

By: _____   Dated: _____

Printed name: _____

By: _____   Dated: _____

Printed name: _____

Promissory Note
(Amortized Monthly or Annual Payments)

1. **Names.**

   Borrower: _____

   Address: _____

   _____

   Lender: _____

   Address: _____

   _____

2. **Promise to Pay.** For value received, Borrower promises to pay Lender $_____ and interest at the yearly rate of _____% on the unpaid balance as specified below.

3. **Installments.**

   ☐ Monthly Installments: Borrower will pay _____ monthly installments of $ _____ each. Payment shall be made at Lender's address above.

   ☐ Annual Installments: Borrower will make _____ annual installments of $ _____ each. Payment shall be made at Lender's address above.

4. **Date of Installment Payments.**

   ☐ Monthly Installments: Borrower will make an installment payment on the _____ day of each month beginning _____ until the principal and interest have been paid in full.

   ☐ Annual Installments: Borrower will make an installment payment on _____ of each year beginning _____ until the principal and interest have been paid in full.

5. **Application of Payments.** Payments will be applied first to interest and then to principal.

6. **Prepayment.** Borrower may prepay all or any part of the principal without penalty.

7. **Loan Acceleration.** If Borrower is more than _____ days late in making any payment, Lender may declare that the entire balance of unpaid principal is due immediately, together with the interest that has accrued.

8. **Security.**

   ☐ This is an unsecured note.

   ☐ Borrower agrees that until the principal and interest owed under this promissory note are paid in full, this note will be secured by a security agreement and Uniform Commercial Code Financing Statement giving Lender a security interest in certain equipment, fixtures, inventory, or other assets, as described in the security agreement, of the business known as _____

   _____ .

   ☐ Borrower agrees that until the principal and interest owed under this promissory note are paid in full, this note will be secured by the ☐ mortgage ☐ deed of trust covering the real estate commonly known as _____

   and more fully described as follows: _____

   _____ .

9. **Collection Costs.** If Lender prevails in a lawsuit to collect on this note, Borrower will pay Lender's costs and lawyers' fees in an amount the court finds to be reasonable.

NOLO
www.nolo.com
©nolo

Form 4A: Promissory Note
(Amortized Monthly or Annual Payments)

Page 1 of 2

10. **Notices.** All notices must be in writing. A notice may be delivered to Borrower or Lender at the address specified in Section 1, above, or to a new address Borrower or Lender has designated in writing. A notice may be delivered:

    (1) in person

    (2) by certified mail, or

    (3) by overnight courier.

11. **Governing Law.** This promissory note will be governed by and construed in accordance with the laws of the state of _____ .

12. **Severability.** If any court determines that any provision of this promissory note is invalid or unenforceable, any invalidity or unenforceability will affect only that provision and will not make any other provision of this agreement invalid or unenforceable and such provision shall be modified, amended, or limited only to the extent necessary to render it valid and enforceable.

Dated: _____

Name of business: _____

a _____

By: _____

Printed name: _____

Title: _____

Address: _____

Promissory Note
(Balloon Payment)

1. **Names.**

   Borrower: _____

   Address: _____

   _____

   Lender: _____

   Address: _____

   _____

2. **Promise to Pay.** For value received, Borrower promises to pay Lender $_____ and interest at the yearly rate of _____% on the unpaid balance as specified below.

3. **Monthly Installments.** Borrower will pay _____ monthly installments of $_____ each.

4. **Date of Installment Payments.** Borrower will make an installment payment on the _____ day of each month beginning _____ . On or before _____ , Borrower will make a lump-sum payment for the entire balance of accrued principal and interest.

5. **Application of Payments.** Payments will be applied first to interest and then to principal.

6. **Prepayment.** Borrower may prepay all or any part of the principal without penalty.

7. **Loan Acceleration.** If Borrower is more than _____ days late in making any payment, Lender may declare that the entire balance of unpaid principal is due immediately, together with the interest that has accrued.

8. **Security.**

   ☐ This is an unsecured note.

   ☐ Borrower agrees that until the principal and interest owed under this promissory note are paid in full, this note will be secured by a security agreement and Uniform Commercial Code Financing Statement giving Lender a security interest in certain equipment, fixtures, inventory, or other assets, as described in the security agreement, of the business known as _____

   _____ .

   ☐ Borrower agrees that until the principal and interest owed under this promissory note are paid in full, this note will be secured by the ☐ mortgage ☐ deed of trust covering the real estate commonly known as and more fully described as follows: _____

   _____

   _____ .

9. **Collection Costs.** If Lender prevails in a lawsuit to collect on this note, Borrower will pay Lender's costs and lawyers' fees in an amount the court finds to be reasonable.

10. **Notices.** All notices must be in writing. A notice may be delivered to Borrower or Lender at the address specified in Section 1, above, or to a new address Borrower or Lender has designated in writing. A notice may be delivered:

    (1) in person

    (2) by certified mail, or

    (3) by overnight courier.

11. **Governing Law.** This promissory note will be governed by and construed in accordance with the laws of the state of _____ .

12. **Severability.** If any court determines that any provision of this promissory note is invalid or unenforceable, any invalidity or unenforceability will affect only that provision and will not make any other provision of this agreement invalid or unenforceable and such provision shall be modified, amended, or limited only to the extent necessary to render it valid and enforceable.

Dated: _____

Name of business: _____ ,

a _____

By: _____

Printed name: _____

Title: _____

Address: _____

Promissory Note
(Interest-Only Payments)

1. **Names.**

   Borrower: _____

   Address: _____

   _____

   Lender: _____

   Address: _____

   _____

2. **Promise to Pay.** For value received, Borrower promises to pay Lender $_____ and interest at the yearly rate of _____% on the unpaid balance as specified below.

3. **Interest Payments.**

   ☐ Annual Payments: Borrower will pay interest on _____ of each year beginning in _____ . The amount of each interest payment will be $_____ .

   ☐ Monthly Payments: Borrower will pay interest on the _____ day of each month beginning in _____ . The amount of each interest payment will be
   $_____ .

   ☐ Other: Borrower will pay interest as follows: _____
   _____ .

4. **Principal Payment.** Borrower will pay the principal in full on or before _____ , together with any accrued interest.

5. **Prepayment.** Borrower may prepay all or any part of the principal without penalty.

6. **Loan Acceleration.** If Borrower is more than _____ days late in making any payment, Lender may declare that the entire balance of unpaid principal is due immediately, together with the interest that has accrued.

7. **Security.**

   ☐ This is an unsecured note.

   ☐ Borrower agrees that until the principal and interest owed under this promissory note are paid in full, this note will be secured by a security agreement and Uniform Commercial Code Financing Statement giving Lender a security interest in certain equipment, fixtures, inventory, or other assets, as described in the security agreement, of the business known as _____
   _____ .

   ☐ Borrower agrees that until the principal and interest owed under this promissory note are paid in full, this note will be secured by the ☐ mortgage ☐ deed of trust   covering the real estate commonly known as _____
   more fully described as follows: _____
   _____
   _____
   _____
   _____ .

8. **Collection Costs.** If Lender prevails in a lawsuit to collect on this note, Borrower will pay Lender's costs and lawyers' fees in an amount the court finds to be reasonable.

9. **Notices.** All notices must be in writing. A notice may be delivered to Borrower or Lender at the address specified in Section 1, above, or to a new address Borrower or Lender has designated in writing. A notice may be delivered:

    (1) in person

    (2) by certified mail, or

    (3) by overnight courier.

10. **Governing Law.** This promissory note will be governed by and construed in accordance with the laws of the state of _____ .

11. **Severability.** If any court determines that any provision of this promissory note is invalid or unenforceable, any invalidity or unenforceability will affect only that provision and will not make any other provision of this agreement invalid or unenforceable and such provision shall be modified, amended, or limited only to the extent necessary to render it valid and enforceable.

Dated: _____

Name of business: _____ ,

a _____

By: _____   Dated: _____

Printed name: _____

Title: _____

Address: _____

_____

Promissory Note
(Lump-Sum Payment)

1. Names.

Borrower: _____

Address: _____

_____

Lender: _____

Address: _____

_____

2. Promise to Pay. For value received, Borrower promises to pay Lender $_____ and interest at the yearly rate of _____% on the unpaid balance as specified below.

3. Payment Date.

☐ Borrower will pay the entire amount of principal and interest on or before _____ .

☐ Borrower will pay the entire amount of principal and interest on or before the earlier of (1) the occurrence of_____ , or

(2) _____ .

4. Prepayment. Borrower may prepay all or any part of the principal without penalty.

5. Security.

☐ This is an unsecured note.

☐ Borrower agrees that until the principal and interest owed under this promissory note are paid in full, this note will be secured by a security agreement and Uniform Commercial Code Financing Statement giving Lender a security interest in certain equipment, fixtures, inventory, or other assets, as described in the security agreement, of the business known as _____

_____ .

☐ Borrower agrees that until the principal and interest owed under this promissory note are paid in full, this note will be secured by the ☐ mortgage ☐ deed of trust covering the real estate commonly known as _____

more fully described as follows: _____

_____

_____ .

6. Collection Costs. If Lender prevails in a lawsuit to collect on this note, Borrower will pay Lender's costs and lawyers' fees in an amount the court finds to be reasonable.

7. Notices. All notices must be in writing. A notice may be delivered to Borrower or Lender at the address specified in Section 1, above, or to a new address Borrower or Lender has designated in writing. A notice may be delivered:

(1) in person

(2) by certified mail, or

(3) by overnight courier.

8. **Governing Law.** This promissory note will be governed by and construed in accordance with the laws of the state of _____ .

9. **Severability.** If any court determines that any provision of this promissory note is invalid or unenforceable, any invalidity or unenforceability will affect only that provision and will not make any other provision of this agreement invalid or unenforceable and such provision shall be modified, amended, or limited only to the extent necessary to render it valid and enforceable.

Dated: _____

Name of business: _____ ,

a _____

By: _____

Printed name: _____

Title: _____

Address: _____

Security Agreement for Borrowing Money

1. **Names.** This Security Agreement is between _____ , Borrower, and _____ , Lender.

2. **Grant of Security Interest.** Borrower grants to Lender a continuing security interest in the following property (the Secured Property), which consists of

   ☐ the tangible personal property owned by Borrower's business known as _____

   _____ ,

   _____ as listed in attached Attachment 1.

   ☐ any additional tangible personal property that Borrower now owns or later acquires in connection with Borrower's business, including replacement inventory.

   ☐ Other: _____

   _____ .

3. **Security for Promissory Note.** Borrower is granting this security interest to secure performance of a promissory note dated _____ that Borrower executed in favor of Lender. The promissory note obligates Borrower to pay Lender $_____ with interest at the rate of _____% a year, on the terms stated in the promissory note.

4. **Financing Statement.** Borrower agrees that until the principal and interest owed under the promissory note are paid in full, the note will be further secured by a Uniform Commercial Code Financing Statement. Borrower will sign any other documents that Lender reasonably requests to protect Lender's security interest in the Secured Property.

5. **Use and Care of the Secured Property.** Until the promissory note is fully paid, Borrower agrees to:

   A. keep at Borrower's premises the Secured Property owned by the Borrower's business and use it only in the operation of the business

   B. maintain the Secured Property in good repair

   C. not sell, transfer, or release the Secured Property unless Lender consents. Borrower may sell inventory in the ordinary course of Borrower's business, but will reasonably renew and replenish inventory to keep it at its current level

   D. pay all taxes on the Secured Property as taxes become due

   E. insure the Secured Property against normal risks, with an insurance policy that names Borrower and Lender as beneficiaries as their interests appear

   F. deliver to Lender a copy of the insurance policy insuring the Secured Property and provide annual proof to the Lender that Borrower has paid the premiums on the policy, and

   G. allow Lender to inspect the Secured Property at any reasonable time.

6. **Borrower's Default.** If Borrower is more than _____ days late in making any payment required by the promissory note or if Borrower fails to correct any violations of Paragraph 5 of this Security Agreement within _____ days of receiving written notice from Lender, Borrower will be in default.

7. **Lender's Rights.** If Borrower is in default, Lender may exercise the remedies contained in the Uniform Commercial Code for the state of _____ and any other remedies legally available to Lender. Lender may, for example:

A. remove the Secured Property from the place where it is then located

B. require Borrower to make the Secured Property available to Lender at a place designated by Lender that is reasonably convenient to Borrower and Lender, and

C. sell, lease, or otherwise dispose of the Secured Property.

8. **Notice to Borrower.**

Lender will give Borrower at least ten days' notice of when and where the Secured Property will be sold, leased, or otherwise disposed of. Any notice required by this paragraph or by statute will be deemed given to Borrower if sent by first-class mail to Borrower at the following address: _____ _____ .

9. **Entire Agreement.** This is the entire agreement between the parties. It replaces and supersedes any and all oral agreements between the parties, as well as any prior writings.

10. **Successors and Assignees.** This agreement binds and benefits the heirs, successors, and assignees of the parties.

11. **Governing Law.** This agreement will be governed by and construed in accordance with the laws of the state of _____ .

12. **Counterparts.** This agreement may be signed by the parties in different counterparts and the signature pages combined will create a document binding on all parties.

13. **Modification.** This agreement may be modified only by a written agreement signed by all the parties.

14. **Waiver.** If one party waives any term or provision of this agreement at any time, that waiver will be effective only for the specific instance and specific purpose for which the waiver was given. If either party fails to exercise or delays exercising any of its rights or remedies under this agreement, that party retains the right to enforce that term or provision at a later time.

15. **Severability.** If any court determines that any provision of this agreement is invalid or unenforceable, any invalidity or unenforceability will affect only that provision and will not make any other provision of this agreement invalid or unenforceable and such provision shall be modified, amended, or limited only to the extent necessary to render it valid and enforceable.

Lender

Name of business: _____ ,

a _____

By: _____ Dated: _____

Printed name: _____

Title: _____

Address: _____

_____

Borrower

Name of business: _____ ,

a _____

By: _____ Dated: _____

Printed name: _____

Title: _____

Address: _____

Attachment 1
to Security Agreement

1. **Names.** This attachment is made by _____ ,
    Borrower, and _____ , Lender.

2. **Terms of Attachment.** We agree that the tangible personal property covered by Paragraph 2 of our
    Security Agreement dated _____ includes the following:

    _____

    _____

    _____

    _____

    _____

    _____

    _____

    _____ .

Lender

Name of business: _____ ,

a _____

By: _____ Dated: _____

Printed name: _____

Title: _____

Address: _____

_____

Borrower

Name of business: _____ ,

a _____

By: _____ Dated: _____

Printed name: _____

Title: _____

Address: _____

_____

Contract for Purchase of Assets From an Unincorporated Business

1. Names. _____ ,
Seller, and _____ ,
Buyer, agree to the following sale.

2. Sale of Business Assets. Seller is selling to Buyer and Buyer is buying from Seller the assets of the
business known as _____
located at _____
_____ .

3. Assets Being Sold. The assets being sold consist of:

☐ A. The inventory of goods.

☐ B. The furniture, fixtures, and equipment listed in attached Schedule A.

☐ C. The lease dated _____ , between _____
_____ , Seller, and
_____ ,
Landlord, covering the premises at _____
_____ .

☐ D. The contracts listed in attached Schedule B.

☐ E. The goodwill of the business, including the current business name and domain name.

☐ F. Other: _____
_____ .

4. Purchase Price. The purchase price is $_____ , allocated as follows:

A.	Furniture, fixtures, and equipment	$_____
B.	Assignment of lease	$_____
C.	Assignment of contracts	$_____
D.	Goodwill	$_____
E.	Other: _____	$_____
	Total	$_____

☐ The total purchase price will be adjusted by prorating rent, taxes, insurance premiums, utility
costs, and security deposits as of the date of closing.

☐ The total purchase price will be adjusted at closing by adding the price of the inventory as
covered in Paragraph 5.

☐ **5. Price of Inventory.** (*Optional*)

At closing, in addition to the total purchase price listed in Paragraph 4, Buyer will buy the inventory by
paying Seller the amount Seller paid for those goods. A physical count of the goods will be made by

☐ Seller and Buyer.

☐ an inventory service company mutually agreed upon by Seller and Buyer.

The count will be made _____ days before closing and will include only
unopened and undamaged goods. If an inventory service company is used, Seller and Buyer will share
the cost of the service equally.

☐ Buyer will pay no more than $ _____ for the goods.

6. **Accounts Receivable.**

☐ Seller's accounts receivable will remain Seller's property. Buyer will within ten days send Seller the proceeds of any of Seller's accounts receivable that Buyer may collect after closing.

☐ At closing, Buyer will purchase all of Seller's accounts receivable that are no more than _____ days old. Buyer will pay Seller the balances owed on these accounts less _____%.

7. **Deposit.** Buyer will pay Seller a deposit of $_____ when Buyer and Seller sign this contract. This amount will be applied toward the amount listed in Paragraph 4. Seller will return this deposit to Buyer if the purchase is not completed because Seller cannot or does not meet its commitments.

8. **Payments at Closing.** At closing, Buyer will pay Seller the following amounts, using a cashier's check:

☐ $_____ to be applied toward the amount listed in Paragraph 4.

☐ The value of the inventory as determined under Paragraph 5.

☐ The value of the accounts receivable as determined under Paragraph 6.

9. **Promissory Note.** *(Optional)*

At closing, Buyer will give Seller a promissory note for the balance of the purchase price. The promissory note will be signed by Buyer.

☐ **Buyer is a sole proprietor and a cosigner will personally guarantee payment.** _____ _____ will sign the promissory note along with Buyer. Each signer will be jointly and individually liable for payment.

☐ **Buyer is a partnership.** Each partner will cosign the promissory note and will be jointly and individually liable for payment.

☐ **Buyer is a corporation or an LLC and the owners will personally guarantee payment.** The following people will personally guarantee the promissory note and will be jointly and individually liable for payment: _____ _____ _____ .

The promissory note will contain the following terms:

A. The unpaid balance will be subject to interest at the rate of _____% a year.

B. Buyer will pay $_____ on the _____ day of each month beginning one month after the closing until the principal and interest have been paid in full.

C. The entire amount of principal and interest will be paid by _____ .

D. Payments will be applied first to interest and then to principal.

E. Buyer may prepay all or any part of the principal without penalty.

F. If Buyer is more than _____ days late in making a payment, Seller may declare that the entire balance of the unpaid principal is due immediately, together with the interest that has accrued.

10. **Security for Payment.** At closing, to secure the payment of the promissory note, Buyer will sign a security agreement giving Seller a security interest in

☐ the assets that Buyer is purchasing.

☐ the lease that is being assigned to Buyer.

Seller may file a Uniform Commercial Code Financing Statement to further protect Seller's security interest in the Secured Property.

11. **Seller's Debts.** Buyer is not assuming any of Seller's debts or liabilities. At or before closing, Seller will pay all debts and liabilities that are or may become a lien on the assets being bought by Buyer.

At closing, Seller will confirm in an affidavit that Seller has paid all debts and liabilities of the business, including those that are known and those that are in dispute.

12. **Closing.** The closing will take place:

Date: _____

Time: _____

Location: _____

_____

At closing, Buyer and Seller will sign the documents specified in this contract and all other documents reasonably needed to transfer the business assets to Buyer. Buyer will pay Seller the amounts required by this contract and Seller will transfer the business assets to Buyer.

13. **Documents for Transferring Assets.** At closing, Seller will deliver to Buyer these signed documents:

☐ A. A bill of sale for the tangible assets being bought, with a warranty of good title.

☐ B. An assignment of the lease, with the landlord's written consent.

☐ C. Assignment of any other contracts that are being transferred to Buyer, with the written consent of the other contracting person, if such consent is required.

☐ D. Assignments of all trademarks, patents, and copyrights that are part of this purchase.

Seller will also deliver to Buyer at closing all other documents reasonably needed to transfer the business assets to Buyer.

14. **Seller's Representations.** Seller warrants and represents that:

☐ A. Seller has good and marketable title to the assets being sold. The assets will be free from encumbrances at closing.

☐ B. At closing, Seller will have paid all taxes affecting the business and its assets.

☐ C. There are no judgments, claims, liens, or proceedings pending against Seller, the business, or the assets being sold and none will be pending at closing.

☐ D. Seller has given Buyer complete and accurate information, in writing, about the earnings of the business, its assets and liabilities, and its financial condition.

☐ E. Until closing, Seller will not enter into any new contracts or incur any new obligations and will continue to conduct its business in a normal manner.

☐ F. Other: _____

_____.

These warranties and representations will survive the closing.

15. **Buyer's Representations.** Buyer warrants and represents that:

A. Buyer has inspected the tangible assets that Buyer is purchasing and the premises covered by the lease, as applicable, and is satisfied with their condition except for: _____

_____.

B. Buyer has given Seller accurate information about Buyer's financial condition.

These warranties and representations will survive the closing.

---

16. **Covenant Not to Compete.** *(Optional)*

For _____ ☐ years ☐ months following the closing, the individual owners of the business being sold ("former owners") and the spouses of former owners who sign this contract will not directly or indirectly participate in a business that is similar to a business now or later operated by Buyer in the same geographical area. This includes participating in former owner's own business or in former owner's spouse's business or acting as a co-owner, director, officer, consultant, independent contractor, employee, or agent of another business.

In particular, the former owners and the spouses of former owners who sign this contract will not:

(a) solicit or attempt to solicit any business or trade from Buyer's actual or prospective customers or clients

(b) employ or attempt to employ any employee of Buyer

(c) divert or attempt to divert business away from Buyer, or

(d) encourage any independent contractor or consultant to end a relationship with Buyer.

The former owners and the spouses of former owners acknowledge and agree that if any former owner or spouse of a former owner breaches or threatens to breach any of the terms of this Paragraph 16, Buyer will sustain irreparable harm and will be entitled to obtain an injunction to stop any breach or threatened breach of this Paragraph 16.

Each former owner and each spouse of a former owner, by signing this agreement, accepts and agrees to be bound by this covenant not to compete. At closing, Buyer will pay each former owner and each spouse of a former owner $_____ for this covenant not to compete.

17. **Risk of Loss.** If business assets are damaged or destroyed before closing, Buyer may cancel this contract, in which case Seller will promptly return the deposit.

18. **Disputes.**

☐ **Litigation.** If a dispute arises, either party may take the matter to court.

☐ **Mediation and Possible Litigation.** If a dispute arises, the parties will try in good faith to settle it through mediation conducted by:

☐ _____ .

☐ a mediator to be mutually selected.

The parties will share the costs of the mediator equally. Each party will cooperate fully and fairly with the mediator and will attempt to reach a mutually satisfactory compromise to the dispute. If the dispute is not resolved within 30 days after it is referred to the mediator, either party may take the matter to court.

☐ **Mediation and Possible Arbitration.** If a dispute arises, the parties will try in good faith to settle it through mediation conducted by:

☐ _____ .

☐ a mediator to be mutually selected.

The parties will share the costs of the mediator equally. Each party will cooperate fully and fairly with the mediator and will attempt to reach a mutually satisfactory compromise to the dispute. If the dispute is not resolved within 30 days after it is referred to the mediator, it will be arbitrated by:

☐ _____ .

☐ an arbitrator to be mutually selected.

Judgment on the arbitration award may be entered in any court that has jurisdiction over the matter. Costs of arbitration, including lawyers' fees, will be allocated by the arbitrator.

☐ **Attorneys' Fees.** If either party brings a legal action arising out of a dispute over this agreement, the losing party will reimburse the prevailing party for all reasonable costs and attorneys' fees incurred by the prevailing party in the lawsuit.

19. **Additional Agreements.** Seller and Buyer additionally agree that _____

_____ .

20. **Entire Agreement.** This is the entire agreement between the parties. It replaces and supersedes any and all oral agreements between the parties, as well as any prior writings.

21. **Successors and Assignees.** This agreement binds and benefits the heirs, successors, and assignees of the parties.

22. **Notices.** All notices must be in writing. A notice may be delivered to a party at the address that follows a party's signature or to a new address that a party designates in writing. A notice may be delivered:

    (1) in person

    (2) by certified mail, or

    (3) by overnight courier.

23. **Governing Law.** This agreement will be governed by and construed in accordance with the laws of the state of _____ .

24. **Counterparts.** This agreement may be signed by the parties in different counterparts and the signature pages combined will create a document binding on all parties.

25. **Modification.** This agreement may be modified only by a written agreement signed by all the parties.

26. **Waiver.** If one party waives any term or provision of this agreement at any time, that waiver will be effective only for the specific instance and specific purpose for which the waiver was given. If either party fails to exercise or delays exercising any of its rights or remedies under this agreement, that party retains the right to enforce that term or provision at a later time.

27. **Severability.** If any court determines that any provision of this agreement is invalid or unenforceable, any invalidity or unenforceability will affect only that provision and will not make any other provision of this agreement invalid or unenforceable and such provision shall be modified, amended, or limited only to the extent necessary to render it valid and enforceable.

Seller

Name of business: _____ ,

a _____

By: _____ Dated: _____

Printed name: _____

Title: _____

Address: _____

_____

Buyer

Name of business: _____ ,

a _____

By: _____ Dated: _____

Printed name: _____

Title: _____

Address: _____

_____

☐ **Signatures of all partners or members of business being sold** (*For use where Seller is a partnership or multimember LLC*)

Signature: _____ Dated: _____

Printed name: _____

Address: _____

_____

Signature: _____ Dated: _____

Printed name: _____

Address: _____

_____

☐ **Signatures of spouses of owners of business being sold**

Signature: _____ Dated: _____

Printed name: _____

Address: _____

_____

Spouse of: _____

Signature: _____ Dated: _____

Printed name: _____

Address: _____

_____

Spouse of: _____

☐ **Signature of cosigner for buyer**

I will sign the promissory note for the unpaid balance due under this purchase contract on the terms and conditions set forth in Paragraph 9.

Signature: _____ Dated: _____

Printed name: _____

Address: _____

_____

Contract for Purchase of Assets From a Corporation

1. **Names.** _____ , a _____ corporation,
   Seller, and _____ ,
   Buyer, agree to the following sale.

2. **Sale of Business Assets.** Seller is selling to Buyer and Buyer is buying from Seller the assets of the
   business known as _____
   located at _____
   _____ .

3. **Assets Being Sold.** The assets being sold consist of:
   ☐ A. The inventory of goods
   ☐ B. The furniture, fixtures, and equipment listed in attached Schedule A
   ☐ C. The lease dated _____ , between _____
   _____ , Seller,
   and _____ ,
   Landlord, covering the premises at _____
   _____

   ☐ D. The contracts listed in attached Schedule B
   ☐ E. The goodwill of the business, including the current business name and domain name
   ☐ F. Other: _____
   _____
   _____

4. **Purchase Price.** The purchase price is $_____ , allocated as follows:

A. Furniture, fixtures, and equipment	$_____
B. Assignment of lease	$_____
C. Assignment of contracts	$_____
D. Goodwill	$_____
E. Other: _____	$_____
Total	$_____

   ☐ The total purchase price will be adjusted by prorating rent, taxes, insurance premiums, utility
   costs, and security deposits as of the date of closing.
   ☐ The total purchase price will be adjusted at closing by adding the price of the inventory as
   covered in Paragraph 5.

5. **Price of Inventory.** (*Optional*)
   At closing, in addition to the total purchase price listed in Paragraph 4, Buyer will buy the inventory by
   paying Seller the amount Seller paid for those goods. A physical count of the goods will be made by:
   ☐ Seller and Buyer.
   ☐ an inventory service company mutually agreed upon by Seller and Buyer.
   The count will be made _____ days before closing and will include only
   unopened and undamaged goods. If an inventory service company is used, Seller and Buyer will share
   the cost of the service equally.
   ☐ Buyer will pay no more than $_____ for the goods.

6. **Accounts Receivable.**

☐ Seller's accounts receivable will remain Seller's property. Buyer will, within ten days, send Seller the proceeds of any of Seller's accounts receivable that Buyer may collect after closing.

☐ At closing, Buyer will purchase all of Seller's accounts receivable that are no more than _____ days old. Buyer will pay Seller the balances owed on these accounts less _____%.

7. **Deposit.** Buyer will pay Seller a deposit of $_____ when Buyer and Seller sign this contract. This amount will be applied toward the amount listed in Paragraph 4. Seller will return this deposit to Buyer if the purchase is not completed because Seller cannot or does not meet its commitments.

8. **Payments at Closing.** At closing, Buyer will pay Seller the following amounts, using a cashier's check:

☐ $_____ to be applied toward the amount listed in Paragraph 4.

☐ the value of the inventory as determined under Paragraph 5.

☐ the value of the accounts receivable as determined under Paragraph 6.

9. **Promissory Note.** *(Optional)*

At closing, Buyer will give Seller a promissory note for the balance of the purchase price. The promissory note will be signed by Buyer.

☐ **Buyer is a sole proprietor, and a cosigner will personally guarantee payment.** _____ _____ will sign the promissory note along with Buyer. Each signer will be jointly and individually liable for payment.

☐ **Buyer is a partnership.** Each partner will cosign the promissory note and will be jointly and individually liable for payment.

☐ **Buyer is a corporation or an LLC and the owners will personally guarantee payment.** The following people will personally guarantee the promissory note and will be jointly and individually liable for payment: _____ _____ _____ .

The promissory note will contain the following terms:

A. The unpaid balance will be subject to interest at the rate of _____% a year.

B. Buyer will pay $_____ on the _____ day of each month beginning one month after the closing until the principal and interest have been paid in full.

C. The entire amount of principal and interest will be paid by _____ .

D. Payments will be applied first to interest and then to principal.

E. Buyer may prepay all or any part of the principal without penalty.

F. If Buyer is more than _____ days late in making a payment, Seller may declare that the entire balance of the unpaid principal is due immediately, together with the interest that has accrued.

10. **Security for Payment.** At closing, to secure the payment of the promissory note, Buyer will sign a security agreement giving Seller a security interest in:

☐ the assets that Buyer is purchasing.

☐ the lease that is being assigned to Buyer.

Seller may file a Uniform Commercial Code Financing Statement to further protect Seller's security interest in the Secured Property.

11. **Seller's Debts.** Buyer is not assuming any of Seller's debts or liabilities. At or before closing, Seller will pay all debts and liabilities that are or may become a lien on the assets being bought by Buyer.

At closing, Seller will confirm in an affidavit that Seller has paid all debts and liabilities of the business, including those that are known and those that are in dispute.

12. **Closing.** The closing will take place:

Date: _____

Time: _____

Location: _____

_____.

At closing, Buyer and Seller will sign the documents specified in this contract and all other documents reasonably needed to transfer the business assets to Buyer. Buyer will pay Seller the amounts required by this contract and Seller will transfer the business assets to Buyer.

13. **Documents for Transferring Assets.** At closing, Seller will deliver to Buyer these signed documents:

☐ A. A bill of sale for the tangible assets being bought, with a warranty of good title.

☐ B. An assignment of the lease, with the landlord's written consent.

☐ C. Assignment of any other contracts that are being transferred to Buyer, with the written consent of the other contracting person, if such consent is required.

☐ D. Assignments of all trademarks, patents, and copyrights that are part of this purchase.

Seller will also deliver to Buyer at closing all other documents reasonably needed to transfer the business assets to Buyer.

14. **Seller's Representations.** Seller warrants and represents that:

A. Seller has good and marketable title to the assets being sold. The assets will be free from encumbrances at closing.

B. At closing, Seller will have paid all taxes affecting the business and its assets.

C. There are no judgments, claims, liens, or proceedings pending against Seller, the business, or the assets being sold and none will be pending at closing.

D. Seller has given Buyer complete and accurate information, in writing, about the earnings of the business, its assets and liabilities, and its financial condition.

E. Until closing, Seller will not enter into any new contracts or incur any new obligations and will continue to conduct its business in a normal manner.

F. Other: _____

_____.

These warranties and representations will survive the closing.

15. **Buyer's Representations.** Buyer warrants and represents that:

A. Buyer has inspected the tangible assets that Buyer is purchasing and the premises covered by the lease, as applicable, and is satisfied with their condition except for: _____

_____.

B. Buyer has given Seller accurate information about Buyer's financial condition.

These warranties and representations will survive the closing.

16. **Covenant Not to Compete.** *(Optional)*

For _____ ☐ years ☐ months following the closing, the individual owners of the business being sold ("former owners") and the spouses of former owners who sign this contract will not directly or indirectly participate in a business that is similar to a business now or later operated by Buyer in the same geographical area. This includes participating in former owner's own business or in former owner's spouse's business or acting as a co-owner, director, officer, consultant, independent contractor, employee, or agent of another business.

In particular, the former owners and the spouses of former owners who sign this contract will not:

   (a) solicit or attempt to solicit any business or trade from Buyer's actual or prospective customers or clients

   (b) employ or attempt to employ any employee of Buyer

   (c) divert or attempt to divert business away from Buyer, or

   (d) encourage any independent contractor or consultant to end a relationship with Buyer.

The former owners and the spouses of former owners acknowledge and agree that if any former owner or spouse of a former owner breaches or threatens to breach any of the terms of this Paragraph 16, Buyer will sustain irreparable harm and will be entitled to obtain an injunction to stop any breach or threatened breach of this Paragraph 16.

Each former owner and each spouse of a former owner, by signing this agreement, accepts and agrees to be bound by this covenant not to compete. At closing, Buyer will pay each former owner and each spouse of a former owner $_____ for this covenant not to compete.

17. **Risk of Loss.** If business assets are damaged or destroyed before closing, Buyer may cancel this contract, in which case Seller will promptly return the deposit.

18. **Disputes.**

   ☐ **Litigation.** If a dispute arises, either party may take the matter to court.

   ☐ **Mediation and Possible Litigation.** If a dispute arises, the parties will try in good faith to settle it through mediation conducted by:

      ☐ _____ .

      ☐ a mediator to be mutually selected.

      The parties will share the costs of the mediator equally. Each party will cooperate fully and fairly with the mediator and will attempt to reach a mutually satisfactory compromise to the dispute. If the dispute is not resolved within 30 days after it is referred to the mediator, either party may take the matter to court.

   ☐ **Mediation and Possible Arbitration.** If a dispute arises, the parties will try in good faith to settle it through mediation conducted by:

      ☐ _____ .

      ☐ a mediator to be mutually selected.

      The parties will share the costs of the mediator equally. Each party will cooperate fully and fairly with the mediator and will attempt to reach a mutually satisfactory compromise to the dispute. If the dispute is not resolved within 30 days after it is referred to the mediator, it will be arbitrated by:

      ☐ _____ .

☐ an arbitrator to be mutually selected.

Judgment on the arbitration award may be entered in any court that has jurisdiction over the matter. Costs of arbitration, including lawyers' fees, will be allocated by the arbitrator.

☐ **Attorneys' Fees.** If either party brings a legal action arising out of a dispute over this agreement, the losing party will reimburse the prevailing party for all reasonable costs and attorneys' fees incurred by the prevailing party in the lawsuit.

19. **Additional Agreements.** Seller and Buyer additionally agree that _____
_____
_____
_____ .

20. **Entire Agreement.** This is the entire agreement between the parties. It replaces and supersedes any and all oral agreements between the parties, as well as any prior writings.

21. **Successors and Assignees.** This agreement binds and benefits the heirs, successors, and assignees of the parties.

22. **Notices.** All notices must be in writing. A notice may be delivered to a party at the address that follows a party's signature or to a new address that a party designates in writing. A notice may be delivered:

(1) in person

(2) by certified mail, or

(3) by overnight courier.

23. **Governing Law.** This agreement will be governed by and construed in accordance with the laws of the state of _____ .

24. **Counterparts.** This agreement may be signed by the parties in different counterparts and the signature pages combined will create a document binding on all parties.

25. **Modification.** This agreement may be modified only by a written agreement signed by all the parties.

26. **Waiver.** If one party waives any term or provision of this agreement at any time, that waiver will be effective only for the specific instance and specific purpose for which the waiver was given. If either party fails to exercise or delays exercising any of its rights or remedies under this agreement, that party retains the right to enforce that term or provision at a later time.

27. **Severability.** If any court determines that any provision of this agreement is invalid or unenforceable, any invalidity or unenforceability will affect only that provision and will not make any other provision of this agreement invalid or unenforceable and such provision shall be modified, amended, or limited only to the extent necessary to render it valid and enforceable.

Seller

Name of business: _____ ,

a _____

By: _____ Dated: _____

Printed name: _____

Title: _____

Address: _____

_____

Buyer

Name of business: _____ ,

a _____

By: _____ Dated: _____

Printed name: _____

Title: _____

Address: _____

_____

☐ **Signatures of all shareholders**

Signature: _____ Dated: _____

Printed name: _____

Address: _____

_____

Signature: _____ Dated: _____

Printed name: _____

Address: _____

_____

☐ **Signatures of spouses of shareholders**

Signature: _____ Dated: _____

Printed name: _____

Address: _____

_____

Spouse of: _____

Signature: _____ Dated: _____

Printed name: _____

Address: _____

_____

Spouse of: _____

☐ **Signature of cosigner for buyer**

I will sign the promissory note for the unpaid balance due under this purchase contract on the terms and conditions set forth in Paragraph 9.

Signature: _____ Dated: _____

Printed name: _____

Address: _____

_____

Corporate Resolution Authorizing Sale of Assets

All of the shareholders and directors of _____
_____ , a _____
corporation, consent to the sale of the corporation's assets on the terms stated in the purchase
agreement attached to this resolution.

The corporation's president is authorized to sign the purchase agreement on behalf of the
corporation and to take such actions as the president deems necessary or appropriate to carry out the
terms of the purchase agreement.

Shareholders

Signature: _____ Dated: _____

Printed name: _____

Signature: _____ Dated: _____

Printed name: _____

Directors

Signature: _____ Dated: _____

Printed name: _____

Signature: _____ Dated: _____

Printed name: _____

Contract for Purchase of Corporate Stock

1. **Names.**

   Seller: _____

   _____

   Buyer: _____

   _____

   The above-listed Seller and Buyer agree to the terms of this contract.

2. **Sale of Corporate Stock.** Seller is selling to Buyer and Buyer is buying from Seller all the issued and

   outstanding stock of _____,

   a _____ corporation, free of encumbrances. This sale

   includes the corporate assets listed in attached Schedule A.

   The corporation has issued _____ shares of common stock, which are owned as

   follows:

   | | Shares of Common |
Name of Shareholder	Stock Owned
_____	_____
_____	_____
_____	_____
_____	_____

3. **Purchase Price.** The purchase price is $_____ per share, for a total of $_____.

   At closing, Buyer will pay the purchase price to each shareholder by cashier's check.

4. **Provision for Payment of Undisclosed or Unpaid Liabilities.** *(Optional)*

   At closing, to provide for payment of undisclosed or unpaid liabilities incurred prior to closing but

   which have not yet been determined:

   ☐ A. Seller and Buyer will place an agreed-upon portion of the purchase price in escrow for 90 days with

       ☐ _____.

       ☐ a person to be agreed upon.

   ☐ B. Buyer will withhold an agreed-upon portion of the purchase price for 90 days.

   Any portion of these funds not used to pay undisclosed or unpaid liabilities will be returned to

   Seller at the end of the 90 days.

5. **Closing.** The closing will take place:

   Date: _____

   Time: _____

   Location: _____

   _____.

6. **Documents for Buyer.** At closing, Seller will deliver these signed documents to Buyer:

   A. Stock certificates for all the corporation's stock endorsed for transfer by shareholders. Stock
      certificates will be coendorsed by the spouse of each married shareholder.

   B. The written resignations of the corporation's officers and directors.

   C. The corporation's minute book and business records.

D. The corporation's contracts and leases.

E. The landlord's written consent to the assignment of the lease, if such consent is required.

F. The written consent of any other party, if such consent is required.

G. All other documents reasonably needed to transfer the corporation to Buyer.

7. **Seller's Representations.** Each shareholder warrants and represents that:

A. Shareholders listed above own all of the issued and outstanding shares of the corporation's stock. The shares are free of any liens or encumbrances.

B. The corporation has good and marketable title to the assets listed in attached Schedule A. The assets will be free from liens or encumbrances at closing.

C. The debts and liabilities of the corporation are listed in attached Schedule B. There will be no other debts or liabilities at closing.

D. At closing, the corporation will have paid all taxes affecting the business and its assets, to the extent known at closing.

E. Any judgments, claims, liens, or proceedings pending against the corporation or its assets have been disclosed to Buyer in writing. No others will be pending at closing.

F. Seller has given Buyer, in writing, complete and accurate information about the earnings of the corporation, its assets and liabilities, and its financial condition.

G. The corporation is properly incorporated and is in good standing.

H. The corporation will not enter into any new contracts or incur any new obligations from now until closing and will continue to conduct its business in a normal manner.

I. The corporation owes no outstanding dividends and will declare no dividends from now until closing.

J. Between now and closing, the corporation will not increase the compensation of any employee, consultant, independent contractor, director, or officer, or hire any new employee, consultant, independent contractor, director, or officer.

These warranties and representations will survive the closing.

8. **Covenant Not to Compete.** *(Optional)*

For _____ ☐ years ☐ months following the closing, the shareholders of the corporation being sold ("former owners") and the spouses of former owners who sign this contract will not directly or indirectly participate in a business that is similar to a business now or later operated by Buyer in the same geographical area. This includes participating in former owner's own business or in former owner's spouse's business or acting as a co-owner, director, officer, consultant, independent contractor, employee, or agent of another business.

In particular, the former owners and the spouses of former owners who sign this contract will not:

(a) solicit or attempt to solicit any business or trade from Buyer's actual or prospective customers or clients

(b) employ or attempt to employ any employee of Buyer

(c) divert or attempt to divert business away from Buyer, or

(d) encourage any independent contractor or consultant to end a relationship with Buyer. The former owners and the spouses of former owners acknowledge and agree that if any former owner or spouse of a former owner breaches or threatens to breach any of the terms of this Paragraph 8, Buyer will sustain irreparable harm and will be entitled to obtain an injunction to stop any breach or threatened breach of this Paragraph 8.

Each former owner and each spouse of a former owner, by signing this agreement, accepts and agrees to be bound by this covenant not to compete. At closing, Buyer will pay each former owner and each spouse of a former owner $_____ for this covenant not to compete.

9. **Risk of Loss.** Until closing, Seller assumes the risk of loss or damage to the corporation's physical assets caused by fire or other casualty. If corporate assets are lost or destroyed by fire or other casualty before closing, Buyer may cancel this contract.

10. **Disputes**

☐ **Litigation.** If a dispute arises, either party may take the matter to court.

☐ **Mediation and Possible Litigation.** If a dispute arises, the parties will try in good faith to settle it through mediation conducted by:

☐ _____ .

☐ a mediator to be mutually selected.

The parties will share the costs of the mediator equally. Each party will cooperate fully and fairly with the mediator and will attempt to reach a mutually satisfactory compromise to the dispute. If the dispute is not resolved within 30 days after it is referred to the mediator, either party may take the matter to court.

☐ **Mediation and Possible Arbitration.** If a dispute arises, the parties will try in good faith to settle it through mediation conducted by:

☐ _____ .

☐ a mediator to be mutually selected.

The parties will share the costs of the mediator equally. Each party will cooperate fully and fairly with the mediator and will attempt to reach a mutually satisfactory compromise to the dispute. If the dispute is not resolved within 30 days after it is referred to the mediator, it will be arbitrated by:

☐ _____ .

☐ an arbitrator to be mutually selected.

Judgment on the arbitration award may be entered in any court that has jurisdiction over the matter. Costs of arbitration, including lawyers' fees, will be allocated by the arbitrator.

☐ **Attorneys' Fees.** If either party brings a legal action arising out of a dispute over this agreement, the losing party will reimburse the prevailing party for all reasonable costs and attorneys' fees incurred by the prevailing party in the lawsuit.

11. **Additional Agreements.** Seller and Buyer additionally agree that _____

_____

_____

_____

_____

_____ .

12. **Required Signatures.** This contract is valid only if signed by all the persons owning shares in the

_____ corporation.

13. **Entire Agreement.** This is the entire agreement between the parties. It replaces and supersedes any and all oral agreements between the parties, as well as any prior writings.

14. **Successors and Assignees.** This agreement binds and benefits the heirs, successors, and assignees of the parties.

15. **Notices.** All notices must be in writing. A notice may be delivered to a party at the address that follows a party's signature or to a new address that a party designates in writing. A notice may be delivered:

     (1) in person

     (2) by certified mail, or

     (3) by overnight courier.

16. **Governing Law.** This agreement will be governed by and construed in accordance with the laws of the state of _____ .

17. **Counterparts.** This agreement may be signed by the parties in different counterparts and the signature pages combined will create a document binding on all parties.

18. **Modification.** This agreement may be modified only by a written agreement signed by all the parties.

19. **Waiver.** If one party waives any term or provision of this agreement at any time, that waiver will be effective only for the specific instance and specific purpose for which the waiver was given. If either party fails to exercise or delays exercising any of its rights or remedies under this agreement, that party retains the right to enforce that term or provision at a later time.

20. **Severability.** If any court determines that any provision of this lease is invalid or unenforceable, any invalidity or unenforceability will affect only that provision and will not make any other provision of this lease invalid or unenforceable. Instead, the court shall modify, amend, or limit the provision to the extent necessary to render it valid and enforceable.

Buyer

Signature: _____ Dated: _____

Printed name: _____

Address: _____

_____

Seller (Shareholders)

Signature: _____ Dated: _____

Printed name: _____

Address: _____

_____

Signature: _____ Dated: _____

Printed name: _____

Address: _____

_____

☐ **Spouses of shareholders**

Signature: _____ Dated: _____

Printed name: _____

Signature: _____ Dated: _____

Printed name: _____

Bill of Sale for Business Assets

1. **Names.** _____ ,
    Seller, transfers to _____ , Buyer,
    full ownership of the property listed on Attachment 1.

2. **Acknowledgment of Payment.** Seller acknowledges receiving payment for this property in the form of
    ☐ a cashier's check.
    ☐ a cashier's check and a promissory note secured by a security interest.

3. **Warranty of Ownership.** Seller warrants that Seller is the legal owner of the property and that the
    property is:
    ☐ free of all liens and encumbrances.
    ☐ free of all liens and encumbrances except the security interest granted by Buyer to Seller.

Seller

Name of business: _____ ,

a _____

By: _____ Dated: _____

Printed name: _____

Title: _____

Address: _____

_____

☐ **Signatures of spouses of owners of business being sold**

Signature: _____ Dated: _____

Printed name: _____

Spouse of: _____

Signature: _____ Dated: _____

Printed name: _____

Spouse of: _____

☐ **Signatures of all owners of business being sold** (*for use where Seller is a partnership,
   multimember LLC, or corporation*)

Personal Responsibility for Warranty. The following are all of Seller's ☐ partners ☐ LLC members
☐ corporate shareholders. Each will be personally responsible for the warranty in Paragraph 3 of this Bill
of Sale.

Signature: _____ Dated: _____

Printed name: _____

Address: _____

_____

Signature: _____ Dated: _____

Printed name: _____

Address: _____

_____

Attachment 1
to Bill of Sale

This is an attachment to the Bill of Sale given by _____

_____ , Seller, to _____

_____ , Buyer.

Seller is transferring to Buyer full ownership of the following property:

_____

_____

_____

_____

_____

_____

_____

_____

_____

_____

_____

_____

_____

_____

_____

_____

_____

_____

_____

_____

_____

_____

_____ .

Dated: _____

Seller

Name of business: _____ ,

a _____

By: _____

Printed name: _____

Title: _____

Address: _____

_____

Seller's Affidavit—No Creditors

State of _____

County of _____

I, _____ ,

state under oath:

1. **Entity Selling Assets.** I make this affidavit on behalf of

   ☐ myself, a sole proprietor,

   ☐ _____ , a partnership,

   ☐ _____ , a limited liability
   company,

   ☐ _____ , a corporation,

   as Seller of business assets to _____ , Buyer.

2. **No Security Interests.** The assets that Seller is transferring to Buyer by a bill of sale are free of all
   security interests and other liens.

3. **No Creditors.** Seller has paid all debts and liabilities of Seller's business. There are no debts or
   liabilities of the individual owner(s) of Seller's business that affect Seller's assets or the right of Seller
   to transfer Seller's assets to Buyer.

4. **No Claims.** There are no claims or liens (either disputed or undisputed) against Seller, Seller's assets,
   or the individual owner(s) of Seller's business that affect Seller's assets or the right of Seller to transfer
   Seller's assets to Buyer.

5. **Indemnification.** If, contrary to Paragraphs 2, 3, or 4 of this Affidavit, there are any security interests
   or other liens, debts, liabilities, or claims, Seller and the signer of this affidavit will immediately
   remove the encumbrances or liens, pay the debts, liabilities, or claims, and indemnify, defend, hold
   harmless, and protect Buyer from any loss or liability arising out of such security interest, lien, debt,
   liability, or claim.

Dated: _____

Seller

Name of business: _____ ,

a _____

By: _____

Printed name: _____

Title: _____

Address: _____

_____

[NOTARIZATION]

Security Agreement for Buying Business Assets

1. **Names.** _____ ,
   Buyer, grants to _____ ,
   Seller, a continuing security interest in the following property (the Secured Property), which consists of
   - ☐ the property listed in Attachment 1.
   - ☐ any additional tangible personal property that Buyer now owns or later acquires in connection with Buyer's business, including replacement inventory.

2. **Security for Promissory Note.** Buyer is granting this security interest to secure performance of a promissory note that Buyer executed on _____ as partial payment for certain business assets. The promissory note obligates Buyer to pay Seller $_____ with interest at the rate of _____% a year, on the terms stated in the promissory note.

3. **Financing Statement.** Buyer agrees that the promissory note will be further secured by a Uniform Commercial Code Financing Statement. Buyer will sign any other documents that Seller reasonably requests to protect Seller's security interest in the Secured Property.

4. **Use and Care of the Secured Property.** Until the promissory note is fully paid, Buyer agrees to:
   - ☐ A. Keep the Secured Property at Buyer's premises and use it only in the operation of Buyer's business.
   - ☐ B. Maintain the Secured Property in good repair.
   - ☐ C. Not sell, transfer, or release the Secured Property unless Seller consents. Buyer may sell inventory in the ordinary course of Buyer's business, but will reasonably renew and replenish inventory to keep it at its current level.
   - ☐ D. Pay all taxes on the Secured Property as taxes become due.
   - ☐ E. Insure the Secured Property against normal risks, with an insurance policy that names Buyer and Seller as beneficiaries.
   - ☐ F. Deliver to Seller a copy of the insurance policy insuring the Secured Property and provide to Seller annual proof that Buyer has paid the premiums on the policy.
   - ☐ G. Allow Seller to inspect the Secured Property at any reasonable time.

5. **Buyer's Default.** If Buyer is more than ten days late in making any payment required by the promissory note or if Buyer fails to correct any violations of Paragraph 4 within ten days of receiving written notice from Seller, Buyer will be in default.

6. **Seller's Rights.** If Buyer is in default, Seller may exercise the remedies contained in the Uniform Commercial Code for the State of _____ and any other remedies legally available to Seller. Seller may, for example:
   - ☐ A. Remove the Secured Property from the place where it is then located.
   - ☐ B. Require Buyer to assemble the Secured Property and make it available to Seller at a place designated by Seller that is reasonably convenient to Buyer and Seller.
   - ☐ C. Sell or lease the Secured Property, or otherwise dispose of it.

7. **Notice to Buyer.** Seller will give Buyer at least ten days' notice of when and where the Secured Property will be sold, leased, or otherwise disposed of. Any notice required here or by statute will be

deemed given to Buyer if sent by first-class mail to Buyer at the following address: _____

_____ ,

_____ or to a new address that Buyer designates in writing.

8. **Entire Agreement.** This is the entire agreement between the parties. It replaces and supersedes any and all oral agreements between the parties, as well as any prior writings.

9. **Successors and Assignees.** This agreement binds and benefits the heirs, successors, and assignees of the parties.

10. **Governing Law.** This agreement will be governed by and construed in accordance with the laws of the state of _____ .

11. **Counterparts.** This agreement may be signed by the parties in different counterparts and the signature pages combined will create a document binding on all parties.

12. **Modification.** This agreement may be modified only by a written agreement signed by all the parties.

13. **Waiver.** If one party waives any term or provision of this agreement at any time, that waiver will be effective only for the specific instance and specific purpose for which the waiver was given. If either party fails to exercise or delays exercising any of its rights or remedies under this agreement, that party retains the right to enforce that term or provision at a later time.

14. **Severability.** If any court determines that any provision of this agreement is invalid or unenforceable, any invalidity or unenforceability will affect only that provision and will not make any other provision of this agreement invalid or unenforceable and such provision shall be modified, amended, or limited only to the extent necessary to render it valid and enforceable.

Seller

Name of business: _____ ,

a _____

By: _____   Dated: _____

Printed name: _____

Title: _____

Address: _____

_____

Buyer

Name of business: _____ ,

a _____

By: _____   Dated: _____

Printed name: _____

Title: _____

Address: _____

_____

Attachment 1
to Security Agreement

This is an attachment to the Security Agreement given by _____

_____ , Buyer, to _____

_____ , Seller.

The Secured Property consists of the following: _____

_____

_____

_____

_____

_____

_____

_____

_____

_____

_____

_____

_____

_____

_____

_____

_____

_____

_____

_____

Seller

Name of business: _____ ,

a _____

By: _____ Dated: _____

Printed name: _____

Title: _____

Address: _____

_____

Buyer

Name of business: _____ ,

a _____

By: _____ Dated: _____

Printed name: _____

Title: _____

Address: _____

_____

Gross Lease

1. **Names.** This lease is made by _____ ,
   Landlord, and _____ , Tenant.

2. **Premises Being Leased.** Landlord is leasing to Tenant and Tenant is leasing from Landlord the
   following premises: _____
   _____ .

   ☐ **Part of Building Only.** Specifically, Tenant is leasing the _____
   _____ of the building.

   ☐ **Shared Facilities.** Tenant and Tenant's employees and customers may use the following additional
   facilities in common with other tenants, employees, and customers:

   ☐ Parking spaces: _____
   ☐ Restroom facilities: _____
   ☐ Storage areas: _____
   ☐ Hallways, stairways, and elevators: _____
   ☐ Conference rooms: _____
   ☐ Other: _____

3. **Term of Lease.** This lease begins on _____ and ends on
   _____ .

4. **Rent.** Tenant will pay rent in advance on the _____ day of each month. Tenant's first rent
   payment will be on _____ in the amount of $_____ .
   Tenant will pay rent of $_____ per month thereafter.

   ☐ Tenant will pay this rental amount for the entire term of the lease.

   ☐ Rent will increase each year, on the anniversary of the starting date in Paragraph 3, as follows:
   _____
   _____ .

5. **Option to Extend Lease.**

   ☐ **First Option.** Landlord grants Tenant the option to extend this lease for an additional _____
   years. Tenant will pay Landlord $_____ in consideration for this option right, understood
   as additional rent and payable with Tenant's first full rent payment. To exercise this option,
   Tenant must give Landlord written notice on or before _____ . Tenant may exercise this
   option only if Tenant is in substantial compliance with the terms of this lease. Tenant will lease
   the premises on the same terms as in this lease except as follows: _____
   _____
   _____ .

   ☐ **Second Option.** If Tenant exercises the option granted above, Tenant will then have the option
   to extend this lease for _____ years beyond the first option period. Tenant will pay
   Landlord $_____ in consideration for this second option right, understood as additional
   rent and payable with Tenant's first full rent payment. To exercise this option, Tenant must give
   Landlord written notice on or before _____ . Tenant may exercise this option only if

Tenant is in substantial compliance with the terms of this lease. Tenant will lease the premises on the same terms as in this lease except as follows: _____
_____ .

6. **Security Deposit.** Tenant has deposited $_____ with Landlord as security for Tenant's performance of this lease. Landlord will refund the full security deposit to Tenant within 14 days following the end of the lease if Tenant returns the premises to Landlord in good condition (except for reasonable wear and tear) and Tenant has paid Landlord all sums due under this lease. Otherwise, Landlord may deduct any amounts required to place the premises in good condition and to pay for any money owed to Landlord under the lease.

7. **Improvements by Landlord.**

☐ Before the lease term begins, Landlord (at Landlord's expense) will make the repairs and improvements listed in Attachment 1 to this contract.

☐ Tenant accepts the premises in "as is" condition. Landlord need not provide any repairs or improvements before the lease term begins.

8. **Improvements by Tenant.** Tenant may make alterations and improvements to the premises after obtaining the Landlord's written consent, which will not be unreasonably withheld. At any time before this lease ends, Tenant may remove any of Tenant's alterations and improvements, as long as Tenant repairs any damage caused by attaching the items to or removing them from the premises.

9. **Tenant's Use of Premises.** Tenant will use the premises for the following business purposes: _____
_____ .

Tenant may also use the premises for purposes reasonably related to the main use.

10. **Landlord's Representations.** Landlord represents that:

☐ A. At the beginning of the lease term, the premises will be properly zoned for Tenant's stated use and will be in compliance with all applicable laws and regulations.

☐ B. The premises have not been used for the storage or disposal of any toxic or hazardous substance and Landlord has received no notice from any governmental authority concerning removal of any toxic or hazardous substance from the property.

11. **Utilities and Services.** Landlord will pay for the following utilities and services:

☐ Water   ☐ Heat

☐ Electricity   ☐ Air-conditioning

☐ Gas

Any items not checked will be the responsibility of Tenant.

12. **Maintenance and Repairs.**

☐ A. Landlord will maintain and make all necessary repairs to: (1) the roof, structural components, exterior walls, and interior common walls of the premises, and (2) the plumbing, electrical, heating, ventilating, and air-conditioning systems.

☐ B. Landlord will regularly clean and maintain (including snow removal) the parking areas, yards, common areas, and exterior of the building and remove all litter so that the premises will be kept in an attractive condition.

☐ C. Tenant will clean and maintain Tenant's portion of the building so that it will be kept in an attractive condition.

13. **Insurance.**

    ☐ A. Landlord will carry fire and extended coverage insurance on the building.

    ☐ B. Tenant will carry public liability insurance; this insurance will include Landlord as an insured party. The public liability coverage for personal injury will be in at least the following amounts:

        $_____ per occurrence

        $_____ in any one year

    ☐ C. Landlord and Tenant release each other from any liability to the other for any property loss, property damage, or personal injury to the extent covered by insurance carried by the party suffering the loss, damage, or injury.

    ☐ D. Tenant will give Landlord a certificate of insurance for all insurance policies that this lease requires Tenant to obtain.

14. **Taxes.**

    A. Landlord will pay all real property taxes levied and assessed against the premises.

    B. Tenant will pay all personal property taxes levied and assessed against Tenant's personal property.

15. **Subletting and Assignment.** Tenant will not assign this lease or sublet any part of the premises without the written consent of Landlord. Landlord will not unreasonably withhold such consent.

16. **Damage to Premises.**

    A. If the premises are damaged through fire or other cause not the fault of Tenant, Tenant will owe no rent for any period during which Tenant is substantially deprived of the use of the premises.

    B. If Tenant is substantially deprived of the use of the premises for more than 90 days because of such damage, Tenant may terminate this lease by delivering written notice of termination to Landlord.

17. **Notice of Default.** Before starting a legal action to recover possession of the premises based on Tenant's default, Landlord will notify Tenant in writing of the default. Landlord will take legal action only if Tenant does not correct the default within ten days after written notice is given or mailed to Tenant.

18. **Quiet Enjoyment.** As long as Tenant is not in default under the terms of this lease, Tenant will have the right to occupy the premises peacefully and without interference.

19. **Eminent Domain.** This lease will become void if any part of the leased premises or the building in which the leased premises are located is taken by eminent domain. Tenant has the right to receive and keep any amount of money that the agency taking the premises by eminent domain pays for the value of Tenant's lease, its loss of business, and for moving and relocation expenses.

20. **Holding Over.** If Tenant remains in possession after this lease ends, the continuing tenancy will be from month to month.

21. **Disputes.**

    ☐ **Litigation.** If a dispute arises, either party may take the matter to court.

    ☐ **Mediation and Possible Litigation.** If a dispute arises, the parties will try in good faith to settle it through mediation conducted by

        ☐ _____ .

        ☐ a mediator to be mutually selected.

        The parties will share the costs of the mediator equally. Each party will cooperate fully and fairly with the mediator and will attempt to reach a mutually satisfactory compromise to the dispute. If the dispute is not resolved within 30 days after it is referred to the mediator, either party may take the matter to court.

☐ **Mediation and Possible Arbitration.** If a dispute arises, the parties will try in good faith to settle it through mediation conducted by

☐ _____ .

☐ a mediator to be mutually selected.

The parties will share the costs of the mediator equally. Each party will cooperate fully and fairly with the mediator and will attempt to reach a mutually satisfactory compromise to the dispute. If the dispute is not resolved within 30 days after it is referred to the mediator, it will be arbitrated by

☐ _____ .

☐ an arbitrator to be mutually selected.

Judgment on the arbitration award may be entered in any court that has jurisdiction over the matter. Costs of arbitration, including lawyers' fees, will be allocated by the arbitrator.

Landlord need not participate in mediation or arbitration of a dispute unless Tenant has paid the rent called for by this lease or has placed any unpaid rent in escrow with an agreed-upon mediator or arbitrator.

☐ **Attorneys' Fees.** If either party brings a legal action arising out of a dispute over this agreement, the losing party will reimburse the prevailing party for all reasonable costs and attorneys' fees incurred by the prevailing party in the lawsuit.

22. **Additional Agreements.** Landlord and Tenant additionally agree that _____

_____

_____

_____

_____

_____

_____

_____

_____

_____ .

23. **Entire Agreement.** This is the entire agreement between the parties. It replaces and supersedes any and all oral agreements between the parties, as well as any prior writings.

24. **Successors and Assignees.** This lease binds and benefits the heirs, successors, and assignees of the parties.

25. **Notices.** All notices must be in writing. A notice may be delivered to a party at the address that follows a party's signature or to a new address that a party designates in writing. A notice may be delivered:

(1) in person

(2) by certified mail, or

(3) by overnight courier.

26. **Governing Law.** This lease will be governed by and construed in accordance with the laws of the state of _____ .

27. **Counterparts.** This lease may be signed by the parties in different counterparts and the signature pages combined will create a document binding on all parties.

28. **Modification.** This lease may be modified only by a written agreement signed by all the parties.

29. **Waiver.** If one party waives any term or provision of this lease at any time, that waiver will be effective only for the specific instance and specific purpose for which the waiver was given. If either party fails to exercise or delays exercising any of its rights or remedies under this lease, that party retains the right to enforce that term or provision at a later time.

30. **Severability.** If any court determines that any provision of this lease is invalid or unenforceable, any invalidity or unenforceability will affect only that provision and will not make any other provision of this lease invalid or unenforceable and shall be modified, amended, or limited only to the extent necessary to render it valid and enforceable.

Landlord

Name of business: _____

a _____

By: _____ Dated: _____

Printed name: _____

Title: _____

Address: _____

_____

Tenant

Name of business: _____

a _____

By: _____ Dated: _____

Printed name: _____

Title: _____

Address: _____

☐ **Guarantor**

By signing this lease, I personally guarantee the performance of all financial obligations of _____

_____ under this lease.

By: _____ Dated: _____

Printed name: _____

Address: _____

_____

Net Lease for Entire Building

1. **Names.** This lease is made by _____ , Landlord, and _____ , Tenant.

2. **Premises Being Leased.** Landlord is leasing to Tenant and Tenant is leasing from Landlord the following premises: _____
_____ .

3. **Term of Lease.** This lease begins on _____ and ends on _____ .

4. **Rent.** Tenant will pay rent in advance on the _____ day of each month. Tenant's first rent payment will be on _____ in the amount of $ _____ . Tenant will pay rent of $ _____ per month thereafter.

   ☐ Tenant will pay this rental amount for the entire term of the lease.

   ☐ Rent will increase each year, on the anniversary of the starting date in Paragraph 3, as follows:
   _____
   _____ .

5. **Option to Extend Lease.**

   ☐ **First Option.** Landlord grants Tenant the option to extend this lease for an additional _____ years. To exercise this option, Tenant must give Landlord written notice on or before _____ . Tenant may exercise this option only if Tenant is in substantial compliance with the terms of this lease. Tenant will lease the premises on the same terms as in this lease except as follows: _____
   _____
   _____ .

   ☐ **Second Option.** If Tenant exercises the option granted above, Tenant will then have the option to extend this lease for _____ years beyond the first option period. To exercise this option, Tenant must give Landlord written notice on or before _____ . Tenant may exercise this option only if Tenant is in substantial compliance with the terms of this lease. Tenant will lease the premises on the same terms as in this lease except as follows: _____
   _____
   _____ .

6. **Security Deposit.** Tenant has deposited $ _____ with Landlord as security for Tenant's performance of this lease. Landlord will refund the full security deposit to Tenant within 14 days following the end of the lease if Tenant returns the premises to Landlord in good condition (except for reasonable wear and tear) and Tenant has paid Landlord all sums due under this lease. Otherwise, Landlord may deduct any amounts required to place the premises in good condition and to pay for any money owed to Landlord under the lease.

7. **Improvements by Landlord.**

   ☐ Before the lease term begins, Landlord (at Landlord's expense) will make the repairs and improvements listed in Attachment _____ to this contract.

   ☐ Tenant accepts the premises in "as is" condition. Landlord need not provide any repairs or improvements before the lease term begins.

8. **Improvements by Tenant.** Tenant may make alterations and improvements to the premises after obtaining the Landlord's written consent. At any time before this lease ends, Tenant may remove any of Tenant's alterations and improvements, as long as Tenant repairs any damage caused by attaching the items to or removing them from the premises.

9. **Tenant's Use of Premises.** Tenant will use the premises for the following business purposes: _____
_____

_____ .

Tenant may also use the premises for purposes reasonably related to the main use.

10. **Landlord's Representations.** Landlord represents that:

    A. At the beginning of the lease term, the premises will be properly zoned for Tenant's stated use and will be in compliance with all applicable laws and regulations.

    B. The premises have not been used for the storage or disposal of any toxic or hazardous substance and Landlord has received no notice from any governmental authority concerning removal of any toxic or hazardous substance from the property.

11. **Utilities and Services.** Tenant will pay for all utilities and services, including water, electricity, and gas, including the electricity or gas needed for heating and air-conditioning.

12. **Maintenance and Repairs.**

    A. Tenant will maintain and make all necessary repairs to: (1) the roof, structural components, exterior walls, and interior walls of the premises, and (2) the plumbing, electrical, heating, ventilating, and air-conditioning systems.

    B. Tenant will clean and maintain (including snow removal) the parking areas, yards, common areas, and exterior of the premises so that the premises will be kept in a safe and attractive condition.

13. **Insurance.**

    A. Tenant will carry fire and extended coverage insurance on the building in the amount of at least $_____ ; this insurance will include Landlord as an insured party.

    B. Tenant will carry public liability insurance, which will include Landlord as an insured party. The public liability coverage for personal injury will be in at least the following amounts:

    $_____ per occurrence

    $_____ in any one year

    C. Landlord and Tenant release each other from any liability to the other for any property loss, property damage, or personal injury to the extent covered by insurance carried by the party suffering the loss, damage, or injury.

    D. Tenant will give Landlord a certificate of insurance for all insurance policies that this lease requires Tenant to obtain.

14. **Taxes.**

    A. Tenant will pay all real property taxes levied and assessed against the premises during the term of this lease.

    B. Tenant will pay all personal property taxes levied and assessed against Tenant's personal property.

15. **Subletting and Assignment.** Tenant will not assign this lease or sublet any part of the premises without the written consent of Landlord. Landlord will not unreasonably withhold such consent.

16. **Notice of Default.** Before starting a legal action to recover possession of the premises based on Tenant's default, Landlord will notify Tenant in writing of the default. Landlord will take legal action only if Tenant does not correct the default within ten days after written notice is given or mailed to Tenant.

17. **Quiet Enjoyment.** As long as Tenant is not in default under the terms of this lease, Tenant will have the right to occupy the premises peacefully and without interference.

18. **Eminent Domain.** This lease will become void if any part of the leased premises or the building in which the leased premises are located is taken by eminent domain. Tenant has the right to receive and keep any amount of money that the agency taking the premises by eminent domain pays for the value of Tenant's lease, its loss of business, and for moving and relocation expenses.

19. **Holding Over.** If Tenant remains in possession after this lease ends, the continuing tenancy will be from month to month.

20. **Disputes.**

    ☐ **Litigation.** If a dispute arises, either party may take the matter to court.

    ☐ **Mediation and Possible Litigation.** If a dispute arises, the parties will try in good faith to settle it through mediation conducted by:

    ☐ _____ .

    ☐ a mediator to be mutually selected.

      The parties will share the costs of the mediator equally. Each party will cooperate fully and fairly with the mediator and will attempt to reach a mutually satisfactory compromise to the dispute. If the dispute is not resolved within 30 days after it is referred to the mediator, either party may take the matter to court.

    ☐ **Mediation and Possible Arbitration.** If a dispute arises, the parties will try in good faith to settle it through mediation conducted by:

    ☐ _____ .

    ☐ a mediator to be mutually selected.

      The parties will share the costs of the mediator equally. Each party will cooperate fully and fairly with the mediator and will attempt to reach a mutually satisfactory compromise to the dispute. If the dispute is not resolved within 30 days after it is referred to the mediator, it will be arbitrated by:

    ☐ _____ .

    ☐ an arbitrator to be mutually selected.

      Judgment on the arbitration award may be entered in any court that has jurisdiction over the matter. Costs of arbitration, including lawyers' fees, will be allocated by the arbitrator.

      Landlord need not participate in mediation or arbitration of a dispute unless Tenant has paid the rent called for by this lease or has placed any unpaid rent in escrow with an agreed-upon mediator or arbitrator.

    ☐ **Attorneys' Fees.** If either party brings a legal action arising out of a dispute over this agreement, the losing party will reimburse the prevailing party for all reasonable costs and attorneys' fees incurred by the prevailing party in the lawsuit.

21. **Additional Agreements.** Landlord and Tenant additionally agree that _____

    _____

    _____

_____

_____

_____

_____

_____

_____

_____

_____

_____ .

22. **Entire Agreement.** This is the entire agreement between the parties. It replaces and supersedes any and all oral agreements between the parties, as well as any prior writings.

23. **Successors and Assignees.** This lease binds and benefits the heirs, successors, and assignees of the parties.

24. **Notices.** All notices must be in writing. A notice may be delivered to a party at the address that follows a party's signature or to a new address that a party designates in writing. A notice may be delivered:

    (1) in person

    (2) by certified mail, or

    (3) by overnight courier.

25. **Governing Law.** This lease will be governed by and construed in accordance with the laws of the state of _____ .

26. **Counterparts.** This lease may be signed by the parties in different counterparts and the signature pages combined will create a document binding on all parties.

27. **Modification.** This agreement may be modified only by a written agreement signed by all the parties.

28. **Waiver.** If one party waives any term or provision of this lease at any time, that waiver will be effective only for the specific instance and specific purpose for which the waiver was given. If either party fails to exercise or delays exercising any of its rights or remedies under this lease, that party retains the right to enforce that term or provision at a later time.

29. **Severability.** If any court determines that any provision of this lease is invalid or unenforceable, any invalidity or unenforceability will affect only that provision and will not make any other provision of this lease invalid or unenforceable and shall be modified, amended, or limited only to the extent necessary to render it valid and enforceable.

Landlord

Name of business: _____

a _____

By: _____   Dated: _____

Printed name: _____

Title: _____

Address: _____

_____

Tenant

Name of business: _____

a _____

By: _____ Dated: _____

Printed name: _____

Title: _____

Address: _____

_____

☐ **Guarantor**

By signing this lease, I personally guarantee the performance of all financial obligations of _____

_____ under this lease.

By: _____ Dated: _____

Printed name: _____

Address: _____

_____

Net Lease for Part of Building

1. **Names.** This lease is made by _____ , Landlord, and _____ , Tenant.

2. **Premises Being Leased.** Landlord is leasing to Tenant and Tenant is leasing from Landlord the following premises: _____
   _____ .

   Specifically, Tenant is leasing _____
   _____ .

   ☐ **Shared Facilities.** Tenant and Tenant's employees and customers may use the following additional facilities in common with other tenants, employees, and customers:

      ☐ Parking spaces: _____
      ☐ Restroom facilities: _____
      ☐ Storage areas: _____
      ☐ Hallways, stairways, and elevators: _____
      ☐ Conference rooms: _____
      ☐ Other: _____

3. **Term of Lease.** This lease begins on _____ and ends on _____ .

4. **Rent.** Tenant will pay rent in advance on the _____ day of each month. Tenant's first rent payment will be on _____ in the amount of $ _____ .
   Tenant will pay rent of $ _____ per month thereafter.

   ☐ Tenant will pay this rental amount for the entire term of the lease.

   ☐ Rent will increase each year, on the anniversary of the starting date in Paragraph 3, as follows:
   _____
   _____
   _____ .

5. **Option to Extend Lease.**

   ☐ **First Option.** Landlord grants Tenant the option to extend this lease for an additional _____ years. To exercise this option, Tenant must give Landlord written notice on or before _____ . Tenant may exercise this option only if Tenant is in substantial compliance with the terms of this lease. Tenant will lease the premises on the same terms as in this lease except as follows: _____
   _____
   _____ .

   ☐ **Second Option.** If Tenant exercises the option granted above, Tenant will then have the option to extend this lease for _____ years beyond the first option period. To exercise this option, Tenant must give Landlord written notice on or before _____ .
   Tenant may exercise this option only if Tenant is in substantial compliance with the terms of this lease. Tenant will lease the premises on the same terms as in this lease except as follows:
   _____
   _____
   _____ .

6. **Security Deposit.** Tenant has deposited $ _____ with Landlord as security for Tenant's performance of this lease. Landlord will refund the full security deposit to Tenant within 14 days

following the end of the lease if Tenant returns the premises to Landlord in good condition (except for reasonable wear and tear) and Tenant has paid Landlord all sums due under this lease. Otherwise, Landlord may deduct any amounts required to place the premises in good condition and to pay for any money owed to Landlord under the lease.

7. **Improvements by Landlord.**

☐ Before the lease term begins, Landlord (at Landlord's expense) will make the repairs and improvements listed in Attachment 1 to this contract.

☐ Tenant accepts the premises in "as is" condition. Landlord need not provide any repairs or improvements before the lease term begins.

8. **Improvements by Tenant.** Tenant may make alterations and improvements to the premises after obtaining the Landlord's written consent. At any time before this lease ends, Tenant may remove any of Tenant's alterations and improvements, as long as Tenant repairs any damage caused by attaching the items to or removing them from the premises.

9. **Tenant's Use of Premises.** Tenant will use the premises for the following business purposes: _____

_____

_____

_____ .

  Tenant may also use the premises for purposes reasonably related to the main use.

10. **Landlord's Representations.** Landlord represents that:

A. At the beginning of the lease term, the premises will be properly zoned for Tenant's stated use and will be in compliance with all applicable laws and regulations.

B. The premises have not been used for the storage or disposal of any toxic or hazardous substance and Landlord has received no notice from any governmental authority concerning removal of any toxic or hazardous substance from the property.

11. **Utilities and Services.**

A. **Separately Metered Utilities.** Tenant will pay for the following utilities and services that are separately metered or billed to Tenant:

☐ Water

☐ Electricity

☐ Gas

☐ Heating oil

☐ Trash collection

☐ Other: _____

B. **Other Utilities.** Tenant will pay _____% of the following utilities and services that are not separately metered to Tenant:

☐ Water

☐ Electricity

☐ Gas

☐ Heating oil

☐ Trash collection

☐ Other: _____

Tenant will pay for these utilities in monthly installments on or before the _____ day of each month, in advance, in an amount estimated by Landlord. Every _____ months, Landlord will give Tenant copies of the bills sent to Landlord. If Tenant's share of the actual costs for utilities and services exceeds the amount paid in advance by Tenant, Tenant will pay Landlord the difference within 30 days. If Tenant has paid more than Tenant's share of the actual costs, Tenant will receive a credit for the overage, which will be applied to reduce the next installment due from Tenant.

12. **Maintenance and Repair of Common Areas.** Landlord will maintain and make all necessary repairs to the common areas of the building and adjacent premises and keep these areas safe and free of trash. This includes:

☐ On-site parking areas

☐ Off-site parking areas

☐ Restroom facilities

☐ Storage areas

☐ Hallways, stairways, and elevators

☐ Conference rooms

☐ Sidewalks and driveways

☐ Other: _____

Tenant will pay Landlord _____% of the cost of such maintenance and repairs. Tenant will pay these amounts in monthly installments on or before the _____ day of each month, in advance, in an amount estimated by Landlord. Within 90 days after the end of each lease year, Landlord will give Tenant a statement of the actual amount of Tenant's share of such costs for such period. If Tenant's share of the actual costs exceeds the amount paid in advance by Tenant, Tenant will pay Landlord the difference within 30 days. If Tenant has paid more than Tenant's share of the actual costs, Tenant will receive a credit for the overage that will be applied to reduce the next installment due from Tenant.

13. **Maintenance and Repair of Leased Premises.** Landlord will maintain and make all necessary repairs to the following parts of the building in which the leased premises are located:

☐ Roof

☐ Foundation and structural components

☐ Exterior walls

☐ Interior common walls

☐ Exterior doors and windows

☐ Plumbing system

☐ Sewage disposal system

☐ Electrical system

☐ Heating, ventilating, and air-conditioning systems

☐ Sprinkler system

☐ Other: _____

Tenant will maintain and repair the leased premises and keep the leased premises in good repair except for those items specified above as being Landlord's responsibility.

14. **Insurance.**

   A. Landlord will carry fire and extended coverage insurance on the building. Tenant will pay Tenant's proportionate share (_____%) of such insurance within ten days after receiving a statement from Landlord as to the cost.

   B. Tenant will carry public liability insurance, which will include Landlord as an "additional insured" party. The public liability coverage for personal injury will be in at least the following amounts:

   $_____ per occurrence

   $_____ in any one year

   C. Landlord and Tenant release each other from any liability to the other for any property loss, property damage, or personal injury to the extent covered by insurance carried by the party suffering the loss, damage, or injury.

   D. Tenant will give Landlord a certificate of insurance for all insurance policies that this lease requires Tenant to obtain.

15. **Taxes.**

   A. Tenant will pay _____% of all taxes and assessments that may be levied or assessed against the building and the land for the period of the lease. Tenant will pay these taxes and assessments in monthly installments on or before the _____ day of each month, in advance, in an amount estimated by Landlord. Landlord will give Tenant copies of the tax bills and assessments as Landlord receives them. If Tenant's share of the actual taxes and assessments exceeds the amount paid in advance by Tenant, Tenant will pay Landlord the difference within 30 days. If Tenant has paid more than Tenant's share of the actual taxes and assessment, Tenant will receive a credit for the overage, which will be applied to reduce the next installment due from Tenant. Taxes and assessments to be paid by Tenant will be prorated on a due-date basis and will be assumed to cover a period of one year from the due date.

   B. Tenant will pay all personal property taxes levied and assessed against Tenant's personal property.

16. **Subletting and Assignment.** Tenant will not assign this lease or sublet any part of the premises without the written consent of Landlord. Landlord will not unreasonably withhold such consent.

17. **Damage to Premises.**

   A. If the premises are damaged through fire or other cause not the fault of Tenant, Tenant will owe no rent for any period during which Tenant is substantially deprived of the use of the premises.

   B. If Tenant is substantially deprived of the use of the premises for more than 90 days because of such damage, Tenant may terminate this lease by delivering written notice of termination to Landlord.

18. **Notice of Default.** Before starting a legal action to recover possession of the premises based on Tenant's default, Landlord will notify Tenant in writing of the default. Landlord will take legal action only if Tenant does not correct the default within ten days after written notice is given or mailed to Tenant.

19. **Quiet Enjoyment.** As long as Tenant is not in default under the terms of this lease, Tenant will have the right to occupy the premises peacefully and without interference.

20. **Eminent Domain.** This lease will become void if any part of the leased premises or the building in which the leased premises are located is taken by eminent domain. Tenant has the right to receive and keep any amount of money that the agency taking the premises by eminent domain pays for the value of Tenant's lease, its loss of business, and for moving and relocation expenses.

21. **Holding Over.** If Tenant remains in possession after this lease ends, the continuing tenancy will be from month to month.

22. **Disputes.**

☐ **Litigation.** If a dispute arises, either party may take the matter to court.

☐ **Mediation and Possible Litigation.** If a dispute arises, the parties will try in good faith to settle it through mediation conducted by:

☐ _____ .

☐ a mediator to be mutually selected.

The parties will share the costs of the mediator equally. Each party will cooperate fully and fairly with the mediator and will attempt to reach a mutually satisfactory compromise to the dispute. If the dispute is not resolved within 30 days after it is referred to the mediator, either party may take the matter to court.

☐ **Mediation and Possible Arbitration.** If a dispute arises, the parties will try in good faith to settle it through mediation conducted by:

☐ _____ .

☐ a mediator to be mutually selected.

The parties will share the costs of the mediator equally. Each party will cooperate fully and fairly with the mediator and will attempt to reach a mutually satisfactory compromise to the dispute. If the dispute is not resolved within 30 days after it is referred to the mediator, it will be arbitrated by:

☐ _____ .

☐ an arbitrator to be mutually selected.

Judgment on the arbitration award may be entered in any court that has jurisdiction over the matter. Costs of arbitration, including lawyers' fees, will be allocated by the arbitrator.

Landlord need not participate in mediation or arbitration of a dispute unless Tenant has paid the rent called for by this lease or has placed any unpaid rent in escrow with an agreed-upon mediator or arbitrator.

☐ **Attorneys' Fees.** If either party brings a legal action arising out of a dispute over this agreement, the losing party will reimburse the prevailing party for all reasonable costs and attorneys' fees incurred by the prevailing party in the lawsuit.

23. **Additional Agreements.** Landlord and Tenant additionally agree that _____

_____

_____

_____ .

24. **Entire Agreement.** This is the entire agreement between the parties. It replaces and supersedes any and all oral agreements between the parties, as well as any prior writings.

25. **Successors and Assignees.** This lease binds and benefits the heirs, successors, and assignees of the parties.

26. **Notices.** All notices must be in writing. A notice may be delivered to a party at the address that follows a party's signature or to a new address that a party designates in writing. A notice may be delivered:

(1) in person

(2) by certified mail, or

(3) by overnight courier.

27. **Governing Law.** This lease will be governed by and construed in accordance with the laws of the state of _____ .

28. **Counterparts.** This lease may be signed by the parties in different counterparts and the signature pages combined will create a document binding on all parties.

29. **Modification.** This agreement may be modified only by a written agreement signed by all the parties.

30. **Waiver.** If one party waives any term or provision of this lease at any time, that waiver will be effective only for the specific instance and specific purpose for which the waiver was given. If either party fails to exercise or delays exercising any of its rights or remedies under this lease, that party retains the right to enforce that term or provision at a later time.

31. **Severability.** If any court determines that any provision of this lease is invalid or unenforceable, any invalidity or unenforceability will affect only that provision and will not make any other provision of this lease invalid or unenforceable and shall be modified, amended, or limited only to the extent necessary to render it valid and enforceable.

Landlord

Name of business: _____

a _____

By: _____ Dated: _____

Printed name: _____

Title: _____

Address: _____

_____

Tenant

Name of business: _____

a _____

By: _____ Dated: _____

Printed name: _____

Title: _____

Address: _____

_____

☐ **Guarantor**

By signing this lease, I personally guarantee the performance of all financial obligations of _____

_____ under this lease.

By: _____ Dated: _____

Printed name: _____

Title, if any: _____

Address: _____

_____

Sublease

1. **Names.** This sublease is made by _____ , Sublandlord, and _____ , Subtenant.

2. **Property Subleased.** Sublandlord is subleasing to Subtenant, and Subtenant is subleasing from Sublandlord

   ☐ all of the premises at _____

   _____ .

   ☐ the following part of the premises at _____

   _____ .

   Specifically, Subtenant is leasing _____

   _____

3. **Original Lease.**

   A. This subtenancy is subject to all the terms and conditions of the attached Original Lease dated

   _____ between _____

   _____ , Landlord, and _____

   _____ , Tenant, except for the following:

   _____

   _____

   _____

   _____ .

   B. Except as specified in this sublease, Subtenant will perform and observe all of the terms and conditions of the Original Lease as if Subtenant were named as Tenant in the Original Lease. Subtenant will do nothing that will create a breach by Sublandlord of any of the terms or conditions of the Original Lease.

4. **Term of Sublease.** This sublease begins on _____ and ends on

   _____ .

5. **Rent.** Subtenant will pay rent in advance on the _____ day of each month. Subtenant's first rent payment will be on _____ in the amount of $_____ . Subtenant will pay rent of $_____ per month thereafter.

   ☐ Subtenant will pay this rental amount for the entire term of the lease.

   ☐ Rent will increase each year, on the anniversary of the starting date in Paragraph 3, as follows:

   _____

   _____ .

6. **Option to Extend Sublease.** For the sum of $_____ , which Landlord and Tenant designate as additional rent and which is due and payable with Tenant's first full rent payment, Sublandlord grants Subtenant the option to extend this lease for an additional _____ years. To exercise this option, Subtenant must give Sublandlord written notice on or before _____ . Subtenant may exercise this option only if Sublandlord's own lease has been extended to encompass Subtenant's proposed extended term, and only if Subtenant is in substantial compliance with the terms of this sublease. Subtenant will lease the premises on the same terms as in this sublease except as follows: _____

7. **Security Deposit.** Subtenant has deposited $_____ with Sublandlord as security for Subtenant's performance of this sublease. Sublandlord will refund the full security deposit to Subtenant at the end of the sublease if Subtenant returns the premises to Sublandlord in good condition (except for reasonable wear and tear) and Subtenant has paid Sublandlord all sums due under this sublease. Otherwise, Sublandlord may deduct any amounts required to place the premises in good condition and to pay for any sums due under the sublease.

8. **Notices From Landlord.** If Landlord notifies Subtenant of any breach of the terms or conditions of the Original Lease that Subtenant is obligated to perform, Subtenant will immediately notify Sublandlord in writing. Subtenant will promptly cure any breach.

   If Landlord notifies Sublandlord of any breach of the terms or conditions of the Original Lease that Subtenant is obligated to perform, Sublandlord will immediately notify Subtenant in writing. Subtenant will promptly cure any breach.

9. **Subletting and Assignment.** Subtenant will not assign this sublease or further sublet any part of the premises without the written consent of both Sublandlord and Landlord. Sublandlord will not unreasonably withhold such consent.

10. **Insurance.**
    A. Subtenant will indemnify Sublandlord and hold Sublandlord harmless from all claims and liabilities arising because of Subtenant's failure to meet the terms of the sublease.
    B. Subtenant will carry public liability insurance; this insurance policy will include Sublandlord and Landlord as additional insured parties. The public liability coverage for personal injury will be in at least the following amounts:

     $_____ per occurrence

     $_____ in any one year

    C. Subtenant will give Sublandlord a certificate of insurance for all insurance policies that this sublease requires Subtenant to obtain.

11. **Condition of Premises.**
    ☐ Before the sublease term begins, Sublandlord (at Sublandlord's expense) will make the following modifications or improvements to the premises: _____
    _____
    _____
    _____.

    ☐ Subtenant accepts the premises in "as is" condition. Sublandlord need not provide any repairs or improvements before the lease term begins.

12. **Landlord's Consent.** This sublease will not be effective unless Landlord signs the Landlord's Consent attached to this sublease.

13. **Disputes.**
    ☐ **Litigation.** If a dispute arises, either party may take the matter to court.
    ☐ **Mediation and Possible Litigation.** If a dispute arises, the parties will try in good faith to settle it through mediation conducted by:

☐ _____ .

☐ a mediator to be mutually selected.

 The parties will share the costs of the mediator equally. Each party will cooperate fully and fairly with the mediator and will attempt to reach a mutually satisfactory compromise to the dispute. If the dispute is not resolved within 30 days after it is referred to the mediator, either party may take the matter to court.

☐ **Mediation and Possible Arbitration.** If a dispute arises, the parties will try in good faith to settle it through mediation conducted by:

☐ _____ .

☐ a mediator to be mutually selected.

 The parties will share the costs of the mediator equally. Each party will cooperate fully and fairly with the mediator and will attempt to reach a mutually satisfactory compromise to the dispute. If the dispute is not resolved within 30 days after it is referred to the mediator, it will be arbitrated by:

☐ _____ .

☐ an arbitrator to be mutually selected.

Judgment on the arbitration award may be entered in any court that has jurisdiction over the matter. Costs of arbitration, including lawyers' fees, will be allocated by the arbitrator.

Sublandlord need not participate in mediation or arbitration of a dispute unless Subtenant has paid the rent called for by this lease or has placed any unpaid rent in escrow with an agreed-upon mediator or arbitrator.

☐ **Attorneys' Fees.** If either party brings a legal action arising out of a dispute over this agreement, the losing party will reimburse the prevailing party for all reasonable costs and attorneys' fees incurred by the prevailing party in the lawsuit.

14. **Additional Agreements.** Sublandlord and Subtenant additionally agree that _____

_____

_____

_____

_____

_____

_____

_____

_____ .

15. **Entire Agreement.** This is the entire agreement between the parties. It replaces and supersedes any and all oral agreements between the parties, as well as any prior writings.

16. **Successors and Assignees.** This agreement binds and benefits the heirs, successors, and assignees of the parties.

17. **Notices.** All notices must be in writing. A notice may be delivered to a party at the address that follows a party's signature or to a new address that a party designates in writing. A notice may be delivered:

(1) in person

(2) by certified mail, or

(3) by overnight courier.

18. **Governing Law.** This agreement will be governed by and construed in accordance with the laws of the state of _____ .

19. **Counterparts.** This sublease may be signed by the parties in different counterparts and the signature pages combined will create a document binding on all parties.

20. **Modification.** This sublease may be modified only by a written agreement signed by all the parties.

21. **Waiver.** If one party waives any term or provision of this sublease at any time, that waiver will be effective only for the specific instance and specific purpose for which the waiver was given. If either party fails to exercise or delays exercising any of its rights or remedies under this sublease, that party retains the right to enforce that term or provision at a later time.

22. **Severability.** If any court determines that any provision of this agreement is invalid or unenforceable, any invalidity or unenforceability will affect only that provision and will not make any other provision of this agreement invalid or unenforceable and shall be modified, amended, or limited only to the extent necessary to render the provision valid and enforceable.

Sublandlord

Name of business: _____

a _____

By: _____ Dated: _____

Printed name: _____

Title: _____

Address: _____

Subtenant

Name of business: _____

a _____

By: _____ Dated: _____

Printed name: _____

Title: _____

Address: _____

Landlord's Consent to Sublease

1. **Names.** _____ , Landlord,

   gives this consent to _____ , Tenant,

   and _____ , Subtenant.

2. **Consent to Sublease.** Landlord consents to the attached sublease dated _____ ,

   which has been signed by Tenant and Subtenant for the following premises: _____

   _____

   _____

   _____ .

3. **Status of Original Lease.**

   A. The Original Lease referred to in the Sublease, and any modifications or amendments attached to it, remain in full effect.

   B. Tenant has currently paid all rent due under the Original Lease.

   C. Tenant is not in default under the Original Lease.

   D. The Original Lease will not be modified without Subtenant's written consent.

4. **Notice of Default.** If Tenant or Subtenant defaults in the performance of any obligations under the Original Lease, Landlord will send a written notice to both Tenant and Subtenant by certified mail or overnight delivery (return receipt requested). If Original Lease provides for a specified cure period following notice of default, Tenant and Subtenant will have that amount of time in which to cure the default. If Original Lease does not provide for a cure period, Tenant and Subtenant will have _____ days after the notice is mailed or delivered to the overnight carrier to cure the default.

Tenant

Name of business: _____

a _____

By: _____ Dated: _____

Printed name: _____

Title: _____

Address: _____

_____

Subtenant

Name of business: _____

a _____

By: _____ Dated: _____

Printed name: _____

Title: _____

Address: _____

_____

Landlord

Name of business: _____

a _____

By: _____   Dated: _____

Printed name: _____

Title: _____

Address: _____

_____

Assignment of Lease

1. **Names.** This lease assignment is made by _____ ,
   Original Tenant and Assignor, and _____ ,
   New Tenant and Assignee, with the consent of _____ , Landlord.

2. **Assignment.** Original Tenant assigns to New Tenant all of Original Tenant's rights in the attached
   lease dated _____ , which covers

   ☐ all of the premises at _____
   _____ .

   ☐ the following part of the premises at _____
   _____

   Specifically, New Tenant is leasing _____
   _____ .

3. **Effective Date.** This assignment will take effect on _____ .

4. **Acceptance.** New Tenant accepts this assignment and assumes the lease. From the effective date
   of this assignment, New Tenant will pay all rents and will perform all of Original Tenant's other
   obligations under the lease.

5. **Condition of Premises.** New Tenant has inspected the premises and accepts the premises in "as is"
   condition.

6. **Landlord's Certification.** Landlord certifies that:

   A. Original Tenant has paid all rents and other sums due through _____ .

   B. Landlord is holding a security deposit in the amount of $_____ , which Landlord
      will now hold for New Tenant under the terms of the lease.

   C. Original Tenant is not in default in performing any obligations under the lease.

   D. The lease as attached is in full effect.

7. **Reimbursement.** New Tenant will immediately reimburse Original Tenant for

   ☐ the security deposit held by the Landlord under the lease.

   ☐ any rent and other items that Original Tenant has paid in advance under the lease covering the
     period following the effective date of this assignment.

8. **Landlord's Consent.** Landlord consents to this assignment and to New Tenant's taking over Original
   Tenant's obligations.

9. **Release.** *(Optional)*
   Landlord releases Original Tenant from liability for the payment of rents and from the performance
   of all other lease obligations from the effective date of this assignment.

10. **Entire Agreement.** This is the entire agreement between the parties. It replaces and supersedes any
    and all oral agreements between the parties, as well as any prior writings.

11. **Successors and Assignees.** This lease assignment binds and benefits the heirs, successors, and
    assignees of the parties.

12. **Notices.** All notices must be in writing. A notice may be delivered to a party at the address that follows
    a party's signature or to a new address that a party designates in writing. A notice may be delivered:

    (1) in person

    (2) by certified mail, or

    (3) by overnight courier.

13. **Governing Law.** This lease assignment will be governed by and construed in accordance with the laws of the state of _____ .

14. **Counterparts.** This lease assignment may be signed by the parties in different counterparts and the signature pages combined will create a document binding on all parties. Any fully signed counterpart shall be treated as an original.

15. **Modification.** This lease assignment may be modified only by a written agreement signed by all the parties.

16. **Waiver.** If one party waives any term or provision of this lease assignment at any time, that waiver will be effective only for the specific instance and specific purpose for which the waiver was given. If either party fails to exercise or delays exercising any of its rights or remedies under this lease assignment, that party retains the right to enforce that term or provision at a later time.

17. **Severability.** If any court determines that any provision of this lease assignment is invalid or unenforceable, any invalidity or unenforceability will affect only that provision and will not make any other provision of this lease assignment invalid or unenforceable and shall be modified, amended, or limited only to the extent necessary to render it valid and enforceable.

Original Tenant

Name of business: _____

a _____

By: _____ Dated: _____

Printed name: _____

Title: _____

Address: _____

_____

New Tenant

Name of business: _____

a _____

By: _____ Dated: _____

Printed name: _____

Title: _____

Address: _____

_____

Landlord

Name of business: _____

a _____

By: _____ Dated: _____

Printed name: _____

Title: _____

Address: _____

_____

Notice of Exercise of Lease Option
Extension 1

To _____ , Landlord:

1. Exercise of Lease Option

_____ , Tenant,

exercises its option to extend through _____ its tenancy of the following premises.

_____

_____

_____

_____

_____

_____ .

2. Notice to Landlord

This notice is given in accordance with the lease covering Tenant's current tenancy of the premises,

dated _____ and originally ending _____ .

Tenant

Name of business: _____

a _____

By: _____ Dated: _____

Printed name: _____

Title: _____

Address: _____

_____

☐ **Guarantor**

By signing this lease, I personally guarantee the performance of all financial obligations of _____

_____ under this lease.

By: _____ Dated: _____

Printed name: _____

Address: _____

_____

Extension 1
of Lease

1. **Names.** This extension of lease is made by _____ ,
   Landlord, and _____ , Tenant.

2. **New Lease Term.** The lease between Landlord and Tenant dated _____
   and originally ending _____ for the following premises: _____
   _____
   _____ is extended through _____ .

3. **Modifications to Lease.** The terms and conditions of the existing lease will apply during the
   extension period, except as follows: _____
   _____
   _____
   _____
   _____
   _____
   _____ .

Landlord

Name of business: _____

a _____

By: _____   Dated: _____

Printed name: _____

Title: _____

Address: _____

_____

Tenant

Name of business: _____

a _____

By: _____   Dated: _____

Printed name: _____

Title: _____

Address: _____

_____

☐ Guarantor

By signing this lease, I personally guarantee the performance of all financial obligations of _____
_____ under this lease.

By: _____   Dated: _____

Printed name: _____

Title, if any: _____

Address: _____

_____

Amendment _____ to Lease

1. **Names.** This Amendment to lease is made by _____ ,

    Landlord, and _____ , Tenant.

2. **Terms Amended.** The lease dated _____ covering the premises at

    _____

    is amended as follows: _____

    _____

    _____

    _____

    _____

    _____ .

3. **Effective Date.** This Amendment will take effect on _____ .

4. **Other Terms of Lease.** In all other respects, the terms of the original lease and any earlier
    amendments will remain in effect. If there is a conflict between this Amendment and the original
    lease or any earlier amendment, the terms of this Amendment will prevail.

Landlord

Name of business: _____

a _____

By: _____   Dated: _____

Printed name: _____

Title: _____

Address: _____

_____

Tenant

Name of business: _____

a _____

By: _____   Dated: _____

Printed name: _____

Title: _____

Address: _____

_____

☐ Guarantor

By signing this lease, I personally guarantee the performance of all financial obligations of _____

_____ under this lease.

By: _____   Dated: _____

Printed name: _____

Title, if any: _____

Address: _____

_____

Attachment _____ to Lease

1. **Names.** This Attachment to lease is made by _____ ,
_____ Landlord, and _____
_____ , Tenant.

2. **Terms of Attachment.** Landlord and Tenant agree to the following Attachment to the lease dated
_____ covering the premises at _____
_____
_____ :

_____
_____
_____
_____
_____
_____
_____
_____
_____
_____
_____
_____
_____ .

Landlord

Name of business: _____

a _____

By: _____ Dated: _____

Printed name: _____

Title: _____

Address: _____

_____

Tenant

Name of business: _____

a _____

By: _____ Dated: _____

Printed name: _____

Title: _____

Address: _____

_____

Contract to Purchase Building

1. **Names.** This contract is made by _____ ,
Seller, and _____ , Buyer.

2. **Purchase of Real Estate.** Seller is selling and Buyer is buying the property commonly known as
_____ , located at _____
_____ .

   ☐ The legal description of the property is as follows: _____
   _____
   _____ .

   ☐ The legal description of the property is given in Attachment 1.

   Seller will transfer the property to Buyer subject to easements and restrictions of record.

3. **Purchase Price.** The purchase price is $_____ . Seller acknowledges that Buyer has
deposited $_____ with _____ ,
as escrow agent, upon the signing of this agreement. This deposit is to be credited against the
purchase price. Buyer will pay the balance of $_____ at closing in cash or by electronic funds
transfer or by cashier's check.

4. **Financing Contingency.** This contract is contingent upon Buyer qualifying for and obtaining
a commitment for a mortgage or deed of trust loan in the amount of $_____ , with terms
acceptable to the Buyer. Buyer will apply for such financing within _____ business days from the
date of this agreement and pursue the application in good faith. This financing contingency is to be
removed by _____ .

5. **Inclusions.** This contract includes all improvements and fixtures (including lighting, plumbing,
heating, and cooling fixtures) on the property as of the date of this contract, unless excluded under
Section 6 of this contract, and the following personal property: _____
_____
_____
_____
_____ .

   All personal property will be conveyed at closing free and clear of all taxes (except personal
   property taxes for the year of the closing), liens, and encumbrances, except: _____
   _____ .

   At closing, Seller will give Buyer a bill of sale for the listed personal property.

6. **Exclusions.** The following items are excluded from this contract: _____
_____
_____
_____ .

7. **Condition of Equipment.** Seller warrants that all equipment will be in good working condition at the
time of closing, except for _____
_____
_____
_____ .

8. **Physical Problems With Property.** To the best of Seller's knowledge, there are no physical problems with the property that would not be apparent upon inspection, except for the following: _____

_____

_____

_____ .

9. **Cleaning of Premises.** Seller warrants that the property will be free of trash and will be left in broom-clean condition at the time of closing.

10. **Special Assessments.** Seller will pay any special assessments and/or liens that are imposed on the property on or before the date of closing. Buyer will pay any special assessments and/or liens that are imposed on the property after the date of closing.

11. **Other Government Charges.** Seller will pay any other charges made against the property by any government authority for installation or extension of water, sanitary, or sewer service, if such charges have been incurred up to and including the date of closing. Buyer will pay for such charges incurred after the date of closing.

12. **Real Estate Taxes.** Real estate taxes will be prorated on a 30-day-month, 360-day-year basis to the date of closing based on the due date of the taxing authority. For proration purposes, these taxes will be deemed to be paid in advance.

13. **Other Prorations.** _____, where applicable, will be prorated to the date of closing.

14. **Closing and Possession.** The purchase will be closed on _____ . Possession will be given at closing.

15. **Transfer of Title.** Seller will transfer marketable title to the property to Buyer by a warranty deed. Seller will pay any transfer tax when title passes.

16. **Title Insurance.** Buyer will receive an owner's policy of title insurance, including a policy commitment before closing, in the amount of the purchase price.

    ☐ The cost of the owner's insurance policy will be paid by Buyer.

    ☐ The cost of the owner's insurance policy will be paid by Seller.

    ☐ The cost of the owner's insurance policy will be split equally between Buyer and Seller.

17. **Additional Contingencies.** This contract is contingent upon satisfactory completion of the following items:

    ☐ A contractor's inspection of the property at Buyer's expense resulting in a report satisfactory to Buyer. This contingency is to be removed by _____ .

    ☐ An architect's inspection of the property at Buyer's expense resulting in a report satisfactory to Buyer. This contingency is to be removed by _____ .

    ☐ An environmental inspection of the property at Buyer's expense resulting in findings satisfactory to Buyer. This contingency is to be removed by _____ .

    ☐ A review of public and private building and use requirements affecting the property at Buyer's expense resulting in findings satisfactory to Buyer. This contingency is to be removed by _____ .

    ☐ A stake survey or survey report at Buyer's expense resulting in findings satisfactory to Buyer. This contingency is to be removed by _____ .

    ☐ Approval of the title insurance commitment by Buyer or Buyer's lawyer. This contingency is to be removed within _____ days after the title insurance commitment is received by Buyer.

☐ A written appraisal of the property by a licensed or certified appraiser, obtained at Buyer's expense, that is no less than the purchase price. This contingency is to be removed within _____ days after Buyer receives the written appraisal report.

☐ A review and approval of common interest community documents by Buyer or Buyer's lawyer. This contingency is to be removed within _____ days after Seller provides Buyer with the common interest community documents.

☐ Other: _____.

18. **Removal of Contingencies.** If any contingency in this contract is not removed in writing by the required date, this contract becomes voidable. After the required date and until the contingency is removed, either party may cancel this contract by written notice to the other. In that case, Seller will return the deposit to Buyer or authorize the escrow agent to do so.

19. **Loss Before Closing.** Until the purchase is closed and the warranty deed delivered to Buyer, the risk of loss by fire, windstorm, earthquake, flood, or other casualty is assumed by Seller.

20. **Default.** If Buyer defaults, Seller may (1) pursue legal remedies or (2) cancel this contract and claim the deposit as liquidated damages.

    If Seller defaults, Buyer may (1) enforce this contract, (2) demand a refund of the deposit in termination of this contract, or (3) pursue legal remedies.

21. **Disputes.**

    ☐ **Litigation.** If a dispute arises, either party may take the matter to court.

    ☐ **Mediation and Possible Litigation.** If a dispute arises, the parties will try in good faith to settle it through mediation conducted by:

    ☐ _____.

    ☐ a mediator to be mutually selected.

    The parties will share the costs of the mediator equally. Each party will cooperate fully and fairly with the mediator and will attempt to reach a mutually satisfactory compromise to the dispute. If the dispute is not resolved within 30 days after it is referred to the mediator, either party may take the matter to court.

    ☐ **Mediation and Possible Arbitration.** If a dispute arises, the parties will try in good faith to settle it through mediation conducted by:

    ☐ _____.

    ☐ a mediator to be mutually selected.

    The parties will share the costs of the mediator equally. Each party will cooperate fully and fairly with the mediator and will attempt to reach a mutually satisfactory compromise to the dispute. If the dispute is not resolved within 30 days after it is referred to the mediator, it will be arbitrated by:

    ☐ _____.

    ☐ an arbitrator to be mutually selected.

    Judgment on the arbitration award may be entered in any court that has jurisdiction over the matter. Costs of arbitration, including lawyers' fees, will be allocated by the arbitrator.

    ☐ **Attorneys' Fees.** If either party brings a legal action arising out of a dispute over this agreement, the losing party will reimburse the prevailing party for all reasonable costs and attorneys' fees incurred by the prevailing party in the lawsuit.

22. **Additional Agreements.** Seller and Buyer additionally agree that _____

_____

_____

_____

_____ .

23. **Entire Agreement.** This is the entire agreement between the parties. It replaces and supersedes any and all oral agreements between the parties, as well as any prior writings.

24. **Successors and Assignees.** This contract binds and benefits the heirs, successors, and assignees of the parties.

25. **Notices.** All notices must be in writing. A notice may be delivered to a party at the address that follows a party's signature or to a new address that a party designates in writing. A notice may be delivered:

    (1) in person

    (2) by certified mail, or

    (3) by overnight courier.

26. **Governing Law.** This contract will be governed by and construed in accordance with the laws of the state of _____ .

27. **Counterparts.** This contract may be signed by the parties in different counterparts and the signature pages combined will create a document binding on all parties.

28. **Modification.** This contract may be modified only by a written agreement signed by all the parties.

29. **Waiver.** If one party waives any term or provision of this contract at any time, that waiver will be effective only for the specific instance and specific purpose for which the waiver was given. If either party fails to exercise or delays exercising any of its rights or remedies under this contract, that party retains the right to enforce that term or provision at a later time.

30. **Severability.** If any court determines that any provision of this contract is invalid or unenforceable, any invalidity or unenforceability will affect only that provision and will not make any other provision of this contract invalid or unenforceable and such provision shall be modified, amended, or limited only to the extent necessary to render it valid and enforceable.

Seller

Name of business: _____

a _____

By: _____ Dated: _____

Printed name: _____

Title: _____

Address: _____

Buyer

Name of business: _____

a _____

By: _____ Dated: _____

Printed name: _____

Title: _____

Address: _____

Option to Purchase Building

1. **Names.** This contract is made by _____
    _____ , Seller, and _____
    _____ , Buyer.

2. **Option to Purchase Building.** In exchange for $_____ , which Buyer has paid to Seller as
    an option fee, Seller grants to Buyer the option to purchase the property commonly known as
    _____ , located at
    _____ .

    ☐ The legal description of the property is as follows: _____
    _____
    _____
    _____

    ☐ The legal description of the property is given in Attachment 1 to this contract.
       If Buyer exercises this option, Seller will transfer the property to Buyer on the terms stated in this
    contract. The conveyance will be subject to easements and restrictions of record.

3. **Exercise of Option.** Buyer may exercise this option by delivering to Seller on or before
    _____ a written notice of exercise of option. Buyer may deliver the notice by:

    ☐ handing it to Seller.
    ☐ sending it to Seller's office at _____ by certified
       mail or private overnight mail service, in which case the notice will be treated as delivered when
       placed in the possession of the U.S. Postal Service or the private carrier.

4. **Purchase Price.** If Buyer exercises the option, the purchase price is $_____ .
    The option fee ☐ will ☐ will not be applied toward the purchase price. The purchase price
    will be paid at closing in cash or by electronic funds transfer or cashier's check.

5. **Inclusions.** This contract includes all improvements and fixtures (including lighting, plumbing,
    heating, and cooling fixtures) on the property as of the date of this closing, unless excluded under
    Section 6 of this contract, and the following personal property: _____
    _____
    _____
    _____
    _____

    All personal property will be conveyed at closing free and clear of all taxes (except personal
    property taxes for the year of the closing), liens, and encumbrances, except: _____
    _____

    At closing, Seller will give Buyer a bill of sale for the listed personal property.

6. **Exclusions.** The following items are excluded from this contract: _____
    _____
    _____

7. **Condition of Equipment.** Seller warrants that all equipment will be in good working condition at the time of closing, except for _____

_____

_____

_____

_____ .

8. **Access to Property.** Upon reasonable notice to Seller, Buyer and others chosen by Buyer may enter the property at reasonable times to perform a contractor's inspection, an architect's inspection, an environmental inspection, and a boundary line survey, as desired by Buyer. Such inspections will be at Buyer's expense.

9. **Physical Problems With Property.** To the best of Seller's knowledge, there are no physical problems with the property that would not be apparent upon inspection, except for the following: _____

_____

_____

_____ .

10. **Cleaning of Premises.** Seller warrants that the property will be free of trash and will be left in broom-clean condition at the time of closing.

11. **Special Assessments.** Seller will pay any special assessments and/or liens that are imposed on the property on or before the date of closing. Buyer will pay any special assessments and/or liens that are imposed on the property after the date of closing.

12. **Other Government Charges.** Seller will pay any other charges made against the property by any government authority for installation or extension of water, sanitary, or sewer service, if such charges have been incurred before the date of closing. Buyer will pay for the charges incurred after the date of closing.

13. **Real Estate Taxes.** Real estate taxes will be prorated on a 30-day-month, 360-day-year basis to the date of closing based on the due date of the taxing authority. For proration purposes, these taxes will be deemed to be paid in advance.

14. **Other Prorations.** _____, where applicable, will be prorated to the date of closing.

15. **Closing and Possession.** The purchase will be closed on _____ . Possession will be given at closing.

16. **Transfer of Title.** Seller will transfer marketable title to the property to Buyer by a warranty deed. Seller will pay any transfer tax due when title passes.

17. **Title Insurance.**

    A. Buyer will receive an owner's policy of title insurance, including a policy commitment before closing, in the amount of the purchase price.

        ☐ The cost of the owner's insurance policy will be paid by Buyer.

        ☐ The cost of the owner's insurance policy will be paid by Seller.

        ☐ The cost of the owner's insurance policy will be split equally between Buyer and Seller.

    B. The purchase is contingent upon Buyer or Buyer's lawyer approving:

        ☐ the title insurance commitment.

        ☐ a survey of the property to be provided by Seller.

Seller will deliver these documents to Buyer on or before _____ .

This contingency is to be removed within _____ days after Buyer receives the documents called for above. If the contingency is not removed, Seller will refund the option fee to Buyer.

18. **Loss Before Closing.** Until the purchase is closed and the warranty deed delivered to Buyer, the risk of loss by fire, windstorm, earthquake, flood, or other casualty is assumed by Seller.

19. **Default.** If Buyer defaults, Seller may (1) pursue legal remedies or (2) cancel this contract and claim the option fee as liquidated damages.

If Seller defaults, Buyer may (1) enforce this contract, (2) demand a refund of the option fee in termination of this contract, or (3) pursue legal remedies.

20. **Disputes.**

☐ **Litigation.** If a dispute arises, either party may take the matter to court.

☐ **Mediation and Possible Litigation.** If a dispute arises, the parties will try in good faith to settle it through mediation conducted by:

☐ _____ .

☐ a mediator to be mutually selected.

The parties will share the costs of the mediator equally. Each party will cooperate fully and fairly with the mediator and will attempt to reach a mutually satisfactory compromise to the dispute. If the dispute is not resolved within 30 days after it is referred to the mediator, either party may take the matter to court.

☐ **Mediation and Possible Arbitration.** If a dispute arises, the parties will try in good faith to settle it through mediation conducted by:

☐ _____ .

☐ a mediator to be mutually selected.

The parties will share the costs of the mediator equally. Each party will cooperate fully and fairly with the mediator and will attempt to reach a mutually satisfactory compromise to the dispute. If the dispute is not resolved within 30 days after it is referred to the mediator, it will be arbitrated by:

☐ _____ .

☐ an arbitrator to be mutually selected.

Judgment on the arbitration award may be entered in any court that has jurisdiction over the matter. Costs of arbitration, including lawyers' fees, will be allocated by the arbitrator.

☐ **Attorneys' Fees.** If either party brings a legal action arising out of a dispute over this agreement, the losing party will reimburse the prevailing party for all reasonable costs and attorneys' fees incurred by the prevailing party in the lawsuit.

21. **Additional Agreements.** Seller and Buyer additionally agree that _____

_____

_____

_____

_____

_____

_____

22. **Entire Agreement.** This is the entire agreement between the parties. It replaces and supersedes any and all oral agreements between the parties, as well as any prior writings.

23. **Successors and Assignees.** This contract binds and benefits the heirs, successors, and assignees of the parties.

24. **Notices.** All notices must be in writing. A notice may be delivered to a party at the address that follows a party's signature or to a new address that a party designates in writing. A notice may be delivered:

    (1) in person

    (2) by certified mail, or

    (3) by overnight courier.

25. **Governing Law.** This contract will be governed by and construed in accordance with the laws of the state of _____ .

26. **Counterparts.** This contract may be signed by the parties in different counterparts and the signature pages combined will create a document binding on all parties.

27. **Modification.** This contract may be modified only by a written agreement signed by all the parties.

28. **Waiver.** If one party waives any term or provision of this contract at any time, that waiver will be effective only for the specific instance and specific purpose for which the waiver was given. If either party fails to exercise or delays exercising any of its rights or remedies under this contract, that party retains the right to enforce that term or provision at a later time.

29. **Severability.** If any court determines that any provision of this contract is invalid or unenforceable, any invalidity or unenforceability will affect only that provision and will not make any other provision of this contract invalid or unenforceable and such provision shall be modified, amended, or limited only to the extent necessary to render it valid and enforceable.

Seller

Name of business: _____

a _____

By: _____ Dated: _____

Printed name: _____

Title: _____

Address: _____

_____

Buyer

Name of business: _____

a _____

By: _____ Dated: _____

Printed name: _____

Title: _____

Address: _____

_____

Contract to Purchase Vacant Land

1. **Names.** This contract is made by _____ ,
    Seller, and _____ , Buyer.

2. **Purchase of Real Estate.** Seller is selling and Buyer is buying the property commonly known as
    _____ , located at _____
    _____ .

    ☐ The legal description of the property is as follows: _____
    _____
    _____
    _____ .

    ☐ The legal description of the property is given in Attachment 1.

    Seller will transfer the property to Buyer subject to easements and restrictions of record.

3. **Purchase Price.** The purchase price is $_____ . Seller acknowledges that Buyer has
    deposited $_____ with _____ ,
    as escrow agent, upon the signing of this agreement. This deposit is to be credited against the
    purchase price. Buyer will pay the balance of $_____ at closing in cash or by electronic funds
    transfer or by cashier's check.

4. **Financing Contingency.** This contract is contingent upon Buyer qualifying for and obtaining
    a commitment for a mortgage or deed of trust loan in the amount of $_____ , with terms
    acceptable to the Buyer. Buyer will apply for such financing within _____ business days from the
    date of this agreement and pursue the application in good faith. This financing contingency is to be
    removed by _____ .

5. **Special Assessments.** Seller will pay any special assessments and/or liens that are imposed on the
    property on or before the date of closing. Buyer will pay any special assessments and/or liens that are
    imposed on the property after the date of closing.

6. **Other Government Charges.** Seller will pay any other charges made against the property by any
    government authority for installation or extension of water, sanitary, or sewer service, if such charges
    have been incurred before the date of closing. Buyer will pay for such charges incurred after the date
    of closing.

7. **Real Estate Taxes.** Real estate taxes will be prorated on a 30-day-month, 360-day-year basis to the
    date of closing based on the due date of the taxing authority. For proration purposes, these taxes will
    be deemed to be paid in advance.

8. **Closing and Possession.** The purchase will be closed on _____ . Possession will
    be given at closing.

9. **Transfer of Title.** Seller will transfer marketable title to the property to Buyer by a warranty deed.
    Seller will pay any transfer tax due when title passes.

10. **Title Insurance.** Buyer will receive an owner's policy of title insurance, including a policy
    commitment before closing, in the amount of the purchase price.

    ☐ The cost of the owner's insurance policy will be paid by Buyer.

    ☐ The cost of the owner's insurance policy will be paid by Seller.

    ☐ The cost of the owner's insurance policy will be split equally between Buyer and Seller.

11. **Additional Contingencies.** This contract is contingent upon satisfactory completion of the following items:

☐ A contractor's inspection of the property at Buyer's expense resulting in a report satisfactory to Buyer. This contingency is to be removed by _____ .

☐ An architect's inspection of the property at Buyer's expense resulting in a report satisfactory to Buyer. This contingency is to be removed by _____ .

☐ An environmental inspection of the property at Buyer's expense resulting in findings satisfactory to Buyer. This contingency is to be removed by _____ .

☐ A review of public and private building and use requirements affecting the property at Buyer's expense resulting in findings satisfactory to Buyer. This contingency is to be removed by

_____ .

☐ A stake survey or survey report at Buyer's expense resulting in findings satisfactory to Buyer. This contingency is to be removed by _____ .

☐ Approval of the title insurance commitment by Buyer's lawyer. This contingency is to be removed within _____ days after the title insurance commitment is received by Buyer.

☐ A written appraisal of the property by a licensed or certified appraiser, obtained at Buyer's expense, that is no less than the purchase price. This contingency is to be removed within _____ days after Buyer receives the written appraisal report.

☐ A review and approval of common interest community documents by Buyer or Buyer's lawyer. This contingency is to be removed within _____ days after Seller provides Buyer with the common interest community documents.

☐ Other: _____ .

12. **Removal of Contingencies**. If any contingency in this contract is not removed in writing by the required date, this contract becomes voidable. After the required date and until the contingency is removed, either party may cancel this contract by written notice to the other. In that case, Seller will return the deposit to Buyer.

13. **Default.** If Buyer defaults, Seller may (1) pursue legal remedies or (2) cancel this contract and claim the deposit as liquidated damages.

   If Seller defaults, Buyer may (1) enforce this contract, (2) demand a refund of the deposit in termination of this contract, or (3) pursue legal remedies.

14. **Disputes.**

☐ **Litigation.** If a dispute arises, either party may take the matter to court.

☐ **Mediation and Possible Litigation.** If a dispute arises, the parties will try in good faith to settle it through mediation conducted by:

   ☐ _____ .

   ☐ a mediator to be mutually selected.

   The parties will share the costs of the mediator equally. Each party will cooperate fully and fairly with the mediator and will attempt to reach a mutually satisfactory compromise to the dispute. If the dispute is not resolved within 30 days after it is referred to the mediator, either party may take the matter to court.

☐ **Mediation and Possible Arbitration.** If a dispute arises, the parties will try in good faith to settle it through mediation conducted by:

☐ _____ .

☐ a mediator to be mutually selected.

The parties will share the costs of the mediator equally. Each party will cooperate fully and fairly with the mediator and will attempt to reach a mutually satisfactory compromise to the dispute. If the dispute is not resolved within 30 days after it is referred to the mediator, it will be arbitrated by:

☐ _____ .

☐ an arbitrator to be mutually selected.

Judgment on the arbitration award may be entered in any court that has jurisdiction over the matter. Costs of arbitration, including lawyers' fees, will be allocated by the arbitrator.

☐ **Attorneys' Fees.** If either party brings a legal action arising out of a dispute over this agreement, the losing party will reimburse the prevailing party for all reasonable costs and attorneys' fees incurred by the prevailing party in the lawsuit.

15. **Additional Agreements.** Seller and Buyer additionally agree that _____

_____

_____

_____

_____

_____

_____

_____

_____

_____

_____

_____ .

16. **Entire Agreement.** This is the entire agreement between the parties. It replaces and supersedes any and all oral agreements between the parties, as well as any prior writings.

17. **Successors and Assignees.** This contract binds and benefits the heirs, successors, and assignees of the parties.

18. **Notices.** All notices must be in writing. A notice may be delivered to a party at the address that follows a party's signature or to a new address that a party designates in writing. A notice may be delivered:

    (1) in person

    (2) by certified mail, or

    (3) by overnight courier.

19. **Governing Law.** This contract will be governed by and construed in accordance with the laws of the state of _____ .

20. **Counterparts.** This contract may be signed by the parties in different counterparts and the signature pages combined will create a document binding on all parties.

21. **Modification.** This contract may be modified only by a written agreement signed by all the parties.

22. **Waiver.** If one party waives any term or provision of this contract at any time, that waiver will be effective only for the specific instance and specific purpose for which the waiver was given. If either party fails to exercise or delays exercising any of its rights or remedies under this contract, that party retains the right to enforce that term or provision at a later time.

23. **Severability.** If any court determines that any provision of this contract is invalid or unenforceable, any invalidity or unenforceability will affect only that provision and will not make any other provision of this contract invalid or unenforceable and such provision shall be modified, amended, or limited only to the extent necessary to render it valid and enforceable.

Seller

Name of business: _____

a _____

By: _____ Dated: _____

Printed name: _____

Title: _____

Address: _____

_____

Buyer

Name of business: _____

a _____

By: _____ Dated: _____

Printed name: _____

Title: _____

Address: _____

_____

Option to Purchase Vacant Land

1. **Names.** This contract is made by _____
_____ , Seller, and _____
_____ , Buyer.

2. **Option to Purchase Vacant Land.** In exchange for $_____, which Buyer has paid to Seller
as an option fee, Seller grants to Buyer the option to purchase the property commonly known as
_____ , located at
_____ .

   ☐ The legal description of the property is as follows: _____
   _____
   _____
   _____ .

   ☐ The legal description of the property is given in Attachment 1 to this contract.
   If Buyer exercises this option, Seller will transfer the property to Buyer on the terms stated in this
   contract. The conveyance will be subject to easements and restrictions of record.

3. **Exercise of Option.** Buyer may exercise this option by delivering to Seller on or before
_____ a written notice of exercise of option. Buyer may deliver the notice by:
   ☐ handing it to Seller.
   ☐ sending it to Seller's office at _____ by certified mail or
   private overnight mail service, in which case the notice will be treated as delivered when placed in
   the possession of the U.S. Postal Service or the private carrier.

4. **Purchase Price.** If Buyer exercises the option, the purchase price is $_____ .
The option fee   ☐ will   ☐ will not   be applied toward the purchase price. The purchase price
will be paid at closing in cash or by electronic funds transfer or by cashier's check.

5. **Access to Property.** Upon reasonable notice to Seller, Buyer and others chosen by Buyer may enter
the property at reasonable times to perform a contractor's inspection, an architect's inspection, an
environmental inspection, and a boundary line survey, as desired by Buyer. Such inspections will be
at Buyer's expense.

6. **Special Assessments.** Seller will pay any special assessments and/or liens that are imposed on the
property on or before the date of closing. Buyer will pay any special assessments and/or liens that are
imposed on the property after the date of closing.

7. **Other Government Charges.** Seller will pay any other charges made against the property by any
government authority for installation or extension of water, sanitary, or sewer service, if such charges
have been incurred before the date of closing. Buyer will pay for the charges incurred after the date
of closing.

8. **Real Estate Taxes.** Real estate taxes will be prorated on a 30-day-month, 360-day-year basis to the
date of closing based on the due date of the taxing authority. For proration purposes, these taxes will
be deemed to be paid in advance.

9. **Closing and Possession.** The purchase will be closed on _____ . Possession
of the premises will be given to Buyer at closing.

10. **Transfer of Title.** Seller will transfer marketable title to the property to Buyer by a warranty deed. Seller will pay any transfer tax due when title passes.

11. **Title Insurance.**

   A. Buyer will receive an owner's policy of title insurance, including a policy commitment before closing, in the amount of the purchase price.

   ☐ The cost of the owner's insurance policy will be paid by Buyer.

   ☐ The cost of the owner's insurance policy will be paid by Seller.

   ☐ The cost of the owner's insurance policy will be split equally between Buyer and Seller.

   B. The purchase is contingent upon Buyer or Buyer's lawyer approving

   ☐ the title insurance commitment.

   ☐ a survey of the property to be provided by Seller.

   Seller will deliver these documents to Buyer on or before _____ . This contingency is to be removed within _____ days after Buyer receives the documents called for above. If the contingency is not removed, Seller will refund the option fee to Buyer.

12. **Default.** If Buyer defaults, Seller may (1) pursue legal remedies or (2) cancel this contract and claim the option fee as liquidated damages.

   If Seller defaults, Buyer may (1) enforce this contract, (2) demand a refund of the option fee in termination of this contract, or (3) pursue legal remedies.

13. **Disputes.**

   ☐ **Litigation.** If a dispute arises, either party may take the matter to court.

   ☐ **Mediation and Possible Litigation.** If a dispute arises, the parties will try in good faith to settle it through mediation conducted by:

   ☐ _____ .

   ☐ a mediator to be mutually selected.

   The parties will share the costs of the mediator equally. Each party will cooperate fully and fairly with the mediator and will attempt to reach a mutually satisfactory compromise to the dispute. If the dispute is not resolved within 30 days after it is referred to the mediator, either party may take the matter to court.

   ☐ **Mediation and Possible Arbitration.** If a dispute arises, the parties will try in good faith to settle it through mediation conducted by:

   ☐ _____ .

   ☐ a mediator to be mutually selected.

   The parties will share the costs of the mediator equally. Each party will cooperate fully and fairly with the mediator and will attempt to reach a mutually satisfactory compromise to the dispute. If the dispute is not resolved within 30 days after it is referred to the mediator, it will be arbitrated by:

   ☐ _____ .

   ☐ an arbitrator to be mutually selected.

   Judgment on the arbitration award may be entered in any court that has jurisdiction over the matter. Costs of arbitration, including lawyers' fees, will be allocated by the arbitrator.

☐ **Attorneys' Fees.** If either party brings a legal action arising out of a dispute over this agreement, the losing party will reimburse the prevailing party for all reasonable costs and attorneys' fees incurred by the prevailing party in the lawsuit.

14. **Additional Agreements.** Seller and Buyer additionally agree that _____

_____

_____

_____

_____

_____

_____

_____

_____

_____

_____

_____

_____

_____ .

15. **Entire Agreement.** This is the entire agreement between the parties. It replaces and supersedes any and all oral agreements between the parties, as well as any prior writings.

16. **Successors and Assignees.** This contract binds and benefits the heirs, successors, and assignees of the parties.

17. **Notices.** All notices must be in writing. A notice may be delivered to a party at the address that follows a party's signature or to a new address that a party designates in writing. A notice may be delivered:

    (1) in person

    (2) by certified mail, or

    (3) by overnight courier.

18. **Governing Law.** This contract will be governed by and construed in accordance with the laws of the state of _____ .

19. **Counterparts.** This contract may be signed by the parties in different counterparts and the signature pages combined will create a document binding on all parties.

20. **Modification.** This contract may be modified only by a written agreement signed by all the parties.

21. **Waiver.** If one party waives any term or provision of this contract at any time, that waiver will be effective only for the specific instance and specific purpose for which the waiver was given. If either party fails to exercise or delays exercising any of its rights or remedies under this contract, that party retains the right to enforce that term or provision at a later time.

22. **Severability.** If any court determines that any provision of this contract is invalid or unenforceable, any invalidity or unenforceability will affect only that provision and will not make any other provision of this contract invalid or unenforceable and such provision shall be modified, amended, or limited only to the extent necessary to render it valid and enforceable.

Seller

Name of business: _____

a _____

By: _____ Dated: _____

Printed name: _____

Title: _____

Address: _____

_____

Buyer

Name of business: _____

a _____

By: _____ Dated: _____

Printed name: _____

Title: _____

Address: _____

_____

Attachment _____ to _____

1. **Names.** This attachment is made by _____
_____ , Seller, and _____
_____ , Buyer.

2. **Terms of Attachment.** We agree to the following attachment to _____ dated
_____ , covering the property described as _____
_____
_____ :

_____
_____
_____
_____
_____
_____
_____
_____
_____
_____
_____
_____
_____ .

Seller

Name of business: _____

a _____

By: _____ Dated: _____

Printed name: _____

Title: _____

Address: _____

_____

Buyer

Name of business: _____

a _____

By: _____ Dated: _____

Printed name: _____

Title: _____

Address: _____

_____

Amendment _____ of _____

1. **Names.** This amendment is made by _____
_____ , Seller, and _____
_____ , Buyer.

2. **Terms of Amendment. The** _____ dated _____ , covering
the property described as _____
_____
_____

is amended as follows: _____
_____
_____
_____
_____
_____
_____
_____
_____
_____
_____
_____
_____
_____
_____
_____
_____
_____ .

In all other respects, the terms of the original contract and any earlier amendments will remain in effect. If there is a conflict between this amendment and the original contract or any earlier amendment, the terms of this amendment will prevail.

Seller

Name of business: _____

a _____

By: _____ Dated: _____

Printed name: _____

Title: _____

Address: _____
_____

Buyer

Name of business: _____

a _____

By: _____ Dated: _____

Printed name: _____

Title: _____

Address: _____

_____

Removal of Contingency

In accordance with the terms and conditions in the _____ ,

dated _____ , for the property known as _____ ,

between _____ , Buyer, and

_____ , Seller:

Buyer removes the following contingencies:

☐ Contingency regarding financing (Contract paragraph #_____)

☐ Contingency regarding contractor's inspection and/or report (Contract paragraph #_____)

☐ Contingency regarding architect's inspection and/or report (Contract paragraph #_____)

☐ Contingency regarding environmental inspection and/or report (Contract paragraph #_____)

☐ Contingency regarding use requirements (Contract paragraph #_____)

☐ Contingency regarding survey report (Contract paragraph #_____)

☐ Contingency regarding title insurance commitment (Contract paragraph #_____)

☐ Contingency regarding appraisal (Contract paragraph #_____)

☐ Contingency regarding common interest community documents (Contract paragraph #_____)

☐ Other: _____

_____

_____

Dated: _____

Buyer

Name of business: _____

a _____

By: _____   Dated: _____

Printed name: _____

Title: _____

Address: _____

_____

Extension of Time to Remove Contingencies

This Extension of Time to Remove Contingencies relates to the _____ ,

dated, _____ , for the property known as

_____ , between

_____ , Buyer, and

_____ , Seller:

Buyer and Seller agree that the dates for removal of contingencies are extended as follows:

☐ Contingency regarding financing (Contract paragraph # _____) is extended to _____ .

☐ Contingency regarding contractor's inspection and/or report (Contract paragraph # _____) is extended to

_____ .

☐ Contingency regarding architect's inspection and/or report (Contract paragraph # _____) is extended to

_____ .

☐ Contingency regarding environmental inspection and/or report (Contract paragraph # _____) is

extended to _____ .

☐ Contingency regarding use requirements (Contract paragraph # _____) is extended to _____ .

☐ Contingency regarding survey report (Contract paragraph # _____) is extended to _____ .

☐ Contingency regarding title insurance commitment (Contract paragraph # _____) is extended to

_____ .

☐ Contingency regarding appraisal (Contract paragraph # _____) is extended to _____ .

☐ Contingency regarding common interest community documents (Contract paragraph # _____) is

extended to _____ .

☐ Other: _____

_____ is extended to _____ .

Any contingency removal date not changed here will remain as previously agreed.

Seller

Name of business: _____

a _____

By: _____ Dated: _____

Printed name: _____

Title: _____

Address: _____

_____

Buyer

Name of business: _____

a _____

By: _____ Dated: _____

Printed name: _____

Title: _____

Address: _____

_____

Exercise of Option to Purchase Real Estate

To _____ , Seller:

_____ , Buyer,

exercises its option to purchase the following property: _____

_____ .

This notice is given in accordance with the _____

between Seller and Buyer, dated _____ .

Dated: _____

Buyer

Name of business: _____

a _____

By: _____

Printed name: _____

Title: _____

Address: _____

_____

Sales Contract
(Lump-Sum Payment)

1. **Names.** _____ , Seller,
   and _____ , Buyer,
   agree to the following sale.

2. **Property Being Sold.** Seller agrees to sell to Buyer, and Buyer agrees to buy from Seller, the following
   property: _____
   _____ (the Property).

3. **Condition of Property.**

   ☐ The Property is new.

   ☐ The Property is used. Buyer has inspected the Property and will accept it.

   ☐ The Property is used. Buyer has inspected the Property and will accept it except for the following
   modifications, which Seller agrees to make before delivery: _____
   _____
   _____ .

   ☐ Seller discloses the following defects: _____
   _____
   _____ .

4. **Purchase Price.** The purchase price of the Property is $_____ .

5. **Down Payment.**

   ☐ Buyer will make a down payment of $_____ when this contract is signed.
   This down payment will be applied toward the purchase price.

   ☐ Buyer will not make a down payment.

6. **Time of Payment.** Buyer will pay Seller the purchase price (less any down payment)

   ☐ upon delivery of the property to Buyer, assuming any modifications in the condition called for in
   Paragraph 3 have been made.

   ☐ on _____ .

7. **Method of Payment.** *(Optional)*
   Buyer will pay Seller by

   ☐ personal or business check.

   ☐ cashier's check.

   ☐ credit card.

   ☐ cash.

8. **Delivery.** Seller will deliver the Property to Buyer on _____ at
   _____ .

9. **Ownership.** Seller has legal title to the Property and is selling the Property free of any liens or liabilities.

10. **Transfer of Ownership.** Seller will transfer ownership of the Property to Buyer through

    ☐ a receipt.

    ☐ a bill of sale.

    ☐ such documents as may be required by the state of _____ to legally
    transfer the ownership of the Property.

11. **Other Terms and Conditions.** _____

_____

_____

_____ .

12. **Entire Agreement.** This is the entire agreement between the parties. It replaces and supersedes any and all oral agreements between the parties, as well as any prior writings.

13. **Successors and Assignees.** This agreement binds and benefits the heirs, successors, and assignees of the parties.

14. **Notices.** All notices must be in writing. A notice may be delivered to a party at the address that follows a party's signature or to a new address that a party designates in writing. A notice may be delivered:

    (1) in person

    (2) by certified mail, or

    (3) by overnight courier.

15. **Governing Law.** This agreement will be governed by and construed in accordance with the laws of the state of _____ .

16. **Counterparts.** This agreement may be signed by the parties in different counterparts and the signature pages combined will create a document binding on all parties.

17. **Modification.** This agreement may be modified only by a written agreement signed by all the parties.

18. **Waiver.** If one party waives any term or provision of this agreement at any time, that waiver will be effective only for the specific instance and specific purpose for which the waiver was given. If either party fails to exercise or delays exercising any of its rights or remedies under this agreement, that party retains the right to enforce that term or provision at a later time.

19. **Severability.** If any court determines that any provision of this agreement is invalid or unenforceable, any invalidity or unenforceability will affect only that provision and will not make any other provision of this agreement invalid or unenforceable and shall be modified, amended, or limited only to the extent necessary to render it valid and enforceable.

Seller

Name of business: _____

a _____

By: _____ Dated: _____

Printed name: _____

Title: _____

Address: _____

_____

Buyer

Name of business: _____

a _____

By: _____ Dated: _____

Printed name: _____

Title: _____

Address: _____

_____

Sales Contract
(Installment Payments)

1. **Names.** _____ , Seller,
and _____ , Buyer,
agree to the following sale.

2. **Property Being Sold.** Seller agrees to sell to Buyer, and Buyer agrees to buy from Seller, the following
property: _____
_____ (the Property).

3. **Condition of Property.**
   ☐ The Property is new.
   ☐ The Property is used. Buyer has inspected the Property and will accept it.
   ☐ The Property is used. Buyer has inspected the Property and will accept it except for the following
   modifications, which Seller agrees to make before delivery: _____
   _____
   _____
   _____ .

   ☐ Seller discloses the following defects: _____
   _____
   _____ .

4. **Purchase Price.** The purchase price of the Property is $_____ .

5. **Down Payment.**
   ☐ Buyer will make a down payment of $_____ when this contract is signed.
   This down payment will be applied toward the purchase price.
   ☐ Buyer will not make a down payment.

6. **Time of Payment.** Buyer will pay Seller the purchase price (less any down payment) in installments as
   follows: _____
   _____ .

7. **Method of Payment.** (*Optional*)
   Buyer will pay Seller by
   ☐ personal or business check.
   ☐ cashier's check.
   ☐ credit card.
   ☐ cash.

8. **Delivery.** Seller will deliver the Property to Buyer on _____ at
   _____ .

9. **Ownership.** Seller has legal title to the Property and is selling the Property free of any liens or liabilities.

10. **Transfer of Ownership.** Seller will transfer ownership of the Property to Buyer through
    ☐ a receipt.
    ☐ a bill of sale.
    ☐ such documents as may be required by the state of _____ to legally
    transfer the ownership of the Property.

11. **Security Interest.**

☐ Seller will not retain a security interest in the property.

☐ Seller will retain a security interest in the property. At the time the property is delivered to Buyer, Buyer will sign and deliver to Seller a security agreement. Buyer also acknowledges that Seller will file a Uniform Commercial Code Financing Statement, which will secure Seller's interest in the Property until the purchase price has been paid in full.

12. **Other Terms and Conditions.** _____

_____

_____

_____ .

13. **Entire Agreement.** This is the entire agreement between the parties. It replaces and supersedes any and all oral agreements between the parties, as well as any prior writings.

14. **Successors and Assignees.** This agreement binds and benefits the heirs, successors, and assignees of the parties.

15. **Notices.** All notices must be in writing. A notice may be delivered to a party at the address that follows a party's signature or to a new address that a party designates in writing. A notice may be delivered:

(1) in person

(2) by certified mail, or

(3) by overnight courier.

16. **Governing Law.** This agreement will be governed by and construed in accordance with the laws of the state of _____ .

17. **Counterparts.** This agreement may be signed by the parties in different counterparts and the signature pages combined will create a document binding on all parties.

18. **Modification.** This agreement may be modified only by a written agreement signed by all the parties.

19. **Waiver.** If one party waives any term or provision of this agreement at any time, that waiver will be effective only for the specific instance and specific purpose for which the waiver was given. If either party fails to exercise or delays exercising any of its rights or remedies under this agreement, that party retains the right to enforce that term or provision at a later time.

20. **Severability.** If any court determines that any provision of this agreement is invalid or unenforceable, any invalidity or unenforceability will affect only that provision and will not make any other provision of this agreement invalid or unenforceable and shall be modified, amended, or limited only to the extent necessary to render it valid and enforceable.

Seller

Name of business: _____

a _____

By: _____ Dated: _____

Printed name: _____

Title: _____

Address: _____

_____

Buyer

Name of business: _____

a _____

By: _____ Dated: _____

Printed name: _____

Title: _____

Address: _____

_____

Bill of Sale for Goods

1. **Names.**

   Seller: _____

   Buyer: _____

2. **Transfer of Ownership.** Seller sells and transfers to Buyer the following property: _____

   _____

   _____

   _____ (the Property).

   ☐ Seller acknowledges receiving $ _____ and other consideration from Buyer as payment for this transfer of ownership.

   ☐ Seller acknowledges receiving $ _____ as a down payment for the Property. Buyer agrees to pay the balance of $ _____ in installments as provided in the sales contract dated _____ between Buyer and Seller.

3. **Condition of Property.**

   ☐ The Property is new.

   ☐ The Property is used.

4. **Warranty of Ownership.** Seller warrants that Seller is the legal owner of the Property and that the Property is free of all liens and encumbrances.

Dated: _____

Seller

Name of business: _____

a _____

By: _____

Printed name: _____

Title: _____

Address: _____

_____

Security Agreement for Buying Goods

1. **Names.**

   Seller: _____

   Buyer: _____

2. **Grant of Security Interest.** Buyer grants to Seller a continuing security interest in the following property (the Secured Property), which consists of _____

   _____

   _____

   _____ ,

   and all proceeds, products, and accessions of and to the property listed in this paragraph, including any money, property, or insurance proceeds Buyer receives from the loss, sale, transfer, or damage of or to the listed property.

3. **Installment Payments.** Buyer is granting this security interest to secure performance of Buyer's promise to make the following installment payments on the Secured Property as listed in the sales contract between Buyer and Seller dated _____ :

   _____

   _____

   _____ .

4. **Financing Statement.** Seller may file a Uniform Commercial Code Financing Statement to further protect Seller's security interest in the Secured Property.

5. **Use and Care of the Secured Property.** Until all installment payments have been made, Buyer agrees to:

   A. Keep the Secured Property at Buyer's premises.

   B. Maintain the Secured Property in good repair.

   C. Not sell, transfer, or release the Secured Property unless Seller consents.

   D. Pay all taxes on the Secured Property as taxes become due.

   E. Insure the Secured Property against normal risks with an insurance policy that names Buyer and Seller as beneficiaries based on their respective interests in the property.

   F. Deliver to Seller a copy of the insurance policy insuring the Secured Property and provide annual proof to Seller that Buyer has paid the premiums on the policy.

   G. Allow Seller to inspect the Secured Property at any reasonable time.

6. **Default of Buyer.** Buyer will be in default if either of the following occurs:

   A. Buyer is late in making any payment required by the sales contract and does not pay within ten days of Seller sending written notice of late payment.

   B. Buyer fails to correct any actual violations of Paragraph 5 within ten days of receiving written notice from Seller.

7. **Rights of Seller.** If Buyer is in default, Seller may exercise the remedies contained in the Uniform Commercial Code for the state of _____ and any other remedies legally available to Seller. Seller may, for example:

   A. Remove the Secured Property from the place where it is then located.

B. Require Buyer to make the Secured Property available to Seller at a place designated by Seller that is reasonably convenient to Buyer and Seller.

C. Sell or lease the Secured Property, or otherwise dispose of it.

8. **Notice to Buyer.** Seller will give Buyer at least five days' notice of when and where the Secured Property will be sold, leased, or otherwise disposed of. Any notice required here or by statute will be deemed given to Buyer if sent by first-class mail to Buyer at the following address: _____ _____ .

9. **Entire Agreement.** This is the entire agreement between the parties. It replaces and supersedes any and all oral agreements between the parties, as well as any prior writings.

10. **Successors and Assignees.** This agreement binds and benefits the heirs, successors, and assignees of the parties.

11. **Governing Law.** This agreement will be governed by and construed in accordance with the laws of the state of _____ .

12. **Counterparts.** This agreement may be signed by the parties in different counterparts and the signature pages combined will create a document binding on all parties.

13. **Modification.** This agreement may be modified only by a written agreement signed by all the parties.

14. **Waiver.** If one party waives any term or provision of this agreement at any time, that waiver will be effective only for the specific instance and specific purpose for which the waiver was given. If either party fails to exercise or delays exercising any of its rights or remedies under this agreement, that party retains the right to enforce that term or provision at a later time.

15. **Severability.** If any court determines that any provision of this agreement is invalid or unenforceable, any invalidity or unenforceability will affect only that provision and will not make any other provision of this agreement invalid or unenforceable and shall be modified, amended, or limited only to the extent necessary to render it valid and enforceable.

Seller

Name of business: _____

a _____

By: _____ Dated: _____

Printed name: _____

Title: _____

Address: _____

_____

Buyer

Name of business: _____

a _____

By: _____ Dated: _____

Printed name: _____

Title: _____

Address: _____

_____

Contract for Manufacture of Goods

1. **Names.** _____ , Seller,

   and _____ , Buyer,

   agree to the following terms.

2. **Property Description.** Seller agrees to ☐ manufacture ☐ customize and sell to Buyer, and

   Buyer agrees to buy from Seller, the following property: _____

   _____ (the Property).

   ☐ Seller will ☐ manufacture ☐ customize the Property according to the specifications that are

   designated in Attachment 1 to this contract.

3. **Purchase Price.** The purchase price of the Property is $ _____ .

4. **Down Payment.**

   ☐ Buyer will make a down payment of $ _____ when this contract is signed.

   This down payment will be applied toward the purchase price.

   ☐ Buyer will not make a down payment.

5. **Time of Payment.** Buyer will pay Seller the purchase price (less any down payment)

   ☐ upon delivery of the property to Buyer.

   ☐ on _____ .

   ☐ in installments according to schedule established in Attachment _____ .

6. **Method of Payment.** *(Optional)*

   Buyer will pay Seller by

   ☐ personal or business check.

   ☐ cashier's check.

   ☐ credit card.

   ☐ cash.

7. **Delivery.** Seller will deliver the Property to Buyer by _____ at

   ☐ Seller's place of business, _____ .

   ☐ Buyer's place of business, _____ .

   ☐ Other: _____ .

8. **Ownership.** Seller has legal title to the Property and is selling the property free of any liens or

   liabilities.

9. **Bill of Sale.** Concurrently with the delivery of the Property to the Buyer, Seller will transfer

   ownership of the Property to Buyer through a bill of sale.

10. **Security Interest.**

    ☐ Seller will not retain a security interest in the Property.

    ☐ Seller will retain a security interest in the Property. At the time the Property is delivered to Buyer,

    Buyer will sign and deliver to Seller a security agreement. Buyer acknowledges that Seller may file a

    Uniform Commercial Code Financing Statement to further protect Seller's interest in the Property.

11. **Other Terms and Conditions.** _____

    _____

    _____

    _____ .

12. **Entire Agreement.** This is the entire agreement between the parties. It replaces and supersedes any and all oral agreements between the parties, as well as any prior writings.

13. **Successors and Assignees.** This agreement binds and benefits the heirs, successors, and assignees of the parties.

14. **Notices.** All notices must be in writing. A notice may be delivered to a party at the address that follows a party's signature or to a new address that a party designates in writing. A notice may be delivered:

    (1) in person

    (2) by certified mail, or

    (3) by overnight courier.

15. **Governing Law.** This agreement will be governed by and construed in accordance with the laws of the state of _____ .

16. **Counterparts.** This agreement may be signed by the parties in different counterparts and the signature pages combined will create a document binding on all parties.

17. **Modification.** This agreement may be modified only by a written agreement signed by all the parties.

18. **Waiver.** If one party waives any term or provision of this agreement at any time, that waiver will be effective only for the specific instance and specific purpose for which the waiver was given. If either party fails to exercise or delays exercising any of its rights or remedies under this agreement, that party retains the right to enforce that term or provision at a later time.

19. **Severability.** If any court determines that any provision of this agreement is invalid or unenforceable, any invalidity or unenforceability will affect only that provision and will not make any other provision of this agreement invalid or unenforceable and shall be modified, amended, or limited only to the extent necessary to render it valid and enforceable.

Seller

Name of business: _____

a _____

By: _____ Dated: _____

Printed name: _____

Title: _____

Address: _____

_____

Buyer

Name of business: _____

a _____

By: _____ Dated: _____

Printed name: _____

Title: _____

Address: _____

_____

Equipment Rental Contract

1. **Names.** _____ , Owner,
   and _____ , Renter,
   agree to the following rental.

2. **Equipment Being Rented.** Owner agrees to rent to Renter, and Renter agrees to rent from Owner,
   the following equipment: _____
   _____ (the Equipment).

3. **Duration of Rental Period.** The rental will begin at _____ on _____
   and will end at _____ on _____ .

4. **Rental Amount.** The rental amount is $_____ per ☐ day ☐ week ☐ year.

5. **Payment.** Renter has paid $ _____ to Owner to cover the rental period specified in
   Paragraph 3.

   ☐ **Security Deposit.** In addition to the rent, Renter has deposited $ _____ with Owner.
   This deposit will be applied toward any additional rent and any amounts owed for damage to or
   loss of the Equipment, which Owner and Renter agree has the current value stated in Paragraph
   9. Owner will return to Renter any unused portion of the deposit.

6. **Delivery.** Owner will deliver the Equipment to Renter on _____ at
   ☐ the Owner's place of business, _____ .
   ☐ the Renter's place of business, _____ .
   ☐ Other: _____
   _____ .

7. **Late Return.** If Renter returns the equipment to Owner after the time and date the rental period
   ends, Renter will pay Owner a rental charge of $_____ per day for each day or partial day
   beyond the end of the rental period until the Equipment is returned. Owner can subtract these rental
   charges from the security deposit.

8. **Damage or Loss.** Renter acknowledges receiving the Equipment in good condition, except as follows:
   _____
   _____
   _____ .

   Renter will return the Equipment to Owner in good condition except as noted above. If the
   Equipment is damaged while in Renter's possession, Renter will be responsible for the cost of repair,
   up to the current value of the Equipment. If the Equipment is lost while in Renter's possession,
   Renter will pay Owner its current value.

9. **Value of Equipment.** Owner and Renter agree that the current value of the Equipment is $ _____ .

10. **Use of Equipment.** *(Optional)*
    Renter acknowledges that use of the Equipment creates some risk of personal injury to Renter and third
    parties, as well as a risk of damage to property, and Renter expressly assumes that risk. Renter therefore
    agrees to use the Equipment safely and only in the manner for which it is intended to be used. Owner
    is not responsible for any personal injury or property damage resulting from Renter's misuse, unsafe
    use, or reckless use of the Equipment. Renter will indemnify and defend Owner from and against any
    injury or damage claims arising out of Renter's misuse, unsafe use, or reckless use of the Equipment.

11. **Entire Agreement.** This is the entire agreement between the parties. It replaces and supersedes any and all oral agreements between the parties, as well as any prior writings.

12. **Successors and Assignees.** This agreement binds and benefits the heirs, successors, and assignees of the parties.

13. **Notices.** All notices must be in writing. A notice may be delivered to a party at the address that follows a party's signature or to a new address that a party designates in writing. A notice may be delivered:

    (1) in person

    (2) by certified mail, or

    (3) by overnight courier.

14. **Governing Law.** This agreement will be governed by and construed in accordance with the laws of the state of _____ .

15. **Counterparts.** This agreement may be signed by the parties in different counterparts and the signature pages combined will create a document binding on all parties.

16. **Modification.** This agreement may be modified only by a written agreement signed by all the parties.

17. **Waiver.** If one party waives any term or provision of this agreement at any time, that waiver will be effective only for the specific instance and specific purpose for which the waiver was given. If either party fails to exercise or delays exercising any of its rights or remedies under this agreement, that party retains the right to enforce that term or provision at a later time.

18. **Severability.** If any court determines that any provision of this agreement is invalid or unenforceable, any invalidity or unenforceability will affect only that provision and will not make any other provision of this agreement invalid or unenforceable and shall be modified, amended, or limited only to the extent necessary to render it valid and enforceable.

Owner

Name of business: _____

a _____

By: _____ Dated: _____

Printed name: _____

Title: _____

Address: _____

_____

Renter

Name of business: _____

a _____

By: _____ Dated: _____

Printed name: _____

Title: _____

Address: _____

_____

Storage Contract

1. **Names.** _____ , Customer,

   and _____ , Storer,

   agree to the following storage arrangements.

2. **Property Being Stored.** Storer agrees to store the following Property for Customer: _____

   _____ .

   _____ (the Property).

3. **Storage Period.** The storage will begin on _____ and continue until

   _____ , unless Customer takes back the Property before then.

4. **Storage Fees.** Customer has paid Storer $ _____ , which covers all storage fees

   through the storage period set out in Paragraph 3.

5. **Additional Fees.** If Customer does not take back the Property by the end of the stated storage period,

   Storer will continue to store the Property until Customer does take back the Property or Storer

   terminates the contract, whichever occurs first. The fee for storage beyond the stated storage period

   will be $ _____ per ☐ month ☐ week ☐ day to be paid in advance by Customer.

6. **Refunds.** The unused portion of storage fees paid by Customer is not refundable, unless Storer

   terminates the storage contract.

7. **End of Storage.** Following the end of the stated storage period, Storer may end this storage contract

   by sending written notice to Customer at least _____ days in advance of the date Storer

   wishes the contract to terminate. If Customer does not pay any unpaid balance of storage fees and

   take back the Property by the termination date specified in the notice, the Property will be treated

   as abandoned. Storer will sell the Property in a commercially reasonable manner and apply the

   proceeds to the costs of sale and any unpaid storage fees. Storer will mail the balance of the proceeds

   to Customer.

8. **Storage Location.** Storer will store the Property at _____

   _____ .

9. **Value of Property.** *(Optional)*

   Customer and Storer agree that the replacement value of the Property is $ _____ .

10. **Condition of Property.** The parties agree that the Property is in good condition except for the

    following: _____

    _____

    _____ .

11. **Reasonable Care.** Storer will use reasonable care to protect the Property. Customer will bear the

    expense of any damage to or loss of the Property not caused by Storer's actions or negligence.

12. **Other Terms and Conditions.** _____

    _____

    _____

    _____

    _____

    _____ .

13. **Entire Agreement.** This is the entire agreement between the parties. It replaces and supersedes any and all oral agreements between the parties, as well as any prior writings.

14. **Successors and Assignees.** This agreement binds and benefits the heirs, successors, and assignees of the parties.

15. **Notices.** All notices must be in writing. A notice may be delivered to a party at the address that follows a party's signature or to a new address that a party designates in writing. A notice may be delivered:

    (1) in person

    (2) by certified mail, or

    (3) by overnight courier.

16. **Governing Law.** This agreement will be governed by and construed in accordance with the laws of the state of _____ .

17. **Counterparts.** This agreement may be signed by the parties in different counterparts and the signature pages combined will create a document binding on all parties.

18. **Modification.** This agreement may be modified only by a written agreement signed by all the parties.

19. **Waiver.** If one party waives any term or provision of this agreement at any time, that waiver will be effective only for the specific instance and specific purpose for which the waiver was given. If either party fails to exercise or delays exercising any of its rights or remedies under this agreement, that party retains the right to enforce that term or provision at a later time.

20. **Severability.** If any court determines that any provision of this agreement is invalid or unenforceable, any invalidity or unenforceability will affect only that provision and will not make any other provision of this agreement invalid or unenforceable and shall be modified, amended, or limited only to the extent necessary to render it valid and enforceable.

Storer

Name of business: _____

a _____

By: _____ Dated: _____

Printed name: _____

Title: _____

Address: _____

_____

Customer

Name of business: _____

a _____

By: _____ Dated: _____

Printed name: _____

Title: _____

Address: _____

_____

Consignment Contract

1. **Names.** _____ , Customer,
   and _____ , Consignee,
   agree to the following consignment.

2. **Property Consigned.** Customer ☐ has delivered ☐ will deliver the following goods to Consignee
   on consignment (the Goods):

   Description of Goods   Sale Price

   _____   _____

   _____   _____

   _____   _____

   _____   _____

   _____   _____

   _____   _____

   _____   _____

3. **Efforts to Sell.** Consignee will display the Goods and attempt to sell them at or above the sale prices
   listed in Paragraph 2. Consignee will obtain the written consent of Customer before selling the
   Goods at prices lower than those listed in Paragraph 2.

4. **Proceeds of Sale.** Following a sale, Consignee will retain from the sale proceeds a commission of
   _____% of the sale price. In computing the commission, sales tax will not be added to the sale
   price. Consignee will send the balance of the sale proceeds to Customer within five days of the sale.

5. **Ownership Before Sale.** Customer will retain ownership of the Goods until they are sold.

6. **Risk of Loss.** While the Goods are in Consignee's possession, Consignee will bear the risk of damage
   to or loss of the Goods. If the Goods are damaged or lost, Consignee will pay Customer the selling
   price listed above less the stated commission.

7. **Termination of Consignment.** Customer or Consignee may terminate this contract at any time. If
   either party terminates the agreement, Consignee will return the Goods to Customer as soon as
   practicable at

   ☐ Customer's place of business at _____ .
   ☐ Consignee's place of business at _____ .
   ☐ Other: _____
   _____ .

8. **Other Terms and Conditions.** _____
   _____
   _____
   _____
   _____
   _____
   _____
   _____ .

9. **Entire Agreement.** This is the entire agreement between the parties. It replaces and supersedes any and all oral agreements between the parties, as well as any prior writings.

10. **Successors and Assignees.** This agreement binds and benefits the heirs, successors, and assignees of the parties.

11. **Notices.** All notices must be in writing. A notice may be delivered to a party at the address that follows a party's signature or to a new address that a party designates in writing. A notice may be delivered:

    (1) in person

    (2) by certified mail, or

    (3) by overnight courier.

12. **Governing Law.** This agreement will be governed by and construed in accordance with the laws of the state of _____ .

13. **Counterparts.** This agreement may be signed by the parties in different counterparts and the signature pages combined will create a document binding on all parties.

14. **Modification.** This agreement may be modified only by a written agreement signed by all the parties.

15. **Waiver.** If one party waives any term or provision of this agreement at any time, that waiver will be effective only for the specific instance and specific purpose for which the waiver was given. If either party fails to exercise or delays exercising any of its rights or remedies under this agreement, that party retains the right to enforce that term or provision at a later time.

16. **Severability.** If any court determines that any provision of this agreement is invalid or unenforceable, any invalidity or unenforceability will affect only that provision and will not make any other provision of this agreement invalid or unenforceable and shall be modified, amended, or limited only to the extent necessary to render it valid and enforceable.

Customer

Name of business: _____

a _____

By: _____ Dated: _____

Printed name: _____

Title: _____

Address: _____

_____

Consignee

Name of business: _____

a _____

By: _____ Dated: _____

Printed name: _____

Title: _____

Address: _____

_____

Employment Application

Position _____

Full name: _____

Address: _____

_____

Telephone number: _____ Social Security number: _____

Are you legally entitled to work in the United States? ☐ Yes ☐ No

Are you 18 years old or older? ☐ Yes ☐ No

If not, please give your date of birth: _____

Education

High School

Name of school: _____

Location: _____

Number of years attended: _____   Did you graduate? ☐ Yes ☐ No

Date of graduation: _____

Trade School

Name of school: _____

Location: _____

Number of years attended: _____   Did you graduate? ☐ Yes ☐ No

Date of graduation: _____

College

Name of school: _____

Location: _____

Number of years attended: _____   Did you graduate? ☐ Yes ☐ No

Date of graduation: _____   What degree did you earn? _____

Graduate

Name of school: _____

Location: _____

Number of years attended: _____   Did you graduate? ☐ Yes ☐ No

Date of graduation: _____   What degree did you earn? _____

Employment History

Beginning with your most recent employment and working back in time, please give the following information:

Employer: _____

Address: _____

_____

Job title: _____

Duties: _____

_____

_____

_____

Dates of employment: _____ Salary: _____

Supervisor: _____

Telephone number: _____ Email address: _____

Reason for leaving, if not still employed: _____

_____

_____

_____

If still employed, can we contact this employer?   ☐ Yes   ☐ No

Employer: _____

Address: _____

_____

Job title: _____

Duties: _____

_____

_____

Dates of employment: _____ Salary: _____

Supervisor: _____

Telephone number: _____ Email address: _____

Reason for leaving, if not still employed: _____

_____

_____

If still employed, can we contact this employer?   ☐ Yes   ☐ No

Employer: _____

Address: _____

_____

Job title: _____

Duties: _____

_____

_____

Dates of employment: _____   Salary: _____

Supervisor: _____

Telephone number: _____   Email address: _____

Reason for leaving, if not still employed: _____

_____

_____

_____

If still employed, can we contact this employer?   ☐ Yes   ☐ No

Personal References

Please provide the names of two references who have not employed you and are not related to you.

Reference Name: _____   Relationship: _____

Address: _____

_____

Telephone number: _____   Email Address: _____

Reference Name: _____   Relationship: _____

Address: _____

_____

Telephone number: _____   Email Address: _____

Additional Qualifications

Please describe any other training, education, skills, or achievements that you feel should be considered.

_____

_____

_____

_____

_____

_____

_____

_____

☐ Attached to this application is a complete job description. Please review it carefully.

I understand that if I am hired, my employment will be at will. My employment may be terminated—or I may resign—at any time, with or without cause.

I have carefully reviewed this application form, and I verify that all the information that I have provided is accurate and complete. I understand that if I am hired, any false or incomplete statements on this application may result in termination of my employment.

Date application completed: _____

Applicant's signature: _____

Authorization to Release Information

I, the undersigned, hereby authorize _____ , my Prospective

Employer, to obtain information about me from my previous employers and schools.

    I authorize my previous employers and schools that I have attended to disclose such information

about me as Prospective Employer may request.

    I further authorize my previous employers to candidly disclose to Prospective Employer all facts and

opinions concerning my work performance, cooperativeness, and ability to get along well with others.

Date: _____

Signature: _____

Printed name: _____

Address: _____

_____

Offer Letter

Date: _____

Full name: _____

Address: _____

_____

Dear _____ :

I am pleased to offer you a position of _____

at _____ .

The purpose of this letter is to set forth the terms of your employment.

Your first day of work will be _____ . Your compensation will be

$ _____ per _____ .

We look forward to working with you, and sincerely hope you are happy as an employee at

_____ . However, we cannot make any

guarantees about your continued employment here. _____

is an at-will employer. While we hope things work out, you are free to quit at any time, for any reason, just

as _____ is free to terminate your

employment at any time, for any reason. This policy can be changed only by a written contract signed by

_____ .

Please sign and return the enclosed copy of this letter, acknowledging your acceptance of employment

with _____ under the

terms set forth here. Welcome aboard!

Sincerely,

Signature: _____

Printed name: _____

Title: _____

Company: _____

Acceptance of Offer of Employment

I accept your offer of employment dated _____ . I understand that my

employment with your company is at will. No representations regarding the terms and conditions of my

employment have been made to me other than those recited in this letter.

Signature: _____

Printed name: _____

Date: _____

Confidentiality Agreement

This Confidentiality Agreement is between _____
(Employer), and _____ (Employee).

In consideration of _____ , Employee agrees as follows:

1. **Agreement Not to Disclose Confidential Information.** I acknowledge that Employer may disclose to me or give me access to confidential information so that I may perform my employment duties. I agree that the confidential information includes Employer's trade secrets, sales and profit figures, customer lists, relationships with contractors, customers, or suppliers, and opportunities for new or developing business. The confidential information may be contained in written materials, such as computer hardware and software, documents, files, drawings, and product specifications. It may also consist of unwritten knowledge, including ideas, research, processes, practices, or know-how. While I am employed by Employer, and afterward, I will not use or disclose to any other person or entity any confidential information or materials (either written or unwritten) except when I am required to do so to properly perform my duties to Employer or as required by law.

    Information in the public domain, information generally known in the trade, and information that I acquire completely independently of my services for Employer is not considered to be confidential.

2. **Return of Confidential Information.** While I am employed by Employer and afterward, I will not, except in performing my duties, remove or copy any confidential information or materials or assist anyone in doing so without Employer's written permission. Upon my termination by Employer, or at any time that Employer requests it, I will immediately return all confidential information and materials to Employer.

3. **Right to an Injunction.** I acknowledge that in addition to receiving or having access to confidential information as part of my employment, I will be in a position of confidence and trust with employees, clients, and customers of Employer. I acknowledge and agree that if I breach or threaten to breach any of the terms of this agreement, Employer will sustain irreparable harm and will be entitled to obtain an injunction to stop any breach or threatened breach of this agreement.

4. **Reasonableness.** I acknowledge that the restrictions in this agreement are reasonable and necessary to protect Employer and its confidential information.

5. **Survivability.** This agreement will survive the termination, for any reason, of my employment with Employer.

6. **Entire Agreement.** This is the entire agreement between the parties. It replaces any and all oral agreements between the parties, as well as any prior writings.

7. **Successors and Assignees.** This agreement binds and benefits the heirs, successors, and assignees of the parties.

8. **Notices.** All notices must be in writing. A notice may be delivered to a party at the address below or to a new address that a party designates in writing. A notice may be delivered:

    (1) in person

    (2) by certified mail, or

    (3) by overnight courier.

Employer address: _____

_____

Employee address: _____

_____

9. **Governing Law.** This agreement will be governed by and construed in accordance with the laws of the state of _____ .

10. **Modification.** This agreement may be modified only by a written agreement signed by all the parties.

11. **Waiver.** If one party waives any term or provision of this agreement at any time, that waiver will be effective only for the specific instance and specific purpose for which the waiver was given. If either party fails to exercise or delays exercising any of its rights or remedies under this agreement, that party retains the right to enforce that term or provision at a later time.

12. **Severability.** If any court determines that any provision of this lease is invalid or unenforceable, any invalidity or unenforceability will affect only that provision and will not make any other provision of this lease invalid or unenforceable and shall be modified, amended, or limited only to the extent necessary to render it valid and enforceable.

Date: _____

Signed: _____

Printed name: _____

Covenant Not to Compete

This agreement is between _____
(Employer), and _____ (Employee).
In consideration of _____ , Employee agrees as follows:

1. **Agreement Not to Compete.** While I, the Employee, am employed by Employer, and for _____
   ☐ years   ☐ months   afterward, I will not directly or indirectly participate in a business that
   is similar to a business now or later operated by Employer in the same geographical area. This
   includes participating in my own business or as a co-owner, director, officer, consultant, independent
   contractor, employee, or agent of another business.

   In particular, I will not:

   (a) solicit or attempt to solicit any business or trade from Employer's actual or prospective
       customers or clients

   (b) employ or attempt to employ any employee of Employer

   (c) divert or attempt to divert business away from Employer, or

   (d) encourage any independent contractor or consultant to end a relationship with Employer.

2. **Right to an Injunction.** I acknowledge and agree that if I breach or threaten to breach any of the
   terms of this agreement, Employer will sustain irreparable harm and will be entitled to obtain an
   injunction to stop any breach or threatened breach of this agreement.

3. **Reasonableness.** I acknowledge that the restrictions in this agreement are reasonable and necessary
   for the protection of Employer.

4. **Survivability.** This agreement will survive the termination, for any reason, of my employment with
   Employer.

5. **Entire Agreement.** This is the entire agreement between the parties. It replaces and supersedes any
   and all oral agreements between the parties, as well as any prior writings.

6. **Successors and Assignees.** This agreement binds and benefits the heirs, successors, and assignees of
   the parties.

7. **Notices.** All notices must be in writing. A notice may be delivered to a party at the address below or
   to a new address that a party designates in writing. A notice may be delivered:

   (1) in person

   (2) by certified mail, or

   (3) by overnight courier.

   Employer address: _____

   _____

   Employee address: _____

   _____

8. **Governing Law.** This agreement will be governed by and construed in accordance with the laws of
   the state of _____ .

9. **Modification.** This agreement may be modified only by a written agreement signed by Employer and
   Employee.

10. **Waiver.** If one party waives any term or provision of this agreement at any time, that waiver will be effective only for the specific instance and specific purpose for which the waiver was given. If either party fails to exercise or delays exercising any of its rights or remedies under this agreement, that party retains the right to enforce that term or provision at a later time.

11. **Severability.** If any court determines that any provision of this lease is invalid or unenforceable, any invalidity or unenforceability will affect only that provision and will not make any other provision of this lease invalid or unenforceable and shall be modified, amended, or limited only to the extent necessary to render it valid and enforceable.

Date: _____

Signed:_____

Printed name: _____

Contract With Independent Contractor

1. **Names.** This agreement is between _____ ,
   Client, and _____ , Contractor.

2. **Services to Be Performed.** Contractor agrees to perform the following services for Client: _____
   _____
   _____ .

3. **Time for Performance.**

   ☐ Contractor will complete the performance of these services on or before _____ .

   ☐ Contractor will perform the services according to the following schedule: _____
   _____ .

4. **Payment.** Client will pay Contractor as follows: _____
   _____ .

5. **State and Federal Taxes.** Client will not:

   (a) withhold Social Security and Medicare taxes from Contractor's payments or make such tax payments on Contractor's behalf, or

   (b) withhold state or federal income tax from Contractor's payments or make state or federal unemployment contributions on Contractor's behalf.

   Contractor will pay all applicable taxes related to the performance of services under this contract. This includes income, Social Security, Medicare, and self-employment taxes. Contractor will also pay any unemployment contributions related to the performance of services under this contract.

6. **Fringe Benefits.** Neither Contractor nor Contractor's employees are eligible to participate in any employee pension, health, vacation pay, sick pay, or other fringe benefit plan of Client.

7. **Invoices.** Contractor will submit invoices to Client for all services performed.

8. **Independent Contractor Status.** The parties intend Contractor to be an independent contractor in the performance of the services. Contractor will have the right to control and determine the methods and means of performing the contractual services.

9. **Other Clients.** Contractor retains the right to perform services for other clients.

10. **Assistants.** Contractor, at Contractor's expense, may employ assistants as Contractor deems appropriate to perform the contractual services. Contractor will be responsible for paying these assistants as well as any expense attributable to them, including income, Social Security, and Medicare taxes, and unemployment contributions. Contractor will maintain workers' compensation insurance for all of its employees.

11. **Equipment and Supplies.**

    A. Contractor, at Contractor's expense, will provide all equipment, tools, and supplies necessary to perform the contractual services, except for the following, which will be provided by Client:
    _____
    _____
    _____ .

B. Contractor will be responsible for all expenses required for the performance of the contractual services, except for the following, which will be paid for by Client: _____

_____

_____.

12. **Disputes.**

☐ **Litigation.** If a dispute arises, either party may take the matter to court.

☐ **Mediation and Possible Litigation.** If a dispute arises, the parties will try in good faith to settle it through mediation conducted by:

☐ _____.

☐ a mediator to be mutually selected.

The parties will share the costs of the mediator equally. Each party will cooperate fully and fairly with the mediator and will attempt to reach a mutually satisfactory compromise to the dispute. If the dispute is not resolved within 30 days after it is referred to the mediator, either party may take the matter to court.

☐ **Mediation and Possible Arbitration.** If a dispute arises, the parties will try in good faith to settle it through mediation conducted by:

☐ _____.

☐ a mediator to be mutually selected.

The parties will share the costs of the mediator equally. Each party will cooperate fully and fairly with the mediator and will attempt to reach a mutually satisfactory compromise to the dispute. If the dispute is not resolved within 30 days after it is referred to the mediator, it will be arbitrated by:

☐ _____.

☐ an arbitrator to be mutually selected.

Judgment on the arbitration award may be entered in any court that has jurisdiction over the matter. Costs of arbitration, including lawyers' fees, will be allocated by the arbitrator.

☐ **Attorneys' Fees.** If either party brings a legal action arising out of a dispute over this agreement, the losing party will reimburse the prevailing party for all reasonable costs and attorneys' fees incurred by the prevailing party in the lawsuit.

13. **Entire Agreement.** This is the entire agreement between the parties. It replaces and supersedes any and all oral agreements between the parties, as well as any prior writings.

14. **Successors and Assignees.** This agreement binds and benefits the heirs, successors, and assignees of the parties.

15. **Notices.** All notices must be in writing. A notice may be delivered to a party at the address that follows a party's signature or to a new address that a party designates in writing. A notice may be delivered:

(1) in person

(2) by certified mail, or

(3) by overnight courier.

16. **Governing Law.** This agreement will be governed by and construed in accordance with the laws of the state of _____.

17. **Counterparts.** This agreement may be signed by the parties in different counterparts and the signature pages combined will create a document binding on all parties.

18. **Modification.** This agreement may be modified only by a written agreement signed by all the parties.

19. **Waiver.** If one party waives any term or provision of this agreement at any time, that waiver will be effective only for the specific instance and specific purpose for which the waiver was given. If either party fails to exercise or delays exercising any of its rights or remedies under this agreement, that party retains the right to enforce that term or provision at a later time.

20. **Severability.** If any court determines that any provision of this agreement is invalid or unenforceable, any invalidity or unenforceability will affect only that provision and will not make any other provision of this agreement invalid or unenforceable and such provision shall be modified, amended, or limited only to the extent necessary to render it valid and enforceable.

Client

Name of business: _____

a_____

By: _____ Dated: _____

Printed name: _____

Title: _____

Address: _____

_____

Contractor

Name of business: _____

a_____

By: _____ Dated: _____

Printed name: _____

Title: _____

Address: _____

_____

Credit Application for an Individual Customer

I am applying for credit with _____ .

I agree to abide by the terms and conditions stated below.

Name _____

Address _____

Phone _____ Fax _____

Email _____

Social Security number (needed for credit reports) _____

Employer

Name _____

Address _____

_____

Contact person _____

Your position _____

How long employed with this employer _____

Credit References

Reference #1

Name _____

Address _____

_____

_____ Phone _____

Reference #2

Name _____

Address _____

_____ Phone _____

Reference #3

Name _____

Address _____

_____ Phone _____

Bank References

Bank #1

Name of bank _____

Address _____

_____

Account number _____

Contact person _____ Phone _____

Bank #2

Name of bank _____

Address _____

Account number _____

Contact person _____ Phone _____

    I represent that the above information is true and is given to induce your business to extend credit to me. I authorize your business to make such credit investigation as you see fit, including contacting the above employer, credit references, and banks and obtaining credit reports. I authorize my employer and all credit references, banks, and credit reporting agencies to disclose to your business any and all information concerning my financial and credit history.

    I have read the terms and conditions stated below. I agree to those terms and conditions.

Date: _____

Signature: _____

Printed name: _____

Terms and Conditions

1. Bills are sent on the first day of each month.

2. All bills become payable in full on the 11th day of the month and, if not paid by the end of the month, are considered past due.

3. A service charge of 2% per month will be added to all amounts billed if not paid by the end of the month.

4. No additional credit will be extended to past-due accounts unless satisfactory arrangements are made with our business.

5. If collection action is required for an overdue payment, customer is responsible for costs of the action.

[Date] _____

[Applicant's name] _____
[Applicant's street address] _____
[Applicant's city/state/zip] _____

Dear _*[applicant's name]*_ _____ ,

Thank you for your credit application. Unfortunately, after reviewing your application, we have decided not to extend credit to you at this time. We will, of course, be happy to accept cash, a check, or a credit or debit card in payment for any goods or services you wish to purchase from us.

We did not approve your application for the following reason(s):

☐ Your income

    ☐ is below our minimum requirement.

    ☐ is insufficient to sustain payments on the amount of credit requested.

    ☐ could not be verified.

☐ Your employment

    ☐ is not of sufficient length to qualify.

    ☐ could not be verified.

☐ Your credit history

    ☐ of making payments on time was not satisfactory.

    ☐ could not be verified.

☐ Your application

    ☐ lacks a sufficient number of credit references.

    ☐ lacks acceptable types of credit references.

☐ Other _____
_____ .

Sources of Information

☐ Consumer Reporting Agency. We obtained information from a consumer reporting agency as part of our consideration of your application. That information influenced our decision in whole or in part. The reporting agency played no part in our decision and is unable to provide specific reasons why we have denied credit to you. You have a right under the Fair Credit Reporting Act to know the information contained in your credit file at the credit reporting agency. You also have a right to a free copy of your report from the reporting agency if you request it no later than 60 days after you receive this letter. In addition, if you find that any information in the report you receive is inaccurate or incomplete, you have the right to dispute the matter with the reporting agency. The name, address, and phone number of the reporting agency are as follows: _____
_____ .

Any questions regarding such information should be directed to the credit reporting agency.

☐ Credit Scoring Company. We also obtained your credit score from this consumer reporting agency and used it in making our credit decision. Your credit score is a number that reflects the information in your consumer report. Your credit score can change, depending on how the information in your consumer report changes.

Your credit score: _____

Date: _____

Scores range from a low of _____ to a high of _____ .

Key factors that adversely affected your credit score: _____

_____

_____

_____

_____ .

    If you have any questions regarding your credit score, you should contact the consumer reporting agency that provided the credit score at:

Name of agency providing credit score: _____

Address: _____

_____

Telephone number: _____

☐ Other Information. Our credit decision was based in whole or in part on information obtained from an affiliate or an outside source other than a credit reporting agency, such as your employer or a credit reference named in your application. Under the Fair Credit Reporting Act, you have the right to make a written request, no later than 60 days after you receive this letter, for disclosure of the nature of this information.

Notice

The federal Equal Credit Opportunity Act prohibits creditors from discriminating against credit applicants on the basis of race, color, religion, national origin, sex, marital status, age (provided the applicant has the capacity to enter into a binding contract); because all or part of the applicant's income derives from any public assistance program; or because the applicant has in good faith exercised any right under the Consumer Credit Protection Act. The federal agency that administers compliance with this law concerning this creditor is the Federal Trade Commission at Federal Trade Commission, Equal Credit Opportunity, Washington, DC 20580.

    If you have any questions regarding this letter, please contact me at the address or phone number shown at the beginning of letter.

Sincerely,

[Your signature]

[Your printed name]

[Your title]

Credit Application for a Business Customer

My company, _____ ,

is applying for credit with your business, _____ .

My company and I agree to abide by the terms and conditions stated below.

Company name _____

Business name (if different) _____

Federal Tax ID or Social Security No. _____

Contact person _____

Address _____

Phone _____ Fax _____

Email _____

Type of business _____

Date business established _____ No. of employees _____

Types of products or services to be purchased _____

Amount of credit requested: $_____

Type of Company

☐ **Corporation**

State of incorporation _____

Names, titles, and addresses of the three chief corporate officers

_____

_____

_____

_____

_____

_____

_____

_____

Name and address of the resident agent

_____

_____

☐ **Limited Liability Company (LLC)**

State where formed _____

Names, titles, and addresses of the three chief managers or members

_____

_____

_____

_____

_____

_____

_____

_____

Name and address of the resident agent

_____

_____

☐ **Partnership**

Names and addresses of the partners

_____

_____

_____

_____

_____

_____

_____

_____

_____

_____

_____

_____

☐ **Sole Proprietorship**

Are you sales-tax exempt? ☐ Yes   ☐ No

Have you ever had credit with us before? ☐ Yes   ☐ No

If yes, under what name? _____

Authorized purchasers _____

_____

Purchase order required? ☐ Yes   ☐ No

Trade References

Reference #1

Name _____

Address _____

_____Phone _____

Reference #2

Name _____

Address _____

_____Phone _____

Reference #3

Name _____

Address _____

_____Phone _____

Bank References

Bank #1

Name of bank _____

Address _____

_____

Account number _____

Contact person _____ Phone _____

Bank #2

Name of bank _____

Address _____

_____

Account number _____

Contact person _____ Phone _____

I represent that the above information is true and is given to induce your business to extend credit to my company. My company and I authorize your business to make such credit investigation as you see fit, including contacting the above trade references and banks and obtaining credit reports. My company and I authorize all trade references, banks, and credit reporting agencies to disclose to your business any and all information concerning the financial and credit history of my company.

I have read the terms and conditions stated below. My company and I agree to those terms and conditions.

Authorized signature: _____

Printed name: _____

Title: _____

Date: _____

Personal Guarantee of Corporate or LLC Officer

In consideration of your business extending credit to _____

_____ , I personally guarantee payment for all items and services purchased on credit by that corporation or LLC.

Signature: _____

Printed name: _____

Date: _____

General Terms and Conditions

1. Bills are sent on the first day of each month.

2. All bills become payable in full on the 11th day of the month and, if not paid by the end of the month, are considered past due.

3. A service charge of 2% per month will be added to all amounts billed if not paid by the end of the month.

4. No additional credit will be extended to past-due accounts.

5. If collection action is required for an overdue payment, customer is responsible for costs of the action.

[Date] _____

[Customer's or client's name] _____

[Customer's or client's street address] _____

[Customer's or client's city/state/zip] _____

Dear _[Customer's or client's name]_____ ,

Our records show that you have an outstanding balance with our company of $_____ . This is

for _____

_____ .

    Is there a problem with this bill? If so, please call me so that we can resolve the matter. Otherwise, please send your payment at this time to bring your account current.

    Until you bring your account current, it's our policy to put further purchases on a cash basis. To facilitate your payment, I am enclosing a self-addressed envelope.

Sincerely,

Signature: _____

Printed name: _____

Title: _____

P.S. Paying your bill at this time will help you to maintain your good credit rating.

[*Date*] _____

_[*Customer's or client's name*] _____

_[*Customer's or client's street address*] _____

_[*Customer's or client's city/state/zip*] _____

Dear __[*Customer's or client's name*] _____ ,

Your bill for $_____ is seriously overdue. You have not paid us yet for the _____

_____ we supplied to you in

_____ . More than 60 days have gone by since we sent you our invoice.

You did not respond to the letter I sent you last month.

   We value your patronage, but must insist that you bring your account up to date. Doing so will help

you protect your reputation for prompt payment.

   Please send your check today for the full balance. If this is not feasible, please call me to discuss a

possible payment plan. I need to hear from you as soon as possible. To facilitate your payment, I am

enclosing a self-addressed envelope.

Sincerely,

Signature: _____

Printed name: _____

Title: _____

[Date] _____

[Customer's or client's name] _____

[Customer's or client's street address] _____

[Customer's or client's city/state/zip] _____

Dear ___ *[Customer's or client's name]* _____ ,

We show an unpaid balance of $ _____ on your account that is over 90 days old.

This is for the _____

_____ we supplied you in _____ .

 I have repeatedly tried to contact you, but my calls and letters have gone unheeded.

 You must send full payment by _____ or contact me by that date to discuss your intentions. If I do not hear from you, I plan to turn over the account for collection.

 As you know, collection action can only have an adverse effect on your credit rating, and, according to our credit agreement, you will be responsible for collection costs. I hope to hear from you immediately so that the matter can be resolved without taking that step. To facilitate your payment, I am enclosing a self-addressed envelope.

Sincerely,

Signature: _____

Printed name: _____

Title: _____

Form **SS-4** (Rev. December 2017) Department of the Treasury Internal Revenue Service	**Application for Employer Identification Number** (For use by employers, corporations, partnerships, trusts, estates, churches, government agencies, Indian tribal entities, certain individuals, and others.) ▶ Go to *www.irs.gov/FormSS4* for instructions and the latest information. ▶ See separate instructions for each line. ▶ Keep a copy for your records.	OMB No. 1545-0003 EIN

Type or print clearly.

1	Legal name of entity (or individual) for whom the EIN is being requested	
2	Trade name of business (if different from name on line 1)	**3** Executor, administrator, trustee, "care of" name
4a	Mailing address (room, apt., suite no. and street, or P.O. box)	**5a** Street address (if different) (Do not enter a P.O. box.)
4b	City, state, and ZIP code (if foreign, see instructions)	**5b** City, state, and ZIP code (if foreign, see instructions)
6	County and state where principal business is located	
7a	Name of responsible party	**7b** SSN, ITIN, or EIN

8a	Is this application for a limited liability company (LLC) (or a foreign equivalent)? . . . . ☐ Yes ☐ No	**8b** If 8a is "Yes," enter the number of LLC members . . . . ▶

8c	If 8a is "Yes," was the LLC organized in the United States? . . . . ☐ Yes ☐ No

9a Type of entity (check only one box). **Caution.** If 8a is "Yes," see the instructions for the correct box to check.

☐ Sole proprietor (SSN) _____
☐ Partnership
☐ Corporation (enter form number to be filed) ▶ _____
☐ Personal service corporation
☐ Church or church-controlled organization
☐ Other nonprofit organization (specify) ▶ _____
☐ Other (specify) ▶ _____

☐ Estate (SSN of decedent) _____
☐ Plan administrator (TIN) _____
☐ Trust (TIN of grantor) _____
☐ Military/National Guard ☐ State/local government
☐ Farmers' cooperative ☐ Federal government
☐ REMIC ☐ Indian tribal governments/enterprises
Group Exemption Number (GEN) if any ▶

9b	If a corporation, name the state or foreign country (if applicable) where incorporated	State	Foreign country

10 **Reason for applying** (check only one box)

☐ Started new business (specify type) ▶ _____
☐ Hired employees (Check the box and see line 13.)
☐ Compliance with IRS withholding regulations
☐ Other (specify) ▶

☐ Banking purpose (specify purpose) ▶ _____
☐ Changed type of organization (specify new type) ▶ _____
☐ Purchased going business
☐ Created a trust (specify type) ▶ _____
☐ Created a pension plan (specify type) ▶ _____

11	Date business started or acquired (month, day, year). See instructions.	**12** Closing month of accounting year
13	Highest number of employees expected in the next 12 months (enter -0- if none). If no employees expected, skip line 14.	**14** If you expect your employment tax liability to be $1,000 or less in a full calendar year **and** want to file Form 944 annually instead of Forms 941 quarterly, check here. (Your employment tax liability generally will be $1,000 or less if you expect to pay $4,000 or less in total wages.) If you do not check this box, you must file Form 941 for every quarter. ☐

Agricultural	Household	Other

15	First date wages or annuities were paid (month, day, year). **Note**: If applicant is a withholding agent, enter date income will first be paid to nonresident alien (month, day, year) . . . . ▶

16 Check **one** box that best describes the principal activity of your business.

☐ Construction ☐ Rental & leasing ☐ Transportation & warehousing
☐ Real estate ☐ Manufacturing ☐ Finance & insurance
☐ Health care & social assistance ☐ Wholesale-agent/broker
☐ Accommodation & food service ☐ Wholesale-other ☐ Retail
☐ Other (specify) ▶

17	Indicate principal line of merchandise sold, specific construction work done, products produced, or services provided.

18	Has the applicant entity shown on line 1 ever applied for and received an EIN? ☐ Yes ☐ No If "Yes," write previous EIN here ▶

Complete this section **only** if you want to authorize the named individual to receive the entity's EIN and answer questions about the completion of this form.

Third Party Designee	Designee's name	Designee's telephone number (include area code)
	Address and ZIP code	Designee's fax number (include area code)

Under penalties of perjury, I declare that I have examined this application, and to the best of my knowledge and belief, it is true, correct, and complete.

Name and title (type or print clearly) ▶

Signature ▶   Date ▶

Applicant's telephone number (include area code)
Applicant's fax number (include area code)

For Privacy Act and Paperwork Reduction Act Notice, see separate instructions.   Cat. No. 16055N   Form **SS-4** (Rev. 12-2017)

Do I Need an EIN?

File Form SS-4 if the applicant entity does not already have an EIN but is required to show an EIN on any return, statement, or other document.[1] See also the separate instructions for each line on Form SS-4.

IF the applicant...	AND...	THEN...
Started a new business	Does not currently have (nor expect to have) employees	Complete lines 1, 2, 4a–8a, 8b–c (if applicable), 9a, 9b (if applicable), and 10–14 and 16–18.
Hired (or will hire) employees, including household employees	Does not already have an EIN	Complete lines 1, 2, 4a–6, 7a–b (if applicable), 8a, 8b–c (if applicable), 9a, 9b (if applicable), 10–18.
Opened a bank account	Needs an EIN for banking purposes only	Complete lines 1–5b, 7a–b (if applicable), 8a, 8b–c (if applicable), 9a, 9b (if applicable), 10, and 18.
Changed type of organization	Either the legal character of the organization or its ownership changed (for example, you incorporate a sole proprietorship or form a partnership)[2]	Complete lines 1–18 (as applicable).
Purchased a going business[3]	Does not already have an EIN	Complete lines 1–18 (as applicable).
Created a trust	The trust is other than a grantor trust or an IRA trust[4]	Complete lines 1–18 (as applicable).
Created a pension plan as a plan administrator[5]	Needs an EIN for reporting purposes	Complete lines 1, 3, 4a–5b, 9a, 10, and 18.
Is a foreign person needing an EIN to comply with IRS withholding regulations	Needs an EIN to complete a Form W-8 (other than Form W-8ECI), avoid withholding on portfolio assets, or claim tax treaty benefits[6]	Complete lines 1–5b, 7a–b (SSN or ITIN optional), 8a, 8b–c (if applicable), 9a, 9b (if applicable), 10, and 18.
Is administering an estate	Needs an EIN to report estate income on Form 1041	Complete lines 1–6, 9a, 10–12, 13–17 (if applicable), and 18.
Is a withholding agent for taxes on non-wage income paid to an alien (i.e., individual, corporation, or partnership, etc.)	Is an agent, broker, fiduciary, manager, tenant, or spouse who is required to file Form 1042, Annual Withholding Tax Return for U.S. Source Income of Foreign Persons	Complete lines 1, 2, 3 (if applicable), 4a–5b, 7a–b (if applicable), 8a, 8b–c (if applicable), 9a, 9b (if applicable), 10, and 18.
Is a state or local agency	Serves as a tax reporting agent for public assistance recipients under Rev. Proc. 80-4, 1980-1 C.B. 581[7]	Complete lines 1, 2, 4a–5b, 9a, 10, and 18.
Is a single-member LLC (or similar single-member entity)	Needs an EIN to file Form 8832, Classification Election, for filing employment tax returns and excise tax returns, or for state reporting purposes[8], or is a foreign-owned U.S. disregarded entity and needs an EIN to file Form 5472, Information Return of a 25% Foreign-Owned U.S. Corporation or a Foreign Corporation Engaged in a U.S. Trade or Business (Under Sections 6038A and 6038C of the Internal Revenue Code)	Complete lines 1–18 (as applicable).
Is an S corporation	Needs an EIN to file Form 2553, Election by a Small Business Corporation[9]	Complete lines 1–18 (as applicable).

[1] For example, a sole proprietorship or self-employed farmer who establishes a qualified retirement plan, or is required to file excise, employment, alcohol, tobacco, or firearms returns, must have an EIN. A partnership, corporation, REMIC (real estate mortgage investment conduit), nonprofit organization (church, club, etc.), or farmers' cooperative must use an EIN for any tax-related purpose even if the entity does not have employees.

[2] However, do not apply for a new EIN if the existing entity only (a) changed its business name, (b) elected on Form 8832 to change the way it is taxed (or is covered by the default rules), or (c) terminated its partnership status because at least 50% of the total interests in partnership capital and profits were sold or exchanged within a 12-month period. The EIN of the terminated partnership should continue to be used. See Regulations section 301.6109-1(d)(2)(iii).

[3] Do not use the EIN of the prior business unless you became the "owner" of a corporation by acquiring its stock.

[4] However, grantor trusts that do not file using Optional Method 1 and IRA trusts that are required to file Form 990-T, Exempt Organization Business Income Tax Return, must have an EIN. For more information on grantor trusts, see the Instructions for Form 1041.

[5] A plan administrator is the person or group of persons specified as the administrator by the instrument under which the plan is operated.

[6] Entities applying to be a Qualified Intermediary (QI) need a QI-EIN even if they already have an EIN. See Rev. Proc. 2000-12.

[7] See also *Household employer* on page 4 of the instructions. **Note**: State or local agencies may need an EIN for other reasons, for example, hired employees.

[8] See *Disregarded entities* on page 4 of the instructions for details on completing Form SS-4 for an LLC.

[9] An existing corporation that is electing or revoking S corporation status should use its previously-assigned EIN.

Form W-4 (2019)

Future developments. For the latest information about any future developments related to Form W-4, such as legislation enacted after it was published, go to *www.irs.gov/FormW4*.

Purpose. Complete Form W-4 so that your employer can withhold the correct federal income tax from your pay. Consider completing a new Form W-4 each year and when your personal or financial situation changes.

Exemption from withholding. You may claim exemption from withholding for 2019 if **both** of the following apply.

• For 2018 you had a right to a refund of **all** federal income tax withheld because you had **no** tax liability, **and**

• For 2019 you expect a refund of **all** federal income tax withheld because you expect to have **no** tax liability.

If you're exempt, complete **only** lines 1, 2, 3, 4, and 7 and sign the form to validate it. Your exemption for 2019 expires February 17, 2020. See Pub. 505, Tax Withholding and Estimated Tax, to learn more about whether you qualify for exemption from withholding.

General Instructions

If you aren't exempt, follow the rest of these instructions to determine the number of withholding allowances you should claim for withholding for 2019 and any additional amount of tax to have withheld. For regular wages, withholding must be based on allowances you claimed and may not be a flat amount or percentage of wages.

You can also use the calculator at *www.irs.gov/W4App* to determine your tax withholding more accurately. Consider using this calculator if you have a more complicated tax situation, such as if you have a working spouse, more than one job, or a large amount of nonwage income not subject to withholding outside of your job. After your Form W-4 takes effect, you can also use this calculator to see how the amount of tax you're having withheld compares to your projected total tax for 2019. If you use the calculator, you don't need to complete any of the worksheets for Form W-4.

Note that if you have too much tax withheld, you will receive a refund when you file your tax return. If you have too little tax withheld, you will owe tax when you file your tax return, and you might owe a penalty.

Filers with multiple jobs or working spouses. If you have more than one job at a time, or if you're married filing jointly and your spouse is also working, read all of the instructions including the instructions for the Two-Earners/Multiple Jobs Worksheet before beginning.

Nonwage income. If you have a large amount of nonwage income not subject to withholding, such as interest or dividends, consider making estimated tax payments using Form 1040-ES, Estimated Tax for Individuals. Otherwise, you might owe additional tax. Or, you can use the Deductions, Adjustments, and Additional Income Worksheet on page 3 or the calculator at *www.irs.gov/W4App* to make sure you have enough tax withheld from your paycheck. If you have pension or annuity income, see Pub. 505 or use the calculator at *www.irs.gov/W4App* to find out if you should adjust your withholding on Form W-4 or W-4P.

Nonresident alien. If you're a nonresident alien, see Notice 1392, Supplemental Form W-4 Instructions for Nonresident Aliens, before completing this form.

Specific Instructions
Personal Allowances Worksheet

Complete this worksheet on page 3 first to determine the number of withholding allowances to claim.

Line C. *Head of household please note:* Generally, you may claim head of household filing status on your tax return only if you're unmarried and pay more than 50% of the costs of keeping up a home for yourself and a qualifying individual. See Pub. 501 for more information about filing status.

Line E. Child tax credit. When you file your tax return, you may be eligible to claim a child tax credit for each of your eligible children. To qualify, the child must be under age 17 as of December 31, must be your dependent who lives with you for more than half the year, and must have a valid social security number. To learn more about this credit, see Pub. 972, Child Tax Credit. To reduce the tax withheld from your pay by taking this credit into account, follow the instructions on line E of the worksheet. On the worksheet you will be asked about your total income. For this purpose, total income includes all of your wages and other income, including income earned by a spouse if you are filing a joint return.

Line F. Credit for other dependents. When you file your tax return, you may be eligible to claim a credit for other dependents for whom a child tax credit can't be claimed, such as a qualifying child who doesn't meet the age or social security number requirement for the child tax credit, or a qualifying relative. To learn more about this credit, see Pub. 972. To reduce the tax withheld from your pay by taking this credit into account, follow the instructions on line F of the worksheet. On the worksheet, you will be asked about your total income. For this purpose, total

---

Separate here and give Form W-4 to your employer. Keep the worksheet(s) for your records.

Form W-4
Department of the Treasury
Internal Revenue Service

Employee's Withholding Allowance Certificate

▶ Whether you're entitled to claim a certain number of allowances or exemption from withholding is subject to review by the IRS. Your employer may be required to send a copy of this form to the IRS.

OMB No. 1545-0074

2019

1 Your first name and middle initial	Last name		2 Your social security number

Home address (number and street or rural route)	3 ☐ Single ☐ Married ☐ Married, but withhold at higher Single rate.
	Note: If married filing separately, check "Married, but withhold at higher Single rate."
City or town, state, and ZIP code	4 If your last name differs from that shown on your social security card, check here. You must call 800-772-1213 for a replacement card. ▶ ☐

5	Total number of allowances you're claiming (from the applicable worksheet on the following pages)	**5**	
6	Additional amount, if any, you want withheld from each paycheck	**6**	$

7 I claim exemption from withholding for 2019, and I certify that I meet **both** of the following conditions for exemption.
• Last year I had a right to a refund of **all** federal income tax withheld because I had **no** tax liability, **and**
• This year I expect a refund of **all** federal income tax withheld because I expect to have **no** tax liability.
If you meet both conditions, write "Exempt" here . . . . ▶ | **7** |

Under penalties of perjury, I declare that I have examined this certificate and, to the best of my knowledge and belief, it is true, correct, and complete.

Employee's signature
(This form is not valid unless you sign it.) ▶

Date ▶

8 Employer's name and address (**Employer:** Complete boxes 8 and 10 if sending to IRS and complete boxes 8, 9, and 10 if sending to State Directory of New Hires.)	9 First date of employment	10 Employer identification number (EIN)

For Privacy Act and Paperwork Reduction Act Notice, see page 4.   Cat. No. 10220Q   Form **W-4** (2019)

income includes all of your wages and other income, including income earned by a spouse if you are filing a joint return.

Line G. Other credits. You may be able to reduce the tax withheld from your paycheck if you expect to claim other tax credits, such as tax credits for education (see Pub. 970). If you do so, your paycheck will be larger, but the amount of any refund that you receive when you file your tax return will be smaller. Follow the instructions for Worksheet 1-6 in Pub. 505 if you want to reduce your withholding to take these credits into account. Enter "-0-" on lines E and F if you use Worksheet 1-6.

Deductions, Adjustments, and Additional Income Worksheet

Complete this worksheet to determine if you're able to reduce the tax withheld from your paycheck to account for your itemized deductions and other adjustments to income, such as IRA contributions. If you do so, your refund at the end of the year will be smaller, but your paycheck will be larger. You're not required to complete this worksheet or reduce your withholding if you don't wish to do so.

You can also use this worksheet to figure out how much to increase the tax withheld from your paycheck if you have a large amount of nonwage income not subject to withholding, such as interest or dividends.

Another option is to take these items into account and make your withholding more accurate by using the calculator at *www.irs.gov/W4App*. If you use the calculator, you don't need to complete any of the worksheets for Form W-4.

Two-Earners/Multiple Jobs Worksheet

Complete this worksheet if you have more than one job at a time or are married filing jointly and have a working spouse. If you don't complete this worksheet, you might have too little tax withheld. If so, you will owe tax when you file your tax return and might be subject to a penalty.

Figure the total number of allowances you're entitled to claim and any additional amount of tax to withhold on all jobs using worksheets from only one Form W-4. Claim all allowances on the W-4 that you or your spouse file for the highest paying job in your family and claim zero allowances on Forms W-4 filed for all other jobs. For example, if you earn $60,000 per year and your spouse earns $20,000, you should complete the worksheets to determine what to enter on lines 5 and 6 of your Form W-4, and your spouse should enter zero ("-0-") on lines 5 and 6 of his or her Form W-4. See Pub. 505 for details.

Another option is to use the calculator at *www.irs.gov/W4App* to make your withholding more accurate.

Tip: If you have a working spouse and your incomes are similar, you can check the "Married, but withhold at higher Single rate" box instead of using this worksheet. If you choose this option, then each spouse should fill out the Personal Allowances Worksheet and check the "Married, but withhold at higher Single rate" box on Form W-4, but only one spouse should claim any allowances for credits or fill out the Deductions, Adjustments, and Additional Income Worksheet.

Instructions for Employer

Employees, do not complete box 8, 9, or 10. Your employer will complete these boxes if necessary.

New hire reporting. Employers are required by law to report new employees to a designated State Directory of New Hires. Employers may use Form W-4, boxes 8, 9, and 10 to comply with the new hire reporting requirement for a newly hired employee. A newly hired employee is an employee who hasn't previously been employed by the employer, or who was previously employed by the employer but has been separated from such prior employment for at least 60 consecutive days. Employers should contact the appropriate State Directory of New Hires to find out how to submit a copy of the completed Form W-4. For information and links to each designated State Directory of New Hires (including for U.S. territories), go to *www.acf.hhs.gov/css/employers*.

If an employer is sending a copy of Form W-4 to a designated State Directory of New Hires to comply with the new hire reporting requirement for a newly hired employee, complete boxes 8, 9, and 10 as follows.

Box 8. Enter the employer's name and address. If the employer is sending a copy of this form to a State Directory of New Hires, enter the address where child support agencies should send income withholding orders.

Box 9. If the employer is sending a copy of this form to a State Directory of New Hires, enter the employee's first date of employment, which is the date services for payment were first performed by the employee. If the employer rehired the employee after the employee had been separated from the employer's service for at least 60 days, enter the rehire date.

Box 10. Enter the employer's employer identification number (EIN).

Personal Allowances Worksheet (Keep for your records.)

A   Enter "1" for yourself . . . .   **A** _____

B   Enter "1" if you will file as married filing jointly . . . .   **B** _____

C   Enter "1" if you will file as head of household . . . .   **C** _____

D   Enter "1" if: {
• You're single, or married filing separately, and have only one job; or
• You're married filing jointly, have only one job, and your spouse doesn't work; or
• Your wages from a second job or your spouse's wages (or the total of both) are $1,500 or less.   }   **D** _____

E   **Child tax credit.** See Pub. 972, Child Tax Credit, for more information.

• If your total income will be less than $71,201 ($103,351 if married filing jointly), enter "4" for each eligible child.

• If your total income will be from $71,201 to $179,050 ($103,351 to $345,850 if married filing jointly), enter "2" for each eligible child.

• If your total income will be from $179,051 to $200,000 ($345,851 to $400,000 if married filing jointly), enter "1" for each eligible child.

• If your total income will be higher than $200,000 ($400,000 if married filing jointly), enter "-0-" . . . .   **E** _____

F   **Credit for other dependents.** See Pub. 972, Child Tax Credit, for more information.

• If your total income will be less than $71,201 ($103,351 if married filing jointly), enter "1" for each eligible dependent.

• If your total income will be from $71,201 to $179,050 ($103,351 to $345,850 if married filing jointly), enter "1" for every two dependents (for example, "-0-" for one dependent, "1" if you have two or three dependents, and "2" if you have four dependents).

• If your total income will be higher than $179,050 ($345,850 if married filing jointly), enter "-0-" . . . .   **F** _____

G   **Other credits.** If you have other credits, see Worksheet 1-6 of Pub. 505 and enter the amount from that worksheet here. If you use Worksheet 1-6, enter "-0-" on lines E and F . . . .   **G** _____

H   Add lines A through G and enter the total here . . . . ▶ **H** _____

For accuracy, **complete all worksheets that apply.**   {
• If you plan to **itemize** or **claim adjustments to income** and want to reduce your withholding, or if you have a large amount of nonwage income not subject to withholding and want to increase your withholding, see the **Deductions, Adjustments, and Additional Income Worksheet** below.

• If you **have more than one job at a time** or are **married filing jointly and you and your spouse both work,** and the combined earnings from all jobs exceed $53,000 ($24,450 if married filing jointly), see the **Two-Earners/Multiple Jobs Worksheet** on page 4 to avoid having too little tax withheld.

• If **neither** of the above situations applies, **stop here** and enter the number from line H on line 5 of Form W-4 above.   }

Deductions, Adjustments, and Additional Income Worksheet

Note: Use this worksheet *only* if you plan to itemize deductions, claim certain adjustments to income, or have a large amount of nonwage income not subject to withholding.

1   Enter an estimate of your 2019 itemized deductions. These include qualifying home mortgage interest, charitable contributions, state and local taxes (up to $10,000), and medical expenses in excess of 10% of your income. See Pub. 505 for details . . . .   **1** $ _____

2   Enter: {
$24,400 if you're married filing jointly or qualifying widow(er)
$18,350 if you're head of household
$12,200 if you're single or married filing separately   }   . . . .   **2** $ _____

3   **Subtract** line 2 from line 1. If zero or less, enter "-0-" . . . .   **3** $ _____

4   Enter an estimate of your 2019 adjustments to income, qualified business income deduction, and any additional standard deduction for age or blindness (see Pub. 505 for information about these items) . .   **4** $ _____

5   **Add** lines 3 and 4 and enter the total . . . .   **5** $ _____

6   Enter an estimate of your 2019 nonwage income not subject to withholding (such as dividends or interest) .   **6** $ _____

7   **Subtract** line 6 from line 5. If zero, enter "-0-". If less than zero, enter the amount in parentheses . . .   **7** $ _____

8   **Divide** the amount on line 7 by $4,200 and enter the result here. If a negative amount, enter in parentheses. Drop any fraction . . . .   **8** _____

9   Enter the number from the **Personal Allowances Worksheet,** line H, above . . . .   **9** _____

10   **Add** lines 8 and 9 and enter the total here. If zero or less, enter "-0-". If you plan to use the **Two-Earners/Multiple Jobs Worksheet,** also enter this total on line 1 of that worksheet on page 4. Otherwise, **stop here** and enter this total on Form W-4, line 5, page 1 . . . .   **10** _____

Two-Earners/Multiple Jobs Worksheet

Note: Use this worksheet *only* if the instructions under line H from the **Personal Allowances Worksheet** direct you here.

1	Enter the number from the **Personal Allowances Worksheet,** line H, page 3 (or, if you used the **Deductions, Adjustments, and Additional Income Worksheet** on page 3, the number from line 10 of that worksheet)	**1** _____
2	Find the number in **Table 1** below that applies to the **LOWEST** paying job and enter it here. **However,** if you're married filing jointly and wages from the highest paying job are $75,000 or less and the combined wages for you and your spouse are $107,000 or less, don't enter more than "3"	**2** _____
3	If line 1 is **more than or equal to** line 2, subtract line 2 from line 1. Enter the result here (if zero, enter "-0-") and on Form W-4, line 5, page 1. **Do not** use the rest of this worksheet	**3** _____

Note: If line 1 is **less than** line 2, enter "-0-" on Form W-4, line 5, page 1. Complete lines 4 through 9 below to figure the additional withholding amount necessary to avoid a year-end tax bill.

4	Enter the number from line 2 of this worksheet . . . . **4** _____	
5	Enter the number from line 1 of this worksheet . . . . **5** _____	
6	**Subtract** line 5 from line 4	**6** _____
7	Find the amount in **Table 2** below that applies to the **HIGHEST** paying job and enter it here	**7** $ _____
8	**Multiply** line 7 by line 6 and enter the result here. This is the additional annual withholding needed . . .	**8** $ _____
9	**Divide** line 8 by the number of pay periods remaining in 2019. For example, divide by 18 if you're paid every 2 weeks and you complete this form on a date in late April when there are 18 pay periods remaining in 2019. Enter the result here and on Form W-4, line 6, page 1. This is the additional amount to be withheld from each paycheck	**9** $ _____

Table 1				Table 2			
Married Filing Jointly		**All Others**		**Married Filing Jointly**		**All Others**	
If wages from **LOWEST** paying job are—	Enter on line 2 above	If wages from **LOWEST** paying job are—	Enter on line 2 above	If wages from **HIGHEST** paying job are—	Enter on line 7 above	If wages from **HIGHEST** paying job are—	Enter on line 7 above
$0 - $5,000	0	$0 - $7,000	0	$0 - $24,900	$420	$0 - $7,200	$420
5,001 - 9,500	1	7,001 - 13,000	1	24,901 - 84,450	500	7,201 - 36,975	500
9,501 - 19,500	2	13,001 - 27,500	2	84,451 - 173,900	910	36,976 - 81,700	910
19,501 - 35,000	3	27,501 - 32,000	3	173,901 - 326,950	1,000	81,701 - 158,225	1,000
35,001 - 40,000	4	32,001 - 40,000	4	326,951 - 413,700	1,330	158,226 - 201,600	1,330
40,001 - 46,000	5	40,001 - 60,000	5	413,701 - 617,850	1,450	201,601 - 507,800	1,450
46,001 - 55,000	6	60,001 - 75,000	6	617,851 and over	1,540	507,801 and over	1,540
55,001 - 60,000	7	75,001 - 85,000	7				
60,001 - 70,000	8	85,001 - 95,000	8				
70,001 - 75,000	9	95,001 - 100,000	9				
75,001 - 85,000	10	100,001 - 110,000	10				
85,001 - 95,000	11	110,001 - 115,000	11				
95,001 - 125,000	12	115,001 - 125,000	12				
125,001 - 155,000	13	125,001 - 135,000	13				
155,001 - 165,000	14	135,001 - 145,000	14				
165,001 - 175,000	15	145,001 - 160,000	15				
175,001 - 180,000	16	160,001 - 180,000	16				
180,001 - 195,000	17	180,001 and over	17				
195,001 - 205,000	18						
205,001 and over	19						

Form **2553**

(Rev. December 2017)

Department of the Treasury
Internal Revenue Service

Election by a Small Business Corporation

(Under section 1362 of the Internal Revenue Code)
(Including a late election filed pursuant to Rev. Proc. 2013-30)

▶ You can fax this form to the IRS. See separate instructions.
▶ Go to *www.irs.gov/Form2553* for instructions and the latest information.

OMB No. 1545-0123

Note: This election to be an S corporation can be accepted only if all the tests are met under *Who May Elect* in the instructions, all shareholders have signed the consent statement, an officer has signed below, and the exact name and address of the corporation (entity) and other required form information have been provided.

Part I	Election Information

Type or Print

Name (see instructions)	**A** Employer identification number
Number, street, and room or suite no. If a P.O. box, see instructions.	**B** Date incorporated
City or town, state or province, country, and ZIP or foreign postal code	**C** State of incorporation

D Check the applicable box(es) if the corporation (entity), after applying for the EIN shown in **A** above, changed its ☐ name or ☐ address

E Election is to be effective for tax year beginning (month, day, year) (see instructions) . . . . . . ▶ _____

Caution: A corporation (entity) making the election for its first tax year in existence will usually enter the beginning date of a short tax year that begins on a date other than January 1.

F Selected tax year:
(1) ☐ Calendar year
(2) ☐ Fiscal year ending (month and day) ▶ _____
(3) ☐ 52-53-week year ending with reference to the month of December
(4) ☐ 52-53-week year ending with reference to the month of ▶ _____
If box (2) or (4) is checked, complete Part II.

G If more than 100 shareholders are listed for item J (see page 2), check this box if treating members of a family as one shareholder results in no more than 100 shareholders (see test 2 under *Who May Elect* in the instructions) ▶ ☐

H Name and title of officer or legal representative whom the IRS may call for more information | Telephone number of officer or legal representative

I If this S corporation election is being filed late, I declare I had reasonable cause for not filing Form 2553 timely. If this late election is being made by an entity eligible to elect to be treated as a corporation, I declare I also had reasonable cause for not filing an entity classification election timely and the representations listed in Part IV are true. See below for my explanation of the reasons the election or elections were not made on time and a description of my diligent actions to correct the mistake upon its discovery. See instructions.

Sign Here

Under penalties of perjury, I declare that I have examined this election, including accompanying documents, and, to the best of my knowledge and belief, the election contains all the relevant facts relating to the election, and such facts are true, correct, and complete.

▶ _____ _____ _____
Signature of officer   Title   Date

For Paperwork Reduction Act Notice, see separate instructions.   Cat. No. 18629R   Form **2553** (Rev. 12-2017)

Name					Employer identification number	

| Part I | Election Information *(continued)* **Note:** If you need more rows, use additional copies of page 2. | | | | | |

J Name and address of each shareholder or former shareholder required to consent to the election. (see instructions)	K Shareholder's Consent Statement Under penalties of perjury, I declare that I consent to the election of the above-named corporation (entity) to be an S corporation under section 1362(a) and that I have examined this consent statement, including accompanying documents, and, to the best of my knowledge and belief, the election contains all the relevant facts relating to the election, and such facts are true, correct, and complete. I understand my consent is binding and may not be withdrawn after the corporation (entity) has made a valid election. If seeking relief for a late filed election, I also declare under penalties of perjury that I have reported my income on all affected returns consistent with the S corporation election for the year for which the election should have been filed (see beginning date entered on line E) and for all subsequent years.		L Stock owned or percentage of ownership (see instructions)		M Social security number or employer identification number (see instructions)	N Shareholder's tax year ends (month and day)
	Signature	Date	Number of shares or percentage of ownership	Date(s) acquired		

Name	Employer identification number

Part II — Selection of Fiscal Tax Year (see instructions)

Note: All corporations using this part must complete item O and item P, Q, or R.

O   Check the applicable box to indicate whether the corporation is:

     1. ☐   A new corporation **adopting** the tax year entered in item F, Part I.

     2. ☐   An existing corporation **retaining** the tax year entered in item F, Part I.

     3. ☐   An existing corporation **changing** to the tax year entered in item F, Part I.

P   Complete item P if the corporation is using the automatic approval provisions of Rev. Proc. 2006-46, 2006-45 I.R.B. 859, to request (1) a natural business year (as defined in section 5.07 of Rev. Proc. 2006-46) or (2) a year that satisfies the ownership tax year test (as defined in section 5.08 of Rev. Proc. 2006-46). Check the applicable box below to indicate the representation statement the corporation is making.

     1. Natural Business Year ▶ ☐   I represent that the corporation is adopting, retaining, or changing to a tax year that qualifies as its natural business year (as defined in section 5.07 of Rev. Proc. 2006-46) and has attached a statement showing separately for each month the gross receipts for the most recent 47 months. See instructions. I also represent that the corporation is not precluded by section 4.02 of Rev. Proc. 2006-46 from obtaining automatic approval of such adoption, retention, or change in tax year.

     2. Ownership Tax Year ▶ ☐   I represent that shareholders (as described in section 5.08 of Rev. Proc. 2006-46) holding more than half of the shares of the stock (as of the first day of the tax year to which the request relates) of the corporation have the same tax year or are concurrently changing to the tax year that the corporation adopts, retains, or changes to per item F, Part I, and that such tax year satisfies the requirement of section 4.01(3) of Rev. Proc. 2006-46. I also represent that the corporation is not precluded by section 4.02 of Rev. Proc. 2006-46 from obtaining automatic approval of such adoption, retention, or change in tax year.

Note: If you do not use item P and the corporation wants a fiscal tax year, complete either item Q or R below. Item Q is used to request a fiscal tax year based on a business purpose and to make a back-up section 444 election. Item R is used to make a regular section 444 election.

Q   Business Purpose—To request a fiscal tax year based on a business purpose, check box Q1. See instructions for details including payment of a user fee. You may also check box Q2 and/or box Q3.

     1. Check here ▶ ☐   if the fiscal year entered in item F, Part I, is requested under the prior approval provisions of Rev. Proc. 2002-39, 2002-22 I.R.B. 1046. Attach to Form 2553 a statement describing the relevant facts and circumstances and, if applicable, the gross receipts from sales and services necessary to establish a business purpose. See the instructions for details regarding the gross receipts from sales and services. If the IRS proposes to disapprove the requested fiscal year, do you want a conference with the IRS National Office?

     ☐ Yes   ☐ No

     2. Check here ▶ ☐   to show that the corporation intends to make a back-up section 444 election in the event the corporation's business purpose request is not approved by the IRS. See instructions for more information.

     3. Check here ▶ ☐   to show that the corporation agrees to adopt or change to a tax year ending December 31 if necessary for the IRS to accept this election for S corporation status in the event (1) the corporation's business purpose request is not approved and the corporation makes a back-up section 444 election, but is ultimately not qualified to make a section 444 election, or (2) the corporation's business purpose request is not approved and the corporation did not make a back-up section 444 election.

R   Section 444 Election—To make a section 444 election, check box R1. You may also check box R2.

     1. Check here ▶ ☐   to show that the corporation will make, if qualified, a section 444 election to have the fiscal tax year shown in item F, Part I. To make the election, you must complete **Form 8716,** Election To Have a Tax Year Other Than a Required Tax Year, and either attach it to Form 2553 or file it separately.

     2. Check here ▶ ☐   to show that the corporation agrees to adopt or change to a tax year ending December 31 if necessary for the IRS to accept this election for S corporation status in the event the corporation is ultimately not qualified to make a section 444 election.

Name	Employer identification number

Part III — Qualified Subchapter S Trust (QSST) Election Under Section 1361(d)(2)* Note: If you are making more than one QSST election, use additional copies of page 4.

Income beneficiary's name and address	Social security number

Trust's name and address	Employer identification number

Date on which stock of the corporation was transferred to the trust (month, day, year) . . . . ▶

In order for the trust named above to be a QSST and thus a qualifying shareholder of the S corporation for which this Form 2553 is filed, I hereby make the election under section 1361(d)(2). Under penalties of perjury, I certify that the trust meets the definitional requirements of section 1361(d)(3) and that all other information provided in Part III is true, correct, and complete.

Signature of income beneficiary or signature and title of legal representative or other qualified person making the election	Date

*Use Part III to make the QSST election only if stock of the corporation has been transferred to the trust on or before the date on which the corporation makes its election to be an S corporation. The QSST election must be made and filed separately if stock of the corporation is transferred to the trust **after** the date on which the corporation makes the S election.

Part IV — Late Corporate Classification Election Representations (see instructions)

If a late entity classification election was intended to be effective on the same date that the S corporation election was intended to be effective, relief for a late S corporation election must also include the following representations.

1   The requesting entity is an eligible entity as defined in Regulations section 301.7701-3(a);

2   The requesting entity intended to be classified as a corporation as of the effective date of the S corporation status;

3   The requesting entity fails to qualify as a corporation solely because Form 8832, Entity Classification Election, was not timely filed under Regulations section 301.7701-3(c)(1)(i), or Form 8832 was not deemed to have been filed under Regulations section 301.7701-3(c)(1)(v)(C);

4   The requesting entity fails to qualify as an S corporation on the effective date of the S corporation status solely because the S corporation election was not timely filed pursuant to section 1362(b); **and**

5a   The requesting entity timely filed all required federal tax returns and information returns consistent with its requested classification as an S corporation for all of the years the entity intended to be an S corporation and no inconsistent tax or information returns have been filed by or with respect to the entity during any of the tax years, **or**

b   The requesting entity has not filed a federal tax or information return for the first year in which the election was intended to be effective because the due date has not passed for that year's federal tax or information return.

Form **940 for 2018:** Employer's Annual Federal Unemployment (FUTA) Tax Return

850113

Department of the Treasury — Internal Revenue Service

OMB No. 1545-0028

Employer identification number (EIN) ☐☐ – ☐☐☐☐☐☐☐

Name *(not your trade name)*

Trade name *(if any)*

Address

Number   Street   Suite or room number

City   State   ZIP code

Foreign country name   Foreign province/county   Foreign postal code

Type of Return
(Check all that apply.)

☐ **a.** Amended

☐ **b.** Successor employer

☐ **c.** No payments to employees in 2018

☐ **d.** Final: Business closed or stopped paying wages

Go to *www.irs.gov/Form940* for instructions and the latest information.

Read the separate instructions before you complete this form. Please type or print within the boxes.

Part 1:   Tell us about your return. If any line does NOT apply, leave it blank. See instructions before completing Part 1.

1a If you had to pay state unemployment tax in one state only, enter the state abbreviation .   **1a** ☐ ☐

1b If you had to pay state unemployment tax in more than one state, you are a multi-state employer . . . .   **1b** ☐ Check here. Complete Schedule A (Form 940).

2 If you paid wages in a state that is subject to **CREDIT REDUCTION** . . . .   **2** ☐ Check here. Complete Schedule A (Form 940).

Part 2:   Determine your FUTA tax before adjustments. If any line does NOT apply, leave it blank.

3 Total payments to all employees . . . . **3** ☐.

4 Payments exempt from FUTA tax . . . . . . **4** ☐.

Check all that apply: **4a** ☐ Fringe benefits   **4c** ☐ Retirement/Pension   **4e** ☐ Other
                4b ☐ Group-term life insurance   **4d** ☐ Dependent care

5 Total of payments made to each employee in excess of $7,000 . . . . **5** ☐.

6 Subtotal (line 4 + line 5 = line 6) . . . . **6** ☐.

7 Total taxable FUTA wages (line 3 – line 6 = line 7). See instructions . . . . . . **7** ☐.

8 FUTA tax before adjustments (line 7 x 0.006 = line 8) . . . . **8** ☐.

Part 3:   Determine your adjustments. If any line does NOT apply, leave it blank.

9 If ALL of the taxable FUTA wages you paid were excluded from state unemployment tax, multiply line 7 by 0.054 (line 7 × 0.054 = line 9). Go to line 12 . . . . **9** ☐.

10 If SOME of the taxable FUTA wages you paid were excluded from state unemployment tax, OR you paid ANY state unemployment tax late (after the due date for filing Form 940), complete the worksheet in the instructions. Enter the amount from line 7 of the worksheet . . **10** ☐.

11 If credit reduction applies, enter the total from Schedule A (Form 940) . . . . . . **11** ☐.

Part 4:   Determine your FUTA tax and balance due or overpayment. If any line does NOT apply, leave it blank.

12 Total FUTA tax after adjustments (lines 8 + 9 + 10 + 11 = line 12) . . . . **12** ☐.

13 FUTA tax deposited for the year, including any overpayment applied from a prior year . **13** ☐.

14 Balance due. If line 12 is more than line 13, enter the excess on line 14.
- If line 14 is more than $500, you must deposit your tax.
- If line 14 is $500 or less, you may pay with this return. See instructions . . . . . . **14** ☐.

15 Overpayment. If line 13 is more than line 12, enter the excess on line 15 and check a box below **15** ☐.

▶ You **MUST** complete both pages of this form and **SIGN** it.   Check one: ☐ Apply to next return.   ☐ Send a refund.

Next ▶

    Cat. No. 11234O   Form **940** (2018)

Name *(not your trade name)*	Employer identification number (EIN)

Part 5: Report your FUTA tax liability by quarter only if line 12 is more than $500. If not, go to Part 6.

16 Report the amount of your FUTA tax liability for each quarter; do NOT enter the amount you deposited. If you had no liability for a quarter, leave the line blank.

16a **1st quarter** (January 1 – March 31) . . . . **16a** | · |

16b **2nd quarter** (April 1 – June 30) . . . . **16b** | · |

16c **3rd quarter** (July 1 – September 30) . . . . **16c** | · |

16d **4th quarter** (October 1 – December 31) . . . . **16d** | · |

17 **Total tax liability for the year** (lines 16a + 16b + 16c + 16d = line 17) **17** | · | **Total must equal line 12.**

Part 6: May we speak with your third-party designee?

Do you want to allow an employee, a paid tax preparer, or another person to discuss this return with the IRS? See the instructions for details.

☐ **Yes.** Designee's name and phone number | | | |

Select a 5-digit Personal Identification Number (PIN) to use when talking to IRS | | | | |

☐ **No.**

Part 7: Sign here. You MUST complete both pages of this form and SIGN it.

Under penalties of perjury, I declare that I have examined this return, including accompanying schedules and statements, and to the best of my knowledge and belief, it is true, correct, and complete, and that no part of any payment made to a state unemployment fund claimed as a credit was, or is to be, deducted from the payments made to employees. Declaration of preparer (other than taxpayer) is based on all information of which preparer has any knowledge.

✗ Sign your name here | |

Print your name here | |

Print your title here | |

Date | / / |

Best daytime phone | |

Paid Preparer Use Only

Check if you are self-employed ☐

Preparer's name		PTIN	
Preparer's signature		Date	/ /
Firm's name (or yours if self-employed)		EIN	
Address		Phone	
City		State		ZIP code	

Form **940** (2018)

Form 940-V,
Payment Voucher

Purpose of Form

Complete Form 940-V if you're making a payment with Form 940. We will use the completed voucher to credit your payment more promptly and accurately, and to improve our service to you.

Making Payments With Form 940

To avoid a penalty, make your payment with your 2018 Form 940 **only if** your FUTA tax for the fourth quarter (plus any undeposited amounts from earlier quarters) is $500 or less. If your total FUTA tax after adjustments (Form 940, line 12) is more than $500, you must make deposits by electronic funds transfer. See *When Must You Deposit Your FUTA Tax?* in the Instructions for Form 940. Also see sections 11 and 14 of Pub. 15 for more information about deposits.

 Use Form 940-V when making any payment with Form 940. However, if you pay an amount with Form 940 that should've been deposited, you may be subject to a penalty. See Deposit Penalties *in section 11 of Pub. 15.*

Specific Instructions

Box 1—Employer Identification Number (EIN). If you don't have an EIN, you may apply for one online by visiting the IRS website at *www.irs.gov/EIN*. You may also apply for an EIN by faxing or mailing Form SS-4 to the IRS. If you haven't received your EIN by the due date of Form 940, write "Applied For" and the date you applied in this entry space.

Box 2—Amount paid. Enter the amount paid with Form 940.

Box 3—Name and address. Enter your name and address as shown on Form 940.

• Enclose your check or money order made payable to "United States Treasury." Be sure to enter your EIN, "Form 940," and "2018" on your check or money order. Don't send cash. Don't staple Form 940-V or your payment to Form 940 (or to each other).

• Detach Form 940-V and send it with your payment and Form 940 to the address provided in the Instructions for Form 940.

Note: You must also complete the entity information above Part 1 on Form 940.

✂ ▼ **Detach Here and Mail With Your Payment and Form 940.** ▼ ✂

Form **940-V**

Department of the Treasury
Internal Revenue Service

Payment Voucher

▶ **Don't staple or attach this voucher to your payment.**

OMB No. 1545-0028

20**18**

1 Enter your employer identification number (EIN).	2	Dollars	Cents
	Enter the amount of your payment. ▶ Make your check or money order payable to **"United States Treasury"**		

3 Enter your business name (individual name if sole proprietor).

Enter your address.

Enter your city, state, and ZIP code or your city, foreign country name, foreign province/county, and foreign postal code.

Privacy Act and Paperwork Reduction Act Notice.
We ask for the information on this form to carry out the Internal Revenue laws of the United States. We need it to figure and collect the right amount of tax. Chapter 23, Federal Unemployment Tax Act, of Subtitle C, Employment Taxes, of the Internal Revenue Code imposes a tax on employers with respect to employees. This form is used to determine the amount of the tax that you owe. Section 6011 requires you to provide the requested information if you are liable for FUTA tax under section 3301. Section 6109 requires you to provide your identification number. If you fail to provide this information in a timely manner or provide a false or fraudulent form, you may be subject to penalties.

You're not required to provide the information requested on a form that is subject to the Paperwork Reduction Act unless the form displays a valid OMB control number. Books and records relating to a form or instructions must be retained as long as their contents may become material in the administration of any Internal Revenue law.

Generally, tax returns and return information are confidential, as required by section 6103. However, section 6103 allows or requires the IRS to disclose or give the information shown on your tax return to others as described in the Code. For example, we may disclose your tax information to the Department of Justice for civil and criminal litigation, and to cities, states, the District of Columbia, and U.S. commonwealths and possessions to administer their tax laws. We may also disclose this information to other countries under a tax treaty, to federal and state agencies to enforce federal nontax criminal laws, or to federal law enforcement and intelligence agencies to combat terrorism.

The time needed to complete and file this form will vary depending on individual circumstances. The estimated average time is:

Recordkeeping . . . . 9 hr., 19 min.

Learning about the law or the form . . 1 hr., 23 min.

Preparing, copying, assembling, and sending the form to the IRS . . . . . 1 hr., 36 min.

If you have comments concerning the accuracy of these time estimates or suggestions for making Form 940 simpler, we would be happy to hear from you. You can send us comments from *www.irs.gov/FormComments.* Or you can send your comments to Internal Revenue Service, Tax Forms and Publications Division, 1111 Constitution Ave. NW, IR-6526, Washington, DC 20224. Don't send Form 940 to this address. Instead, see *Where Do You File?* in the Instructions for Form 940.

Form **8594**

(Rev. December 2012)

Department of the Treasury
Internal Revenue Service

Asset Acquisition Statement
Under Section 1060

▶ Attach to your income tax return.
▶ Information about Form 8594 and its separate instructions is at *www.irs.gov/form8594*

OMB No. 1545-1021

Attachment
Sequence No. **169**

Name as shown on return

Identifying number as shown on return

Check the box that identifies you:
☐ Purchaser   ☐ Seller

Part I   General Information

1   Name of other party to the transaction

Other party's identifying number

Address (number, street, and room or suite no.)

City or town, state, and ZIP code

2   Date of sale

3   Total sales price (consideration)

Part II   Original Statement of Assets Transferred

4 Assets	Aggregate fair market value (actual amount for Class I)	Allocation of sales price
Class I	$	$
Class II	$	$
Class III	$	$
Class IV	$	$
Class V	$	$
Class VI and VII	$	$
Total	$	$

5   Did the purchaser and seller provide for an allocation of the sales price in the sales contract or in another written document signed by both parties? . . . . ☐ Yes   ☐ No

If "Yes," are the aggregate fair market values (FMV) listed for each of asset Classes I, II, III, IV, V, VI, and VII the amounts agreed upon in your sales contract or in a separate written document? . . . . ☐ Yes   ☐ No

6   In the purchase of the group of assets (or stock), did the purchaser also purchase a license or a covenant not to compete, or enter into a lease agreement, employment contract, management contract, or similar arrangement with the seller (or managers, directors, owners, or employees of the seller)? . . . . ☐ Yes   ☐ No

If "Yes," attach a statement that specifies **(a)** the type of agreement and **(b)** the maximum amount of consideration (not including interest) paid or to be paid under the agreement. See instructions.

Part III **Supplemental Statement**—Complete only if amending an original statement or previously filed supplemental statement because of an increase or decrease in consideration. See instructions.

7   Tax year and tax return form number with which the original Form 8594 and any supplemental statements were filed.

8 Assets	Allocation of sales price as previously reported	Increase or (decrease)	Redetermined allocation of sales price
Class I	$	$	$
Class II	$	$	$
Class III	$	$	$
Class IV	$	$	$
Class V	$	$	$
Class VI and VII	$	$	$
Total	$		$

9   Reason(s) for increase or decrease. Attach additional sheets if more space is needed.

_____

_____

_____

_____

_____

_____

_____

_____

_____

_____

_____

_____

_____

_____

_____

_____

_____

_____

Instructions for Form I-9, Employment Eligibility Verification

Department of Homeland Security
U.S. Citizenship and Immigration Services

USCIS
Form I-9
OMB No. 1615-0047
Expires 08/31/2019

Anti-Discrimination Notice. It is illegal to discriminate against work-authorized individuals in hiring, firing, recruitment or referral for a fee, or in the employment eligibility verification (Form I-9 and E-Verify) process based on that individual's citizenship status, immigration status or national origin. Employers **CANNOT** specify which document(s) the employee may present to establish employment authorization and identity. The employer must allow the employee to choose the documents to be presented from the Lists of Acceptable Documents, found on the last page of Form I-9. The refusal to hire or continue to employ an individual because the documentation presented has a future expiration date may also constitute illegal discrimination. For more information, call the Immigrant and Employee Rights Section (IER) in the Department of Justice's Civil Rights Division at 1-800-255-7688 (employees), 1-800-255-8155 (employers), or 1-800-237-2515 (TTY), or visit https://www.justice.gov/crt/immigrant-and-employee-rights-section.

What is the Purpose of This Form?

Employers must complete Form I-9 to document verification of the identity and employment authorization of each new employee (both citizen and noncitizen) hired after November 6, 1986, to work in the United States. In the Commonwealth of the Northern Mariana Islands (CNMI), employers must complete Form I-9 to document verification of the identity and employment authorization of each new employee (both citizen and noncitizen) hired after November 27, 2011.

General Instructions

Both employers and employees are responsible for completing their respective sections of Form I-9. For the purpose of completing this form, the term "employer" means all employers, including those recruiters and referrers for a fee who are agricultural associations, agricultural employers, or farm labor contractors, as defined in section 3 of the Migrant and Seasonal Agricultural Worker Protection Act, Public Law 97-470 (29 U.S.C. 1802). An "employee" is a person who performs labor or services in the United States for an employer in return for wages or other remuneration. The term "Employee" does not include those who do not receive any form of remuneration (volunteers), independent contractors or those engaged in certain casual domestic employment. Form I-9 has three sections. Employees complete Section 1. Employers complete Section 2 and, when applicable, Section 3. Employers may be fined if the form is not properly completed. See 8 USC § 1324a and 8 CFR § 274a.10. Individuals may be prosecuted for knowingly and willfully entering false information on the form. Employers are responsible for retaining completed forms. **Do not mail completed forms to U.S. Citizenship and Immigration Services (USCIS) or Immigration and Customs Enforcement (ICE).**

These instructions will assist you in properly completing Form I-9. The employer must ensure that all pages of the instructions and Lists of Acceptable Documents are available, either in print or electronically, to all employees completing this form. When completing the form on a computer, the English version of the form includes specific instructions for each field and drop-down lists for universally used abbreviations and acceptable documents. To access these instructions, move the cursor over each field or click on the question mark symbol (ⓘ) within the field. Employers and employees can also access this full set of instructions at any time by clicking the Instructions button at the top of each page when completing the form on a computer that is connected to the Internet.

Employers and employees may choose to complete any or all sections of the form on paper or using a computer, or a combination of both. Forms I-9 obtained from the USCIS website are not considered electronic Forms I-9 under DHS regulations and, therefore, cannot be electronically signed. Therefore, regardless of the method you used to enter information into each field, you must print a hard copy of the form, then sign and date the hard copy by hand where required.

Employers can obtain a blank copy of Form I-9 from the USCIS website at https://www.uscis.gov/sites/default/files/files/form/i-9.pdf. This form is in portable document format (.pdf) that is fillable and savable. That means that you may download it, or simply print out a blank copy to enter information by hand. You may also request paper Forms I-9 from USCIS.

Certain features of Form I-9 that allow for data entry on personal computers may make the form appear to be more than two pages. When using a computer, Form I-9 has been designed to print as two pages. Using more than one preparer and/or translator will add an additional page to the form, regardless of your method of completion. You are not required to print, retain or store the page containing the Lists of Acceptable Documents.

Form I-9 Instructions 07/17/17 N

Page 1 of 15

The form will also populate certain fields with N/A when certain user choices ensure that particular fields will not be completed. The Print button located at the top of each page that will print any number of pages the user selects. Also, the Start Over button located at the top of each page will clear all the fields on the form.

The Spanish version of Form I-9 does not include the additional instructions and drop-down lists described above. Employers in Puerto Rico may use either the Spanish or English version of the form. Employers outside of Puerto Rico must retain the English version of the form for their records, but may use the Spanish form as a translation tool. Additional guidance to complete the form may be found in the <u>Handbook for Employers: Guidance for Completing Form I-9 (M-274)</u> and on USCIS' Form I-9 website, <u>I-9 Central.</u>

Completing Section I: Employee Information and Attestation

You, the employee, must complete each field in Section 1 as described below. Newly hired employees must complete and sign Section 1 no later than the first day of employment. Section 1 should never be completed before you have accepted a job offer.

Entering Your Employee Information

Last Name *(Family Name)*: Enter your full legal last name. Your last name is your family name or surname. If you have two last names or a hyphenated last name, include both names in the Last Name field. *Examples of correctly entered last names include De La Cruz, O'Neill, Garcia Lopez, Smith-Johnson, Nguyen.* If you only have one name, enter it in this field, then enter "Unknown" in the First Name field. You may not enter "Unknown" in both the Last Name field and the First Name field.

First Name *(Given Name)*: Enter your full legal first name. Your first name is your given name. *Some examples of correctly entered first names include Jessica, John-Paul, Tae Young, D'Shaun, Mai.* If you only have one name, enter it in the Last Name field, then enter "Unknown" in this field. You may not enter "Unknown" in both the First Name field and the Last Name field.

Middle Initial: Your middle initial is the first letter of your second given name, or the first letter of your middle name, if any. If you have more than one middle name, enter the first letter of your first middle name. If you do not have a middle name, enter N/A in this field.

Other Last Names Used: Provide all other last names used, if any (e.g., maiden name). Enter N/A if you have not used other last names. For example, if you legally changed your last name from Smith to Jones, you should enter the name Smith in this field.

Address (Street Name and Number): Enter the street name and number of the current address of your residence. If you are a border commuter from Canada or Mexico, you may enter your Canada or Mexico address in this field. If your residence does not have a physical address, enter a description of the location of your residence, such as "3 miles southwest of Anytown post office near water tower."

Apartment: Enter the number(s) or letter(s) that identify(ies) your apartment. If you do not live in an apartment, enter N/A.

City or Town: Enter your city, town or village in this field. If your residence is not located in a city, town or village, enter your county, township, reservation, etc., in this field. If you are a border commuter from Canada, enter your city and province in this field. If you are a border commuter from Mexico, enter your city and state in this field.

State: Enter the abbreviation of your state or territory in this field. If you are a border commuter from Canada or Mexico, enter your country abbreviation in this field.

ZIP Code: Enter your 5-digit ZIP code. If you are a border commuter from Canada or Mexico, enter your 5- or 6-digit postal code in this field.

Date of Birth: Enter your date of birth as a 2-digit month, 2-digit day, and 4-digit year (mm/dd/yyyy). For example, enter January 8, 1980 as 01/08/1980.

U.S. Social Security Number: Providing your 9-digit Social Security number is voluntary on Form I-9 unless your employer participates in E-Verify. If your employer participates in E-Verify and:

1. You have been issued a Social Security number, you must provide it in this field; or

2. You have applied for, but have not yet received a Social Security number, leave this field blank until you receive a Social Security number.

Employee's E-mail Address (Optional): Providing your e-mail address is optional on Form I-9, but the field cannot be left blank. To enter your e-mail address, use this format: name@site .domain. One reason Department of Homeland Security (DHS) may e-mail you is if your employer uses E-Verify and DHS learns of a potential mismatch between the information provided and the information in government records. This e-mail would contain information on how to begin to resolve the potential mismatch. You may use either your personal or work e-mail address in this field. Enter N/A if you do not enter your e-mail address.

Employee's Telephone Number (Optional): Providing your telephone number is optional on Form I-9, but the field cannot be left blank. If you enter your area code and telephone number, use this format: 000-000-0000. Enter N/A if you do not enter your telephone number.

Attesting to Your Citizenship or Immigration Status

You must select one box to attest to your citizenship or immigration status.

1. **A citizen of the United States.**

2. **A noncitizen national of the United States:** An individual born in American Samoa, certain former citizens of the former Trust Territory of the Pacific Islands, and certain children of noncitizen nationals born abroad.

3. **A lawful permanent resident**: An individual who is not a U.S. citizen and who resides in the United States under legally recognized and lawfully recorded permanent residence as an immigrant. This term includes conditional residents. Asylees and refugees should not select this status, but should instead select "An Alien authorized to work" below.

   If you select "lawful permanent resident," enter your 7- to 9-digit Alien Registration Number (A-Number), including the "A," or USCIS Number in the space provided. When completing this field using a computer, use the dropdown provided to indicate whether you have entered an Alien Number or a USCIS Number. At this time, the USCIS Number is the same as the A-Number without the "A" prefix.

4. **An alien authorized to work**: An individual who is not a citizen or national of the United States, or a lawful permanent resident, but is authorized to work in the United States.

   If you select this box, enter the date that your employment authorization expires, if any, in the space provided. In most cases, your employment authorization expiration date is found on the document(s) evidencing your employment authorization. Refugees, asylees and certain citizens of the Federated States of Micronesia, the Republic of the Marshall Islands, or Palau, and other aliens whose employment authorization does not have an expiration date should enter N/A in the Expiration Date field. In some cases, such as if you have Temporary Protected Status, your employment authorization may have been automatically extended; in these cases, you should enter the expiration date of the automatic extension in this space.

   Aliens authorized to work must enter one of the following to complete Section1:
   1. Alien Registration Number (A-Number)/USCIS Number; or
   2. Form I-94 Admission Number; or
   3. Foreign Passport Number and the Country of Issuance

   Your employer may not ask you to present the document from which you supplied this information.

   Alien Registration Number/USCIS Number: Enter your 7- to 9-digit Alien Registration Number (A-Number), including the "A," or your USCIS Number in this field. At this time, the USCIS Number is the same as your A-Number without the "A" prefix. When completing this field using a computer, use the dropdown provided to indicate whether you have entered an Alien Number or a USCIS Number. If you do not provide an A-Number or USCIS Number, enter N/A in this field then enter either a Form I-94 Admission Number, or a Foreign Passport and Country of Issuance in the fields provided.

   Form I-94 Admission Number: Enter your 11-digit I-94 Admission Number in this field. If you do not provide an I-94 Admission Number, enter N/A in this field, then enter either an Alien Registration Number/USCIS Number or a Foreign Passport Number and Country of Issuance in the fields provided.

   Foreign Passport Number: Enter your Foreign Passport Number in this field. If you do not provide a Foreign Passport Number, enter N/A in this field, then enter either an Alien Number/USCIS Number or a I-94 Admission Number in the fields provided.

   Country of Issuance: If you entered your Foreign Passport Number, enter your Foreign Passport's Country of Issuance. If you did not enter your Foreign Passport Number, enter N/A.

Signature of Employee: After completing Section 1, sign your name in this field. If you used a form obtained from the USCIS website, you must print the form to sign your name in this field. By signing this form, you attest under penalty of perjury (28 U.S.C. § 1746) that the information you provided, along with the citizenship or immigration status you selected, and all information and documentation you provide to your employer, is complete, true and correct, and you are aware that you may face severe penalties provided by law and may be subject to criminal prosecution for knowingly and willfully making false statements or using false documentation when completing this form. Further, falsely attesting to U.S. citizenship may subject employees to penalties, removal proceedings and may adversely affect an employee's ability to seek future immigration benefits. If you cannot sign your name, you may place a mark in this field to indicate your signature. Employees who use a preparer or translator to help them complete the form must still sign or place a mark in the Signature of Employee field on the printed form.

If you used a preparer, translator, and other individual to assist you in completing Form I-9:

- Both you and your preparer(s) and/or translator(s) must complete the appropriate areas of Section 1, and then sign Section 1. If Section 1 was completed on a form obtained from the USCIS website, the form must be printed to sign these fields. You and your preparer(s) and/or translator(s) also should review the instructions for **Completing the Preparer and/or Translator Certification** below.

- If the employee is a minor (individual under 18) who cannot present an identity document, the employee's parent or legal guardian can complete Section 1 for the employee and enter "minor under age 18" in the signature field. If Section 1 was completed on a form obtained from the USCIS website, the form must be printed to enter this information. The minor's parent or legal guardian should review the instructions for Completing the Preparer and/or Translator Certification below. Refer to the Handbook for Employers: Guidance for Completing Form I-9 (M-274) for more guidance on completion of Form I-9 for minors. If the minor's employer participates in E-Verify, the employee must present a list B identity document with a photograph to complete Form I-9.

- If the employee is a person with a disability (who is placed in employment by a nonprofit organization, association or as part of a rehabilitation program) who cannot present an identity document, the employee's parent, legal guardian or a representative of the nonprofit organization, association or rehabilitation program can complete Section 1 for the employee and enter "Special Placement" in this field. If Section 1 was completed on a form obtained from the USCIS website, the form must be printed to enter this information. The parent, legal guardian or representative of the nonprofit organization, association or rehabilitation program completing Section 1 for the employee should review the instructions for Completing the Preparer and/or Translator Certification below. Refer to the Handbook for Employers: Guidance for Completing Form I-9 (M-274) for more guidance on completion of Form I-9 for certain employees with disabilities.

Today's Date: Enter the date you signed Section 1 in this field. Do not backdate this field. Enter the date as a 2-digit month, 2-digit day and 4-digit year (mm/dd/yyyy). For example, enter January 8, 2014 as 01/08/2014. A preparer or translator who assists the employee in completing Section 1 may enter the date the employee signed or made a mark to sign Section 1 in this field. Parents or legal guardians assisting minors (individuals under age 18) and parents, legal guardians or representatives of a nonprofit organization, association or rehabilitation program assisting certain employees with disabilities must enter the date they completed Section 1 for the employee.

Completing the Preparer and/or Translator Certification

If you did not use a preparer or translator to assist you in completing Section 1, you, the employee, must check the box marked **I did not use a Preparer or Translator**. If you check this box, leave the rest of the fields in this area blank.

If one or more preparers and/or translators assist the employee in completing the form using a computer, the preparer and/or translator must check the box marked **"A preparer(s) and/or translator(s) assisted the employee in completing Section 1"**, then select the number of Certification areas needed from the dropdown provided. Any additional Certification areas generated will result in an additional page. Form I-9 Supplement, Section 1 Preparer and/or Translator Certification can be separately downloaded from the USCIS Form I-9 webpage, which provides additional Certification areas for those completing Form I-9 using a computer who need more Certification areas than the 5 provided or those who are completing Form I-9 on paper. The first preparer and/or translator must complete all the fields in the Certification area on the same page the employee has signed. There is no limit to the number of preparers and/or translators an employee can use, but each additional preparer and/or translator must complete and sign a separate Certification area. Ensure the employee's last name, first name and middle initial are entered at the top of any additional pages. The employer must ensure that any additional pages are retained with the employee's completed Form I-9.

Signature of Preparer or Translator: Any person who helped to prepare or translate Section 1 of Form I-9 must sign his or her name in this field. If you used a form obtained from the USCIS website, you must print the form to sign your name in this field. The Preparer and/or Translator Certification must also be completed if "Individual under Age 18" or "Special Placement" is entered in lieu of the employee's signature in Section 1.

Today's Date: The person who signs the Preparer and/or Translator Certification must enter the date he or she signs in this field on the printed form. Do not backdate this field. Enter the date as a 2-digit month, 2-digit day, and 4-digit year (mm/dd/yyyy). For example, enter January 8, 2014 as 01/08/2014.

Last Name *(Family Name):* Enter the full legal last name of the person who helped the employee in preparing or translating Section 1 in this field. The last name is also the family name or surname. If the preparer or translator has two last names or a hyphenated last name, include both names in this field.

First Name *(Given Name):* Enter the full legal first name of the person who helped the employee in preparing or translating Section 1 in this field. The first name is also the given name.

Address (Street Name and Number): Enter the street name and number of the current address of the residence of the person who helped the employee in preparing or translating Section 1 in this field. Addresses for residences in Canada or Mexico may be entered in this field. If the residence does not have a physical address, enter a description of the location of the residence, such as "3 miles southwest of Anytown post office near water tower." If the residence is an apartment, enter the apartment number in this field.

City or Town: Enter the city, town or village of the residence of the person who helped the employee in preparing or translating Section 1 in this field. If the residence is not located in a city, town or village, enter the name of the county, township, reservation, etc., in this field. If the residence is in Canada, enter the city and province in this field. If the residence is in Mexico, enter the city and state in this field.

State: Enter the abbreviation of the state, territory or country of the preparer or translator's residence in this field.

ZIP Code: Enter the 5-digit ZIP code of the residence of the person who helped the employee in preparing or translating Section 1 in this field. If the preparer or translator's residence is in Canada or Mexico, enter the 5- or 6-digit postal code.

Presenting Form I-9 Documents

Within 3 business days of starting work for pay, you must present to your employer documentation that establishes your identity and employment authorization. For example, if you begin employment on Monday, you must present documentation on or before Thursday of that week. However, if you were hired to work for less than 3 business days, you must present documentation no later than the first day of employment.

Choose which unexpired document(s) to present to your employer from the Lists of Acceptable Documents. An employer cannot specify which document(s) you may present from the Lists of Acceptable Documents. You may present either one selection from List A or a combination of one selection from List B and one selection from List C. Some List A documents, which show both identity and employment authorization, are combination documents that must be presented together to be considered a List A document: for example, the foreign passport together with a Form I-94 containing an endorsement of the alien's nonimmigrant status and employment authorization with a specific employer incident to such status. List B documents show identity only and List C documents show employment authorization only. If your employer participates in E-Verify and you present a List B document, the document must contain a photograph. If you present acceptable List A documentation, you should not be asked to present, nor should you provide, List B and List C documentation. If you present acceptable List B and List C documentation, you should not be asked to present, nor should you provide, List A documentation. If you are unable to present a document(s) from these lists, you may be able to present an acceptable receipt. Refer to the Receipts section below.

Your employer must review the document(s) you present to complete Form I-9. If your document(s) reasonably appears to be genuine and to relate to you, your employer must accept the documents. If your document(s) does not reasonably appear to be genuine or to relate to you, your employer must reject it and provide you with an opportunity to present other documents from the Lists of Acceptable Documents. Your employer may choose to make copies of your document(s), but must return the original(s) to you. Your employer must review your documents in your physical presence.

Your employer will complete the other parts of this form, as well as review your entries in Section 1. Your employer may ask you to correct any errors found. Your employer is responsible for ensuring all parts of Form I-9 are properly completed and is subject to penalties under federal law if the form is not completed correctly.

Minors (individuals under age 18) and certain employees with disabilities whose parent, legal guardian or representative completed Section 1 for the employee are only required to present an employment authorization document from List C. Refer to the Handbook for Employers: Guidance for Completing Form I-9 (M-274) for more guidance on minors and certain individuals with disabilities.

Receipts

If you do not have unexpired documentation from the Lists of Acceptable Documents, you may be able to present a receipt(s) in lieu of an acceptable document(s). New employees who choose to present a receipt(s) must do so within three business days of their first day of employment. If your employer is reverifying your employment authorization, and you choose to present a receipt for reverification, you must present the receipt by the date your employment authorization expires. Receipts are not acceptable if employment lasts fewer than three business days.

There are three types of acceptable receipts:

1. A receipt showing that you have applied to replace a document that was lost, stolen or damaged. You must present the actual document within 90 days from the date of hire or, in the case of reverification, within 90 days from the date your original employment authorization expires.

2. The arrival portion of Form I-94/I-94A containing a temporary I-551 stamp and a photograph of the individual. You must present the actual Permanent Resident Card (Form I-551) by the expiration date of the temporary I-551 stamp, or, if there is no expiration date, within 1 year from the date of admission.

3. The departure portion of Form I-94/I-94A with a refugee admission stamp. You must present an unexpired Employment Authorization Document (Form I-766) or a combination of a List B document and an unrestricted Social Security Card within 90 days from the date of hire or, in the case of reverification, within 90 days from the date your original employment authorization expires.

Receipts showing that you have applied for an initial grant of employment authorization, or for renewal of your expiring or expired employment authorization, are not acceptable.

Completing Section 2: Employer or Authorized Representative Review and Verification

You, the employer, must ensure that all parts of Form I-9 are properly completed and may be subject to penalties under federal law if the form is not completed correctly. Section 1 must be completed no later than the employee's first day of employment. You may not ask an individual to complete Section 1 before he or she has accepted a job offer. Before completing Section 2, you should review Section 1 to ensure the employee completed it properly. If you find any errors in Section 1, have the employee make corrections, as necessary and initial and date any corrections made.

You or your authorized representative must complete Section 2 by examining evidence of identity and employment authorization within 3 business days of the employee's first day of employment. For example, if an employee begins employment on Monday, you must review the employee's documentation and complete Section 2 on or before Thursday of that week. However, if you hire an individual for less than 3 business days, Section 2 must be completed no later than the first day of employment.

Entering Employee Information from Section 1

This area, titled, "Employee Info from Section 1" contains fields to enter the employee's last name, first name, middle initial exactly as he or she entered them in Section 1. This area also includes a Citizenship/Immigration Status field to enter the number of the citizenship or immigration status checkbox the employee selected in Section 1. These fields help to ensure that the two pages of an employee's Form I-9 remain together. When completing Section 2 using a computer, the number entered in the Citizenship/Immigration Status field provides drop-downs that directly relate to the employee's selected citizenship or immigration status.

You, the employer or authorized representative, must physically examine, in the employee's physical presence, the unexpired document(s) the employee presents from the Lists of Acceptable Documents to complete the Document fields in Section 2.

You cannot specify which document(s) an employee may present from these lists. If you discriminate in the Form I-9 process based on an individual's citizenship status, immigration status, or national origin, you may be in violation of the law and subject to sanctions such as civil penalties and be required to pay back pay to discrimination victims. A document is acceptable as long as it reasonably appears to be genuine and to relate to the person presenting it. Employees must present one selection from List A or a combination of one selection from List B and one selection from List C.

List A documents show both identity and employment authorization. Some List A documents are combination documents that must be presented together to be considered a List A document, such as a foreign passport together with a Form I-94 containing an endorsement of the alien's nonimmigrant status.

List B documents show identity only, and List C documents show employment authorization only. If an employee presents a List A document, do not ask or require the employee to present List B and List C documents, and vice versa. If an employer participates in E-Verify and the employee presents a List B document, the List B document must include a photograph.

If an employee presents a receipt for the application to replace a lost, stolen or damaged document, the employee must present the replacement document to you within 90 days of the first day of work for pay, or in the case of reverification, within 90 days of the date the employee's employment authorization expired. Enter the word "Receipt" followed by the title of the receipt in Section 2 under the list that relates to the receipt.

When your employee presents the replacement document, draw a line through the receipt, then enter the information from the new document into Section 2. Other receipts may be valid for longer or shorter periods, such as the arrival portion of Form I-94/ I-94A containing a temporary I-551 stamp and a photograph of the individual, which is valid until the expiration date of the temporary I-551 stamp or, if there is no expiration date, valid for one year from the date of admission.

Ensure that each document is an unexpired, original (no photocopies, except for certified copies of birth certificates) document. Certain employees may present an expired employment authorization document, which may be considered unexpired, if the employee's employment authorization has been extended by regulation or a Federal Register Notice. Refer to the Handbook for Employers: Guidance for Completing Form I-9 (M-274) or I-9 Central for more guidance on these special situations.

Refer to the M-274 for guidance on how to handle special situations, such as students (who may present additional documents not specified on the Lists) and H-1B and H-2A nonimmigrants changing employers.

Minors (individuals under age 18) and certain employees with disabilities whose parent, legal guardian or representative completed Section 1 for the employee are only required to present an employment authorization document from List C. Refer to the M-274 for more guidance on minors and certain persons with disabilities. If the minor's employer participates in E-Verify, the minor employee also must present a List B identity document with a photograph to complete Form I-9.

You must return original document(s) to the employee, but may make photocopies of the document(s) reviewed. Photocopying documents is voluntary unless you participate in E-Verify. E-Verify employers are only required to photocopy certain documents. If you are an E-Verify employer who chooses to photocopy documents other than those you are required to photocopy, you should apply this policy consistently with respect to Form I-9 completion for all employees. For more information on the types of documents that an employer must photocopy if the employer uses E-Verify, visit E-Verify's website at www.dhs.gov/e-verify. For non-E-Verify employers, if photocopies are made, they should be made consistently for ALL new hires and reverified employees.

Photocopies must be retained and presented with Form I-9 in case of an inspection by DHS or another federal government agency. You must always complete Section 2 by reviewing original documentation, even if you photocopy an employee's document(s) after reviewing the documentation. Making photocopies of an employee's document(s) cannot take the place of completing Form I-9. You are still responsible for completing and retaining Form I-9.

List A - Identity and Employment Authorization: If the employee presented an acceptable document(s) from List A or an acceptable receipt for a List A document, enter the document(s) information in this column. If the employee presented a List A document that consists of a combination of documents, enter information from each document in that combination in a separate area under List A as described below. All documents must be unexpired. If you enter document information in the List A column, you should not enter document information in the List B or List C columns. If you complete Section 2 using a computer, a selection in List A will fill all the fields in the Lists B and C columns with N/A.

Document Title: If the employee presented a document from List A, enter the title of the List A document or receipt in this field. The abbreviations provided are available in the dropdown when the form is completed on a computer. When completing the form on paper, you may choose to use these abbreviations or any other common abbreviation to enter the document title or issuing authority. If the employee presented a combination of documents, use the second and third Document Title fields as necessary.

Full name of List A Document	Abbreviations
U.S. Passport	U.S. Passport
U.S. Passport Card	U.S. Passport Card
Permanent Resident Card (Form I-551)	Perm. Resident Card (Form I-551)
Alien Registration Receipt Card (Form I-551)	Alien Reg. Receipt Card (Form I-551)
Foreign passport containing a temporary I-551 stamp	1. Foreign Passport 2. Temporary I-551 Stamp
Foreign passport containing a temporary I-551 printed notation on a machine-readable immigrant visa (MRIV)	1. Foreign Passport 2. Machine-readable immigrant visa (MRIV)
Employment Authorization Document (Form I-766)	Employment Auth. Document (Form I-766)
For a nonimmigrant alien authorized to work for a specific employer because of his or her status, a foreign passport with Form I/94/I-94A that contains an endorsement of the alien's nonimmigrant status	1. Foreign Passport, work-authorized non-immigrant 2. Form I-94/I94A 3. "Form I-20" or "Form DS-2019" Note: In limited circumstances, certain J-1 students may be required to present a letter from their Responsible Officer in order to work. Enter the document title, issuing authority, document number and expiration date from this document in the Additional Information field.
Passport from the Federated States of Micronesia (FSM) with Form I-94/I-94A	1. FSM Passport with Form I-94 2. Form I-94/I94A
Passport from the Republic of the Marshall Islands (RMI) with Form I-94/I94A	1. RMI Passport with Form I-94 2. Form I-94/I94A
Receipt: The arrival portion of Form I-94/I-94A containing a temporary I-551 stamp and photograph	Receipt: Form I-94/I-94A w/I-551 stamp, photo
Receipt: The departure portion of Form I-94/I-94A with an unexpired refugee admission stamp	Receipt: Form I-94/I-94A w/refugee stamp
Receipt for an application to replace a lost, stolen or damaged Permanent Resident Card (Form I-551)	Receipt replacement Perm. Res. Card (Form I-551)
Receipt for an application to replace a lost, stolen or damaged Employment Authorization Document (Form I-766)	Receipt replacement EAD (Form I-766)
Receipt for an application to replace a lost, stolen or damaged foreign passport with Form I-94/I-94A that contains an endorsement of the alien's nonimmigrant status	1. Receipt: Replacement Foreign Passport, work-authorized nonimmigrant 2. Receipt: Replacement Form I-94/I-94A 3. Form I-20 or Form DS-2019 (if presented)
Receipt for an application to replace a lost, stolen or damaged passport from the Federated States of Micronesia with Form I-94/I-94A	1. Receipt: Replacement FSM Passport with Form I-94 2. Receipt: Replacement Form I-94/I-94A
Receipt for an application to replace a lost, stolen or damaged passport from the Republic of the Marshall Islands with Form I-94/I-94A	1. Receipt: Replacement RMI Passport with Form I-94 2. Receipt: Replacement Form I-94/I-94A

Issuing Authority: Enter the issuing authority of the List A document or receipt. The issuing authority is the specific entity that issued the document. If the employee presented a combination of documents, use the second and third Issuing Authority fields as necessary.

Document Number: Enter the document number, if any, of the List A document or receipt presented. If the document does not contain a number, enter N/A in this field. If the employee presented a combination of documents, use the second and third Document Number fields as necessary. If the document presented was a Form I-20 or DS-2019, enter the Student and Exchange Visitor Information System (SEVIS) number in the third Document Number field exactly as it appears on the Form I-20 or the DS-2019.

Expiration Date (if any) (mm/dd/yyyy): Enter the expiration date, if any, of the List A document. The document is not acceptable if it has already expired. If the document does not contain an expiration date, enter N/A in this field. If the document uses text rather than a date to indicate when it expires, enter the text as shown on the document, such as "D/S"(which means, "duration of status"). For a receipt, enter the expiration date of the receipt validity period as described above. If the employee presented a combination of documents, use the second and third Expiration Date fields as necessary. If the document presented was a Form I-20 or DS-2019, enter the program end date here.

List B - Identity: If the employee presented an acceptable document from List B or an acceptable receipt for the application to replace a lost, stolen, or destroyed List B document, enter the document information in this column. If a parent or legal guardian attested to the identity of an employee who is an individual under age 18 or certain employees with disabilities in Section 1, enter either "Individual under age 18" or "Special Placement" in this field. Refer to the Handbook for Employers: Guidance for Completing Form I-9 (M-274) for more guidance on individuals under age 18 and certain person with disabilities.

If you enter document information in the List B column, you must also enter document information in the List C column. If an employee presents acceptable List B and List C documents, do not ask the employees to present a List A document. No entries should be made in the List A column. If you complete Section 2 using a computer, a selection in List B will fill all the fields in the List A column with N/A.

Document Title: If the employee presented a document from List B, enter the title of the List B document or receipt in this field. The abbreviations provided are available in the dropdown when the form is completed on a computer. When completing the form on paper, you may choose to use these abbreviations or any other common abbreviations to document the document title or issuing authority.

Full name of List B Document	Abbreviations
Driver's license issued by a State or outlying possession of the United States	Driver's license issued by state/territory
ID card issued by a State or outlying possession of the United States	ID card issued by state/territory
ID card issued by federal, state, or local government agencies or entities	Government ID
School ID card with photograph	School ID
Voter's registration card	Voter registration card
U.S. Military card	U.S. Military card
U.S. Military draft record	U.S. Military draft record
Military dependent's ID card	Military dependent's ID card
U.S. Coast Guard Merchant Mariner Card	USCG Merchant Mariner card
Native American tribal document	Native American tribal document
Driver's license issued by a Canadian government authority	Canadian driver's license
School record (for persons under age 18 who are unable to present a document listed above)	School record (under age 18)
Report card (for persons under age 18 who are unable to present a document listed above)	Report card (under age 18)
Clinic record (for persons under age 18 who are unable to present a document listed above)	Clinic record (under age 18)
Doctor record (for persons under age 18 who are unable to present a document listed above)	Doctor record (under age 18)
Hospital record (for persons under age 18 who are unable to present a document listed above)	Hospital record (under age 18)
Day-care record (for persons under age 18 who are unable to present a document listed above)	Day-care record (under age 18)
Nursery school record (for persons under age 18 who are unable to present a document listed above)	Nursery school record (under age 18)

Full name of List B Document	Abbreviations
Individual under age 18 endorsement by parent or guardian	Individual under Age 18
Special placement endorsement for persons with disabilities	Special Placement
Receipt for the application to replace a lost, stolen or damaged Driver's License issued by a State or outlying possession of the United States	Receipt: Replacement driver's license
Receipt for the application to replace a lost, stolen or damaged ID card issued by a State or outlying possession of the United States	Receipt: Replacement ID card
Receipt for the application to replace a lost, stolen or damaged ID card issued by federal, state, or local government agencies or entities	Receipt: Replacement Gov't ID
Receipt for the application to replace a lost, stolen or damaged School ID card with photograph	Receipt: Replacement School ID
Receipt for the application to replace a lost, stolen or damaged Voter's registration card	Receipt: Replacement Voter reg. card
Receipt for the application to replace a lost, stolen or damaged U.S. Military card	Receipt: Replacement U.S. Military card
Receipt for the application to replace a lost, stolen or damaged Military dependent's ID card	Receipt: Replacement U.S. Military dep. card
Receipt for the application to replace a lost, stolen or damaged U.S. Military draft record	Receipt: Replacement Military draft record
Receipt for the application to replace a lost, stolen or damaged U.S. Coast Guard Merchant Mariner Card	Receipt: Replacement Merchant Mariner card
Receipt for the application to replace a lost, stolen or damaged Driver's license issued by a Canadian government authority	Receipt: Replacement Canadian DL
Receipt for the application to replace a lost, stolen or damaged Native American tribal document	Receipt: Replacement Native American tribal doc
Receipt for the application to replace a lost, stolen or damaged School record (for persons under age 18 who are unable to present a document listed above)	Receipt: Replacement School record (under age 18)
Receipt for the application to replace a lost, stolen or damaged Report card (for persons under age 18 who are unable to present a document listed above)	Receipt: Replacement Report card (under age 18)
Receipt for the application to replace a lost, stolen or damaged Clinic record (for persons under age 18 who are unable to present a document listed above)	Receipt: Replacement Clinic record (under age 18)
Receipt for the application to replace a lost, stolen or damaged Doctor record (for persons under age 18 who are unable to present a document listed above)	Receipt: Replacement Doctor record (under age 18)
Receipt for the application to replace a lost, stolen or damaged Hospital record (for persons under age 18 who are unable to present a document listed above)	Receipt: Replacement Hospital record (under age 18)
Receipt for the application to replace a lost, stolen or damaged Day-care record (for persons under age 18 who are unable to present a document listed above)	Receipt: Replacement Day-care record (under age 18)
Receipt for the application to replace a lost, stolen or damaged Nursery school record (for persons under age 18 who are unable to present a document listed above)	Receipt: Replacement Nursery school record (under age 18)

Issuing Authority: Enter the issuing authority of the List B document or receipt. The issuing authority is the entity that issued the document. If the employee presented a document that is issued by a state agency, include the state as part of the issuing authority.

Document Number: Enter the document number, if any, of the List B document or receipt exactly as it appears on the document. If the document does not contain a number, enter N/A in this field.

Expiration Date (if any) (mm/dd/yyyy): Enter the expiration date, if any, of the List B document. The document is not acceptable if it has already expired. If the document does not contain an expiration date, enter N/A in this field. For a receipt, enter the expiration date of the receipt validity period as described in the Receipt section above.

List C - Employment Authorization: If the employee presented an acceptable document from List C, or an acceptable receipt for the application to replace a lost, stolen, or destroyed List C document, enter the document information in this column. If you enter document information in the List C column, you must also enter document information in the List B column. If an employee presents acceptable List B and List C documents, do not ask the employee to present a list A document. No entries should be made in the List A column.

Document Title: If the employee presented a document from List C, enter the title of the List C document or receipt in this field. The abbreviations provided are available in the dropdown when the form is completed on a computer. When completing the form on paper, you may choose to use these abbreviations or any other common abbreviations to document the document title or issuing authority. If you are completing the form on a computer, and you select an Employment authorization document issued by DHS, the field will populate with List C #7 and provide a space for you to enter a description of the documentation the employee presented. Refer to the M-274 for guidance on entering List C #7 documentation.

Full name of List C Document	Abbreviations
Social Security Account Number card without restrictions	(Unrestricted) Social Security Card
Certification of Birth Abroad (Form FS-545)	Form FS-545
Certification of Report of Birth (Form DS-1350)	Form DS-1350
Consular Report of Birth Abroad (Form FS-240)	Form FS-240
Original or certified copy of a U.S. birth certificate bearing an official seal	Birth Certificate
Native American tribal document	Native American tribal document
U.S. Citizen ID Card (Form I-197)	Form I-197
Identification Card for use of Resident Citizen in the United States (Form I-179)	Form I-179
Employment authorization document issued by DHS (List C #7)	Employment Auth. document (DHS) List C #7
Receipt for the application to replace a lost, stolen or damaged Social Security Account Number Card without restrictions	Receipt: Replacement Unrestricted SS Card
Receipt for the application to replace a lost, stolen or damaged Original or certified copy of a U.S. birth certificate bearing an official seal	Receipt: Replacement Birth Certificate
Receipt for the application to replace a lost, stolen or damaged Native American Tribal Document	Receipt: Replacement Native American Tribal Doc.
Receipt for the application to replace a lost, stolen or damaged Employment Authorization Document issued by DHS	Receipt: Replacement Employment Auth. Doc. (DHS)

Issuing Authority: Enter the issuing authority of the List C document or receipt. The issuing authority is the entity that issued the document.

Document Number: Enter the document number, if any, of the List C document or receipt exactly as it appears on the document. If the document does not contain a number, enter N/A in this field.

Expiration Date (if any) (mm/dd/yyyy): Enter the expiration date, if any, of the List C document. The document is not acceptable if it has already expired, unless USCIS has extended the expiration date on the document. For instance, if a conditional resident presents a Form I-797 extending his or her conditional resident status with the employee's expired Form I-551, enter the future expiration date as indicated on the Form I-797. If the document has no expiration date, enter N/A in this field. For a receipt, enter the expiration date of the receipt validity period as described in the Receipt section above.

Additional Information: Use this space to notate any additional information required for Form I-9 such as:

- Employment authorization extensions for Temporary Protected Status beneficiaries, F-1 OPT STEM students, CAP-GAP, H-1B and H-2A employees continuing employment with the same employer or changing employers, and other nonimmigrant categories that may receive extensions of stay
- Additional document(s) that certain nonimmigrant employees may present
- Discrepancies that E-Verify employers must notate when participating in the IMAGE program
- Employee termination dates and form retention dates
- E-Verify case number, which may also be entered in the margin or attached as a separate sheet per E-Verify requirements and your chosen business process
- Any other comments or notations necessary for the employer's business process

You may leave this field blank if the employee's circumstances do not require additional notations.

Employee's First Day of Employment: Enter the employee's first day of employment as a 2-digit month, 2-digit day and 4-digit year (mm/dd/yyyy).

Signature of Employer or Authorized Representative: Review the form for accuracy and completeness. The person who physically examines the employee's original document(s) and completes Section 2 must sign his or her name in this field. If you used a form obtained from the USCIS website, you must print the form to sign your name in this field. By signing Section 2, you attest under penalty of perjury (28 U.S.C. § 1746) that you have physically examined the documents presented by the employee, the document(s) reasonably appear to be genuine and to relate to the employee named, that to the best of your knowledge the employee is authorized to work in the United States, that the information you entered in Section 2 is complete, true and correct to the best of your knowledge, and that you are aware that you may face severe penalties provided by law and may be subject to criminal prosecution for knowingly and willfully making false statements or knowingly accepting false documentation when completing this form.

Today's Date: The person who signs Section 2 must enter the date he or she signed Section 2 in this field. Do not backdate this field. If you used a form obtained from the USCIS website, you must print the form to write the date in this field. Enter the date as a 2-digit month, 2-digit day and 4-digit year (mm/dd/yyyy). For example, enter January 8, 2014 as 01/08/2014.

Title of Employer or Authorized Representative: Enter the title, position or role of the person who physically examines the employee's original document(s), completes and signs Section 2.

Last Name of the Employer or Authorized Representative: Enter the full legal last name of the person who physically examines the employee's original documents, completes and signs Section 2. Last name refers to family name or surname. If the person has two last names or a hyphenated last name, include both names in this field.

First Name of the Employer or Authorized Representative: Enter the full legal first name of the person who physically examines the employee's original documents, completes, and signs Section 2. First name refers to the given name.

Employer's Business or Organization Name: Enter the name of the employer's business or organization in this field.

Employer's Business or Organization Address (Street Name and Number): Enter an actual, physical address of the employer. If your company has multiple locations, use the most appropriate address that identifies the location of the employer. Do not provide a P.O. Box address.

City or Town: Enter the city or town for the employer's business or organization address. If the location is not a city or town, you may enter the name of the village, county, township, reservation, etc. that applies.

State: Enter the two-character abbreviation of the state for the employer's business or organization address.

ZIP Code: Enter the 5-digit ZIP code for the employer's business or organization address.

Completing Section 3: Reverification and Rehires

Section 3 applies to both reverification and rehires. When completing this section, you must also complete the Last Name, First Name and Middle Initial fields in the Employee Info from Section 1 area at the top of Section 2, leaving the Citizenship/ Immigration Status field blank. When completing Section 3 in either a reverification or rehire situation, if the employee's name has changed, record the new name in Block A.

Reverification

Reverification in Section 3 must be completed prior to the earlier of:

- The expiration date, if any, of the employment authorization stated in Section 1, or
- The expiration date, if any, of the List A or List C employment authorization document recorded in Section 2 (with some exceptions listed below).

Some employees may have entered "N/A" in the expiration date field in Section 1 if they are aliens whose employment authorization does not expire, e.g. asylees, refugees, certain citizens of the Federated States of Micronesia, the Republic of the Marshall Islands, or Palau. Reverification does not apply for such employees unless they choose to present evidence of employment authorization in Section 2 that contains an expiration date and requires reverification, such as Form I-766, Employment Authorization Document.

You should not reverify U.S. citizens and noncitizen nationals, or lawful permanent residents (including conditional residents) who presented a Permanent Resident Card (Form I-551). Reverification does not apply to List B documents.

For reverification, an employee must present an unexpired document(s) (or a receipt) from either List A or List C showing he or she is still authorized to work. You CANNOT require the employee to present a particular document from List A or List C. The employee is also not required to show the same type of document that he or she presented previously. See specific instructions on how to complete Section 3 below.

Rehires

If you rehire an employee within three years from the date that the Form I-9 was previously executed, you may either rely on the employee's previously executed Form I-9 or complete a new Form I-9.

If you choose to rely on a previously completed Form I-9, follow these guidelines.

- If the employee remains employment authorized as indicated on the previously executed Form I-9, the employee does not need to provide any additional documentation. Provide in Section 3 the employee's rehire date, any name changes if applicable, and sign and date the form.

- If the previously executed Form I-9 indicates that the employee's employment authorization from Section 1 or employment authorization documentation from Section 2 that is subject to reverification has expired, then reverification of employment authorization is required in Section 3 in addition to providing the rehire date. If the previously executed Form I-9 is not the current version of the form, you must complete Section 3 on the current version of the form.

- If you already used Section 3 of the employee's previously executed Form I-9, but are rehiring the employee within three years of the original execution of Form I-9, you may complete Section 3 on a new Form I-9 and attach it to the previously executed form.

Employees rehired after three years of original execution of the Form I-9 must complete a new Form I-9.

Complete each block in Section 3 as follows:

Block A - New Name: If an employee who is being reverified or rehired has also changed his or her name since originally completing Section 1 of this form, complete this block with the employee's new name. Enter only the part of the name that has changed, for example: if the employee changed only his or her last name, enter the last name in the Last Name field in this Block, then enter N/A in the First Name and Middle Initial fields. If the employee has not changed his or her name, enter N/A in each field of Block A.

Block B - Date of Rehire: Complete this block if you are rehiring an employee within three years of the date Form I-9 was originally executed. Enter the date of rehire in this field. Enter N/A in this field if the employee is not being rehired.

Block C - Complete this block if you are reverifying expiring or expired employment authorization or employment authorization documentation of a current or rehired employee. Enter the information from the List A or List C document(s) (or receipt) that the employee presented to reverify his or her employment authorization. All documents must be unexpired.

> **Document Title:** Enter the title of the List A or C document (or receipt) the employee has presented to show continuing employment authorization in this field.

> **Document Number:** Enter the document number, if any, of the document you entered in the Document Title field exactly as it appears on the document. Enter N/A if the document does not have a number.

> **Expiration Date (if any) (mm/dd/yyyy):** Enter the expiration date, if any, of the document you entered in the Document Title field as a 2-digit month, 2-digit day, and 4-digit year (mm/dd/yyyy). If the document does not contain an expiration date, enter N/A in this field.

Signature of Employer or Authorized Representative: The person who completes Section 3 must sign in this field. If you used a form obtained from the USCIS website, you must print Section 3 of the form to sign your name in this field. By signing Section 3, you attest under penalty of perjury (28 U.S.C. §1746) that you have examined the documents presented by the employee, that the document(s) reasonably appear to be genuine and to relate to the employee named, that to the best of your knowledge the employee is authorized to work in the United States, that the information you entered in Section 3 is complete, true and correct to the best of your knowledge, and that you are aware that you may face severe penalties provided by law and may be subject to criminal prosecution for knowingly and willfully making false statements or knowingly accepting false documentation when completing this form.

Today's Date: The person who completes Section 3 must enter the date Section 3 was completed and signed in this field. Do not backdate this field. If you used a form obtained from the USCIS website, you must print Section 3 of the form to enter the date in this field. Enter the date as a 2-digit month, 2-digit day, and 4-digit year (mm/dd/yyyy). For example, enter January 8, 2014 as 01/08/2014.

Name of Employer or Authorized Representative: The person who completed, signed and dated Section 3 must enter his or her name in this field.

What is the Filing Fee?

There is no fee for completing Form I-9. This form is not filed with USCIS or any government agency. Form I-9 must be retained by the employer and made available for inspection by U.S. Government officials as specified in the "USCIS Privacy Act Statement" below.

USCIS Forms and Information

For additional guidance about Form I-9, employers and employees should refer to the *Handbook for Employers: Guidance for Completing Form I-9 (M-274)* or USCIS' Form I-9 website at https://www.uscis.gov/i-9-central.

You can also obtain information about Form I-9 by e-mailing USCIS at I-9Central@dhs.gov, or by calling 1-888-464-4218 or 1-877-875-6028 (TTY).

You may download and obtain the English and Spanish versions of Form I-9, the *Handbook for Employers*, or the instructions to Form I-9 from the USCIS website at https://www.uscis.gov/i-9. To complete Form I-9 on a computer, you will need the latest version of Adobe Reader, which can be downloaded for free at http://get.adobe.com/reader/. You may order USCIS forms by calling our toll-free number at 1-800-870-3676. You may also obtain forms and information by contacting the USCIS National Customer Service Center at 1-800-375-5283 or 1-800-767-1833 (TTY).

Information about E-Verify, a fast, free, internet-based system that allows businesses to determine the eligibility of their employees to work in the United States, can be obtained from the USCIS website at http://www.uscis.gov/e-verify, by e-mailing USCIS at E-Verify@dhs.gov or by calling 1-888-464-4218 or 1-877-875-6028 (TTY).

Employees with questions about Form I-9 and/or E-Verify can reach the USCIS employee hotline by calling 1-888-897-7781 or 1-877-875-6028 (TTY).

Photocopying Blank and Completed Forms I-9 and Retaining Completed Forms I-9

Employers may photocopy or print blank Forms I-9 for future use. All pages of the instructions and Lists of Acceptable Documents must be available, either in print or electronically, to all employees completing this form. Employers must retain each employee's completed Form I-9 for as long as the individual works for the employer and for a specified period after employment has ended. Employers are required to retain the pages of the form on which the employee and employer entered data. If copies of documentation presented by the employee are made, those copies must also be retained. Once the individual's employment ends, the employer must retain this form and attachments for either 3 years after the date of hire (i.e., first day of work for pay) or 1 year after the date employment ended, whichever is later. In the case of recruiters or referrers for a fee (only applicable to those that are agricultural associations, agricultural employers, or farm labor contractors), the retention period is 3 years after the date of hire (i.e., first day of work for pay).

Forms I-9 obtained from the USCIS website that are not printed and signed manually (by hand) are not considered complete. In the event of an inspection, retaining incomplete forms may make you subject to fines and penalties associated with incomplete forms.

Employers should ensure that information employees provide on Form I-9 is used only for Form I-9 purposes. Completed Forms I-9 and all accompanying documents should be stored in a safe, secure location.

Form I-9 may be generated, signed, and retained electronically, in compliance with Department of Homeland Security regulations at 8 CFR 274a.2.

Employment Eligibility Verification
Department of Homeland Security
U.S. Citizenship and Immigration Services

USCIS
Form I-9
OMB No. 1615-0047
Expires 08/31/2019

▶ **START HERE:** Read instructions carefully before completing this form. The instructions must be available, either in paper or electronically, during completion of this form. Employers are liable for errors in the completion of this form.

ANTI-DISCRIMINATION NOTICE: It is illegal to discriminate against work-authorized individuals. Employers **CANNOT** specify which document(s) an employee may present to establish employment authorization and identity. The refusal to hire or continue to employ an individual because the documentation presented has a future expiration date may also constitute illegal discrimination.

Section 1. Employee Information and Attestation (Employees must complete and sign Section 1 of Form I-9 no later than the **first day of employment**, but not before accepting a job offer.)

Last Name (Family Name)	First Name (Given Name)	Middle Initial	Other Last Names Used (if any)

Address (Street Number and Name)	Apt. Number	City or Town	State	ZIP Code

Date of Birth (mm/dd/yyyy)	U.S. Social Security Number	Employee's E-mail Address	Employee's Telephone Number
	☐☐☐ - ☐☐ - ☐☐☐☐		

I am aware that federal law provides for imprisonment and/or fines for false statements or use of false documents in connection with the completion of this form.

I attest, under penalty of perjury, that I am (check one of the following boxes):

☐ 1. A citizen of the United States

☐ 2. A noncitizen national of the United States (See instructions)

☐ 3. A lawful permanent resident   (Alien Registration Number/USCIS Number): _____

☐ 4. An alien authorized to work   until (expiration date, if applicable, mm/dd/yyyy): _____
   Some aliens may write "N/A" in the expiration date field. (See instructions)

Aliens authorized to work must provide only one of the following document numbers to complete Form I-9:
An Alien Registration Number/USCIS Number OR Form I-94 Admission Number OR Foreign Passport Number.

1. Alien Registration Number/USCIS Number: _____
OR
2. Form I-94 Admission Number: _____
OR
3. Foreign Passport Number: _____
   Country of Issuance: _____

QR Code - Section 1
Do Not Write In This Space

Signature of Employee	Today's Date (mm/dd/yyyy)

Preparer and/or Translator Certification (check one):
☐ I did not use a preparer or translator.   ☐ A preparer(s) and/or translator(s) assisted the employee in completing Section 1.
(Fields below must be completed and signed when preparers and/or translators assist an employee in completing Section 1.)

I attest, under penalty of perjury, that I have assisted in the completion of Section 1 of this form and that to the best of my knowledge the information is true and correct.

Signature of Preparer or Translator	Today's Date (mm/dd/yyyy)

Last Name (Family Name)	First Name (Given Name)

Address (Street Number and Name)	City or Town	State	ZIP Code

STOP *Employer Completes Next Page* STOP

Employment Eligibility Verification
Department of Homeland Security
U.S. Citizenship and Immigration Services

USCIS
Form I-9
OMB No. 1615-0047
Expires 08/31/2019

Section 2. Employer or Authorized Representative Review and Verification
(Employers or their authorized representative must complete and sign Section 2 within 3 business days of the employee's first day of employment. You must physically examine one document from List A OR a combination of one document from List B and one document from List C as listed on the "Lists of Acceptable Documents.")

Employee Info from Section 1	Last Name *(Family Name)*	First Name *(Given Name)*	M.I.	Citizenship/Immigration Status

List A Identity and Employment Authorization	OR	**List B** Identity	AND	**List C** Employment Authorization

List A	List B	List C
Document Title	Document Title	Document Title
Issuing Authority	Issuing Authority	Issuing Authority
Document Number	Document Number	Document Number
Expiration Date *(if any)(mm/dd/yyyy)*	Expiration Date *(if any)(mm/dd/yyyy)*	Expiration Date *(if any)(mm/dd/yyyy)*
Document Title	Additional Information	QR Code - Sections 2 & 3 Do Not Write In This Space
Issuing Authority		
Document Number		
Expiration Date *(if any)(mm/dd/yyyy)*		
Document Title		
Issuing Authority		
Document Number		
Expiration Date *(if any)(mm/dd/yyyy)*		

Certification: I attest, under penalty of perjury, that (1) I have examined the document(s) presented by the above-named employee, (2) the above-listed document(s) appear to be genuine and to relate to the employee named, and (3) to the best of my knowledge the employee is authorized to work in the United States.

The employee's first day of employment *(mm/dd/yyyy)*: _____ *(See instructions for exemptions)*

Signature of Employer or Authorized Representative	Today's Date *(mm/dd/yyyy)*	Title of Employer or Authorized Representative
Last Name of Employer or Authorized Representative	First Name of Employer or Authorized Representative	Employer's Business or Organization Name

Employer's Business or Organization Address (Street Number and Name)	City or Town	State	ZIP Code

Section 3. Reverification and Rehires *(To be completed and signed by employer or authorized representative.)*

A. New Name *(if applicable)*			**B. Date of Rehire** *(if applicable)*
Last Name *(Family Name)*	First Name *(Given Name)*	Middle Initial	Date *(mm/dd/yyyy)*

C. If the employee's previous grant of employment authorization has expired, provide the information for the document or receipt that establishes continuing employment authorization in the space provided below.

Document Title	Document Number	Expiration Date *(if any) (mm/dd/yyyy)*

I attest, under penalty of perjury, that to the best of my knowledge, this employee is authorized to work in the United States, and if the employee presented document(s), the document(s) I have examined appear to be genuine and to relate to the individual.

Signature of Employer or Authorized Representative	Today's Date *(mm/dd/yyyy)*	Name of Employer or Authorized Representative

LISTS OF ACCEPTABLE DOCUMENTS
All documents must be UNEXPIRED

Employees may present one selection from List A
or a combination of one selection from List B and one selection from List C.

LIST A		LIST B		LIST C
Documents that Establish Both Identity and Employment Authorization	**OR**	**Documents that Establish Identity**	**AND**	**Documents that Establish Employment Authorization**
1. U.S. Passport or U.S. Passport Card		1. Driver's license or ID card issued by a State or outlying possession of the United States provided it contains a photograph or information such as name, date of birth, gender, height, eye color, and address		1. A Social Security Account Number card, unless the card includes one of the following restrictions: (1) NOT VALID FOR EMPLOYMENT (2) VALID FOR WORK ONLY WITH INS AUTHORIZATION (3) VALID FOR WORK ONLY WITH DHS AUTHORIZATION
2. Permanent Resident Card or Alien Registration Receipt Card (Form I-551)				
3. Foreign passport that contains a temporary I-551 stamp or temporary I-551 printed notation on a machine-readable immigrant visa		2. ID card issued by federal, state or local government agencies or entities, provided it contains a photograph or information such as name, date of birth, gender, height, eye color, and address		
4. Employment Authorization Document that contains a photograph (Form I-766)				2. Certification of report of birth issued by the Department of State (Forms DS-1350, FS-545, FS-240)
		3. School ID card with a photograph		
5. For a nonimmigrant alien authorized to work for a specific employer because of his or her status: **a.** Foreign passport; and **b.** Form I-94 or Form I-94A that has the following: (1) The same name as the passport; and (2) An endorsement of the alien's nonimmigrant status as long as that period of endorsement has not yet expired and the proposed employment is not in conflict with any restrictions or limitations identified on the form.		4. Voter's registration card		3. Original or certified copy of birth certificate issued by a State, county, municipal authority, or territory of the United States bearing an official seal
		5. U.S. Military card or draft record		
		6. Military dependent's ID card		
		7. U.S. Coast Guard Merchant Mariner Card		4. Native American tribal document
				5. U.S. Citizen ID Card (Form I-197)
		8. Native American tribal document		6. Identification Card for Use of Resident Citizen in the United States (Form I-179)
		9. Driver's license issued by a Canadian government authority		
		For persons under age 18 who are unable to present a document listed above:		7. Employment authorization document issued by the Department of Homeland Security
6. Passport from the Federated States of Micronesia (FSM) or the Republic of the Marshall Islands (RMI) with Form I-94 or Form I-94A indicating nonimmigrant admission under the Compact of Free Association Between the United States and the FSM or RMI		10. School record or report card		
		11. Clinic, doctor, or hospital record		
		12. Day-care or nursery school record		

Examples of many of these documents appear in Part 13 of the Handbook for Employers (M-274).

Refer to the instructions for more information about acceptable receipts.

Index